D0742298

ASIAN LAW SERIES
SCHOOL OF LAW
UNIVERSITY OF WASHINGTON
Number 6

Asian Law Series
School of Law, University of Washington

The Asian Law Series was initiated with the cooperation of the University of Washington Press and the Institute for Comparative and Foreign Area Studies in 1969 in order to publish the results of several projects under way in Japanese, Chinese, and Korean law. The members of the editorial committee are: Herbert J. Ellison, Director of the Institute for Comparative and Foreign Area Studies; John O. Haley; and Dan Fenno Henderson, chairman.

1. *The Constitution of Japan: Its First Twenty Years, 1947–67*, edited by Dan Fenno Henderson
2. *Village "Contracts" in Tokugawa Japan*, by Dan Fenno Henderson
3. *Chinese Family Law and Social Change in Historic and Comparative Perspective*, edited by David C. Buxbaum
4. *Law and Politics in China's Foreign Trade*, edited by Victor H. Li
5. *Patent and Know-how Licensing in Japan and the United States*, edited by Teruo Doi and Warren L. Shattuck
6. *The Constitutional Case Law of Japan: Selected Supreme Court Decisions, 1961–70*, by Hiroshi Itoh and Lawrence Ward Beer

The Constitutional Case Law of Japan

Selected Supreme Court Decisions, 1961–70

HIROSHI ITOH

and

LAWRENCE WARD BEER

UNIVERSITY OF WASHINGTON PRESS
Seattle and London

Printed in the United States of America

Library of Congress Cataloging in Publication Data

Japan. Saikō Saibansho.
The constitutional case law of Japan.

(Asian law series; no. 6)
Bibliography: p.
Includes index.
1. Japan—Constitutional law—Cases.
I. Itoh, Hiroshi. II. Beer, Lawrence Ward,
1932- III. Title. IV. Series.
LAW 342'.51 77-24669
ISBN 0-295-95571-6

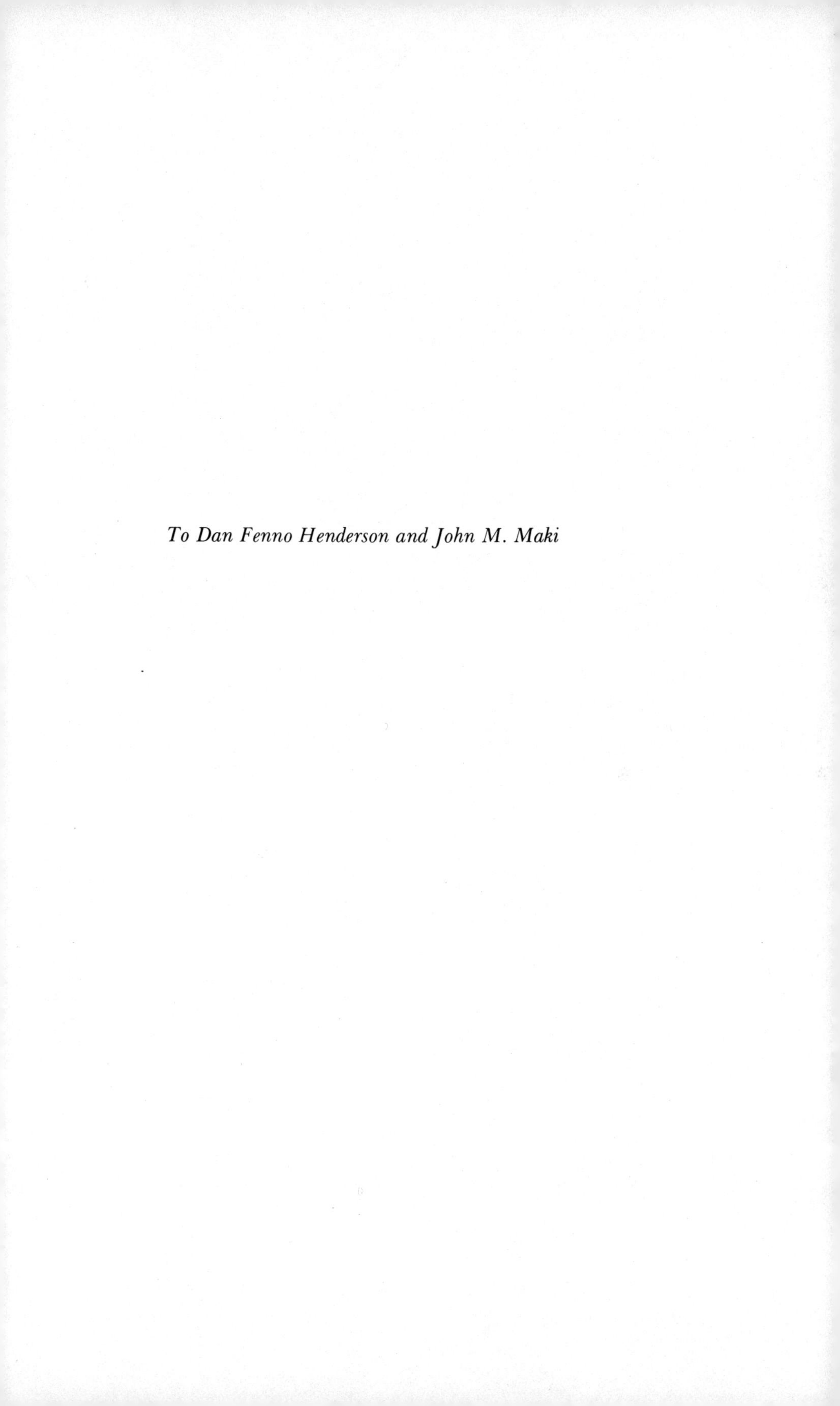

To Dan Fenno Henderson and John M. Maki

Contents

Preface xi

Abbreviations and Legends xv

Introduction 3

Chapter 1. Relationships between Forms, Levels, and Types of Law *(Kokuhō no keishiki)* 22

Case 1. Japan v. *S. Matsumoto (1961).* The Organization Control Ordinance Case. The Political Organization Control Ordinance enacted during the Occupation cannot apply because it was repealed after the act of the accused but before charges were lodged against him for failing to report to the Supreme Public Prosecutor's Office during a criminal investigation. 22

Case 2. T. Matsumoto v. *Japan (1962).* The Osaka Prostitution Ordinance Case. Penal provisions in an Osaka ordinance are held constitutional on grounds that penal provisions need not be in laws passed by the Diet in order to be valid. 36

Chapter 2. The Diet, the Cabinet, and the Courts (*Kokkai-naikaku*) 41

Case 3. Shimizu v. *Governor, Osaka Metropolis (1962).* The Shimizu Police Law Case. A taxpayer's suit challenging the constitutionality of a police law is dismissed because the legislative process inside the Diet is not subject to judicial review in this case. 41

Chapter 3. Local Autonomy (*Chihō jichi*) 45

Case 4. Japan v. *Kobayashi et al (1963).* The Tokyo Ward Autonomy Case. A charge of election campaign bribery is sustained because of peculiarities in the administrative districting of Tokyo's wards (*kū*). 45

Chapter 4. Taxation under the Constitution (*Zaisei*) 50

Case 5. Takano v. *Director, Osaka Office, National Tax Bureau (1961).* The Joint Income Tax Case. The constitutionality of the Income Tax Law is upheld in the face of a challenge on grounds of discriminatory treatment of spouses. 50

Chapter 5. Equality of Rights under the Law (*Hō no moto no byōdo*) 53

Case 6. Koshiyama v. *Chairman, Tokyo Metropolitan Election Supervision Commission (1964).* The Koshiyama Malapportionment Case. The validity of a Diet election is unsuccessfully challenged on the basis of election district malapportionment. 53

Chapter 6. The Economic Freedoms of Citizens (*Keizaiteki jiyū*) 58

Case 7. Nakamura et al v. *Japan (1962).* The Nakamura Case. An application of the Customs Law is held unconstitutional for permitting confiscation of a third-party property related to a crime. 58

Case 8. Japan v. *Iida et al (1963).* The Irrigation Reservoir Case. A limitation on property rights is upheld without compensation, for land at the bank of a reservoir. 73

Case 9. Yoshida v. *Japan (1965).* The Bribery Compensation Case. An order to make payment in lieu of confiscation of bribe money is reversed as unconstitutional. 78

Case 10. Koizumi v. *Japan (1963).* The Gypsy Taxi Cab Case. A challenge to the constitutionality of the taxi licensing system as unreasonably restrictive of the freedom of occupation is dismissed. 80

Case 11. Japan v. *Ki et al (1970).* The Ki Alien Reentry Case. The right of resident aliens to visit their ancestral home (North Korea) and reenter Japan. 81

Chapter 7. Rights Related to the Quality of Socioeconomic Life (*Shakaiken*) 85

Case 12. Toyama et al v. *Japan (1966).* The Tokyo Central Post Office Case. In general, public employees as in this case possess the ordinary rights of workers, although the nature of their assigned duties may dictate special restrictions. 85

Case 13. Japan v. *Sakane et al (1969).* The Court Worker Incitement Case. The special situation of public employees with respect to the rights of workers and freedom of expression. Also, the 1960 United States–Japan Security Treaty is held not obviously unconstitutional on its face. 103

Case 14. Asahi v. *Japan (1967).* The Asahi Tuberculosis Case. Constitutional guarantees of minimum standards of wholesome and cultured living include a guarantee of some medical care, but this right is not inheritable. 130

Case 15. Katō v. *Japan (1964).* The Textbook Fee Case. The state is not obliged to provide students with free textbooks under the compulsory education system. 147

Chapter 8. The Right to Participate in Election Politics (*Sanseiken*) 149

Case 16. Taniguchi v. *Japan (1967).* The Taniguchi Canvassing Case. A prohibition on election canvassing does not violate the freedom of expression. 149

Case 17. Iwasaki v. *Japan (1962).* The Election Invalidation Case. A politician is denied a prefectural assembly seat because his campaign manager is convicted of election law violations. 151

Chapter 9. Procedural Questions 154

Case 18. Kojima v. *Japan (1966).* The Kojima Double Jepoardy Case.

The use of a past criminal record in assessing penalties for later larceny does not constitute double jeopardy. 154

Case 19. Japan v. *Arima (1961).* The Arima Narcotics Seizure Case. An instance of lawful search and seizure attendant to narcotics arrests without a warrant. 157

Case 20. Ichikawa et al v. *Japan (1961).* The Ichikawa Hanging Case. Provisions of an 1873 decree concerning capital punishment by hanging are still in effect and such punishment is constitutional. 161

Case 21. Saitō v. *Japan (1962).* The Saitō Accident Report Case. A driver's duty to report a traffic accident he has caused does not involve an unconstitutional requirement of self-incrimination. 164

Case 22. Abe v. *Japan (1966).* The Abe Confession Case. Evidence obtained under duress from a criminal suspect is held inadmissible. 167

Case 23. Yoshimura v. *Yoshimura (1965).* The Nonlitigious Trial Case. A nonlitigious trial concerning a domestic dispute does not violate the right to a trial, even if confrontation of witnesses in open court is not permitted. 169

Chapter 10. Intellectual Rights and Freedoms (*Seishinteki jiyūken*) 175

Case 24. Kōchi v. *Japan (1969).* The Kōchi Defamation Case. Criminal intent to defame is not present where there is mistaken belief in the truth of allegations and sufficient grounds for the belief. Hearsay evidence is admissible grounds for such belief. 175

Case 25. Hasegawa v. *Japan (1969).* The Right-to-Likeness Case. Police photography of suspects that is necessary for criminal investigation does not violate the right to one's own likeness, which is an aspect of the constitutional right of privacy. 178

Case 26. Ishii et al v. *Japan (1969).* The de Sade Case. Obscene sections render an entire work obscene. A literary work close to, not criminally obscene is possible based on high artistic and intellectual merit. Academic freedom may be limited under the public welfare doctrine. 183

Case 27. Ōno v. *Japan (1961).* The Moxa Advertising Case. Restrictions on advertising, as a protection against misleading ads on such as the medical values of moxa cautery, are not unconstitutional restraints on freedom of expression. 217

Case 28. Nishida v. *Japan (1963).* The Faith Healing Case. Religious practices occasioning injury or death are not defensible on grounds of freedom of religion. 223

Case 29. Tokyo Public Prosecutor v. *Senda (1963).* The Popolo Players Case. University autonomy and academic freedom were allegedly denied in relation to campus police investigations of campus political activities and attendant violence. 226

Case 30. Japan v. *Kanemoto et al (1964).* The Kanemoto Pamphlet Case. Distribution of politically inflammatory pamphlets does not violate the Subversive Activities Prevention Law as instigation to insurrection. 242

Case 31. Yamagishi et al v. *Japan (1970).* The Yamagishi Poster Case. Regulation of poster displays on telephone poles under the Misdemeanor Law does not violate the freedom of expression. 244

Case 32. Kaneko et al v. *Japan (1969).* The Hakata Station Film Case. A court order to present television newsfilm is constitutional when, as in this case, the film is evidence necessary for a fair trial. 246

Appendix 1. Supreme Court Justices of Japan, 1961–70 251

Appendix 2. Organization Chart of Japan's Judicial System, and Map of Court Jurisdictions in Japan 254

Appendix 3. The Constitution of Japan (*Nihonkoku kempō*) 256

Selected Bibliography 270
1. Publications in English
2. Major Legal Journals in Japanese Covering Constitutional Law
3. Selected Publications in Japanese Covering Constitutional Law
4. Selected Japanese Commentaries on the Translated Supreme Court Decisions

Index 279

Preface

Japan is the world's major non-Western industrialized democracy; its law and constitutional experience represent a creative, cumulative synthesis of perennial and modern indigenous elements, the European Civil Law tradition, and the Anglo-American Common Law approach. Comparative legal theories and social science models of democracy and development must take into account, if not test out in relation to, Japan's distinctive constitutional dynamics. Yet the way to knowledge of Japan, in this as in some other fields, has usually been blocked by an obstacle of labyrinthine complexity—the Japanese language. The present volume brings across this great barrier a decade of Japan's major judicial decisions. This book may be considered a sequel to John M. Maki's pioneering *Court and Constitution in Japan: Selected Supreme Court Decisions, 1948–60* (Seattle: University of Washington Press, 1964), which covers early decision-making under the 1947 Constitution of Japan.

The authors selected the thirty-two Supreme Court cases presented here from among the published decisions handed down between 1961 and the end of 1970. Standard Japanese commentaries, such as *Kempō Hanrei Hyakusen-Shimpan* [100 selected Constitutional cases, new edition], (*Jurisuto, bessatsu* no. 21, December 1968), were examined in the process, as were the choices of Isao Sato in *Kempō Kihon Hanreishū* [Basic collection of Constitutional cases], (Ichiryusha, Tokyo, 1967). In addition, the authors consulted at length with two prominent Japanese constitutional lawyers, Professors Masami Ito and Naoki Kobayashi (Faculty of Law, University of Tokyo), before determining upon the final list of cases to be translated. Judicial decisions were selected for inclusion because they fulfilled one or more of the following guidelines: (1) clearly a landmark decision in a particular issue area; (2) generally considered important by specialists in Japan, legally, socially and/or politically; (3) of probable special interest to the foreign legal scholar and/or social scientist because of the nature of the dispute at issue and/or the judicial reasoning.

The book is divided into ten parts, following in general a common system of classifying constitutional cases found in such standard sources as *Jurisuto* (Yuhikaku, Tokyo). We have retained these subdivisions in translation with only the slightest modification instead of fitting the cases into an American legal mold because they are generally quite easy to understand and because we wanted to introduce this system to the reader unfamiliar with Japanese legal categories.

We would emphasize that this is only a casebook, a source to be explored by other interested scholars; adequate commentary and analysis of the legal, socioeconomic, and political significance of each of these decisions are separate tasks. Little or nothing has yet been written in a language other than Japanese about most of the cases discussed. (References to Japanese commentaries on each case, and to a few English-language analyses, can be found in the bibliography.)

Whatever the merits of their respective stands on a particular issue from the reader's standpoint, the justices of the Supreme Court of Japan have provided us with the most authoritative statements of Japan's constitutional law. These statements are sometimes dull with technicalities, sometimes convoluted in phraseology (a trait of the language), sometimes subtle or theoretical in their handling of the interplay of legal norms, sometimes ringing in their advocacy of constitutional principles or public prerogatives, and on occasion even inspiring in their grasp of problems of politics, society, economics, and culture. Be that as it may, these opinions taken together provide the reader with insights into the legal mind of Japan and an understanding of that nation which is based on empirically rooted case law arising from daily life.

In rendering into English the Japanese of the Supreme Court decisions, the authors have labored to convey the precise sense of the Japanese; only rarely and when it would not distort the meaning of the original have they modified the literal sense in the interests of readability. Ellipses are inserted where passages have been omitted because they repeated what is said elsewhere in a decision, because they concerned technicalities not central to the case, or because they were not critical to an understanding of the major positions taken by the justices on an issue. In a few places words are added between brackets to provide brief editorial explanations. Unless otherwise indicated, translations of legal provisions appearing before each case are the authors' own. The Articles of the Constitution of Japan relevant to a given case are listed before the translation of the case; the full text of the Constitution will be found in Appendix 3. We have included only those articles, paragraphs, and items of Codes, laws, ordinances, rules, etc., which are relevant to the particular case. In the heading of each case, the parties to the dispute are indicated, and the popular Japanese name for the case is added.

Where such a popular name has not been invented by the Japanese, the authors have made one up to facilitate future ready reference to the case; the usual formal names of Japanese cases are long and not helpful in this respect. Given names are placed before family names, thus reversing the East Asian name order.

Although we have consulted other translations of a few of the cases in the process of rendering them into English, all the translations in this book are a result of close collaboration between the authors and are the authors' own.

The authors wish to express their gratitude to Professors Masami Ito and Naoki Kobayashi for assistance in case selection; to Kendell A. Whitney and Patrick Stanford for editorial assistance on part of an early draft; to the Faculty of Law, University of Tokyo, for hospitality extended to L. W. Beer in 1970 and 1973; to librarians of the Supreme Court Library in Tokyo who facilitated and assisted H. Itoh's research in Japan during the summers of 1972 and 1974; to the State University of New York Research Foundation for a Faculty Research Fellowship enabling H. Itoh to work in Japan during the summer of 1974; to the Council on Research of the University of Colorado and to the Japan Foundation, for partial support of L. W. Beer's work on this book; and especially to Keiko Beer and the four "short Beers" (David, Chris, Kim, and Larry) for their patient support, and to Nobu Itoh for her contribution to research and useful suggestions, and for typing the manuscript. Finally, the encouragement and interest expressed by professional colleagues in America and Japan have been much appreciated, as we moved from word to word, sentence to sentence, and case to case in the translation work.

Lawrence W. Beer
Boulder, Colorado

Hiroshi Itoh
Plattsburgh, New York

Abbreviations and Legends

*Keishū**	*Saikō saibansho keiji hanreishū* (Collection of Supreme Court Precedents: Criminal Cases)
*Minshū**	*Saikō saibansho minji hanreishū* (Collection of Supreme Court Precedents: Civil Cases)
*Saibanshū Keiji**	*Saikō saibansho saibanshū keiji* (Collection of Supreme Court Decisions: Criminal Cases)
*Saibanshū Minji**	*Saikō saibansho saibanshū minji* (Collection of Supreme Court Decisions: Civil Cases)
Kōsai Keishū	*Kōtō saibansho keiji hanreishū* (Collection of High Court Precedents: Criminal Cases)
Kōsai Minshū	*Kōtō saibansho minji hanreishū* (Collection of High Court Precedents: Civil Cases)
Kakyū Keishū	*Kakyū saibansho keiji saibanreishū* (Collection of Lower Court Decisions: Criminal Cases)
Gyōsai Reishū	*Gyōsei jiken saibanreishū* (Collection of Administrative Cases)
Rōminshū	*Rōdō minji jiken saibanreishū* (Collection of Labor Decisions: Civil Cases)
Jurisuto	*The Jurist*
Hanrei Jihō	*The Case Reporter*
Hanrei Taimuzu	*The Law Times*
Sup. Ct., G.B.	The Supreme Court, Grand Bench

*The *Hanreishū* set does not include as many cases decided by the Supreme Court as the *Saibanshū* set does. But the former is the standard set of reports.

Sup. Ct., P.B.	The Supreme Court, Petty Bench
Dist. Ct.	The District Court
NPEL	The National Public Employees Law
LPEL	The Local Public Employees Law
LRAL	The Labor Relations Adjustment Law
Yen	Roughly 360 yen were equivalent to one U.S. dollar during the period of time covered in this book.
Kōso	A type of appeal that may be lodged against first instance judgments of district courts, family courts, or summary courts. This kind of appeal cannot reach the Supreme Court.
Kōkoku	A complaint lodged against a ruling rendered by a court. An ordinary type of *kōkoku* appeal cannot be carried to the Supreme Court. A special *kōkoku* is allowed to reach as far as the Supreme Court only if the complaint involves alleged unconstitutionality or alleged incompatibility with Supreme Court precedent.
Jōkoku	An appeal that can be carried to the Supreme Court against a judgment of a high court in the first instance court if a claim is made regarding (1) an alleged violation of a constitutional provision, (2) an alleged incompatibility with Supreme Court precedent, or (3) what the Supreme Court deems an important problem in the construction of law or ordinance.

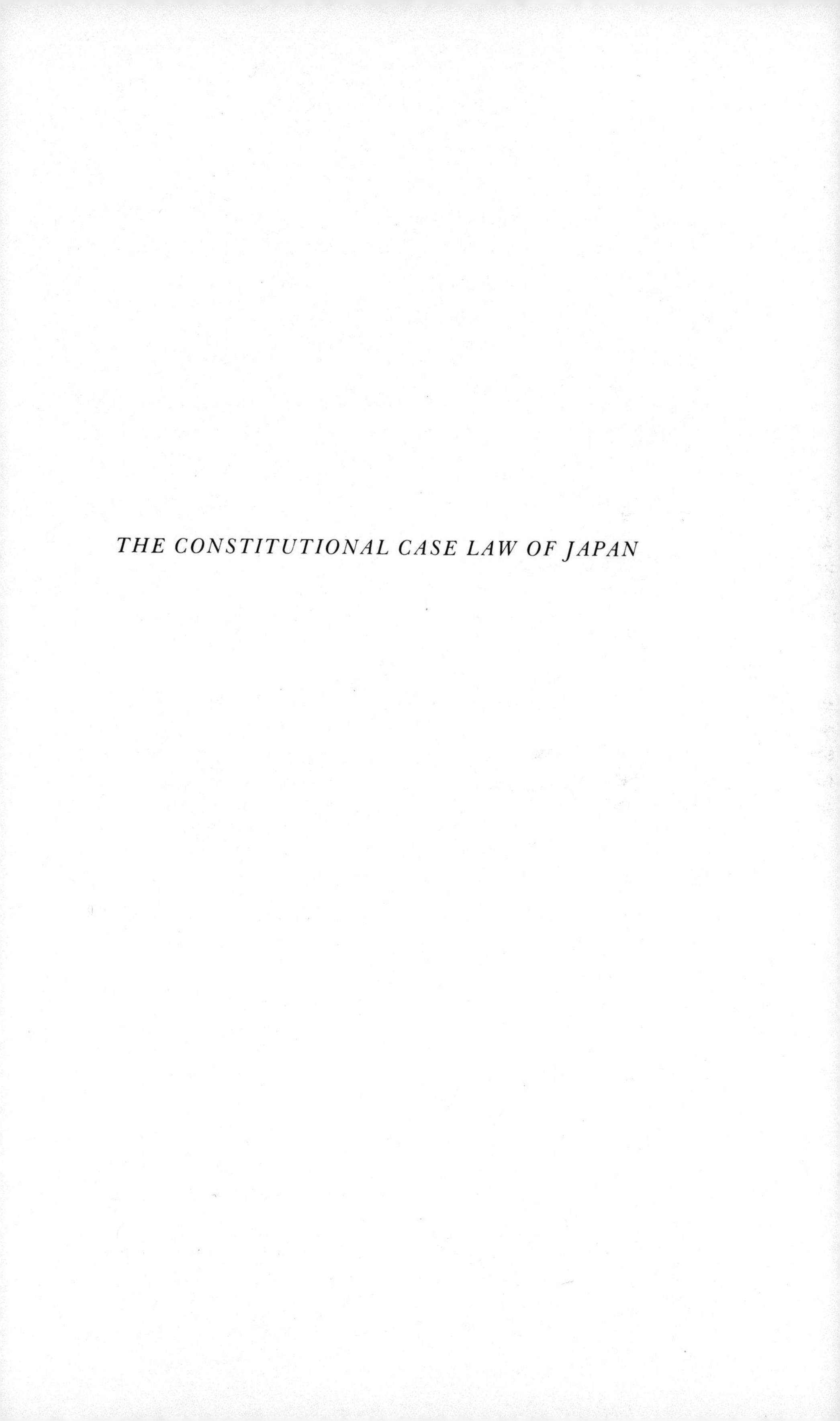

THE CONSTITUTIONAL CASE LAW OF JAPAN

Introduction

The Constitution of Japan came into force on 3 May 1947 as a constitutional amendment that, in effect, replaced the Constitution of the Empire of Japan, the so-called Meiji Constitution of 1889.[1] This book presents the constitutional law of Japan as decided in the courts between 1961 and 1970, a period of awesome economic growth and relative stability in internal politics which contrasts somewhat with the 1950s. In that earlier decade, Japan regained her independence after the Occupation (1945–52), as well as her economic footing, and experienced notable, though not constitutionally dangerous, unrest which reached a high point during the Security Treaty Crisis of 1960.[2] Some of the judicial decisions presented in this volume concern disputes that arose but that were not settled in the 1950s. Before discussing general and specific constitutional trends of the 1961–70 period, some comments on Japan's modern constitutional milieu and judicial system will add perspective for readers new to Japanese constitutionalism.

Japan's Two Constitutions

In the mid-nineteenth century, Japan was subjected to humiliating, yet stimulating, Western encroachments.[3] In the interests of regaining full

1. "Meiji" was the name given to the period during which Emperor Mutsuhito reigned, 1868–1912. Even if the establishment of the present Constitution of Japan is viewed technically as a constitutional amendment, it is the only amendment to either of Japan's modern constitutions.

2. Concerning the Occupation, see KAZUO KAWAI, JAPAN'S AMERICAN INTERLUDE (1960), and Robert E. Ward, *The Origins of the Present Japanese Constitution*, 50 AM. POL. SCI. REV. 980 (1956), and JON LIVINGSTON *et al (eds.)*, POSTWAR JAPAN (1973), especially Part I. On the Security Treaty crisis, see GEORGE R. PACKARD III, PROTEST IN TOKYO: THE SECURITY TREATY CRISIS OF 1960 (1966).

3. HUGH BORTON, JAPAN'S MODERN CENTURY (1955); CHITOSHI YANAGA, JAPAN SINCE PERRY (1949); and GEORGE B. SANSOM, THE WESTERN WORLD AND JAPAN (1949) present the historical context.

independence, attaining equality with Western nations, and making Japan a world power, Japan's leaders ended centuries of rather stringently enforced isolation, and introduced technology and constitutional ideas from the West.[4] After two decades of institutional experimentation and constitutional debate,[5] the Meiji oligarchs established by Japan's first modern constitution a fully centralized state, a bicameral parliamentary arrangement (a House of Peers and a less powerful House of Representatives), a powerful bureaucracy, an ambiguous system of cabinet and military responsibility to the emperor, and a system of laws and rights heavily influenced by both Japanese tradition and European models.[6] The locus of constitutional sovereignty was the emperor, and during nearly six decades of Japanese life under the Meiji Constitution the centrality of the emperor increased, as the transcendent object of loyalty and as the formal basis of legitimate power for competing political interests.[7] In the latter function, the emperor's role resembled the usual status that the imperial house had held in the previous 1,000 years.[8]

In Japan's modern ideology, long and thoroughly disseminated by techniques of education and control, the emperor was viewed with great awe as the more-than-human father of the island family of Japan, with roots deep in Japan's mythical and historical past. The emperor was above and beyond politics, and worthy of the total self-sacrifice of each of his subjects. However ugly politics and war might become, all blood members of the "national family" (a literal translation of the Japanese term for the State, *kokka*) could bask together in his benevolent presence, in a warm aura of security, belonging, solidarity, and mentally isolated superiority over other peoples.[9] Ever suspect in orthodox circles and at times repressed, but co-existing in uneasy tandem with this politico-religious view were many more or less democratic ideas and associations.[10] In the first decades of the twentieth century both democratic and

4. *Id.*; JOSEPH PITTAU, POLITICAL THOUGHT IN EARLY MEIJI JAPAN, 1868–89 (1967); and GEORGE AKITA, FOUNDATIONS OF CONSTITUTIONAL GOVERNMENT IN MODERN JAPAN, 1865–1900 (1967).

5. GEORGE M. BECKMANN, THE MAKING OF THE MEIJI CONSTITUTION (1957).

6. HIROBUMI ITŌ, COMMENTARIES ON THE CONSTITUTION OF THE EMPIRE OF JAPAN (1889), FRANK O. MILLER, MINOBE TATSUKICHI: INTERPRETER OF CONSTITUTIONALISM IN JAPAN (1965).

7. RICHARD H. MINEAR, JAPANESE TRADITION AND WESTERN LAW (1970); MILLER, *op. cit.*: DAVID A. TITUS, PALACE AND POLITICS IN PREWAR JAPAN (1974).

8. GEORGE B. SANSOM, JAPAN: A SHORT CULTURAL HISTORY (1962); DAVID M. EARL, EMPEROR AND NATION IN JAPAN (1964).

9. The atmosphere desired can be sensed by reading NOBUSHIGE HOZUMI, ANCESTOR WORSHIP AND JAPANESE LAW (1912), SHIN'ICHI FUJII, THE ESSENTIALS OF JAPANESE CONSTITUTIONAL LAW (1940), and MASAO MARUYAMA (I. MORRIS, trans. and ed.), THOUGHT AND BEHAVIOR IN MODERN JAPANESE POLITICS (1963).

10. NOBUTAKE IKE, THE BEGINNINGS OF POLITICAL DEMOCRACY IN JAPAN (1950); JOYCE C. LEBRA, OKUMA SHIGENOBU: STATESMAN OF MEIJI JAPAN (1973); SHIGENOBU OKUMA (ed.), FIFTY YEARS OF NEW JAPAN (1910); ROBERT A. SCALAPINO, DEMOCRACY AND THE PARTY MOVEMENT IN PREWAR JAPAN (1953); ROBERT E. WARD (ed.), POLITICAL DEVELOPMENT IN MODERN JAPAN (1968).

authoritarian modes of socialism were added to the mix, with paradoxical effect in the anticapitalist element within militarist thought, but with more long-term impact on postwar Japanese socialism.[11] The period of peak popular dedication to the emperor in all Japanese history and of least democratic influence coincides with the years during which military leaders shunted aside the political parties and the emperor's personal preferences and led Japan to crushing defeat in the Pacific War, in service to emperor and nation.[12]

The "constitutional sense" (*kempō ishiki*) and the Constitution of Japan in the 1960s and 1970s are, we would suggest, *the reverse* of the 1930s and early 1940s, because present Japanese perceptions of the Constitution result from a continuing, radical reaction to Japan's mind-numbing defeat in World War II.[13] The widespread Japanese rejection today of significant military power under the "no war clause" (Article 9) and of imperial power under Chapter I of the Constitution of Japan is intimately linked in the Japanese mind to memories of utter national failure resulting from total and militant loyalty to the emperor. This, in effect, provides democracy in Japan with a powerful ally.

It is easier to say in 1976 what the Japanese people are constitutionally opposed to than to discern the more positive content of Japan's constitutional consensus today, except perhaps in the area of individual rights.[14] An implication commonly associated with the "militarist period" is an antirationalist and severe limitation of freedom of thought and other individual rights in the name of the emperor.[15] The widespread, deep, and genuine loyalty to the emperor-nation of that era is not commonly discussed in contemporary Japan and is perhaps remembered more often with embarrassment than with any pride. Rejection of the entire earlier system, still symbolized by a demanding and oppressive imperial military, seems to explain in part why any efforts to modify the status of either Japan's Self-Defense Forces, or the emperor, or individual rights

11. George O. Totten, The Social Democratic Movement in Prewar Japan (1966); Stephen S. Large, The Yūaikai, 1912–19: The Rise of Labor in Japan (1972). On postwar socialism in Japan, see A. Cole, G. Totten, and C. Uyehara, Socialist Parties in Postwar Japan (1966).

12. Concerning this critical period, see S. Fujii, *op. cit.*; D. Titus, *op. cit.*; Mark R. Peattie, Ishikawa Kanji and Japan's Confrontation with the West (1975); Ben-ami Shillony, Revolt in Japan: The Young Officers in the February 26, 1936 Incident (1973); Richard J. Smethurst, The Social Basis for Prewar Japanese Militarism (1974); and George Wilson (ed.), Crisis Politics in Prewar Japan (1970).

13. Kendell A. Whitney, *Pacifism and Japanese Politics*, unpublished thesis, University of Colorado at Boulder, 1969.

14. Some observers would emphasize the lack of consensus among some élites rather than the popular consensus. For example, J. A. A. Stockwin, Japan: Conflict Politics in a Growth Economy (1975). He notes (p. 190) that at the level of practical politics head-on clashes over constitutional issues among leaders are generally avoided, "a politically sensitive outcome," even if disagreement on fundamentals remains.

15. *See*, for example, Richard Mitchell, Thought Control in Prewar Japan (1976), and Totten, *op. cit.*

are seen as an attempt to rip apart the entire fabric of the new Constitution, and not simply as an attempt to modify one of its elements.[16] More imperial power would imply more military power, which would mean less democratic freedom, and vice versa—or so it seems to many defenders of the Constitution. Fruitless efforts have been made by certain elements in the ruling Liberal-Democratic Party and by other minority groups to revise the Constitution in whole or in part, particularly in the 1950s and early 1960s. From 1957 to 1964 a controversial, but ultimately benign, "Commission on the Constitution" (*Kempō Chōsakai*) studied the operation of each aspect of the Constitution and reported on its investigations to the government without recommendations.[17] "Reformist" politicians ranging from Marxists to democratic socialists to moderate liberals remain cautious rather than optimistic about the future intentions of those who would like to see Japan modify or substantially change her "too foreign"/"imposed" Constitution. Some maintain that the government and the courts, by their allegedly excessive conservatism, have already revised the Constitution in fact, if not formally; but this is at best a doubtful political judgment.[18] The commonly used term "Peace Constitution" is seen in Japan as a reference not just to the antimilitarist provision of the Constitution, but also to its guarantees of civil liberties. Among élites and among activist groups mutual suspicion and fundamental disagreements on the suitability of Japan's Constitution are likely to continue. These concerns may not be shared by the bulk of Japan's rather sophisticated citizenry. Perhaps it may be said that insofar as the Japanese people share basic values that transcend the imperatives inherent in their complex social system, and that replace in some measure and without much emotion their earlier loyalty to the emperor, they share a loyalty to the Constitution of Japan, what it rejects as well as the rights it guarantees.

The Preamble of the Constitution of Japan proclaims that "sovereign power resides with the people." The emperor remains as a quiet "symbol of the State and of the unity of the people" (Article 1) with no governmental powers. Other continuities with the prewar system reflect varying

16. The radical sense of failure in war seemed to combine with a trait already evidenced in the Meiji period—a national capacity for abrupt, pragmatic reversal of prior policy—to discourage backward glances. On the importance of war-failure rejection in Japanese pacifism, *see* WHITNEY, *op. cit.*

17. Concerning the Commission on the Constitution, *see* John M. Maki, *The Documents of Japan's Commission on the Constitution*, and Kenzō Takayanagi, *Some Reminiscences of Japan's Commission on the Constitution*, in D. F. HENDERSON (ed.), THE CONSTITUTION OF JAPAN: ITS FIRST TWENTY YEARS, 1947–67 (1969), and Robert E. Ward, *The Commission on the Constitution and Prospects for Constitutional Change in Japan*, 24 J. ASIAN STUD. 401 (1965).

18. Such judgments seem to exaggerate the functions of a constitution in a nonauthoritarian state (where law interacts with more than educates society). Integrated democratic growth in rights protection comes hard and slow in the law more often than it bursts suddenly full-grown into lasting law. For a different view, *see* R. Neumann, *The Inaba Affair, Constitution Day and Constitutional Revision*, 9 LAW IN JAPAN: AN ANNUAL 129 (1976).

degrees of change: the political party system, more vigorous, more diverse, and stronger than before, but still often viewed as venal and corrupt;[19] a competent, powerful and élitist bureaucracy; a cabinet with clear responsibility to the Diet (Article 66); constitutional rights, sometimes subordinate to informal in-group pressures and administrative presumptions, but more freely exercised than in prewar Japan and vastly expanded in scope;[20] a mass media system that serves as a Fourth Estate; a societal capacity for group work and for deep loyalty to one's community, usually a face-to-face occupational group, but transferable on occasion to a larger occupational entity, or to the nation;[21] a bicameral legislature, the Diet, which is "the highest organ of State power" (Article 41);[22] and a judiciary with a modern tradition of independence in deciding individual cases, but restrained in the use of its new power of judicial review acquired under the 1947 Constitution.

Japan's Courts

A few characteristics that distinguish the Japanese from the American legal and judicial system should be pointed out. Japan is a democratic unitary State and does not have a federal structure. Although cities and prefecture may pass ordinances, within limits established by law, all laws (*hōritsu*) are national laws legislated by the Diet, Japan's parliament. The prime minister is the head of the leading parliamentary party—perennially the Liberal-Democratic Party, a pragmatic changing coalition of moderate-to-conservative factions—he is not elected by the voters, but by his colleagues in the parliament, as in Great Britain.[23] The Supreme Court makes rules for and administers all Japan's courts and entertains appeals from lower court decisions.

During the Meiji constitutional era, the judiciary was tied in rather subordinate manner to the Ministry of Justice, and the jurisdiction and powers of the ordinary courts were very much circumscribed. Many of the constitutional rights of today did not exist and those established in the Meiji Constitution were subject to considerable limitation by law.[24] A

19. On the postwar party system, *see* COLE, TOTTEN and UYEHARA, *op. cit.*; R. SCALAPINO and J. MASUMI, PARTIES AND POLITICS IN CONTEMPORARY JAPAN (1962); NATHANIEL THAYER, HOW THE CONSERVATIVES RULE JAPAN (1969); HARUHIRO FUKUI, PARTY IN POWER (1970); ROBERT A. SCALAPINO, THE JAPAN COMMUNIST PARTY, 1922–66 (1971).

20. Lawrence W. Beer, *Freedom of Expression in Japan with Comparative Reference to the United States*, in R. P. CLAUDE (ed.), COMPARATIVE HUMAN RIGHTS (1976).

21. For a case study of this phenomenon, see Lawrence W. Beer, *Freedom of Information and the Evidentiary Use of Film in Japan. . .* , 65 AM. POL. SCI. REV. 1119 (1971). On Japanese society generally, *see* CHIE NAKANE, JAPANESE SOCIETY (1970).

22. HANS BAERWALD, JAPAN'S PARLIAMENT (1974).

23. Article 65 of the Constitution places the executive power "in the Cabinet." The prime minister appoints the ministers in the Cabinet, a majority of whom must be Diet members (Article 68).

24. Rights were qualified by such phrases as "subject to the limitations imposed by law" and "within limits not prejudicial to peace and order, and not antagonistic to their duties as subjects." See Articles 19 and 22–29, Constitution of the Empire of Japan, and Hirobumi

claim of "unconstitutionality" in prewar Japan was often only a political demand or an academic argument, and was not viable in court.[25] As of 1945, neither judges nor citizenry were accustomed to the notion of a constitutional right—to free speech for example—that was legally binding in and on a court of law.

The shape of Japanese law and judicial decisions today is further affected by the fact that Japan is basically a civil law nation, not a common law country like the United States.[26] The principal external influences on the pre-1945 law and constitution were the French and, especially, German legal traditions. The political history restricting court powers in civil law nations such as France, civil law approaches to the interpretation of law, and European theories of law and the state set the tone of law and legal scholarship when the senior judges, lawyers, prosecutors, and legal scholars of the 1960s received their formative legal experience and technical training. Differing "interpretive methods" (*kaishakuron*) that have no counterpart in American courts and law schools are taken quite seriously in many of Japan's courts and sometimes affect outcome more than other aspects of law and judicial ideology in a case.[27]

The law in Japan arises primarily from codes and laws, not from judicial decisions; this was especially true before 1947. As Akira Mikazuki points out, the earlier modern Japanese judicial system did not arise organically over time from within Japanese legal culture; it was drawn on a *tabula rasa* with an eye more to nineteenth-century Western systems than to Japan, and was then set up by the central government.[28] Like other aspects of Japan's legal system under the Meiji Constitution which filtered down from above into the mental and social interstices of Japan over a period of decades, the judiciary took time to become a familiar feature of Japanese life. Similarly in some respects, the present judicial system did not emerge naturally either from Japanese legal culture or from the relatively new prewar court system; it was designed by Americans and Japanese connected with Occupation agencies in some way after World War II, and put in place with dispatch.[29] Since the

Itō's discussion. *op. cit.*, pp. 41–61. However, identical or analogous provisions are common in the world's constitutions to this day, and are restrictive or democratic in implication depending on the ideology and politico-legal culture of the particular nation in question. *See* Ivo Duchacek, Rights and Liberties in the World Today (1973).

25. Kenzō Takayanagi (Maki trans.), *The Conceptual Background of the Constitutional Revision Debate in the Constitution Investigation Commission*, 1 Law in Japan 1 (1967).

26. John Merryman, The Civil Law Tradition (1969), explains the significance of Civil law–Common law distinctions.

27. Hiroshi Itoh, *How Judges Think in Japan*, 18 Am. J. Comp. L. 775 (1970): Miller, *op. cit.*, at p. 280; and Lawrence W. Beer, *The Public Welfare Standard in Japanese Constitutional Debate*, in The Doctrine of the Public Welfare and the Freedom of Assembly under the Constitution of Japan, unpublished dissertation, University of Washington (1966), at p. 191.

28. Akira Mikazuki (H. Itoh and E. H. Lee trans.), *A Comparative Study of Judicial Systems*, 3 Law in Japan 1 (1969).

29. *Id.*

establishment of the Constitution of Japan, American common law approaches have been intermingling with Japanese civil law methods and concepts to make Japan a distinctively fascinating judicial laboratory of operative comparative law.[30]

Article 81 of the Constitution, with echoes of *Marbury* v. *Madison*, makes the Supreme Court "the court of last resort with power to determine the constitutionality of any law, order, regulation or official act." The courts are given "the whole judicial power" and "no extraordinary tribunal shall be established, nor shall any organ or agency of the Executive be given final judicial power" (Article 76, paragraphs 1 and 2).[31] "All judges shall be independent in the exercise of their conscience and shall be bound only by this Constitution and the laws" (Article 76, paragraph 1). Of the laws, the Codes are central to the system and, in effect, constitutional in nature.[32] Technically, "a conclusion in a decision of a superior court shall bind courts below in respect of the case concerned" (Article 4, Court Organization Law, Law 59 of 16 April 1947) and not in general. The American doctrine of *stare decisis* is not accepted. On the other hand, a principal ground for appeal under the Code of Criminal Procedure (Article 405, paragraphs 2 and 3) is incompatibility with established precedent not only of the Supreme Court but also of the prewar supreme tribunal and the present High Courts in certain instances. The Supreme Court has on rare occasion explicitly reversed itself; but consistency is duly honored in most cases by courts at all levels, and the study and use of precedent, including foreign (especially American) judicial decisions, has become a common feature of judicial life.[33] Some decisions of the pre–1945 supreme court, the Great Court of Cassation (*Daishin'in*), were reported, but under Article 4 of the *Rules for Conduct of Judicial Affairs* (Decree No. 103, 8 June 1875), court decisions were not to be treated as law or precedent for future cases. Nevertheless, the present Supreme Court has on occasion used *Daishin'in* decisions as precedent.[34] Finally, it should be noted that the Supreme Court is not a "constitutional court" and decides issues of constitutionality only in the context of concrete controversies involving parties with proper standing.

30. Charles Stevens, *Modern Japanese Law as an Instrument of Comparison*, 19 AM. J. COMP. L. 665 (1971); L. W. Beer and H. Tomatsu, *A Guide to the Study of Japanese Law*, 23 AM. J. COMP. L. 284 (1975); and Kenzō Takayanagi, *A Century of Innovation: The Development of Japanese Law, 1868–1961*, in A. T. VON MEHREN (ed.), LAW IN JAPAN: THE LEGAL ORDER IN A CHANGING SOCIETY (1963).

31. This contrasts sharply with the Meiji Constitution, "ARTICLE LXI. No suit at law, which relates to rights alleged to have been infringed by the illegal measures of the administrative authorities, and which shall come within the competency of the Court of Administrative Litigation specially established by law, shall be taken cognizance of by a Court of Law."

32. Concerning the *Roppō* (The Six Codes), see Beer and Tomatsu, *op. cit.*, pp. 303–4, 315–16.

33. *Id.*, 306–8, 311–13. Case 7 and Case 24 provide instances of reversal of precedent.

34. For example, the *Lady Chatterley's Lover* Decision, translated in JOHN M. MAKI, COURT AND CONSTITUTION IN JAPAN (1964), at p. 6.

Japan has a "three tier" court system, with the district courts and high courts first deciding the bulk of cases reaching the Supreme Court. However, appeals have also been made to the highest tribunal in cases originating in the summary courts and family courts (see Appendix 2). The organization of the Supreme Court can be simply explained in the context of its disposition of cases coming on appeal. In the late 1960s, for example, about 3,000 criminal cases and 1,500 civil cases reached the Supreme Court each year. These appeals were first sifted through by the thirty or so Supreme Court "research officers" (*chōsakan*), experienced judges assigned for four or five years to this position between stints on the bench in lower courts. Through this process, the research officers eliminated as without legal justification the appeals in roughly 80 percent of the civil cases and 90 percent of the criminal cases. Thus, the court annually accepted for adjudication about 300 cases in each category. To expedite disposition of these cases, the fifteen justices of the Supreme Court divide into three Petty Benches (*Shōhōtei*), each with a minimum of three judges; each bench is able to settle most cases. The Grand Bench (*Daihōtei*) consisting of all fifteen justices (nine is a *quorum*) hears and determines those cases referred to it by one of the Petty Benches, usually because they involve constitutional questions, especially important and complicated issues of law, or, on rare occasion, inconsistent decisions of Petty Benches on similar issues of law. A Grand Bench decision or precedent takes precedence over a Petty Bench decision. The number of cases pending before the Grand Bench at any given time was steadily decreasing by the end of the 1960s, and in 1971 pending cases usually numbered about twenty.[35]

Like the Supreme Court, Japan's high courts and district courts sit as collegiate courts, usually with three members. Family courts and summary courts are single-judge courts. However, there are cases provided for by law in which a district court may be a single-judge court and in which a family court must be a three-judge tribunal. Today, virtually all judges in courts below the Supreme Court enter the judiciary as a lifelong career after about two years at the Legal Training and Research Institute (*Shihō Kenshūjyo*), entrance to which is gained only by passing extremely competitive national examinations conducted by the Supreme Court.[36] The Legal Training and Research Institute is Japan's only post-graduate law school for those pursuing a nonacademic career course, and it is the training ground alike for Japan's judges, prosecutors, and lawyers. Japan does not employ a jury system,[37] so different lawyerly techniques come into play in trial advocacy before the courts.

35. From an address by former Chief Justice Masatoshi Yokota, *Supreme Court Practice in Japan*, University of Colorado, Boulder, 16 September 1971.

36. This institute was established under Article 14 of the Court Organization Law, Law 59 of 16 April 1947. *See* Hakaru Abe, *Education of the Legal Profession in Japan*, in Von Mehren, *op. cit.*, at p. 153. Around 500 of 10,000 applicants enter yearly.

37. J. M. Maki, *op. cit.*, at p. xxxi, and Von Mehren, *op. cit.*, at pp. 21, 318.

Although law professors as a group appear more influential in Japan than in America, the legal profession in general is less powerful and attracts fewer people than in America.[38]

Under the Court Organization Law, the chief justice of the Supreme Court designated by the cabinet is appointed by the emperor, while the other justices are appointed by the cabinet (Article 39). Justices must be at least forty years old at the time of appointment and "persons of broad vision and extensive knowledge of the law" (Article 41). Article 79 of the Constitution requires that appointments to the Supreme Court be reviewed at the subsequent general election for the House of Representatives and similarly thereafter every ten years; in practice to date, the voters have approved all appointments.[39] Most jurists on the Supreme Court have been appointed at a rather elderly age and have thus served for relatively short periods. Justice Toshio Irie, who sat on the bench from 1952 through 1970, is a striking exception to the rule. Retirement is compulsory at age seventy for justices of the Supreme Court and at age sixty-five for most other judges (Article 50). Between 1961 and 1970 a total of thirty-six justices served on the Supreme Court at one time or another, while three chief justices presided: Kisaburo Yokota, October 1960–August 1966; Masatoshi Yokota, August 1966–January 1969; and Kazuto Ishida, from January 1969 (see Appendix 1 for background information on all Japan's justices of this period).

The Japanese Supreme Court and the courts under its authority have a rather technical life of their own that is usually quite independent of the other branches of government in day-to-day operations, and assignments to lower courts as well as nomination lists for the Supreme Court are largely controlled by the Supreme Court itself. Ideological characterization of the judiciary as a whole would be epistemologically questionable. However, the impact of the cabinet over the years on appointments to the Supreme Court has been substantial, and the late 1960s brought a highly politicized atmosphere to judicial administration, as will be explained below. In general, since the Liberal-Democratic Party, which perennially rules Japan, is composed of predominantly conservative factions, most candidates raised to the supreme tribunal have been rather conservative, with notable exceptions such as Jirō Tanaka and Kōtarō Irokawa in the period under review.

Constitutional Developments in Japan, 1961–70

During the 1960s Japan became the world's third-ranking economic

38. Takaaki Hattori, *The Legal Profession in Japan: Its Historical Development and Present State*, in VON MEHREN, *op. cit.*, at p. 111; see especially the comparative statistical table at p. 152.

39. For a critique of the judicial referendum system, see J. M. MAKI, *op. cit.*, at p. xx. In addition, see the Law of Impeachment of Judges, Law 187 of 20 November 1947; Fukio Nakane trans., for Ministry of Justice, Eibun Hōreisha, 1963. Concerning attempts at judicial impeachment, see the discussion below of the 1969–71 judicial crisis.

power, but continued to refrain from developing commensurate military power.[40] Symbolizing the dynamism and prosperity were the Tokyo Olympics of 1964, the sense of economic boom that accompanied the "low posture," the rather conciliatory politics of Prime Minister Hayato Ikeda (1960–64), and the Osaka World's Fair of 1970. While company profits continued to rise rapidly with the explosive growth in Gross National Product, corporate preoccupation with reinvestment for growth purposes declined; public and private employees alike were finally given a series of wage boosts towards affluence, and consumer purchasing grew apace. Though Japan was without significant energy resources or raw materials, chains of supertankers and freighters (made in Japan) were solving those problems. The technical and organizational skills of the citizenry were seen by all but the very cautious as up to any challenge. The yen had not yet been revalued from 360 yen to around 300 yen per U. S. dollar; inflation levels were far below raise and bonus levels.[41] The "Nixon Shocks" of 1971 and 1972, and the "oil shock" of 1973 had not struck.[42] America reshuffled its relations with the People's Republic of China in 1971 without meaningful prior consultations with Japan; in 1972 tensions arose as the trade imbalance favorable to Japan increased and as the United States imposed "voluntary" import quotas on Japan. These problems were dealt with subsequently; but the possibility of political interference with the flow of oil from the Middle East—source of over 80 percent of Japan's oil imports—was only a fist of cloud on a generally clear horizon, and was seen by few in the 1960s.[43]

The prosperous economic climate of the 1960s freed the minds of politicians, intellectuals, and activists for lively debate on sociopolitical issues. Sharply diverse views coexisted in energetic conflict that was reflected at times in cases coming before the bench and in judicial reactions to these disputes. However, the decisions of this decade do not mirror in a simple, short-term manner the visage of the times. Each case is best considered on its own terms and not as a clear manifestation of hypothetical trends in law, society, or politics. With that caution offered, we nevertheless have the temerity to sketch here in broad stroke a few of the main characteristics of the constitutional politics and judicial decisions of 1961 through 1970.

During the 1960s the unique pacifist provisions of Article 9 of the

40. Convenient surveys of the 1960s can be found in *Asahi Nenkan* (Asahi yearbook) and in the January issues of *Asian Survey* (University of California Press). Both law and politics are covered in the *Jurisuto Nenkan* (Jurist yearbook) of the period, published by Yuhikaku in Tokyo. On the Japanese military, *see* JAMES H. BUCK (ed.), THE MODERN JAPANESE MILITARY SYSTEM (1975).

41. For example, consumer prices climbed about 7 percent per annum between 1965 and 1970, while wages and bonuses rose about twice as fast. It should be remembered that from 1945 until the 1960s, personal income levels did not rise quickly.

42. *Asahi Nenkan*, 1972–74.

43. For the mood of the times, *see*, for example, Lawrence W. Beer, *Japan Turning the Corner*, ASIAN SURVEY, January 1971, at p. 74.

Constitution continued to deeply divide Japanese élites, and this division was manifested in many contexts. The Security Treaty Crisis of 1960, the largest mass movement in Japanese history, might be viewed as a rite of affirmation of the legitimacy of the Constitution of Japan and of the necessity for political sensitivity to its demands,[44] rather than as a revolutionary threat to the constitutional order. The primary reason for the outcry against and the political demise of Prime Minister Nobusuke Kishi in 1960 appears to lie neither in irregularities in the Diet passage of the treaty nor in a consensus rejection of the treaty relationship itself but in Kishi's allegedly arrogant disregard for consensus-building with the minority parties, a violation of the unwritten democratic law and communal constitutional sense of Japan.[45] Growing out of the Security Treaty Crisis of 1960 was a pervasive expectation that 1970 would bring an analogous test of the treaty, a similar moment of national truth. From mid–1970 either Japan or the United States could unilaterally abrogate the treaty at any time on a one-year's notice.[46] In the 1960s students on the far left and others came to characterize Japan's entire *status quo* as "the Security establishment" (*anpo taisei*), in reference to the treaty with the United States and, by implication, to Japan's association with America's unpopular involvement in Vietnam. The Japanese student movement became increasingly splintered, and by 1970 an element of nihilism unprecedented in postwar Japan had infected many groups and alienated both the public and most students.[47] In a much more widely supported phenomenon, nationalism and concern for Article 9 combined, as the successful negotiations of Prime Minister Eisaku Sato and the American government on the one hand, and on the other hand, the many demonstrations demanding "reversion" of Okinawa to Japanese sovereignty, led to a historic peaceful transfer of territory.[48] However,

44. On the crisis, *see* PACKARD, *op. cit.* As Edward Seidensticker has noted, the Constitution is now "among the Sacred Books of the East" (*Japan After Vietnam*, Commentary, September 1975, at p. 56). To 1960 and to most periods and contexts of mass protest in recent Japan, Max Gluckman's distinction between "rituals of rebellion" and "revolution" may be applicable. Revolution seeks to overthrow the existing order, while ritual rebellions, a luxury limited to societies like Japan with a firmly established order, reaffirm the system in demonstrating and venting the tensions between leaders and led as well as between different viewpoints coexisting within the system. *See* especially GLUCKMAN'S CUSTOM AND CONFLICT IN AFRICA and POLITICS, LAW, AND RITUAL IN TRIBAL SOCIETY; and TAKEO DOI (Bester trans.), ANATOMY OF DEPENDENCE (1973); DEAN C. BARNLUND, PUBLIC AND PRIVATE SELF IN JAPAN AND THE UNITED STATES, Tokyo, Simul Press, 1975.

45. PACKARD, *op. cit.*; JOHN M. MAKI, GOVERNMENT AND POLITICS IN JAPAN (1962); SCALAPINO and MASUMI, *op. cit.*

46. *Treaty of Mutual Cooperation and Security between the United States and Japan*, Treaty No. 6 of 23 June 1960, ARTICLE 10. For the text of the treaty and a decision upholding its constitutionality, see Case 13, below.

47. Lawrence W. Beer, *Japan, 1969: "My Homeism" and Political Struggle*, ASIAN SURVEY, January 1970, at p. 43; JOURNAL OF SOCIAL AND POLITICAL IDEAS IN JAPAN, vol. 5, Nos. 2 and 3, March 1969.

48. Beer, *Japan, 1969: "My Homeism" and Political Struggle*, and *Japan Turning the Corner*, *op. cit.* Okinawa reverted to Japan in May 1972. *See* Toyohira Yoshiaki, *A New Defense for Okinawa*, 9 THE JAPAN INTERPRETER 353 (1975), on subsequent developments on Okinawa.

Article 9 concerns remained in the 1970s with respect to the military uses of Okinawa. The achievement of reversion agreements in late 1969, and the unpopular violence of rival student factions during the "University Crisis" of the late 1960s seemed to combine with consumer preoccupations to drain away enthusiasm for an anti–Security Treaty effort in 1970. The "University Crisis" paralyzed education for many months on scores of campuses, and for much longer on a few major campuses, in what was perhaps the longest, largest-scale disruption of a system in world university history.[49] Other manifestations of conflict related to Article 9 could be found elsewhere in the educational arena. For example, major constitutional litigation attended by sympathy demonstrations arose over government tampering with the content of high school history texts that allegedly favored revival of the old imperial system and militarism (the Ienaga Textbook Cases).[50] Furthermore, defense of Article 9 was often involved in the motivation for illegal demonstrations issuing in judicial decisions on the constitutionality of restrictions on the political rights of public employees (e.g., Case 13). Article 9 and political rights were commonly intermeshed in political rhetoric and constitutional cases.

A second constitutional trend, one affecting national-local government relations, accompanied the gradual development by the 1970s of a national consensus to the effect that air and water pollution constitute a very serious problem in Japan about which much must be done.[51] Related to this heightened collective awareness and will to act were a notable surge in organized, grassroots political action (*shimin undō*, citizen movements) attacking the specific pollution problems of particular towns and areas, increased denigration of "the god GNP" which had brought a pollution nightmare along with prosperity, and sentiment in all political parties favoring substantial improvement of the welfare system and of public-sector facilities in general. Antipollution laws were significantly toughened by the early 1970s, and innovative systems of legal relief for pollution victims went into operation.[52] Tensions sometimes developed

49. Beer, *Japan, 1969: "My Homeism" and Political Struggle*, at p. 44.

50. L. W. Beer, *Education, Politics, and Freedom in Japan: The Ienaga Textbook Review Cases*, 8 LAW IN JAPAN: AN ANNUAL 67 (1975).

51. Robert L. Seymour, *Pollution Law and Japanese Society*, a paper presented at the Western Conference of the Association for Asian Studies, Boulder, Colorado, 11 October 1975; Julian Gresser, *The 1973 Japanese Law for the Compensation of Pollution-related Health Damage: An Introductory Assessment*, 8 LAW IN JAPAN: AN ANNUAL 91 (1975).

52. KURT STEINER, LOCAL GOVERNMENT IN JAPAN (1965); SEYMOUR, *op cit.*; Matsushita Keiichi, *Politics of Citizen Participation*, and *Irokawa Daikichi*, *The Survival Struggle of the Japanese Community*, 9 THE JAPAN INTERPRETER 451 and 466 (1975); Editor, *Peasant Uprisings and Citizens' Revolts*, 8 THE JAPAN INTERPRETER 279 (1973). These movements include *jūmin undō*, "a local citizens' campaign for some specific objective. The causes vary widely, ranging from disputes over city planning and development programs to opposition to polluting corporations to demands for better public facilities." *Id.*, at p. 279. *See also* Totten and Kuwabara, *Citizens' Movements and Civil Rights: New Interpretations of the Japanese Constitution*, a paper presented at the 28th Annual Meeting, Association for Asian Studies, Toronto,

over proposed solutions, not only among the political parties, but also between national and local government and between the Liberal-Democratic Party and elements of its business constituency. A constitutional shift toward greater powers and responsibilities for "local autonomy" (*chihō jichi*) units seems to be in evidence in some environmental laws and ordinances and related judicial decisions that dovetail with the new vigor of localized antipollution politics.[53]

A third constitutional trend of the 1960s was an increasing sense of separation between the citizens and the political parties of Japan, unprecedented in postwar times.[54] Political parties are a central feature of Japan's unwritten constitution, and no political party is outlawed.[55] Although the conservative party held an overwhelming majority of Diet seats during the 1960s, the Liberal-Democratic Party's popular vote gradually sank below the 50 percent mark; but the opposition parties were unable to combine forces. Votes for a particular party's candidates have often been cast out of distaste for the alternatives rather than for more positive reasons of policy or personality.[56] The public impression of the ruling party and the largest opposition party, the Japan Socialist Party, was often one of factional bickering within the parties and narrow politicking between the parties, with little regard for public needs. One occasionally recurring pattern that has occasioned popular criticisms is the following:[57]

> Rather prolonged debate on a government-sponsored bill, in committee and/or on the floor, resolving into a form of opposition filibuster, which terminates with the LDP 'ramming through' the legislation [in violation of the imperatives of Japanese consensus politics, and in excessive reliance on the questionable principle of majority rule] with party-line voting amidst protests and at times scuffles; and subsequent calls for 'self-examination' and 'normalization' of the Diet from the press and the political parties, which became in time less urgent under the pressure of other political business.

The popular alienation from the political parties in the 1960s may have triggered the later limited collaboration on environmental policy among certain opposition parties, the resurgence of the Japan Communist Party

Canada, 20 March 1976; Roger W. Bowen, *The Narita Conflict*, ASIAN SURVEY, July 1975, p. 598; Toshiaki Kaminogo, *Glory and Misery of Local Autonomies under Progressive Control*, 2 JAPAN ECHO (No. 2) 17 (1975); and Ken'ichi Miyamoto, *The Financial Crisis of Local Governments*, 2 JAPAN ECHO (no. 2) 32 (1975).

53. Discussion with Professor Naoki Kobayashi, Boulder, Colorado, 4 October 1975. *See* Michio Muramatsu, *The Impact of Economic Growth Policies on Local Politics in Japan*, 15 ASIAN SURVEY, September 1975, at p. 799.

54. N. Kobayashi, *id.*

55. John M. Maki, *The Japanese Constitutional Style*, in HENDERSON, *op. cit.*, at p. 16.

56. *See*, for example, Beer, *Japan, 1969. . .* , at p. 48, where poll results indicate, in keeping with normal opinion trends in Japan, that 33.5 percent favored the Liberal Democratic Party, 14.3 percent the Japan Socialist Party, and about 3 percent or less each the other minority parties.

57. *Id.*; and BAERWALD, *op. cit.*

in the 1972 general elections, the diminution of conservative party power in the House of Councillors elections of 1974, the on-again-off-again reports of party coalition and party splintering, and the revision of the Public Office Election Law in 1975.[58]

Despite their institutional preference to be "off to the side" of political life, the courts of Japan have on rare occasion been drawn into the vortex of national politics, but never as in the late 1960s and early 1970s. The fourth major development in constitutional politics, and one that illustrates again the depth of ideological divisions and suspicions coexisting with Japan's cultural homogeneity, is the "judicial crisis." Criticism of the courts and judicial responses were not unknown. On 21 May 1966 an Osaka prosecutor held a press conference criticizing the leniency of a penalty imposed by two judges of the Osaka Summary Court in a traffic accident case. The Osaka District Court expressed regret at the remarks. The two judges were subsequently transferred, and the Osaka Bar Association asked the court and the Osaka Prosecutor's Office to insure the judicial independence of the two judges. In 1967 the Judicial Conference of the Tokyo District Court struck back with an expression of concern about possible impairment of judicial independence when certain labor unions and bar associations illegally distributed fliers and pamphlets. These materials demanded, but did not win, the dismissal of Judge Hidenobu Sonobe for screening those who wanted to be present at trials of labor dispute cases over which he presided.

In the later 1960s conservative criticism fell heavily on *Seihōkyō* [Young Lawyers Association], a predominantly "reformist" group that emerged after the Security Treaty Crisis to defend the Peace Constitution from within the legal and judicial systems against alleged "reverse course" conservative efforts to revise the Constitution.[59] Magazines such as *Zembō* [Comprehensive View] and *Keizai Ōrai* [Economic Currents] termed *Seihōkyō* a "communist-oriented organization" and attacked it, *Jiyū Hōsōdan* [Free Jurists Group], and *Zenshihō* [National Judicial Employees Union; see Case 13] as responsible for many allegedly biased lower court decisions concerning labor disputes and political demonstrations.[60] The *Nikkeiren Taimuzu* [Times of the Japan Federation of

58. N. Kobayashi, *op. cit.* In its successful attempt at achieving greater popularity, the Japan Communist Party has publicly pledged itself to fidelity to the Constitution; strongest have been the party's assurances of respect for individual rights and liberties, 1972–75. *Id.* Regarding the election law changes, *see* THE JAPAN TIMES, 5 July 1975, and 15 April 1976.

59. H. Fukui, *Twenty Years of Revisionism*, in HENDERSON, *op. cit.*, at p. 41. The mood of criticism of *Seihōkyō* (the full name is *Seinen Hōritsuka Kyōkai*) is well conveyed in SHISŌ UNDŌ KENKYŪSHO, *Osorubeki Saiban* (1969), which resulted in at least one defamation suit. *See* ASAHI SHIMBUN, 19 November 1969.

60. *Id.* The most comprehensive study of the judicial crisis in English is Kenneth M. Tagawa, *The Naganuma Nike Missile Site Case: A Study of the Japanese Judicial Crisis, 1969–71*, unpublished thesis, University of Colorado, 1971. In Japanese, *see Shihō no Kiki*, a special issue of HŌGAKU SEMINAH (Law seminar), February 1971.

Employers Associations] maintained that the Japan Communist Party, through *Seihōkyō*, had penetrated judicial circles. In April 1969, the Party Congress of the Liberal Democratic Party resolved to establish a special committee to investigate the politics of the court system and criticized acquittals in political cases by both the Fukuoka District Court and the Supreme Court (Case 12).[61] More important was the suggestion of the Congress that the cabinet use prior judicial opinions as one basis for cabinet appointment and promotion of judges, and that the judge impeachment system be more frequently used.[62] The secretary-general of the Supreme Court warned that this sort of criticism might endanger judicial independence, but also noted that a judge who joins a political organization may create suspicion in the public mind that his judgment may be biased by his political ideology.[63] These remarks led to the withdrawal from *Seihōkyō* of ten younger judges within the Supreme Court Secretariat. The controversy came to a boil when Chief Justice Kazuto Ishida told the press on Constitution Day (3 May 1970) that "those who are extreme militarists, anarchists, or clearly communists, do not make suitable judges, at least from a moral point of view"[64] and urged judicial restraint. These words resulted in an ineffectual impeachment movement against Justice Ishida.[65] In addition, the Judge Impeachment Committee based an inquiry into 213 judges' qualifications on their membership in *Seihōkyō*.[66]

The *Naganuma Nike Missile Site* Case, which came before the Sapporo District Court (Hokkaido) in the late 1960s, brought the courts before the public eye as rarely before, and occasioned some of the above developments.[67] Presiding Judge Shigeo Fukushima received a letter of advice in 1969 from the chief judge of the Sapporo area district courts regarding disposition of the case at hand (the Hiraga Incident). For this, Judge Hiraga was disciplined by the Supreme Court; but later the Diet's

61. Concerning the district court decision, see the related Case 32 below, and Beer, *The Freedom of Information and the Evidentiary Use of Film in Japan*, *op. cit.*

62. Law of Impeachment of Judges, Law 187 of 20 November 1947.

63. *See* SHISŌ UNDŌ KENKYŪSHO, *op. cit.*; TAGAWA, *op. cit.*; and *Shihō no Kiki*, *op. cit.*

64. For the context, *see* TAGAWA, *op. cit.* and Beer, *Japan Turning the Corner*, at p. 78.

65. A petition containing the signatures of 2,208 legalists demanding the resignation of the chief justice was submitted to the Supreme Court by an ad hoc group called the Liaison Conference to Protect Judicial Independence. Like previous attempts to impeach justices, it failed. For example, on 19 November 1963, 103 defense attorneys involved in the Matsukawa Case and the Shiratori Case filed an unsuccessful petition against Justice Masuo Shimoiizaka with the Diet's Judge Impeachment Committee. On the Matsukawa Case, *see* CHALMERS JOHNSON, CONSPIRACY AT MATSUKAWA (1972).

66. This Diet committee stated that although failure to respond to the letter of inquiry would not be interpreted as implying membership in *Seihōkyō*, it would necessitate other means of investigation. TAGAWA, *op. cit.* As expected the Japan Bar Association demanded retraction of the letter, without avail.

67. Robert L. Seymour, *Japan's Self-Defense: The Naganuma Case and Its Implications*, 47 PACIFIC AFFAIRS 421 (1974–75).

Judge Impeachment Committee criticized Judge Fukushima instead, for having revealed the contents of the letter received from Judge Hiraga.[68] In a 1973 decision in *Ito* v. *Minister of Forestry and Agriculture*, Judge Fukushima, a member of *Seihōkyō*, upheld the claims of local farmers at Naganuma that building the missile base violated their land-use rights and declared the Self-Defense Forces of Japan unconstitutional under Article 9.[69] Between 1969 and 1973, numerous other political and judicial happenings surrounded the *Naganuma Nike Missile Site* Case. For example, great concern was evinced by the failure of the Supreme Court to reappoint Assistant Judge Yasuaki Miyamoto in the spring of 1971, presumably for his membership in *Seihōkyō*, although the Court refused to divulge its reasons.[70]

The courts went through some uncomfortable times, but the effects of such controversy on constitutional law were negligible in most issue areas,[71] and reversal of the Fukushima decision was expected in the *Naganuma* Case. Usually, Supreme Court decisions sustained acts of the Diet, the cabinet, administrative agencies, and local autonomy units. Congruence between policies of decision-making bodies was characteristic. Relying on the doctrine of nonjusticiability of matters internal to other branches of government, the Court declined to review the legislative process of the Diet (Case 3). The Court upheld the sublegislative functions of local assemblies as powers appropriately delegated by the Diet (Cases 2 and 4). When the Court ruled, or was felt likely to hold, unlawful or unconstitutional policies of other agencies, the Diet was quick to change the questionable legal provisions, thereby removing the potential for conflict with the courts. For example, in 1960 the Supreme Court upheld the constitutionality of confiscating third-party property used in crime without notice or hearing, but by a narrow eight-to-seven margin. Two years later the Court changed this precedent by a nine-to-five vote and held such confiscation to be an unconstitutional violation of due process and property rights (Case 7). And in 1965 the Court held unconstitutional an order to make payment in lieu of confiscation of bribe money (Case 9). Following the *Nakamura* Case (Case

68. Beer, *Japan Turning the Corner*, at p. 79; TAGAWA, *op. cit.*

69. Seymour, *Japan's Self-Defense*, at p. 428. The decision is in HANREI JIHŌ (No. 712) 26 (1973). A complete translation of the Naganuma Decision has been made in Richard O. Briggs, *The Self-Defense Force and the Japanese Courts: The Naganuma District Court Decision*, unpublished thesis, University of Michigan, 1975. On 5 August 1976 the Sapporo High Court reversed in favor of the government; at time of writing, the case is on appeal in the Supreme Court, ASAHI SHIMBUN (even. ed.), 5 August 1976; JAPAN TIMES, 6 August 1976. Theodore McNelly, *The Constitutionality of Japan's Defense Establishment*, in Buck, *op. cit.* at p. 99.

70. Tagawa, *op. cit.*

71. Holdings related to the *Naganuma* Case have expanded perhaps the range of administrative disputes which can find standing as constitutional cases in the courts. Kenneth M. Tagawa, "Justiciability and Judicial Power in Japan," a paper presented at the Western Conference of the Association for Asian Studies, Boulder, Colorado, 11 October 1975.

7), the Diet promptly passed a law providing a third party to a crime with notice and a hearing before confiscation.[72] In a later case, the Court upheld the new procedures attendant to confiscation. In a malapportionment case (Case 6), the Court upheld the existing system as a matter to be determined at legislative discretion except in extreme cases; the Diet showed some sensitivity to this judicial policy-making by initiating a partial reapportionment in 1964, and similarly in 1975.

In its relations with administrative and law enforcement agencies, the Court usually decides in their favor, but also commonly reasserts its right to review such matters in the process.[73] However, with respect to an ordinance of the Occupation period designed to control political organizations, the Court found aspects of the Supreme Public Prosecutor's investigatory powers a violation of due process (Case 1).

Between 1961 and 1970 a large majority of Supreme Court decisions were unanimous, and the proportion attended by dissenting opinions had decreased by the end of the decade. Some major cases in which the Court split are Cases 1, 7, 8, 12, 21, 25, 26, and 27 in this casebook. Moreover, in the large majority of appeals coming from lower courts, the Court sustained lower court decisions. On the other hand, lower courts took positions not sanctioned by the Supreme Court in some instances. For example, contrary to the 1950 Fukuoka Patricide Decision of the Supreme Court,[74] the Utsunomiya District Court held the provisions of Article 200 of the Criminal Code, which impose capital punishment or life imprisonment for the killing of lineal ascendants, to be in violation of the equal protection clause of the Constitution. The popularity of this lower court decision was a factor when the Supreme Court changed the 1950 precedent in 1973.[75] In the famous Tokyo Ordinance Decision of 1960[76] the Supreme Court settled basic doctrine for the 1960s concerning local ordinances regulating demonstrations and public assemblies. But lower courts found room within the principles laid down in *Tokyo* for holding some ordinances unconstitutional, on their face, or more commonly, in their application.[77]

In a wide range of cases, the Supreme Court continued to base its rationale for limiting individual rights on "the public welfare" (*kōkyō no*

72. Concerning the *Nakamura* Case and the Supreme Court's earlier holding of unconstitutionality in the *Sakagami* Case, see HENDERSON, *op. cit.*, pp. 127–37.

73. For example, Cases 6 and 13, below, and much earlier, the Supreme Court's "May Day Decision" of 1953, which refused to acknowledge unreviewable administrative discretion to regulate collective activities (7 *Minshū* 1561). *See* Lawrence W. Beer, *The Public Welfare Standard and Freedom of Expression in Japan*, in HENDERSON, *op. cit.*, at p. 225, on this point.

74. A translation of the Fukuoka Patricide Decision is in MAKI, COURT AND CONSTITUTION IN JAPAN, at p. 129.

75. Aizawa v. Japan, G. B., Sup. Ct., 4 April 1973, HANREI JIHŌ (No. 697) 3 (1973).

76. Japan v. Itō, G. B. Sup. Ct., 20 July 1960, 14 *Keishū* 1243 (1960), of which a translation is in MAKI, COURT AND CONSTITUTION IN JAPAN, at p. 84; for analysis, *see* Beer, *The Freedom of Expression in Japan with Comparative Reference to the United States, op. cit.*

77. Beer, *id.*

fukushi) provisions of the Constitution (see Articles 12, 13, 22, and 29).[78] Among such decisions herein are Cases 8, 10, and 26.

The Supreme Court in 1969 relied on Article 13 as the basis for its first recognition of a constitutional right of privacy (Case 25), but a 1964 lower court decision in the *After the Banquet* Case first spelled out the doctrine of privacy rights.[79] Similarly, in other areas such as environmental rights and the constitutionality of the government's textbook review system, lower court decisions were leading the way in doctrinal development.[80]

In general, the law of Japan upholds a high degree of freedom of expression; societal restraints seem more important than legal restrictions.[81] While balancing the right to good name against defamation by the press, the Supreme Court gave considerable latitude to the mass media in the 1960s (Case 24). However, as with public employees in the United States, the political rights of Japanese public employees are limited. Although the Court approved of a nonviolent activity of such employees which was allegedly in violation of the National Public Employees Law (Case 12), it later interpreted "incitement" of court workers in a restrictive manner (Case 13). In the 1974 *Sarufutsu* Decision[82] distribution of campaign fliers by a mailman during his leisure hours was held a punishable violation of duty. If the Court was cautious in dealing with other branches of government, and oriented more towards community tranquility than individual assertion in many civil liberties cases, it did show special concern for protection of the constitutional rights of persons accused of crime. The Court reversed some lower court convictions for violation of due process or conviction based solely on confession under duress (Case 22). Finally, although Japan is a code law country, the gradual and cumulative effect of judicial decisions on the constitutional system has been considerable. Japan began to accumulate legal refinements in the practice of new constitutional provisions and principles only in 1947, using both old and new techniques of legal interpretation. Bricks and mortar are being added year by year to the structure of constitutional law, by the courts and by their cogovernors of Japan in national and local assembly. Reading back through the

78. Beer, *The Public Welfare Standard and Freedom of Expression in Japan*, at p. 207.

79. 15 *Kakyū Minshū* (No. 9) 2317 (1964), Tokyo Dist. Ct., 28 September 1964. *See* Lawrence W. Beer, *Defamation, Privacy, and Freedom of Expression in Japan*, 5 LAW IN JAPAN, at p. 203.

80. On environmental decisions, Seymour, *Pollution Law and Japanese Society*, at p. 7; on the Ienaga Textbook Review Cases, *see* BEER, 8 LAW IN JAPAN: AN ANNUAL, *op. cit.*

81. Beer, *Freedom of Expression in Japan with Comparative Reference to the United States*, *op. cit.*, which utilizes the theories of Chie Nakane and Takeo Doi regarding group and dependency (*amae*) behavior. Also, Nobuyoshi Ashibe, *Consciousness of Human Rights and Problems of Equality*, in H. ITOH, JAPANESE POLITICS: AN INSIDE VIEW (1973), at p. 135.

82. Japan v. Osawa, Sup. Ct., G.B., 6 November 1974, HANREI JIHŌ (No. 757) 30 (1974). Concerning the *Sarufutsu* Case and related cases, *see Recent Developments*, 8 LAW IN JAPAN: AN ANNUAL 205 (1975).

judicial decisions of Japan in the past quarter century, we cannot but be struck—whatever our views of particular holdings and doctrines—by the remarkable speed with which Japan's judges, prosecutors, lawyers, and scholars were able to learn, refine, and integrate into legal practice the substantially new approach to law and constitution imported during the Occupation from the common law nations. May this have been Japan's last constitutional revolution.

Chapter 1

Relationships Between Forms, Levels, and Types of Law
(Kokuhō No Keishiki)

This category of Japanese constitutional case law does not correspond precisely to any American category. Kokuhō *refers to the law of the nation; all Japanese laws* (hōritsu) *are national. In German,* Staatsrecht. Kokuhō no keishiki *refers to a wide range of constitutional legal relationships and the ways in which the formalisms into which law is divided intrude upon each other in the theory and practice of constitutional law. See W. Sakae (ed.),* Shinhōritsugaku jiten [*New Japanese legal dictionary*], *(Yuhikaku, 1970) at 411. In common usage,* Kokuhō, *taken by itself and not in combination with* keishiki *or* gaku (studies), *refers to the Constituion. Extensive investigation and discussion with other specialists reveals no perfectly satisfactory English rendering of* Kokuhō no keishiki.

Case 1. Japan v. *S. Matsumoto (1961).* The Organization Control Ordinance Case

15 *Keishū* 11 at p. 1940; Supreme Court, Grand Bench, 20 December 1961; Tokyo Dist. Ct. (First Instance), Tokyo High Ct. (Second Instance), [repeal of penalties under an Occupation-period cabinet order].*

EDITORIAL NOTE: On 3 July 1950 S. Matsumoto, a member of the Central Committee of the Japan Communist Party, was ordered to appear at the Supreme Public Procurator's Office under Article 10, paragraphs 1 and 3 and Article 13, item 3 of the Political Organization Control Ordinance, a cabinet order issued during the Occupation pursuant to the terms of Japan's surrender after World War II. The Ordinance was repealed after the San Francisco Peace Treaty of 1951, but Matsumoto was charged on 4 June 1953 for his earlier failure to report to the procurator's office, in violation of Article 2, paragraph 7, Article 3, and Article 6, paragraph 2 of the Ordinance, as well as provisions supplementary to the Subversive Activities Prevention Law (Law 81 of 1952).

The Tokyo District Court held that punishing the accused for failing to com-

*The translation of judicial opinions in the authors' own, but they have consulted General Secretariat, Supreme Court (trans.), JUDGMENT UPON CASE OF VIOLATION OF THE ORGANIZATIONS CONTROL ORDINANCE: SERIES OF PROMINENT JUDGMENTS OF THE SUPREME COURT UPON QUESTIONS OF CONSTITUTIONALITY, No. 6 (1962).

ply with the order to report would render the related investigation of crime unconstitutional under Articles 31 and 33 of the Constitution. The Tokyo High Court also acquitted Matsumoto, but on grounds that application of the Ordinance after the effective date (28 April 1952) of the peace treaty violated Articles 31 and 33. The high court disposed of the case on analogy to a case in which a penalty has been abolished by a law enacted after the commission of the crime charged. The procurator appealed to the Supreme Court.

REFERENCES

Constitution of Japan [ARTICLES 31 and 39 were at issue in this case. See Appendix 3 for these provisions].

Code of Criminal Procedure (*Law 131 of 1948*, as amended), ARTICLE 198, 1. A public prosecutor, public prosecutor's assistant officer, and judicial police official may ask any suspect to appear in their offices and question him, if it is necessary for pursuing a criminal investigation. However, the suspect may, except in a case where he is under arrest or under detention, refuse to appear or, after he has appeared, may withdraw at any time.

2. In the case of questioning mentioned in the preceding paragraph, the suspect shall be notified in advance that he is not required to make a statement against his will.

3. The statement of the suspect may be recorded in a protocol.

4. The protocol mentioned in the preceding paragraph shall be inspected by or read to the suspect for his verification, and if he makes a motion for any addition or deletion or alteration, his remarks shall be entered in the protocol.

5. If the suspect affirms that the contents of the protocol are correct, he may be asked to sign it and affix his seal. However, this shall not apply if the suspect refuses to do so.

ARTICLE 239, 1. Any person who believes that an offense has been committed may lodge an accusation.

2. When a government or public officer in exercise of his functions believes that an offense has been committed, he must lodge an accusation.

ARTICLE 311, 1. The accused may be silent all the time or refuse to answer to any question during the course of the trial.

2. Where the accused makes a statement voluntarily, the presiding judge may at any time question him about necessary matter.

3. An associate judge, public prosecutor, defense counsel, codefendant or his defense counsel may also, upon notifying the presiding judge, question the accused in cases mentioned in the preceding paragraph.

ARTICLE 337, 1. A pronouncement of acquittal shall be made by a judgment in the following cases:

(1) Where a final judgment has already been rendered;

(2) Where the punishment has been abolished by a law or ordinance enforced subsequent to the commission of the offense;

(3) Where a general amnesty has been proclaimed;

(4) Where the period of limitations has been completed.

ARTICLE 396. Where there exists no grounds for *kōso* appeal prescribed by Articles 377 to 382 and 383, it shall be dismissed by means of a judgment.

ARTICLE 404. The provisions relating to public trial in Book 2 shall apply *mutatis mutandis* to trial on *kōso* appeal, except as otherwise provided in this code.

ARTICLE 414. The provisions of the preceding chapter shall apply *mutatis mutandis* to the trial of *jōkoku* instance, except as otherwise provided in this Code.

*Organization Control Ordinance (Cabinet Order No. 64).** In accordance with the Ordinance (Imperial Ordinance No. 542 of 1945) concerning Orders to be Issued in Consequence of Acceptance of the Potsdam Declaration, the cabinet establishes this cabinet order for amendments to the Ordinance (Imperial Ordinance No. 101 of 1946) concerning the Prohibition, etc. of the Formation of Political Party, Association, Society, or Other Organization in accordance with the former imperial ordinance.

ARTICLE 1, 1. This cabinet order aims to secure public knowledge of the character of political organizations and to prohibit the formation and direction of secret, militaristic, ultranationalistic, terroristic and antidemocratic organizations and such activities of organizations or individuals, in order to attain the healthy development and promotion of pacifism and democracy.

2. This cabinet order shall not be interpreted nor shall it be applied in such a manner as to interfere with freedom of assembly, speech or religion, except with respect to the purposes and activities specifically mentioned in this cabinet order.

ARTICLE 2, 1. It shall be prohibited to form or lead any political party, association, society or other organization whose purpose or activity comes under any of the following items:

(1) Resistance or opposition to the Occupation forces or to orders issued by the Japanese government in response to directions of the Supreme Commander for the Allied Powers;

(2) Support of justification of aggressive Japanese military action abroad;

(7) Alteration of policy by assassination or other terroristic programs, or encouragement or justification of a tradition favoring such terroristic methods.

*The ordinance was abolished when the Peace Treaty came into effect on 28 April 1952.

ARTICLE 3. It shall be prohibited to take part in any activity which comes under any of the items of the preceding Article.

ARTICLE 4, 1. Any organization that falls under any of the following items and is designated by the Supreme Public Procurator shall be dissolved by the said designation:

(1) Organizations that fall under Article 2 (including those regarded as organizations mentioned in Article 2 in accordance with the provisions of Article 5);

(2) Organizations that have taken part in any activity coming under any of the items of Article 2;

2. The Supreme Public Procurator may also designate an organization that falls under any of the items of the preceding paragraph and has already been dissolved without the designation mentioned in the said paragraph (including one dissolved prior to the enforcement of this cabinet order) in accordance with the said paragraph. In this case the organization shall be regarded as being dissolved by the said designation.

ARTICLE 10, 1. The Supreme Public Procurator shall be authorized to make necessary investigations in order to ascertain whether or not the provisions of the present cabinet order are being observed.

2. The Supreme Public Procurator may authorize the governor of the metropolis [Tokyo], Hokkaido, or urban or rural prefecture to transact a part of the business prescribed in the preceding paragraph.

3. The Supreme Public Procurator or the governor of the metropolis, Hokkaido, or urban or rural prefecture shall be authorized, if necessary for conducting investigation prescribed in paragraph 1, to summon the persons concerned, or to cause competent governmental or public officials to hear their explanations and to request the submission of data and other articles to them.

ARTICLE 11, 1. Any person who had such connection as coming under any of the following items, regardless of the length of period, with any of the head office, branch office, or other subordinate organs of the organization dissolved after 11 May 1948 in accordance with the provisions of Article 4 and has been designated by the Supreme Public Procurator shall be removed from public office, following the example of "those falling under the Memorandum" in accordance with the provisions of the Imperial Ordinance concerning Exclusion, Removal, Retirement, etc. from Public Office (Imperial Ordinance No. 1 of 1947; hereinafter called the Imperial Ordinance No. 1):

(1) Founder, officer or director;

(2) Holder of important office;

(3) Compiler of all publications or the organ magazine or paper;

(4) Voluntary contributor of a large sum of money.

ARTICLE 12. Any person coming under the provisions of paragraph 1 of the preceding Article shall be regarded, by the designation mentioned in the said paragraph, as designated as "one falling under the Memorandum" in accordance with the Imperial Ordinance No. 1, and if he is at present in public office stipulated by the said Ordinance, he must retire from the public office in accordance with the provisions of Article 3 of the said Ordinance. The said Ordinance shall also apply to the person in respect to other matters. However, the authority prescribed in the proviso of Article 3, paragraph 2 of the said Ordinance shall be exercised by the Supreme Public Procurator.

ARTICLE 13, 1. Any person mentioned below shall be punished with penal servitude or imprisonment for a period not exceeding ten years. However, he may, taking the extenuating circumstances into consideration, be punished with a fine not exceeding 75,000 yen:

(1) Persons who contravene the provisions of Articles 2 or 3;

(2) Persons who fail to file the declaration stipulated in Article 6 or who make a false declaration;

(3) Persons who do not comply with the request for their appearance, explanation, or submission of data or other articles in accordance with the provisions of Article 10, paragraph 3;

(4) Persons coming under the provisions of paragraph 1 of Article 2 who fail to take steps to retire from public office in accordance with the provisions of the preceding Article or who take any public office mentioned in the Imperial Ordinance No. 1 by concealing the fact of their coming under the said paragraph.

FORMAL JUDGMENT

The appeal in this case is dismissed.

REASONS. The accused is acquitted on the grounds that the penal provision under which he was charged was repealed by a law enacted after the commission of the offense charged. Therefore, the judgment below acquitting the accused is correct in result, and the appeal by the prosecutor lacks proper grounds.

Accordingly, pursuant to Articles 414 and 396 of the Code of Criminal Procedure, this Court renders judgment as stated in the Formal Judgment above.

This judgment is that of all the justices, save for the opinions of Justices Hachirō Fujita, Kiyoshi Takahashi, Matasuke Kawamura, Ken'ichi Okuno, Daisuke Kawamura, Sakunosuke Yamada, Katsumi Tarumi, Kisaburō Yokota, and Tamotsu Shima, and the dissenting opinions of Justices Yūsuke Saitō, Toshio Irie, Katsu Ikeda, Masuo Shimoiizaka, Tsuneshichi Takagi, and Shūichi Ishizaka.

The opinion of Justices Hachirō Fujita and Kiyoshi Takahashi follows.

The accused was charged on 4 June 1953, with violation of Article 10, paragraphs 1 and 3, and Article 13, item 3 of the Organization Control Ordinance (hereinafter referred to as "the Ordinance"), and paragraphs 2 and 3 of the Appendix to the Subversive Activities Prevention Law

(Law 81 of 1952) by reason of the alleged fact that the accused did not obey the order of 3 July 1950, issued by the Supreme Public Procurator under the authority of Article 10 of the abovementioned Ordinance, requesting the accused to appear at the Special Investigation Bureau of the Supreme Public Procurator's Office at 10:00 A.M. of 4 July 1950, or as soon thereafter as convenient, in spite of his knowledge of the issuance of the order by 8 July 1950.

The Ordinance was enacted not only for administrative purposes, expressly provided in Article 1, such as securing public knowledge of political organizations or suppression or dissolution of illegal organizations, but also to proscribe the commission by individuals of the offenses enumerated in Article 2 and offenses provided by Article 3. Articles 2 and 3, with Article 13 (providing punishment for the violation of these two Articles), constitute substantive criminal provisions and, as Article 1 clearly indicates, it is evident that one of the main purposes of this Ordinance is to prevent the commission of offenses by individuals.

Moreover, Article 10 provides that "the Supreme Public Procurator shall conduct necessary investigations to ascertain whether or not the provisions of this Ordinance are being observed." It is clear, in view of the purposes of the Ordinance in Article 1, that the investigation to be performed by the Supreme Public Procurator involves not only investigation for administrative purposes, but also for the prevention of crime. Therefore, the allegation by the prosecutor that an investigation under this Ordinance is solely for administrative purposes, and the opinion by the court below that the objective of an investigation is limited to ascertaining whether the criminal provisions of the Ordinance are being observed, are both incomplete and incorrect, in that each of them observes only one of the two sides of the shield.

The Ordinance is quite different in its nature from other administrative regulations, such as those of the laws regulating narcotics or various laws concerning taxes, in that it confers upon the office of the Supreme Public Procurator, an administrative organ, authority to investigate criminal affairs. Other administrative regulations confer on administrative organs authority, not to investigate criminal affairs, but to investigate for administrative purposes; both Article 53, paragraph 3 of the Law Regulating Narcotics and Article 147, paragraph 2 of the Law Concerning Collection of National Taxes clearly so provide. An administrative organ may not, under administrative regulations, investigate an accused in a criminal matter, regardless of the existence of such a provision as Article 53, paragraph 3 of the Law Regulating Narcotics.

The Supreme Public Procurator's order, with disobedience of which the accused is charged, was issued under the investigatory authority conferred by Article 10 of the Ordinance. It was conclusively found by the court below upon evidence duly examined in this case that the order was issued solely for the purpose of investigating the accused with respect to violations of criminal provisions of the Ordinance, i.e., for the purpose of investigating a criminal matter. (The exception taken by the prosecutor to findings of fact by the court below cannot be proper grounds for appeal, since this is a challenge to the correctness of the findings. The allegation by the accused that the Supreme Public Procurator's order is *ultra vires* and void, on the grounds that issuance of an order for investigating criminal matters is beyond his authority, likewise is not sound, because the Supreme Public Procurator is authorized to issue such an order, as mentioned above.)

However, to punish the accused for disobedience of the order, by applying the penal provision of Article 13 of the Ordinance, is unconstitutional.

According to Article 198, paragraph 1, the proviso of the Code of Criminal Procedure, an accused summoned by a prosecutor, whose function is to investigate criminal affairs, for an investigation of crime, may refuse to appear at the prosecutor's office. This provision is enacted on the basis of Articles 31, 33, and 38 of the Constitution. Article 38, paragraph 1 of the Constitution provides: "No one shall be compelled to make a statement against himself." Needless to say, when an investigatory authority summons an accused, the purpose is to obtain a statement concerning a crime with which he is charged, and it is clear that to compel such attendance would be repugnant to the spirit of Article 38, paragraph 1. Article 33 of the Constitution provides: "No one shall be apprehended except upon a warrant issued by a competent judicial authority." Although this is a provision concerning apprehension, it implies that whenever one is to be restricted in his physical freedom in the context of a criminal investigation, the intervention of a judicial determination authorizing the restriction is to be required. Compelling one to appear for a criminal investigation without this judicial determination violates this implication. Therefore, to compel a suspect to obey a criminal investigatory authority's order to appear before it, is not consistent with the constitutional provision, and it is evident that a provision for such compulsion violates the "due process" clause of Article 31. Thus, Article 198, paragraph 1, the proviso of the Code of Criminal Procedure, which provides that a suspect may refuse to obey a request by a criminal investigatory authority to appear before it, is based upon those constitutional provisions.

Article 10 of the Ordinance provides that "the Supreme Public Procurator shall be authorized to make necessary investigations in order to ascertain whether or not the provisions of the cabinet order are being observed." Article 13 provides that one who disobeys such a request shall be punished with up to ten years imprisonment or with a fine of up to 75,000 yen. As mentioned above, under the provisions of the Code of Criminal Procedure enacted in accordance with the requirements of the

Constitution, a suspect may refuse to appear when summoned by a police officer or a prosecutor. In light of this provision, it is not necessary to use many words to demonstrate the unconstitutionality of a provision compelling a suspect, on pain of disproportionate punishments, to obey a request issued for the purpose of criminal investigation by the Supreme Public Procurator, who is not a criminal investigatory authority but only an administrative authority. Since the Supreme Public Procurator's order involved in this case was issued, as stated above, solely for the sake of criminal investigation, to punish the accused for his violation of this Ordinance by applying the penal provisions of the Ordinance is not permissible under the Constitution.

The Organization Control Ordinance was one of the "Potsdam Cabinet Orders" issued under the authority of Imperial Ordinance No. 542 of 1945, the Imperial Ordinance Concerning Orders to be Issued in Consequence of Acceptance of the Potsdam Declaration. Thus, it had supra-constitutional validity in spite of the Constitution, during the period of the Occupation by the Allied Powers, i.e., before the Peace Treaty became effective. (7 *Keishū* 775; Sup. Ct., G.B., 18 April 1953: 7 *Keishū* 1562; Sup. Ct., G.B., 22 July 1953.) The determination of the constitutional validity of the Supreme Public Procurator's order issued under the Ordinance was thus beyond the jurisdiction of the Japanese courts (6 *Keishū* 584; Sup. Ct., G.B., 9 April 1952). As the Supreme Public Procurator's order involved in this case was issued on 3 July 1950, and the act charged was alleged to have occurred on or about 8 July 1950, the Japanese courts had to hold, during the period of the Occupation, that the facts at the time of commission of the offense charged constituted a violation of the Ordinance. However, at the present time, when our nation has recovered her full sovereignty, to punish the accused for the act charged by application of Article 13 of the Ordinance is unconstitutional. In other words, the act charged had ceased to constitute the offense charged by the time this judgment was rendered. This conclusion is unaffected by the existence of Law 81 of 1952 and paragraphs 2 and 3 of the Appendix of the Subversive Activities Prevention Law.

Therefore, the judgment below acquitting the accused, under Article 337, paragraph 2 of the Code of Criminal Procedure, on the grounds that the penal provision under which the accused had been charged was repealed after commission of the offense charged, is in its conclusion correct (7 *Keishū* 1962; Sup. Ct., G.B., 22 July 1953), and the contentions of the appellant and the appellee based on different views cannot be accepted.

[The brief opinion of Justice Matasuke Kawamura, which accords with the above opinion, has been omitted.]

* * *

The opinion of Justice Ken'ichi Okuno follows.

1. Under the Constitution, especially for the protection of fundamental human rights in criminal proceedings, criminal investigation of a suspect is to be conducted as a rule without using any compulsion, except in cases specifically provided for in the Constitution. An investigation of a suspect conducted by depriving him of his freedom of movement is permissible only when he is properly under arrest or in custody under the authority of a warrant issued by a judicial authority, except in a case where he is arrested during the commission of an offense (Article 33 of the Constitution). Under Article 38 of the Constitution, a suspect is not compelled to make a statement against himself.

A system under which a suspect is compelled to appear to give explanations and to produce materials, and is subjected to physical punishment if he disobeys, leads to a situation where an investigatory authority can obtain a warrant for arrest or detention on the charge of another offense, i.e., disobedience of an order requiring appearance, even in a case where there is no reasonable ground for believing that a suspect has committed an offense under investigation, or where there is no way for an investigatory authority to obtain a warrant charging that offense. On the one hand, this compels a suspect to appear, and on the other hand, enables an investigatory authority to investigate him by depriving him of his freedom of movement without any warrant. This has the effect of compelling a suspect, under threat of prosecution, to appear to provide explanations and to produce materials. Thus, the fundamental human rights protected by Articles 33 and 38 of the Constitution would fall into total disrespect. Therefore, in my opinion, to enable an investigatory authority to conduct a criminal investigation by using such an indirect compulsion is not permissible under the Constitution.

A suspect has the right under Article 198, paragraph 1 of the Code of Criminal Procedure to refuse to appear, and the right under Article 198, paragraph 2 and Article 311 of that Code to refuse to make a statement against himself. If the law imposed on a suspect an obligation to appear and to make a statement against himself, and also provided for physical punishment for disobedience, no one would entertain any doubt that such provisions were unconstitutional.

It is not permissible under the Constitution to compel a suspect to appear and to make a statement against himself under threat of criminal prosecution for an offense, such as disobedience, subject to physical punishment, even in the case of a criminal investigation by a "criminal investigatory authority." The same is true not only in case of a crime investigation by an administrative agency, but also in case of criminal investigation of a suspect by any national agency having the duty of bringing accusations before a "criminal investigatory authority." (Of course, while an agency other than a "criminal investigatory authority" cannot obtain a warrant to arrest a suspect on the charge of "disobedience," it can indirectly compel him to appear under threat of an accusation on the charge of disobedience.) There is no reason why the Constitution, which provides that "no one shall be compelled to make a statement against himself," should be applied solely to an investigation or inquiry by a "criminal investigatory authority" or a judge; the above provision guarantees a suspect the right not to be compelled by any agency of the state to make any self-incriminating statement. Since a request for an appearance may lead to an investigation of a suspect in order to obtain a self-incriminating statement, as a rule the Constitution prohibits compelling a suspect to appear for an investigation of criminal matters by direct arrest or by indirect threat of prosecution, on the charge of a crime of disobedience to the request, punishable by physical penalties. However, it is not always unconstitutional to confer upon an administrative agency the incidental power to investigate matters necessary to the performance of an administrative aim, and to provide a light penalty, as an administrative measure, for the offense of refusal to respond to an administrative investigation, insofar as it may be found to be a reasonable restriction on the guaranteed human rights for the sake of the public welfare, i.e., for the performance of an administrative function, because such investigation does not constitute a compulsory criminal investigation.

2. The purposes behind the Organization Control Ordinance were threefold: (1) to secure public knowledge of political organizations, (2) to prohibit the creation and existence of illegal organizations, and (3) to proscribe illegal acts of individuals. The means to attain these purposes are to prohibit the acts enumerated in Article 2 by providing that organizations whose purpose is to perform these illegal acts shall be proscribed and dissolved, and those persons who have been members of such dissolved organizations shall be excluded from public office. The Supreme Public Procurator may conduct necessary investigations and may, if necessary, request persons connected with such organizations to appear at his office and to give explanations and produce materials, while one who disobeys such a request is punishable with up to ten years imprisonment or confinement under Article 13 of the Ordinance. It is evident that the objectives of an investigation by the Supreme Public Procurator are to inquire whether an organization is one that comes under Article 2, or one whose activities come under the enumerated activities in the provision, and to investigate whether violations of the provision by individuals have occurred. Insofar as the investigation conducted is of activities by individuals, it is for the purpose of detecting criminal offenses. The Ordinance indirectly compels one to appear, to give explanations and to produce materials by providing punishment of up to ten years imprisonment or confinement for disobedience to these requests. On this point, the Ordinance is quite different from other general administrative acts and ordinances incidentally creating an administrative, inves-

tigatory system for the attainment of an administrative aim and providing for a light penalty as an administrative punishment for the sake of the effective conduct of such investigation.

As mentioned above, an investigation conducted by the office of the Supreme Public Procurator, an administrative organ, may result in an administrative disposition, such as the dissolution of an illegal organization or the exclusion of its members from public office. But an investigation of an individual is conducted for the sake of inquiring whether he has committed offenses specified by the Ordinance, and the state official conducting such an investigation is under a duty to make an accusation whenever he believes that an offense has been committed. Furthermore, one to whom the Supreme Public Procurator's order requesting appearance is issued is compelled to obey it under the threat of prosecution on the charge of an offense punishable by up to ten years of imprisonment. Therefore, the provision of the Ordinance empowering the Supreme Public Procurator to issue an order requesting appearance for a criminal investigation is to be declared unconstitutional under Articles 31, 33, and 38. There is no provision in the Subversive Activities Prevention Law equivalent to Article 10, paragraph 3 and Article 13, paragraph 3 of the Organization Control Ordinance.

3. All provisions of the Ordinance were valid during the period of the Occupation, regardless of their repugnance to the Constitution. While there is the opinion that all provisions of the Ordinance became invalid at the time the Peace Treaty became effective, on 28 April 1952, in my opinion those of its provisions not repugnant to the Constitution are still in effect, and those inconsistent with the Constitution became invalid despite the provisions of paragraph 2 of Law 81 of 1952, at the same time the Peace Treaty came into effect. Since Article 13 violates the Constitution in providing up to ten years imprisonment or confinement for disobedience to an order for appearance issuable under Article 10, paragraph 3, the provision became invalid at the time that the Peace Treaty came into effect, and it could not be revived by paragraph 2 of Law 81 of 1952, and paragraph 3 of the Appendix of the Subversive Activities Prevention Law, which became effective on 21 July 1952. Therefore, the judgment below acquitting the accused under Article 404 and Article 337, paragraph 2 of the Code of Criminal Procedure is correct, and the appellant's allegation based on a subjective view is not acceptable.

[The opinion of Justice Daisuke Kawamura has been omitted.]

* * *

The dissenting opinion of Justices Toshio Irie and Tsuneshichi Takagi follows.

In our opinion, the judgment below should be reversed, and the accused acquitted.

The facts constituting the offense charged in this case are [as described above]. . . . According to the court below, the purpose of the investigation for which this request for appearance was served on the accused was solely to ascertain whether he had committed offenses such as violations of Article 2, paragraph 7 and Article 3 (violation of the prohibition on terroristic activities), and of Article 6, paragraph 1 (failing to make a declaration concerning a political organization), and so on.

First, we will consider whether the investigation under Article 10 includes crime detection activity. Article 1 of the Ordinance provides that "this Cabinet Ordinance aims to secure public knowledge of the character of political organizations and to prohibit the formation and direction of secret, militaristic, ultranationalistic, terroristic, and antidemocratic organizations and such activities or organizations or individuals, in order to attain the healthy development and promotion of pacifism and democracy." Furthermore, Article 2 provides that it shall be unlawful to form or lead any political party, association, society, or other organization whose purpose or activity comes under any of the items listed in that Article. Article 3 prohibits taking part in any activity that comes under any of the items of Article 2; Article 4 provides that any organization violating these provisions shall be dissolved upon designation by the Supreme Public Procurator; and Article 10 authorizes the Supreme Public Procurator or the governor of a prefecture to conduct necessary investigations in order to ascertain whether the provisions of the Ordinance have been observed.

In light of these provisions it is reasonable to understand that the investigation under Article 10 is, as the aim of the Ordinance provided in Article 1 shows, the investigation necessary to ascertain whether the provisions of the Ordinance have been observed, and that the investigation is conducted by administrative agencies for securing public knowledge of political organizations, and for effecting dissolution of illegal organizations. In other words, the investigation is not a crime detection activity, but exists solely for an administrative purpose without any crime detection function. Moreover, as acts of an organization are in fact but acts of individuals who are members thereof, the investigation is legal insofar as it is conducted to attain the administrative purpose and within appropriate limits, even if it becomes an investigation of the existence of violations of the Ordinance by individuals who are members of the organization. Although the act of an individual violating the Ordinance is declared by Article 13 of the Ordinance to constitute a punishable offense, we can hardly say that this indicates that such an investigation is a crime-detection activity. This is clear from the terms of Article 10, paragraph 1. Even assuming that the aim of the Ordinance includes the prevention of individuals' acts constituting offenses under Article 13 of the Ordinance, it is necessary to make a leap in logic to think that the investigation under Article 10 is equivalent to a crime-detection activity of the state carried out against a suspect.

The same is true in the case of administrative investigations provided by many administrative statutes other than the Ordinance. Thus, such laws as various tax laws, the Labor Union Law, the Health Insurance Law, the Drug and Narcotics Law, the Gunpowder Law all provide for punishment of violations of their provisions. They authorize at the same time administrative agencies to conduct administrative investigations to discover violations, in aid of the administrative purpose of maintaining the public safety and welfare. There is no reason to regard an investigation under Article 10 of the Ordinance as different in its purpose from those in such statutes; and these provisions, insofar as they relate to an administrative investigation, are not violative of the Constitution.

As stated above, the provision of Article 10 relates solely to an administrative investigation, and it contains nothing concerning investigation as a crime-detection activity. Accordingly, neither the Supreme Public Procurator nor the governor of a prefecture is authorized by the Ordinance to conduct an investigation to discover an offense committed by an accused as an exercise of the function of criminal detection. Nevertheless, according to the facts found by the court below, the sole purpose of the investigation for which the request for appearance was issued to the accused in this case was to detect criminal acts committed by him. On such facts, the request for appearance issued to the accused by the Supreme Public Procurator was, irrespective of its conformity with the Constitution, an act *ultra vires*, not authorized by the Ordinance but merely purporting to be for an investigation under Article 10, paragraph 3, and it was accordingly void. [While there has been a decision of this Court holding that it has no jurisdiction to pass on the validity of a request for appearance issued by the Supreme Public Procurator under Article 10, paragraph 3 (6 *Keishū* 584; Sup. Ct., G.B., 9 April 1952), that case differs in facts from the present one, where the request for appearance is found to be an act *ultra vires* as not authorized by the Ordinance, and it is not pertinent to the present case. In the present case, the court, having jurisdiction at the time of commission of the offense charged, should enter an acquittal in relation to the facts constituting the offense charged.] Accordingly, since the accused in the present case had no obligation to comply with the request for appearance under Article 10, paragraph 3 of the Ordinance, there could be no violation of the Ordinance by his failure to comply. As his act did not constitute an offense, the court should acquit him. On the one hand, while some part of the allegation by the appellant concerning interpretation of Article 10, paragraph 3 is in accordance with our view, its conclusion that a conviction should have been rendered is not acceptable. On the other hand, the judgment below reaching a different conclusion regarding the law erred in its interpretation of the provisions of the Ordinance. This Court should, reversing the judgment below on the application of Article 411 of the Code of Criminal Procedure, pronounce a judgment of "not guilty."

[The three opinions of Chief Justice Kisaburō Yokota and Justices Katsumi Tarumi and Tamotsu Shima have been omitted.]

* * *

The dissenting opinion of Justices Yūsuke Saitō and Masuo Shimoiizaka follows.

As is pointed out in Part 1 of the opinion of Chief Justice Yokota, Article 10 of the Ordinance in question is a provision concerning not a crime-detection activity, but an administrative investigation. Hence, grounds of Appeal 1 and 2 are reasonable. (We cite the first part of the opinion by Justices Irie and Takagi in support of our opinion, as it seems consistent therewith.)

The interpretation given to Articles 1, 2, and 3 of the Ordinance by Justice Fujita and the other justices who concurred in his opinion seems to have been based on a misreading of their provisions. In light of the authority given by Article 10, paragraph 3 of the Ordinance to summon persons concerned, to obtain their explanations and to request the production of data, it is not necessary to have in the Ordinance such precise provisions as Article 53, paragraph 3 of the Drug and Narcotics Law or Article 147, paragraph 2 of the Law Concerning Collection of Taxes, and the justices admit that there is likewise no similar provision in other laws providing for administrative investigation.

Justice Tarumi seems to insist that the provisions at issue violate Article 21 of the Constitution. But he ignores the existence of Article 1, paragraph 2, providing that "this Cabinet Order shall not be interpreted nor shall it be applied in such a manner as to interfere with freedom of assembly, speech, or religion, except with respect to the purpose and activities specifically mentioned herein."

Part 2 of the chief justice's opinion is, in our opinion, also incorrect, in that he overlooks the facts that the body of Article 13, to which paragraph 3 is added, does not provide a simple inflexible penalty, but gives the court wide discretion, and that the court may choose a fine of minimum amount depending on extenuating circumstances, and furthermore, may make a discretionary reduction or may impose a suspended sentence. The opinion holding that the provisions at issue violate Article 13 of the Constitution is, after all, merely useful for future legislation. Accordingly, ground 3 of the appeal is also reasonable. (In this connection, see the decision by the Grand Bench, at 2 *Keishū* 1951, holding that Article 4 of the Ordinance Regulating Poisonous Foods and Liquor does not violate Article 13 of the Constitution in providing that "a person who violates Article 1 of this Ordinance by negligence shall be punished with imprisonment for not more than fifteen and not less than three years, or with a fine not exceeding 10,000 yen and not less than 2,000 yen." Incidentally, Imperial Ordinance No. 325 of 1946 provides that the court may not apply to such a person Article 66 of the Criminal Code, which gave the courts discretion to reduce a punishment.)

While the courts of first and second instance found that the request for appearance in the present case was issued for the sole purpose of crime-detection, there is a gross mistake in this finding which erroneously assumes that such a purpose can be accomplished. Accordingly, the opinions that affirm this obviously erroneous finding and contend that there is a close constitutional and procedural relationship between the request for appearance and coercive crime-detention activities cannot be accepted.

Therefore, in our opinion, all the appellant's grounds of appeal are well founded, and the judgment below should be reversed and the case remanded to the court below.

Justices Kisaburō Yokota (presiding), Yūsuke Saitō, Hachirō Fujita, Matasuke Kawamura, Toshio Irie, Katsu Ikeda, Katsumi Tarumi, Daisuke Kawamura, Masuo Shimoiizaka, Ken'ichi Okuno, Kiyoshi Takahashi, Tsuneshichi Takagi, Shūichi Ishizaka, and Sakunosuke Yamada. Justice Tamotsu Shima did not sign due to retirement.

Case 2. T. Matsumoto v. *Japan (1962).* The Osaka Prostitution Ordinance Case

16 *Keishū* 5 at p. 577; Supreme Court, Grand Bench, 30 May 1962; Osaka Summary Court (First Instance), Osaka High Court (Second Instance), [constitutionality of penalties under a local ordinance].

EDITORIAL NOTE: The Osaka City Ordinance No. 68 prohibited solicitation on the streets for purposes of prostitution (Article 2) and established penalties for violation. The city ordinance was superseded by the Prostitution Prevention Law (Law 118 of 1956), which went into effect 1 April 1958; but the law allowed subsequent punishment under the Ordinance for crimes charged prior to that date in certain cases. The woman in this case was charged with prostitution in February 1956. The Osaka Summary Court (15 March 1956), sustained by the Osaka High Court (18 October 1956), imposed a fine of 5,000 yen (*c.* $14), reasoning as follows: (1) the Ordinance was enacted to maintain public morality, in accordance with Article 2, paragraph 3, item 7 of the Local Autonomy Law; (2) more specificity in the Ordinance would have been desirable, but the generality of the Ordinance does not render it invalid; (3) since the needs of prostitution control vary among large cities and rural areas, such regulation should be left to local discretion.

The accused appealed to the Supreme Court, contending that the imposition of a criminal penalty under the formality of a city ordinance, instead of a law, violates the due process of law required by Article 31 of the Constitution.

REFERENCES

Constitution of Japan [ARTICLES 31, 73, and 94 were at issue in this case. See Appendix 3 for these provisions].

Local Autonomy Law (*Law 67 of 17 April 1947*), ARTICLE 2, 1.

2. The ordinary local public entities shall dispose of such administrative matters as exist within their respective localities, in addition to their own public works and those which laws or ordinances based thereupon assign to the local public entities, and except for those that belong to the state.

3. The matters referred to in the above paragraph roughly include the following, except where provided for specially in a law or an ordinance based thereupon.

(1) Maintaining both the public order, and the safety, health, and welfare of the residents and those who stay in a locality.

(7) Cleaning, sanitation, beautification, and prevention of noise-pollution, and restriction of acts that harm mores or cleanliness, as well as disposition of other matters concerning health, hygiene, and communication of mores.

ARTICLE 14, 1. The ordinary local public entities may enact their own ordinances on matters stipulated in Article 2, paragraph 2, so long as they do not violate laws or ordinances based thereon. . . .

5. Unless especially provided for in a law or ordinance, the ordinary local public entities may set forth in their ordinances provisions to the effect that an offender against the ordinance shall be subject to a penalty not exceeding two years of imprisonment at hard labor, or confinement, and not exceeding 100,000 yen of fine, a small fine, confiscation, or detention.

Ordinance to Control Solicitation for Prostitution on the Street (*Osaka City Ordinance No. 68*, promulgated and effective on 1 December 1950). ARTICLE 2, 1. A person who follows or solicits others on the street or at other public places for purposes of prostitution shall be subject to a fine not exceeding 5,000 yen or detention. . . .

Prostitution Prevention Law, Supplementary Regulations,

(4) Those provisions in a local public entity's ordinance which set forth penalties against the act of prostitution and the like shall lose their force as of 1 April 1958 when the provisions of Chapter 2 of this law become effective.

(5) When a provision of the ordinance mentioned in the preceding item loses its force after the effective date of the provisions in Chapter 2, an offense committed before the expiration date shall still be punished by the application of the expiring penal provision even after the expiration of it, except where otherwise stipulated in an ordinance of the relevant local public entity.

FORMAL JUDGMENT

The appeal in the present case is dismissed.

REASONS. With regard to the reasons for appeal presented by Defense Counsel H. Akiyama, this Court holds as follows:

Legal regulation of social problems is usually conducted under our Constitution by basic laws that have the effectiveness of national uniformity. But it would be more democratic and appropriate to leave some issues to be decided at the discretionary judgment of each local public entity, which would take into account the preference of residents as well as the natural and social conditions in each locality. Because there are other areas that sometimes can be regulated just as well by either method, the Constitution stipulates that "regulations concerning organizations and operations of local public entities shall be fixed by law in accordance with the principle of local autonomy" (Article 92 of the Constitution); and "the local public entities shall establish assemblies" and the members of their assemblies and the chief executive officers of all local public entities shall be elected by direct popular vote (Article 93). In addition, it provides that "local public entities shall have the right to manage" their affairs and administration, and furthermore "to enact their own regulations within law" (Article 94). (12 *Keishū* 3305; Sup. Ct., G.B., 15 October 1958). The regulations enacted by a local public entity are nothing less than a kind of autonomous legislation. The Constitution directly recognizes in its Article 94 the authority to enact within law, in accordance with the principle of local autonomy (Article 92), which is specially guaranteed by the Constitution as an indispensable part of the structure of democratic political organization. Therefore, although the authority and the effectiveness of a regulation cannot exceed the limits recognized by a law, so long as it is within the law, the ordinance must be said to be effective in law. (8 *Keishū* 1866; Sup. Ct., G.B., 24 November 1954).

The regulation applying to the facts ascertained by the judgment of the first instance, and held constitutional and lawful by the court below, was Article 2, paragraph 1 of the Ordinance to Control Solicitation for Prostitution on the Street (hereinafter referred to as "the Ordinance"; Osaka City Ordinance No. 68, promulgated and effective on 1 December 1950). The above provision sets forth punishment by fines not exceeding 5,000 yen or by imprisonment for acts of following or soliciting others on the street or at other public places for the purposes of prostitution. Article 2, paragraphs 2 and 3 of the Local Autonomy Law specify the restriction of acts that harm mores or cleanliness and the disposition of other matters concerning health, hygiene, and the communication of manners (paragraph 3, item 7). These provisions also maintain that the safety, health and the welfare of the residents and those who stay there (paragraph 3, item 1) are among the administrative matters to be dealt with by the relevant local public entity (hereinafter referred to as "a local public entity"). At the same time Article 14, paragraphs 1 and 5 of the said law stipulate that except where provided for specially in a law, a local public entity can prescribe penalties for the violator of an ordinance, of no more than two years imprisonment at hard labor or confinement, or of a fine not exceeding 100,000 yen, detention, a minor fine, or confiscation. It is clear that at the time of the act committed by the accused in the present case there existed no special provision in a law concerning the matters dealt with in Article 2, paragraph 1 of the Ordinance in the present case.

It is contended that Article 14, paragraphs 1 and 5 of the Local Autonomy Law makes it possible to stipulate in an ordinance to the effect that the violator of an ordinance shall be punished in the manner described previously except where specially provided otherwise in a law, and that this would make the limits of the delegation of power uncertain and abstract and any concrete prescriptions impossible. As a result, in general it would become possible to impose any penal provisions in relation to any matter in the form of an ordinance, thereby violating Article 31 of the Constitution which sets forth the principle that a crime shall be punished under the rule of law.

However, Article 31 of the Constitution does not always require that the law stipulate punishments and penalties; it should rather be understood that by a delegation of power, an ordinance or order that is lower than law should be able to prescribe them. This becomes clear from a reading of Article 73, paragraph 6, the proviso, of the constitution. However, needless to say, the delegation in a law should not be an indeterminate, general *carte blanche*. Matters prescribed in Article 2 of the Local Autonomy Law under paragraph 3, items 1 and 7 are related to the instant case; these matters are quite concrete in content, and the penalties and punishments under Article 14, paragraph 5 of the said law are limited as well. Furthermore, as an ordinance is a form of regulation lower than the law, it is autonomous legislation, as noted above, enacted through a resolution of the assembly of a local public entity composed of representatives publicly elected. An ordinance differs from an order issued by the administration, and rather belongs to the same category of law as that enacted by a resolution of the Diet which is composed of representatives publicly elected by the people. Therefore, a proper construction would be that in cases of prescribing penalty and punishment by ordinance, it suffices to make the delegation under law concrete and rather restrictive. A prescription concerning penalty and punishment in a concrete problem area like Article 2, paragraph 3, items 1 and 7 of the Local Autonomy Law, can be established by ordinance within limits placed on the penalty and punishment, like those in Article 14, paragraph 5 of the said law. Such provisions can be said to impose criminal penalties according to procedure established by law within the meaning of Article 31 of the Constitution, and as such cannot be said to be in contravention of the said Article as is argued by the appellant. Therefore, the above provision of the Ordinance in the present instance, which is based upon Article 14, paragraph 5 of the Local Autonomy Law, cannot be said to be in violation of the above Article of the Constitution.

Consequently, this Court decides as stated in the Formal Judgment in accordance with Article 408 of the Code of Criminal Procedure.

This judgment is unanimous save for the supplementary opinions of the Justices Hachirō Fujita, Toshio Irie, Katsumi Tarumi, and Ken'ichi Okuno [which are here omitted].

Justices Kisaburō Yokota (presiding), Yūsuke Saitō, Hachirō Fujita, Matasuke Kawamura, Toshio Irie, Katsu Ikeda, Katsumi Tarumi, Daisuke Kawamura, Masuo Shimoiizaka, Ken'ichi Okuno, Tsuneshichi Takagi, Shūichi Ishizaka, Sakunosuke Yamada, and Kakiwa Gokijyō.

Chapter 2

The Diet, the Cabinet, and the Courts (Kokkai-Naikaku)

Case 3. Shimizu v. *Governor, Osaka Metropolis.* The Shimizu Police Law Case

16 *Minshū* 3 at p. 445; Supreme Court, Grand Bench, 7 March 1962; Osaka Dist. Ct. (First Instance), Osaka High Ct. (Second Instance), [constitutionality of judicial review of the legislative process].

EDITORIAL NOTE: In 1954 a new Police Law was enacted that transformed all city, town, and village police into prefectural police. At the request of the governor, the Osaka Metropolitan Assembly approved a budget supplement for fiscal year 1954, in order to implement the new Police Law. The plaintiff, a resident taxpayer of Osaka Metropolis, challenged this action before the Prefectural Auditor's Commission, which responded as follows: (1) the Police Law was passed in accordance with proper and normal legislative procedures; (2) the governor performed his duty in taking measures to implement the law; (3) the Assembly approved the budget, and the governor was within his authority in administering the budget and approved expenditures.

The plaintiff contended the following in district court: (1) the new Police Law was passed by the House of Councillors on 7 June 1954 and put into effect, despite the fact that the Diet session had ended on 3 June. The Police Law was approved after the session had closed and is therefore invalid. The Speaker of the House of Representatives allegedly extended the session, but he was not seated at the rostrum when he announced the extension on 3 June. He neither called the meeting to order nor distributed the agenda beforehand. He failed to allow time for debate and failed to announce the results of the voting. Thus, the Speaker did not conform to the Rules of the House of Representatives. (2) The law in question violates the constitutional principle of local autonomy by depriving cities, towns and villages of the function of maintaining their own police forces.

The court of first instance dismissed the suit, stating that to warrant a trial under Article 243-2, paragraph 4 of the Local Autonomy Law, an "unlawful expenditure" must be such that a local auditor can request corrective measures of his superior. Moreover, this challenge to the legislative process inside the Diet is not an appropriate matter for judicial review. The Osaka High Court upheld this ruling, and the plaintiff filed an appeal with the Supreme Court.

REFERENCES

Constitution of Japan [ARTICLES 59, 81, and 92 were at issue in this case. See Appendix 3 for these provisions].

Local Autonomy Law (*Law 67 of 17 April 1947*), ARTICLE 243-2, 1. When convinced that the head, treasurer, cashier, or other personnel of an ordinary local public entity is engaged in an unlawful or inappropriate expenditure or waste of public money, an unlawful or inappropriate disposition of property, an expenditure of public money for purposes other than specifically appropriated, incurring an unlawful debt or other obligation, an unlawful use of property or building, or concluding or performing *ultra vires* unlawful contracts, the resident of an ordinary local public entity can request with a written statement of allegations to an auditor of it to audit and take measures necessary to restrict or prohibit the alleged, above-mentioned act.

2. Within twenty days after the complaint in the preceding paragraph has been filed, an auditor shall request the head of an ordinary local public entity to restrict or prohibit the alleged action if he finds the allegation to be true, or notify the complainant in paragraph 1 of his finding showing an absence of such an alleged action.

3. The head of an ordinary local public entity shall immediately take necessary measures upon the auditor's request in the preceding paragraph, and also shall notify both the auditor and the complainant of his actions.

4. If dissatisfied with the measures taken by the auditor or the head of an ordinary local public entity under the provisions of paragraph 2, or in the absence of any measures to be taken by these people, the complainant in paragraph 1 may request a court in a suit, in accordance with the Supreme Court Rules, to restrict, prohibit, revoke, or nullify an unlawful or *ultra vires* action, and to grant compensation for resultant damages to an ordinary local public entity.

5. In a city, town, or village without an auditor, a complaint in paragraph 1 can be made to the head of an ordinary local public entity, and the tasks charged to an auditor or to the head of an ordinary local public entity in paragraphs 2 and 3 shall be carried out by a city mayor or by the head of a town or village.

Police Law (*Law 196 of 1947*), ARTICLE 40, 1. Towns and villages with a population of 5,000 or more and all cities shall be charged with maintaining police forces of their own to carry out law and order in their own jurisdiction.

2. Cities, towns, and villages in the preceding paragraph shall be designated in a government ordinance in accordance with the size of population published in a latest official gazette.

Police Law (*Law 162 of 1954*), ARTICLE 36. The metropolis, Hokkaido, and the urban and rural prefectures shall set up their own police forces, which shall be charged with the duties in Article 2 within their own jurisdiction.

FORMAL JUDGMENT

The appeal in the present case is dismissed.

REASONS. The judgment of the court below did not accept the contention of the appellant on the grounds that the authority of the auditor of a local autonomy entity was limited to determining the adequacy of actions taken by the head and the executive branch under him, and did not extend to determination of the adequacy of actions taken by the legislature. The authority of the auditor under Article 243-2 of the Local Autonomy Law should be similarly construed. Even in a suit under the same Article, the unlawfulness itself of bills passed by the legislature cannot be corrected when such action would exceed the authority vested in the auditor. As long as the expenditure in the present case is based upon a budget passed by the Osaka Assembly, the appellant who contends the expenditure is unlawful cannot seek a judgment on the question by the court. The *jōkoku* appeal contends that the ruling of the judgment below in the above opinion was unlawful by reason of erroneous interpretation of the laws.

As the court below ruled, a request for an audit by a resident, and also a suit under Article 243-2 of the Local Autonomy Law, are remedial steps for actions taken by the head and other personnel concerning public funds or property that belongs to a local autonomy entity, and are not intended for the correction of legislative actions. On the one hand, the expenditure of public funds by the head official or other personnel requires legislative action; on the other hand, it must conform to provisions of the laws. A resolution by an assembly does not make an unlawful expenditure a lawful one.

The court below apparently was of the opinion that in a case like this, a solution must be sought through a request for the conversion of legislation as stipulated in Chapter 5 of the above law; but it is proper to interpret the said law as establishing Article 243-2 apart from Chapter 5, probably because such a method of direct appeal was thought to be insufficient, and partly because giving individual residents a means to seek a restriction and prohibition of unlawful expenditures would rectify expenditures from public funds and the management of public properties. Thus construed, an auditor is not necessarily unable to make the head official take proper measures in its execution, an existing assembly resolution notwithstanding. One should be able to seek by a suit an injunction and restriction of execution based upon the resolution. The judgment below must be said to be unlawful in erroneously interpreting the laws inasmuch as it dismissed the request of the appellant simply on the grounds that the Osaka Assembly had passed a resolution concerning the expenditure in the present case. On the points above, the contentions are not unreasonable.

It would now be appropriate to examine the record in order to review the appellant's contention that the expenditure in the instant case is unlawful. The appellant contends that the Police Law (Law 162 of 1954) is invalid and that an expenditure which is based upon an invalid law is unlawful. He bases his contention that the Police Law is invalid on the grounds that the resolution of the House of Councillors which passed the law was invalid, that the law does not have effect as a law, and furthermore, that the said law in its content is invalid as contrary to the intent of local autonomy stipulated in Article 92 of the Constitution. However, as long as the said law was passed by resolution of both houses and was promulgated through lawful procedure, the court should respect the autonomy of both houses of the Diet, and should not examine and pass its judgment on the validity of facts, as was argued in court, concerning the procedures followed in enacting the said law. Therefore, as argued by the court, the said law cannot be invalidated on these grounds. Furthermore, the appellant contends that the law, in its content, is in violation of Article 92 of the Constitution. But the law cannot be construed as violating the essence of local autonomy, even if it abolished the police of city, town, and village and transferred those responsibilities to the police of the prefectures. Therefore, the law in its content cannot be held in violation of Article 92 of the Constitution.

As is explained above, the Police Law is not invalid. Since the appellant does not contend that the expenditures in this case are unlawful on any other grounds, the claim by the appellant in the instant suit must be considered unreasonable. As was pointed out before, the court below erred in interpreting the provisions of Article 243-2 of the Local Autonomy Law, but it was correct in concluding that the claim of the appellant should not be accepted.

This Court dismisses the appeal in the present case, as stated in the Formal Judgment, in accordance with Articles 396, 384-2, 95, and 89 of the Code of Civil Procedure.

This judgment is unanimous save for the supplementary opinion of Justice Ken'ichi Okuno and dissenting opinions of Justices Kisaburō Yokota, Yūsuke Saitō, Hachirō Fujita, Katsumi Tarumi, Masuo Shimoiizaka and Sakunosuke Yamada [all of whose opinions are omitted here].

Justices Kisaburō Yokota (presiding), Yūsuke Saitō, Hachirō Fujita, Matasuke Kawamura, Toshio Irie, Katsu Ikeda, Katsumi Tarumi, Daisuke Kawamura, Masuo Shimoiizaka, Ken'ichi Okuno, Kiyoshi Takahashi, Tsuneshichi Takagi, Shūichi Ishizaka, and Sakunosuke Yamada.

Chapter 3

Local Autonomy (Chihō Jichi)

Japan has a unitary, centralized democratic government, not a federal system. All laws (hōritsu) *are national laws. Nevertheless, both by tradition and under the impetus of the Allied Occupation (1945–52) and the operative force of the 1947 Constitution, a measure of local autonomy in administrative and legislative, but not judicial, matters is characteristic of constitutional arrangements in Japan.*

Case 4. Japan v. *Kobayashi et al (1963).* The Tokyo Ward Autonomy Case

17 *Keishū* 2 at p. 121; Supreme Court, Grand Bench, 27 March 1963; Tokyo Dist. Ct. (First Instance), [constitutionality of the ward mayoralty election system].*

EDITORIAL NOTE: The defendants in this case received money in connection with the election of the ward mayor by the Shibuya Ward Assembly in August 1963; but they were acquitted by the Tokyo District Court on the following grounds: (1) a special ward in Tokyo is a constitutionally established autonomous unit (Article 93, paragraph 2); (2) it is unconstitutional to abolish by a mere revision of the Local Autonomy Law the system of popular election in a ward; (3) consequently, it was unlawful for the ward assembly to nominate and select the ward leader as it did; (4) since the accused did not have the authority to elect the ward mayor, their receipt of money in connection with such an election did not constitute the crime of bribery. The prosecutor's office lodged an appeal directly to the Supreme Court, omitting an appeal to the Tokyo High Court.

REFERENCES

Constitution of Japan, [ARTICLE 93, paragraph 2 was at issue in this case. See Appendix 3 for this provision].

Local Autonomy Law (*Law 67 of 1947*), ARTICLE 281-2, 1. The mayor of a special ward (*ku*) shall be elected, with the governor's consent, by a spe-

*HANREI JIHŌ, No. 291, p. 8 (Tokyo Dist. Ct., 26 February 1962).

cial ward assembly from among those who are twenty-five years of age and over and who are eligible to vote for the special ward assemblymen.

FORMAL JUDGMENT

1. The decision below is quashed.
2. This case is remanded to the Tokyo District Court.

REASONS. The appeal presented by Prosecutor T. Ishida of the Tokyo District Public Prosecutor's Office, contends that the decision below was unlawful by reason of error in the interpretation of the above provision of the Constitution, when it ruled that Article 281-2, paragraph 1 of the Local Autonomy Law, which voided the public election of the mayor of a special ward in the Tokyo metropolis, was in violation of Article 93, paragraph 2 of the Constitution and invalid.

Article 93, paragraph 2 of the Constitution stipulates that "the chief executive officers of all local public entities, the members of assemblies and such other local officials as may be determined by law shall be elected by direct popular vote within their particular communities." There is no clear indication as to what is meant by "local public entities." But the Constitution has specially established this chapter and has guaranteed a local self-government in order to assure, as part of the democratization that underlies the new Constitution, a type of political structure under which residents of a community would have their own entities manage public matters that are closely connected to their daily lives. In the light of this intent, it takes more than treatment by law as a local public entity in name to be a local public entity in the above sense; the residents must be able to supervise the particular community, both economically and culturally; there must exist a social foundation with the sense of being a communal body; it is required to be a communal body, both historically and in actual administration, vested with such basic powers of local self-government as a considerable degree of autonomous power to legislate, to administer, and to finance. Law should not deny to an entity equipped with such features the function of local self-government guaranteed by the Constitution.

A good example of this autonomy is the Tokyo districts, with wards having a long history and tradition as local entities ever since the administrative system of the county, ward, and town was established under the Village Organization Law of 1878. But the ward has never acquired the position of a completely autonomous body such as a city, town, and village, nor has it ever performed any such functions. With the establishment of the local autonomy system, recognition was also extended to the status of a ward as a legal person, and yet the mayor of a ward was still regarded as a salaried official of the city, appointed by the governor. A ward was not given the right to tax or to issue bonds, or an autonomous right to legislate; it was restricted merely to the management of matters concerning its own property and structures, or matters that belonged to the ward under other legal orders. Particularly after the Sino-Japanese War, the autonomous power of a ward was gradually suppressed, and under the Tokyo metropolitan system established in July 1943, it became merely a substructure of the metropolis.

However, by a partial revision of the metropolitan system of Tokyo after the war in September 1946, a ward was granted, allowing an additional power to manage its own affairs in accordance with prescriptions of legal orders (Article 140), a right to enact ward ordinances and ward regulations, and a right to assess and collect ward taxes and a share of expenses (Article 143 and Article 157 [3 and 5]). A system of publicly electing a ward mayor was adopted in which "the ward head will be installed in a ward" and "he will be elected by electors from among eligible voters" (Article 151 [2]). Even in the Local Autonomy Law enacted in April 1947, provisions concerning the city were to be applied, as a rule, to a special ward, as to "a special local public entity." But the premise of these laws was realized in the business and work of a special ward only to the extent that a ward conducted popular elections of its mayors. Other than that, no difference is discernable from the metropolitan government. Although a special ward carries out its administration directly for its residents, it differs considerably in several respects from a city in its sphere and authority. This will be sufficiently clear from looking at the provisions of various laws listed below.

Under the Local Autonomy Law, the Tokyo metropolis can, by its own ordinances, set up necessary provisions concerning a special ward (Article 282), and a governor of the metropolis can appoint officials of the metropolis in a special ward (Article 210 of an Enforcement Ordinance for the said law). In addition, on the basis of a provision of Article 191 of the Tokyo Metropolitan Government Ordinance, which is still enforced by application of Article 2 in supplementary provisions of the said Law, many responsibilities that had been handled by the metropolis during the period of the prewar metropolitan government were still reserved to the metropolis. In the provisions of a special law certain matters are under the jurisdiction of a city in law; but in metropolitan Tokyo, important matters are excluded from the authority of special wards, or all the special wards are treated as one object. Thus, in many instances the metropolis is given a dual character as both city and prefecture. For example, we might mention Article 51 of the Police Law (Law 196 of 1947); Item 16 of the Fire Prevention Law (Law 226 of 1947); and the Road Traffic Law (Law 58 of 1919). The applicability of these has been completely suspended by Article 4 of the supplementary provision to the Local Autonomy Law Enforcement Ordinance. Other examples are the Water Works Ordinance (Imperial Ordinance 9 of 1890); Article 71 of the Child Welfare Law (Law 164 of 1947); Article 52 of the Board of Education Law (Law 170 of 1948); Article 209 of the Local Autonomy Law Enforcement Ordinance (Cabinet Order 16 of 1947); and Article 2, paragraph 1 of the Local Finance Equalization Grant Law (Law 211 of 1950).

Particularly with regard to the power of a special ward in public finance, as mentioned before, a ward was given the power of autonomous public financing and could assess and collect ward tax independently under the partial revision of the Tokyo Metropolitan Government Ordinance in 1946. But in the Local Taxation Law (Law 16 of 1946) revised the same year, a ward in metropolitan Tokyo was allowed only to tax as a ward the whole or part of taxes that the metropolis was able to impose in accordance with a metropolitan ordinance. Furthermore, a ward was required to get the consent of the metropolis when it wanted to establish any taxes and impose an independent tax (Article 85 [11 and 12]). Thus, a ward was not treated as a local entity having an independent power of taxation. Even in the revised Local Tax Law of 1950 (Law 226 of 1950), this premise has not been changed to date (Article 1, items 734 and 736). Thus, an attempt was made to strengthen the autonomy of a special ward by a modification of the Metropolitan Government Ordinance in September 1946, but by the Local Autonomy Law enacted in April 1947 and other laws, substantial restrictions have been imposed upon its autonomy. This was because of the rapid economic development and the thriving culture in metropolitan Tokyo after the war, and also because the daily life of its residents often went beyond the boundaries of one special ward into other districts. The population differences increased tremendously between daytime and nighttime from the center of the metropolis to the suburbs. Furthermore, the uneven distribution of financial sources in several districts became more and more conspicuous, based upon the need to carry out the administration of a large metropolitan government with unity, balance, and planning, covering all the districts of twenty-three wards. Moreover, it should be said that it was also based on the fact that a special ward forms part of an independent local entity of the unique character of metropolitan Tokyo.

Since the actual situation of a special ward is as described above, even though the direct election of the mayor of a special ward is recognized by law, a special ward could be regarded as a local public entity recognized in Article 93, paragraph 2 of the Constitution neither at the time of the enactment of the Constitution, nor at the time of the revision of the Local Autonomy Law in August 1952. Therefore, the revised Local Autonomy Law, which abolished the above direct election system, and which adopted instead a method by which the assembly of a special ward, with the consent of the metropolitan governor, selects the head of the ward from among those who are over twenty-five years of age and in possession of the right to vote in assembly elections of the special ward, pertains merely to questions of legislative policy and cannot be said to contravene Article 93, paragraph 2 of the Constitution.

The court below held that Article 281-2, Paragraph 1 of the Local

Autonomy Law, which abolished the popular election system for the mayoralty of a special ward, is in violation of Article 93, Paragraph 2 of the Constitution and as such invalid. It follows from what has been said above that the decision below is unlawful by reason of erroneous interpretation of the above provision of the Constitution. The contentions of the appeal are reasonable, and the judgment of the court below must be quashed.

Consequently, this Court decides as stated in the Formal Judgment in accordance with Article 410, Paragraph 1, the Main Text, Article 405, Item 1, and Article 413, Main Text of the Code of Criminal Procedure.

This judgment is unanimous save for the supplementary opinion of Justice Katsumi Tarumi [which is omitted].

Justices Kisaburō Yokota (presiding), Matasuke Kawamura, Toshio Irie, Katsu Ikeda, Katsumi Tarumi, Daisuke Kawamura, Masuo Shimoiizaka, Ken'ichi Okuno, Tsuneshichi Takagi, Shūichi Ishizaka, Sakunosuke Yamada, Kakiwa Gokijyō, Masatoshi Yokota, Kitarō Saitō, and Asanosuke Kusaka.

Chapter 4

Taxation Under the Constitution (Zaisei)

Article 30 of the Constitution: "The people shall be liable to taxation as provided by law." Japanese and resident aliens are subject to national, local, and special taxes established pursuant to law.

Case 5. Takano v. *Director, Osaka Office, National Tax Bureau (1961)*. The Joint Income Tax Case

15 *Minshū* 8 at p. 2047; Supreme Court, Grand Bench, 6 September 1961; Osaka Dist. Ct. (First Instance), Osaka High Ct. (Second Instance), [constitutionality of the joint income tax system].

EDITORIAL NOTE: In filing income tax returns for 1957, the plaintiff divided his wages and business income equally between his wife and himself and filed two separate returns on the grounds that half of the income he had earned belonged to his wife, who had helped him earn by her domestic labor and cooperation. However, the tax office transferred all his income to a single return under his name and reassessed his income tax.

After an unsuccessful complaint to the tax office, the appellant lodged a suit seeking the revocation of the tax office's reassessment. The plaintiff contended that the Income Tax Law, which credits all assets to the husband, allows the husband to monopolize all assets and disregards the wife's domestic labor, thereby failing to recognize her dignity and the equality of the sexes guaranteed in Articles 14, 24, and 30 of the Constitution. The lower courts dismissed this contention, maintaining that taxes on a married couple's income are assessed on the principle of partition of assets between spouses (Article 762, paragraph 1 of the Civil Code) and that the Income Tax Law is reasonable, in view of other provisions available to correct gross inequalities between spouses for purposes of maintaining domestic harmony. The plaintiff appealed to the Supreme Court.

REFERENCES

Constitution of Japan [ARTICLES 14, 24, and 30 were at issue in this case. See Appendix 3 for these provisions].

Civil Code (*Law 9 of 21 June 1898*, as amended), ARTICLE 762, 1. A spouse who acquired certain property before his or her marriage or who acquired it in his or her name after marriage remains its sole owner.

FORMAL JUDGMENT

The appeal in the present case is dismissed.

REASONS. On grounds that the provision of Article 762, paragraph 1 of the Civil Code is in violation of Article 24 of the Constitution, objection is lodged by the plaintiff, as seen in his appeal brief, against the decision below, which held that neither Article 762, paragraph 1 of the Civil Code nor the Income Tax Law based thereon and directed at persons with income is contrary to Article 24 of the Constitution.

The provisions of Article 24 of the Constitution read, "Marriage . . . shall be maintained through mutual cooperation with the equal rights of husband and wife as a basis." And "with regard to choice of spouse, property rights, inheritance, choice of domicile, divorce, and other matters pertaining to marriage and the family, laws shall be enacted from the standpoint of individual dignity and the essential equality of the sexes." Thus, these provisions set forth for marital and domestic relations the individual's dignity and the equality of the sexes, a basic principle of democracy, and allow a husband as husband no rights beyond those enjoyed by a wife as wife. From the standpoint of their general perspective, these provisions call for essentially equal enjoyment of rights in marital relationships. These provisions should not be construed as dictating that in every concrete legal relationship husband and wife should always enjoy the same rights.

According to Article 762, paragraph 1 of the Civil Code, a spouse can claim all the assets that he or she has acquired under his or her marital name. It is true as contended that this provision applies equally to both spouses, who are two-in-one forming one cooperative body and that one spouse often assists the other in accumulating community property. However, the Civil Code also provides for a right to the partition of community property and a claim to inheritance and support. Thus, in dealing with the cooperation and respective contributions of spouses, the legislature was solicitous lest an exercise of those rights should create essential inequalities. Therefore, Article 762, paragraph 1 of the Civil Code does not violate Article 24 of the Constitution, as construed above.

As applied in the present case, the Income Tax Law is no more in contravention of Article 24 of the Constitution than is Article 762, paragraph 1 of the Civil Code, which sets forth the principle of partition of assets between spouses which constitutes the basis for calculating the income of spouses who share living expenses.

Thus the judgment of the court below is correct and is the same as the opinion above. The plaintiff's contentions cannot be accepted.

Consequently, this Court unanimously decides as stated in the Formal

Judgment in accordance with Articles 401, 95, and 89 of the Code of Civil Procedure.

Justices Kisaburō Yokota (presiding), Yūsuke Saitō, Hachirō Fujita, Matasuke Kawamura, Toshio Irie, Katsu Ikeda, Katsumi Tarumi, Daisuke Kawamura, Masuo Shimoiizaka, Ken'ichi Okuno, Kiyoshi Takahashi, Tsuneshichi Takagi, Shūichi Ishizaka, and Sakunosuke Yamada.

Chapter 5

Equality of Rights under the Law *(Hō No Moto No Byōdō)*

Case 6. Koshiyama v. *Chairman, Tokyo Metropolitan Election Supervision Commission (1964).* The Koshiyama Malapportionment Case

18 *Minshū* 2 at p. 270; Supreme Court, Grand Bench, 5 February 1964; Tokyo High Court (First Instance, [constitutionality of the apportionment of seats for the House of Councillors].

EDITORIAL NOTE: A Tokyo voter challenged the 1962 election of Tokyo representatives to the House of Councillors on the grounds that the apportionment of seats was based on a 1946 census and that the Public Office Election Law violated the guarantee of equality under the law. The Tokyo High Court did not agree, and the plaintiff appealed to the Supreme Court, contending that the court below had erred in interpreting Article 14, paragraph 1 of the Constitution. He maintained that the Constitution requires that the number of representatives be proportionate to population and that in the absence of a good reason to allow an imbalance between the number of representatives and the number of voters in terms of the "value of a vote," a law or ordinance that exceeds the maximum limit of tolerable imbalance violates the principle of equality under the law and is accordingly invalid.

REFERENCES

Constitution of Japan [ARTICLES 14, 15, 43, 44, and 47 were at issue in this case. See Appendix 3 for these provisions].

FORMAL JUDGMENT

The appeal in the present case is dismissed.

REASONS. As contended by the appellant, Article 4, paragraph 2 of the Constitution stipulates that "the number of the members of each House shall be fixed by law"; and Article 47 provides that "electoral districts, method of voting and other matters pertaining to the method of election of members of both Houses shall be fixed by law." Thus, the Constitution does not make special provision for the number of members in each House, electoral districts, and other election matters, but rather leaves them to be specified by law, because, in principle, decisions on matters concerning elections should be left to the discretionary power of the legislative branch of government, the Diet. Therefore, the Diet has the power to divide election districts into a national constituency and prefectural constituencies, or even to abolish this distinction, and furthermore to make appropriate decisions concerning the ratio of members from the prefectural constituencies to be allocated to each election district. Neither Article 14 nor Article 44, or any other provision in the Constitution specifically require that the seats in each House be allocated in proportion to the number of electors in each election district.

The apportionment of Diet seats to each election district in proportion to the population of the electorate is definitely desirable in terms of the constitutional principle of equality under the law. However, the fact that the ratio of the population of the electorate is undeniably the principal factor in apportioning seats to an election district implies no impediment to considering many additional factors. For example, with respect to the system under Article 46 of the Constitution of electing half the members of the House of Councillors every three years, it would be difficult to reduce the present minimum of two representatives per district, regardless of the number of seats and the population in each election district. In determining the apportionment of Diet seats, it is important to consider and to take into account such factors as historical background and a balance between the number of members and the number of separate administrative divisions. As mentioned above, the Diet possesses a discretionary authority as the legislature to determine the number of members in each House, the election districts, and the apportionment of members to each election district. Therefore, except in a case in which the number of Diet members in an election district creates an extreme inequality in the voter's enjoyment of the right to elect, the percentage of seats apportioned to each election district is a matter of legislative policy subject to the Diet's authority as the legislative branch. We cannot judge the apportionment of Diet seats void and contrary to Article 14, paragraph 1 of the Constitution based solely on the fact that it is not proportionate to the population of electorates. Although the Public Office Election Law (Appendix II) has not been revised to reflect population distribution in the electorate, and this creates the present degree of imbalance and inequality, the problem is still only one of propriety of legislative policy, and we cannot recognize the emergence of a problem of unconstitutionality. Therefore, the contention of the appellant cannot be accepted.

Consequently, this Court decides as stated in the Formal Judgment in accordance with Article 396, 384, 95, and 89 of the Code of Civil Procedure.

This judgment is the unanimous opinion of the justices, except for the supplementary opinion of Justice Kitarō Saitō.

* * *

The supplementary opinion of Justice Kitarō Saitō follows.

I have no objection to a majority opinion which holds that the percentage of members apportioned to each election district is a question of legislative policy subject to the Diet's authority as the legislative branch. But I have some qualms about the majority opinion's holding that although the present Public Office Election Law (Appendix II) had not been revised to reflect population distribution in the electorate, the present degree of inequality is still only a problem of the propriety of legislative policy, except in a case where the number of Diet members in an election district creates an extreme inequality in the voter's enjoyment of the right to elect. In such an exceptional case, a question of unconstitutionality would arise, and the above appendix would be held void.

The decision of the Grand Bench in the so-called Sunagawa Case (13 *Keishū* 3225 [1959]) revealed a similar way of thinking in ruling that it falls outside "the right of judicial review" by the courts unless there is clearly obvious invalidity or unconstitutionality. Certain matters are outside the courts' power of review, with the qualification that they are subject to such judicial review in an exceptional case; this (latter reservation) should be stated out of respect for the judge's zeal in upholding the prestige of the judicial power and in faithfully performing his duty. In the long run, this policy should also serve to protect the fundamental human rights of the people. Needless to say, this determination is important for a judge, but as a practical matter, can the prestige of the judicial power be enhanced and can the trust of the people be earned by such a court policy? I think it necessary to reflect upon this point. A reading of the long minority (dissenting) opinion by Justice Frankfurter in *Baker* v. *Carr** of the United States Supreme Court deepens this feeling. (In the following discussion, portions of a free translation of the justice's opinion [i.e., into Japanese], and phrases quoted above from the present case, are set off with quotation marks).

"The court's authority—possessed neither of the purse nor of the sword—is ultimately left to a sustained public confidence in its moral sanction. Such feeling must be nourished by the court's complete detachment, in fact and in appearance, from political entanglements, and by abstention from injecting itself into the squash of political forces in political settlements." Expanding the coverage of the judicial review laws

*369 *U.S.* 186 (1962).

cannot always enhance the prestige of the judicial power. It is more important to defend "inherent limits in the effective exercise of the court's 'judicial power' than to expand the scope of judicial review."*

As the majority opinion in the present case indicates, the determining factors in apportioning a number of seats to each election district involve many elements besides population distribution in the electorate. And when we take these elements into account in making judgments, we must note the absence of "accepted criteria for making judicial judgments." Justice Frankfurter in *Baker* v. *Carr* even goes so far as to say that "to charge courts with the task of 'deciding these problems' is to attribute . . . omnicompetence to judges." We must frankly acknowledge that "there is not under our Constitution a judicial remedy for every political mischief, for every undesirable exercise of legislative power." Must we not be content with a situation where "in a democratic society, relief must come through an aroused popular conscience that sears the conscience of the people's representatives?"

In this case, the majority opinion refers to a situation regarding the number of Diet seats alloted to an election district in which an extreme inequality has been created in the voter's enjoyment of the right to elect; but it is not clear exactly what specific condition the opinion is referring to. Invalidation of an election in the future on grounds that it falls under the doctrine in this case will probably not come easily. I believe that we can put more trust in the power of public opinion and in the conscience of the legislative and administrative organs. Even if we give assurances that unconstitutionality can be declared by a court judgment, in the absence of a clear standard, will not a suit filed on those grounds of unconstitutionality be completely rejected as falling short of such a standard? I am afraid that as a result the court would be betraying the trust which the people put in the judiciary, "sounding a word of promise to the ear, sure to be disappointing to the hope."

Suppose an election were held void on grounds that the Public Office Election Law (Appendix II) is in violation of the equality clause of the Constitution. What consequences would arise? The ultimate result might be to deprive the people of the existing legislative machinery without providing any new method for electing the legislative organ to replace it, thereby inviting in the end the destruction of the nation's electoral processes. If a situation were to arise in which the election of half the members of the House of Councillors were completely voided, the functioning of the Diet would be utterly paralyzed. (See Article 10 of the Diet Law.)†

**See* Kitarō Saitō, *Hō to kokka kenryoku* (Law and state power) in *Hōtetsugaku Nempō* (Annual of legal philosophy) (1955):16.

†The Diet Law (Law No. 79 of 1947), Article 10. The term of an ordinary session shall be 150 days; however, in cases where the term of office of members expires during the session, the term of the session shall terminate on the day of such expiration.

Basically, suits instituted under Article 204 of the Public Office Election Law are thought to be designed to correct errors in the management and administration of elections. That is why an election is to be held within forty days when such a suit results in an order to conduct a second election. (Article 109, item 4; Article 110, paragraph 2; and Article 32, paragraph 1 of the Public Office Election Law.) Were Appendix II recognized to be unconstitutional and void in the present case, could we expect to have the appendix revised in such a short period as thirty days? If not, then we cannot help but repeat one invalid election after another. Even granting an extended interpretation within reasonable limits of the above provision of Article 204, to give a judicial solution to those questions that are likely to occasion differences of discretionary judgment between the Diet and the Court is to invite a confusing and complex situation. This line of thinking gives me strong doubts about the legality, in a suit based on Article 204, of the kind of claim that is presented in the instant case.

Justices Kisaburō Yokota (presiding), Toshio Irie, Ken'ichi Okuno, Shūichi Ishizaka, Sakunosuke Yamada, Kakiwa Gokijyō, Masatoshi Yokota, Asanosuke Kusaka, Kingo Osabe, Yoshihiko Kido, Kazuto Ishida, Kitarō Saitō, and Masuo Shimoiizaka.

Chapter 6

The Economic Freedoms of Citizens (Keizaiteki Jiyū)

The "economic freedoms" refer to property rights and their use (Article 29 of the Constitution of Japan; see Appendix 3 for the text of this and the following provisions) and to the freedom to choose one's occupation (Article 22), as well as to other rights included in Article 22: the right to choose and change one's place of residence, and the right to emigrate. These provisions are taken by Japanese writers as primarily concerned with the right to conduct business in Japanese society and are categorized separately from the rights of workers (See Chapter 7), which are considered among the "social rights" (shakaiken) *of individuals. All individual rights in Japan may be legitimately regulated under the general "public welfare"* (kōkyō no fukushi) *provisions of Articles 12 and 13 of the Constitution; but only Articles 22 and 29 mention the public welfare standard as limiting specific rights.*

Case 7. Nakamura et al v. *Japan (1962).* The Nakamura Case

16 *Keishū* 11 at p. 1593; Supreme Court, Grand Bench, 28 November 1962; Fukuoka Dist. Ct. (First Instance), Fukuoka High Ct. (Second Instance), [unconstitutionality of confiscation of third-party property related to a crime].*

EDITORIAL NOTE: The accused attempted to smuggle contraband goods to South Korea in violation of the Customs Law, but failed to transfer the shipment to a fishing boat off the coast of Fukuoka, Kyushu due to stormy weather. The first instance court, upheld by the Fukuoka High Court, convicted the accused and confiscated the motor boat and cargo.

The accused appealed to the Supreme Court, contending in part that some of the property confiscated belonged to a third party who had no prior knowledge that a crime was to be committed, and who was denied any notice, hearing, or means of redress for such confiscation in violation of Article 29, paragraph 1 of the Constitution. Article 118, paragraph 1 of the Customs Law was declared to be in violation of Articles 29 and 31 of the Constitution, marking the first time that the Supreme Court of Japan held a prospective law unconstitutional.

*This translation is taken, with some modifications, from materials prepared by the Asian Law Program of the University of Washington, Seattle, and is included here by permission of Professor Dan Fenno Henderson, director of that program.

REFERENCES

Constitution of Japan [ARTICLES 29 and 31 were at issue in this case. See Appendix 3 for these provisions].

Customs Law, ARTICLE 118, 1. Cargo related to the crimes provided in Articles 109 through 111 (crime of importing prohibited cargo, crime of avoiding customs, etc., and crime of exporting or importing without permit), ships or airplanes used in the commission of such crimes, or cargo related to the crime provided in Article 112 (crime of transport, etc. of smuggled cargo—hereafter referred to as "criminal cargo" in this article) shall be confiscated. However, this shall not apply to criminal cargo owned by a party other than the criminal and when such party comes under any one of the following items:

(1) When it is found that he has continuously maintained the criminal cargo as owner without knowing in advance that one or more of the crimes provided in Articles 109 through 112 were to be committed.

(2) When it is found that he took possession of the criminal cargo without knowing of the circumstances after one or more of the crimes provided in the preceding item were committed.

2. When the criminal cargo that should be confiscated under the provisions of the preceding paragraph cannot be confiscated, or when the criminal cargo is not confiscated according to the provisions of item 2 of that paragraph, an amount equivalent to the value at that time when the crime was committed of such criminal cargo that cannot be confiscated or is not confiscated shall be collected as an additional penalty from the criminal.

3. When tariffs should be collected in cases in which criminal cargo is not confiscated according to the provisions of Article 1(1), such tariffs shall be collected immediately from the owner. However, when criminal cargo is brought into the bonded area as foreign cargo within a period designated by the Chief of Customs, they shall be deemed as having not been imported.

Code of Criminal Procedure, ARTICLE 405, 1. A *jōkoku* appeal may be lodged against a judgment in first or second instance rendered by a High Court in the following cases:

(1) On the ground that there is a violation of the Constitution or an error in construction, interpretation, or application of the Constitution.

FORMAL JUDGMENT

The decision below and decision of first instance are quashed.

Accused, Kazuichi Nakamura, is sentenced to six months of imprisonment at forced labor, and accused, Toshihiro Nakamura, is sentenced to four months of imprisonment at forced labor, except that execution of each of these sentences is to be suspended for three years from the date this judgment becomes final.

The Taiei-maru, a steam-and-sail-driven ship (valued at 431,000 yen or $1,197.00), which is in the custody of the Kokura Branch of the Fukuoka District Prosecutor's Office, shall be confiscated.

REASONS. Regarding the reasons for the respective *jōkoku* appeals presented by Counsel E. Ogata and S. Matsunaga: It is reasonable to say that confiscation as provided in Article 118 (1) of the Customs Law is a disposition forfeiting and appropriating by the national treasury, the ownership of ships and cargo, etc. that are related to the crimes as provided in the same paragraph and that do not come under the proviso of the same paragraph, whether they belong to the accused or not; and that even though the owner is a third party, not an accused, the declaration of confiscation as an additional penalty against the accused does give rise to the effect of forfeiture of such third party's ownership.

1. However, when the property of a third party is confiscated, we must say that to deprive the owner of his ownership without giving him notice or an opportunity for explanation or defense in connection with such confiscation, is extremely unreasonable and cannot be tolerated by the Constitution. For, Article 29 (1) of the Constitution provides that property rights are inviolable, and Article 31 provides that no person shall be deprived of life or liberty, nor shall any other criminal penalty be imposed, except according to procedure established by law; the above confiscation of a third party's property is ordered as an additional penalty against the accused, and the effect of the disposition of the criminal case extends to the third party; thus, it is necessary to give notice and opportunity of explanation and defense to the third party who has his property thus confiscated. To confiscate the property of a third party otherwise is to impose a penalty that would result in violation of property rights without resort to procedure established by law. Accordingly, this is a problem separate from the kind of remedy for such third party that would be recognized afterwards. Nevertheless, Article 118 (1) of the Customs Law, although providing for the confiscation of ships and cargo, etc. related to the crimes as provided in the same paragraph even when they are owned by a third party not an accused, does not provide for giving notice or opportunity for explanation or defense to such third party owners, nor does the Criminal Code nor any other law or order establish provisions concerning such procedure. Consequently, we cannot but judge that to confiscate a third party's property pursuant to Article 118 (1) of the Customs Law violates Articles 31 and 29 of the Constitution.

2. An accused who has suffered such a declaration of confiscation may, as a matter of course, make a *jōkoku* appeal on the grounds of the unconstitutionality of the judgment of confiscation, since it is an additional penalty against him, even in cases concerning a third party's property. Furthermore, since an accused obviously has an interest in the

outcome because he is deprived of his possession of the property so confiscated or he is put in a situation in which he cannot use or take advantage of it or because he is exposed to a possible claim for damages by the third party who had his ownership confiscated, we must hold that he may seek his remedy by *jōkoku* appeal.

We regard it as reasonable to modify the Grand Bench precedents *Ōmachi et al* v. *Japan*, (14 *Keishū* 1574 Sup. Ct., 19 October 1960) and *Kiyonaga* v. *Japan*, (14 *Keishū* 1611 Sup. Ct., 19 October 1960), which are contradictory to the above.

Regarding the present case, because the court below confirmed the fact that the confiscated cargo was owned by a third party not an accused, the judgment of confiscation is unconstitutional for the above reasons, and appellants' points of argument are, in this regard, well taken.

The decision below and decision on first instance must be reversed in this regard.

Therefore, we quash the decision below in accordance with Article 410 (1), main paragraph, Article 405 (1), and Article 413, proviso of the Code of Criminal Procedure and enter new judgment in the present case.

We decide as in the Formal Judgment above; that is, when the law is applied to the facts found in the decision on first instance and confirmed by the court below, the acts of the accused found as above come under Article 111 (1) and (2) [Sic., 118 (1) and (2)] of the Customs Law and Article 60 of the Criminal Code; thus, we choose imprisonment at forced labor out of the penalties provided by law and within the terms of penalties so provided, we sentence accused Kazuichi Nakamura to imprisonment at forced labor for six months and accused Toshihiro Nakamura to imprisonment at forced labor for four months, suspending the execution of each sentence for three years from the date this judgment becomes final by application of Article 25 (1) of the Criminal Code in accordance with the circumstances. The value, 431,000 yen, of the Taiei-maru, the steam-and-sail-driven ship mentioned in the decree is to be confiscated pursuant to Article 118 (1), main paragraph of the Customs Law since it is a ship used in the commission of the crime in this case and is owned by accused Toshihiro Nakamura. Costs are to be determined by applying Article 181 (1), main paragraph and Article 182 of the Code of Criminal Procedure.

This decision is made by the unanimous opinion of all justices except for the concurring opinions of Justices Toshio Irie, Katsumi Tarumi, and Ken'ichi Okuno, and the dissenting opinions of Justices Hachirō Fujita, Masuo Shimoiizaka, Tsuneshichi Takagi, Shuichi Ishizaka, and Sakunosuke Yamada.

* * *

The concurring opinion of Justice Toshio Irie follows.

1. I agree with the majority opinion in this decision holding that: (1) confiscation as provided under Article 118 (1) of the Customs Law is a disposition purporting to transfer ownership of ships and cargo, etc. that are related to the crimes as provided under the same paragraph but do not come under the proviso of the same paragraph, to the national treasury whether they are owned by the accused or not; (2) if a third party, not an accused, is the owner, the declaration of confiscation as an additional penalty against the accused would give rise to the effect of forfeiture of the ownership of such third party; and (3) an accused who suffers such declaration of confiscation may make a *jōkoku* appeal on the grounds of unconstitutionality of the judgment of confiscation, even though the object confiscated is a third party's property. Concerning the reasons therefor, I wish to supplement the above by incorporating by reference my dissenting opinion on these points in the Grand Bench Decision, *Ōmachi et al* v. *Japan*, (14 *Keishū* 1574 Sup. Ct., 19 October 1960).

2. The majority opinion in this judgment states that the confiscation in this case violates Articles 31 and 29 of the Constitution and in this regard, I have decided to amend what I stated in my dissenting opinion concerning the above points in the decision cited above and to agree with the above majority opinion. Although I think that what the majority opinion explains suffices as reasoning, I would supplement it somewhat by additional points just for emphasis.

1. I consider that the guarantee of procedure established by law found in Article 31 of the Constitution should be interpreted as meaning not that merely nominal establishment of procedure by law satisfies the requirements of this Article, but that even though established by some law, that law does not avoid violating this Article, if its content contravenes the fundamental principles of Constitutions in modern democratic states; the guarantee of this Article covers not only procedural provisions but substantive provisions establishing the content of rights; and Article 31 should be interpreted as meaning not only to provide for criminal penalties but also to cover by the words "no person shall be deprived of . . . or liberty" cases in which individual rights or property are infringed upon by the power of the state. (We should consider this Article as also a successor to the intent of Article 23 of the Meiji Constitution, which was generally interpreted as providing guarantees concerning, not only criminal, but also administrative arrest, detention, interrogation, and punishment.)

2. I do not consider, however, that Article 31 of the Constitution requires, in all cases in which the power of the state infringes on the right or interest of an individual, that he be given notice and opportunity to be heard so that he may state his opinion, and explain and defend himself. For punishment, of course, we should find that such requirements are

expressly provided by the other articles of the Constitution, such as Articles 32, 37, and 82, and such guarantees are given by these Articles as well as Article 31; however, I should say that for matters other than criminal punishment, this should not be interpreted to mean that the lack of notice or opportunity to be heard, explain, and defend is, aside from the viewpoint of legislative policy, contrary to Article 31 of the Constitution, unless, judging from the nature of the problem, such notice or opportunity is indispensable to the guarantee of fundamental human rights, as viewed from the premises of the Constitution as a whole.

3. Since the procedure for declaration of confiscation against a third party and procedure for the main penalty declared are inseparable and must be considered as a whole, we must say that it is necessary under Article 31 of the Constitution to join such third party in the trial procedure and to give him, in some way, advance notice and opportunity to be heard so that he may explain and defend himself. My way of thinking concerning Article 31 of the Constitution as stated above in 1 through 3 is in no way different from what I stated in my dissenting opinion in the previous case.

4. In the previous dissenting opinion, however, I insisted on an interpretation of Article 31 of the Constitution, as applied to confiscation of a third party's property, to the effect that the minimum requirement to satisfy this Article would be to summon such third party as a witness to the court and to give him notice of the proposed third party confiscation and thus give him an opportunity to state his opinion, and explain and defend himself; but I have this time decided to amend my view and to agree with the majority opinion in this judgment. For, because there are certain limitations on procedure for examination of witnesses under the present Code of Criminal Procedure, we may hardly say that to question a witness in and of itself amounts to giving him an opportunity to defend himself, and there is no evidentiary requirement, under present trial procedure, that a third party owner be questioned as a witness in order to find him in bad faith. However, although when an accused is punished by confiscation of his property, he is naturally given, as an accused, notice, hearing, and opportunity for defense, there is no institutional guarantee of such opportunity when a third party has his property confiscated, and we must say that there is an unfavorable discrimination in treatment between an accused and a third party. Taking such circumstances into consideration (these points were raised in the minority opinions of Justices Daisuke Kawamura and Ken'ichi Okuno in the previous precedent), I have come to think it appropriate to hold that confiscation of a third party's property should be treated as a penal disposition in relation to such a third party as well, because it is pronounced as an additional penalty against the accused and yet its effect extends to the third party; and I think that, analogous to the case of an

accused, the third party should be joined in the trial procedure and be given notice and opportunity to explain and defend himself, and that it does not satisfy due process in Article 31 of the Constitution merely to examine the third party as a witness, thereby giving him notice and an opportunity of sorts to explain and defend himself.

* * *

The concurring opinion of Justice Katsumi Tarumi follows.

1. Confiscation is a deprivation of ownership on the grounds of a crime. (It was with this idea that the provisions concerning execution of confiscation were established.) Therefore, persons who are to suffer this disadvantageous disposition regarding the things used in a crime or made a constituent element in a crime must, first of all, speaking from the standpoint of substantive law, be limited to offenders themselves, persons with bad faith (accomplices), or persons with such intentions or attitudes that are strongly blameworthy by society (a kind of negligent person). Secondly, speaking from the standpoint of procedural law, to determine the fact that the owner stands in the position of an offender, accomplice, or negligent person, as noted above, such third party must be made a kind of party to the lawsuit when he is not already a party to the suit, unless there are proper reasons to the contrary, and he must be duly given notice of the factual and legal grounds for the threatened confiscation, an opportunity for his case to be heard, and an opportunity by himself or by his representative to prove as a means of defense the factual or legal reasons why confiscation should not be imposed. Only when this has been done may confiscation of the property of a third party be said to follow due process as provided in Article 31 of the Constitution. (This is the same as my concurring opinion in *Ōmachi et al* v. *Japan*; Case Concerning Charge of Violation of Customs Law, 14 *Keishū* 1574; Sup. Ct., G.B., 19 October 1960.)

But the present Code of Criminal Procedure has no such special procedural provisions for protection of the interests of third parties when their property is to be confiscated. Until such special provisions are created by legislation, judgments confiscating a third party's property are contrary to Article 31 and hence Article 29 (1) of the Constitution, even though the provisions of substantive criminal law recognizing third party confiscations are constitutional.

2. The majority opinion, which rejects indiscriminate confiscation and holds that if indiscriminate, there may be no confiscation, does not indicate which article of the present Code of Criminal Procedure violates Article 31 of the Constitution. We must interpret this to mean that if a decision confiscates a third party's property, although the Code of Criminal Procedure lacks provision for due process, it violates Articles 31 and 29 (1) of the Constitution. (Such a decision declaring law or order unconstitutional without clearly indicating any particular provision of the

law or order concerned must surely be contrary to law.) The value of the property to be confiscated does not matter to the majority opinion. The confiscation of a third party's property is thus unconstitutional, except for certain prohibited objects that no one may legally own, objects that have lost their value, or objects the ownership of which may be regarded as abandoned by their owners (objects that an ordinary person may be regarded as having abandoned such as a fish knife used in a murder or a blood-stained towel). Of course, even when the third party confiscation should be allowed by the evidence presented in a criminal case, it would still violate Article 31 of the Constitution to so declare without giving him an opportunity for defense (that is, without so much as hearing the third person's opinion and proof on admissibility and credibility of the evidence).

Perhaps we may ordinarily make a confiscation judgment if the third party has failed to appear without due cause though he has received proper summons to the confiscation proceedings. However, in Japan today, it is generally difficult to successfully serve notice of confiscation by international judicial cooperation to a third party residing abroad for a long time, and even though the third party is in this country, it takes much energy, money, and time, and hence slows down the trial, to give service by public notice on particular property to be confiscated from him when his residence is unknown or unsettled, with the result that it often happens, even though fair procedural rules are established, that they may not be actually operable. Since we can hardly wait a long time for the decision on the principal issue of guilty or not guilty (against the accused) in such a case, we must declare nonconfiscation, unless appropriate legislation for such cases is enacted. In addition, would it not be possible to enact legislation providing remedies by which, after the judgment of confiscation of a third party's property becomes final, its execution be stayed, if the Court regards grounds alleged by the third party owner sufficient?

3. The majority opinion says that ". . . an accused who has suffered a declaration of confiscation against a third party's property may, as a matter of course, make a *jōkoku* appeal on the grounds of the unconstitutionality of the judgment of confiscation since it is an additional penalty against him, even in cases concerning a third party's property. Furthermore, since an accused obviously has an interest in the outcome because he is deprived of his possession of the property so confiscated or he is put in a situation in which he cannot use or take advantage of it or because he is exposed to a possible claim for damages by a third party who has his ownership confiscated, we must interpret that he can seek his remedy by *jōkoku* appeal."*

Yet, there is a problem to this. It is said that the Supreme Court of the

*Though in quotation marks, this is *not* a verbatim quote.

United States as a general rule has come to hold that: "Appeals which allege the unconstitutionality of a law merely by invoking the constitutional rights of another are unlawful. For, one whose constitutional rights are damaged is most qualified to present the constitutional issue before the Court, and the Court also can appropriately render judgment on constitutionality only when that person himself makes such an allegation. When the possessor of constitutional rights endures the infringement on his rights, and perhaps has abandoned or ignores his constitutional rights, it is not appropriate to decide those rights where another (going ahead of their possessor) invokes his rights. It is not desirable to render a constitutional judgment based upon a hypothetical fact situation as yet not arisen in which, although the law has not been applied to a certain other person, when the law is applied to him, his constitutional rights will probably be injured."

It is a general rule, in *kōso* appeals and *jōkoku* appeals, as in suits in the first instance, that it does not constitute proper grounds for appeal to allege infringement of another's interests without alleging concrete facts that involve possible damage to the interests of the accused himself, because otherwise the appellant is not seeking a decision beneficial to himself; that is, a decision modifying the decision below to benefit the appellant himself. The grounds for *jōkoku* appeal in this case says that to confiscate the third party's property as an additional penalty against the accused is unconstitutional. As the grounds for this, the allegation is that the accused have concrete and natural interests since they will avoid the additional penalty by quashment of the confiscation decision. Assuming this, we may for the moment render a substantive judgment on the reasons for the *jōkoku* appeal in this case as follows: "Due process was satisfied for the accused themselves since the accused in this case received confiscation decision as provided by law after they were notified in the first instance of the facts in the information (*kōso jijitsu*), gave opposing pleading in open court, made allegations in their own behalf, were given opportunity to examine the witnesses in court through their counsel, and were defended by their counsel." From the standpoint of substantive law, we may answer the arguments for *jōkoku* appeal as follows: (1) even assuming the owner of the confiscated property was responsible for the crime, which, as a matter of substantive law, justified the confiscation because he was an accomplice or the like, the decision below is proper as a penalty against the accused, since the confiscation was imposed as an additional penalty against the accused themselves on the grounds of their criminal acts; (2) even assuming the owner of the confiscated property had no bad faith nor any kind of negligence that would justify the confiscation, even though the accused were deprived only of their possession as an additional penalty for their own crime, the innocent owner may suffer imposition of penalty more severe than the criminal i.e., confiscation of ownership. Therefore, it is natural that the accused have a duty to compensate him. In any event, the accused cannot be exempted from confiscation for their crime. So far as the accused themselves are concerned, there are no grounds for their arguments for *jōkoku* appeal. This may well be a judgment in accordance with procedure provided by law.

However, were we to dismiss the *jōkoku* appeal and regard the confiscation decision below as proper, the result would be that the third party owner, without being found to be a person to be held liable by lawful procedure would be deprived of his right of ownership by the unconstitutional confiscation decision. Therefore, in this case, it is a matter requiring immediate attention and meeting the demands for justice and equity to resist deprivation of a third party's ownership by an unconstitutional procedure like this, even though it involves escape of the accused, who are criminals.

Thus, in one decision we are in the dilemma that while the confiscation against the accused found to be criminals must be allowed, the same confiscation must be denied because of depriving a third party of his right of ownership. Why this dilemma? While from the standpoint of procedural law we render a decision to deprive a third party of his right based on arguments between the litigants alone and from the standpoint of substantive criminal law confiscation merely deprives the criminal of the right of possession, such deprivation of a third party's right of ownership would mean neither punishment nor education to the criminal, yet we deprive the third party of his right of ownership. Perhaps the dilemma is derived from such absurdity as this. This is particularly clear in the case of indiscriminate confiscation in which it does not matter whether the owner is responsible or not. (Legislation may be justified if confiscation of a third party's property is not allowed, but additional collection may be imposed on the criminal accused instead.) Be that as it may, even when the third party owner has some blameworthy intent or negligence, so long as there is no law providing due process giving the right to such owner to be joined in a lawsuit to secure self-protection and to be able to receive a decision beneficial to himself and in order to find whether such fault existed, it is unconstitutional to treat the third party unfavorably by confiscating his property. Therefore, it cannot be helped that, as said in the majority opinion, such injustice may actually occur in which, for example, the third party owner has had bad intentions or was negligent, or the accused is unjustly exempted from a confiscation decision, until appropriate procedure is legislated.

For the above reasons, I have decided to amend my opinion regarding "lawful grounds for *jōkoku* appeal" in the Grand Bench decision on the case of the accused charged with violation of Customs Law involving Tatsuhei Ōmachi et al, which was cited at the beginning of my opinion and to agree with the majority opinion regarding the substantive question of constitutionality.

* * *

The dissenting opinion of Justice Masuo Shimoiizaka follows.

It is not at all necessary to pass on the question of unconstitutionality in a case like this in which the accused, who are not the owners of the confiscated article, dispute the constitutional effect of a decision, that, as an additional penalty, declared confiscation of a third party's property. Consequently, this decision makes, in spite of this, an unnecessary constitutional judgment, which is against purport of the Grand Bench decisions of this Court, *Ōmachi et al* v. *Japan*, 14 *Keishū* 1574, 19 October 1960, and *Kiyonaga* v. *Japan*, 14 *Keishū* 1611, Supreme Court, 19 October 1960. I, as a person who firmly insisted on the opinion included in the above-cited Grand Bench decisions, still strongly oppose the present decision and wish to point out the errors expressed in the majority opinion of this case and to add the following opinion, as well as to maintain and incorporate by reference those Grand Bench decisions.

The right to review for unconstitutionality given to the Court under Article 81 of the Constitution must be exercised within the scope of judicial power; and for the judicial power to be invoked it is necessary that a contentious case has been instituted concretely. The Court, when there is no concrete contentious case before it, is not empowered to give abstract judgments concerning the dubious arguments existing concerning construction of the Constitution and other laws and orders in anticipation of the future, as has been established by the Grand Bench of this Court (cf. *Suzuki* v. *Japan*; 6 *Minshū* 783, Sup. Ct., G.B., 8 October 1952). In concrete contentious cases when laws and orders that do not apply to oneself or that do apply constitutionally to oneself are unconstitutional if applied to another person, should we allow their attack on the grounds of unconstitutionality and hasten invocation of the right to review for unconstitutionality? In such an event, it is necessary to consider separately two kinds of cases: (1) cases in which the party concerned does not actually suffer concrete detriment under the laws and orders that are being reviewed for unconstitutionality; (2) cases in which the party concerned does actually suffer concrete detriment under the laws and orders that are being reviewed for unconstitutionality. In the former case (when the party concerned does not actually suffer concrete harm under the laws and orders that are being reviewed for unconstitutionality), to give a judgment on the issue of unconstitutionality is nothing but to give an abstract judgment on dubious arguments in anticipation of the future, which is to go outside the scope of the judicial power. To do so is not permissible as an exercise of the right to review for unconstitutionality given to the Court under Article 81 of the Constitution. For the latter case (when the party concerned does actually suffer concrete detriment under the laws and orders that are being reviewed for unconstitutionality), I will later touch upon the propriety of giving a judgment on the issue of unconstitutionality.

Turning to the present case, it was confirmed by the court below that the confiscated cargo was criminal cargo that the accused attempted to smuggle abroad and that it was owned by a third party, not an accused. The majority opinion holds that the accused may dispute the constitutionality of the confiscation judgment on the grounds that the accused, from the judgment for confiscation of the criminal cargo, which became final, obviously have an interest because they are deprived of the right of possession of the confiscated article, or are put in a position unable to use or take profit from it, and further, are exposed to the risk that the third party deprived of his right of ownership may exercise his right to claim damages. The majority opinion points out, as one of the reasons why the accused may contest the confiscation judgment in this case as unconstitutional, the fact that the accused is exposed to the risk that the third party deprived of the right of ownership may exercise his right to claim damages; yet whether the third party owner will exercise his right to claim damages is a pending question and such a risk is but indefinite and abstract. The accused have thus not actually suffered any concrete detriment from the confiscation judgment in this case. A Grand Bench decision of this Court (*Kanashiro* v. *Japan*; 11 *Keishū* 3132, Sup. Ct., G.B., 27 November 1957) has held that the confiscation of the property of a third party who was in bad faith is not contrary to Article 29 of the Constitution. Admitting that the accused are deprived of the right of possession of the confiscated cargo by the final confiscation judgment in this case and are unable to use or take profit from it as pointed out by the majority opinion, since the accused, criminals who attempted to smuggle the confiscated cargo abroad, did act in bad faith, we cannot conclude even if the accused are deprived of the right of possession of the article by the final confiscation judgment in this case or are put in a position unable to use or take profit from it that they, as a result, have been illegally deprived of a property right under Article 29 of the Constitution, or that they actually suffered infringement of their constitutional rights from the confiscation judgment, since the accused were given notice and an opportunity for explanation and defense. Consequently, since the accused have not suffered any actual concrete detriment, from any point of view, from the confiscation judgment in this case, the majority opinion, which, on the issue of unconstitutionality of the confiscation judgment, bases its decision on the petition of these accused who in fact have not suffered actual concrete detriment, I must conclude, is nothing but an abstract judgment on dubious arguments in anticipation of the future, transcending the scope of the right to review for unconstitutionality given to the courts under Article 81 of the Constitution. Since the accused lack any actual concrete interest to argue the unconstitutionality of the confiscation judgment in this case, the grounds for *jōkoku* appeal alleging the confiscation to be unconstitutional are legally insufficient, and the appeal in this case should be dismissed for this reason. Accordingly, I must say a word on the fact that the majority opinion has modified the Grand Bench decisions of 19 October 1960, cited above. Those decisions hold it reasonable to regard that it is impermissible in a lawsuit to interfere with rights of another and seek relief for him; therefore, it should also be regarded that it is impermissible to argue, as in this case, that confiscation is constitutionally invalid as an infringement of fundamental human rights against the property of another. The previous decisions declare in short that it is not permissible under any circumstances to argue that laws and orders are unconstitutional in a concrete contentious case, when they are constitutional as applied to oneself, simply because they would be unconstitutional if applied to another. Presumably, it is sound to say that when a party has not suffered any concrete detriment under the laws and orders that are being reviewed for unconstitutionality, it would result in interfering with the constitutional rights of another person to base one's case on the grounds that such laws and orders, when applied to another, would infringe the constitutional rights of that other person, and such asking for relief for others should not be allowed. In contrast to this, if the party concerned does actually suffer concrete detriment under the laws and orders that are being reviewed for unconstitutionality, I think we must consider, from another angle, whether it should be absolutely forbidden to attack such laws and orders by invoking the constitutional rights of another person on the ground that the laws and orders infringe the constitutional rights of such other person. On this point the expressions in the Grand Bench decision cited above, it seems to me, lacked clarity and breadth. I thus wish to interpret the content of the above Grand Bench decision as having wider meaning and to explain and amplify this point as follows. That is, I think that when a party does actually suffer concrete detriment under the laws and orders that are being reviewed for unconstitutionality, it is proper to say that the law does not prohibit an attack on such laws and orders by invoking the constitutional rights of another person nor does it transcend the scope of the judicial power, even if we adjudicate constitutional issues thus raised. (However, in the present case, the accused have neither alleged nor proved that they suffered any concrete detriment from the confiscation judgment.)

Next, I would like to introduce the thinking of the Supreme Court of the United States of America on this point, which Court is based on a system of review for unconstitutionality that is the same as ours.

On the attitude of the United States Supreme Court, which has long adhered to the principle that it does not have the power to declare laws unconstitutional except when the question is raised for judgments regarding the legal rights of litigants in actual disputes, the Court has said as follows:

> We start with the fundamental purpose of avoiding unnecessary constitutional judgments. This originates from considerations (1) of the delicate function of what is termed review for unconstitutionality, which becomes

> clear when the Court makes a judgment of unconstitutionality and when its effects extend to other organs established under the Constitution, the same as the Court (i.e., the legislative body and executive body); (2) of the relative conclusiveness of the Court's judgment of unconstitutionality, which does not absolutely bind other organizations; (3) of the scrupulous care that should properly be given to judgments concerning the powers of the organs holding legislative power and administrative power under the Constitution along with the Court; (4) of the necessity of the holders of state power to stay within the scope of authority given to each such holder, including the Court, in order to act in accordance with constitutional provisions; (5) of the limitations inherent in the judicial process arising from the negative nature of the judicature, as well as the limited means by which judgments are enforced; and (6) of the important position occupied by the Court's constitutional judgments in the political structure of the United States. . . .

Declared as one of the manifestations of the above fundamental attitude is the principle that "it is impermissible to attack a law that is constitutionally applied to oneself, on the grounds that the law becomes unconstitutional when it is applied to another person or to other facts," and it is declared as an expression incidental to this principle that "the litigant may only argue his own constitutional rights and is not allowed to invoke constitutional rights of another person." This principle may be interpreted to flow from the following reasons: (1) the person who has his own constitutional rights infringed is best able to raise constitutional issues before the Court, and a proper decision can only be made by a constitutional judgment when there is an attack by one whose constitutional rights are damaged; (2) although the possessor of constitutional rights being invoked may tolerate infringement on his rights and may abandon his constitutional rights, it is undesirable to make a constitutional judgment when, in anticipation, such rights are invoked by another on hypothetical facts, yet to occur, that when and if the law in question is applied to another person in the future, his constitutional rights would be infringed. The attitude of the United States Supreme Court has consistently been as stated above, which is said to have proven most wise through time and experience.

Because I think that in Japan, as well, the above principle would be wise and a way of thinking endorsed by reason, it seems to me that the above points might well be considered fully in connection with review for unconstitutionality handled by the courts in our country. However, since the above principle should be interpreted not as a principle ordered by the Constitution to the court, but rather as a frame of mind for the court, or a standard with which to form a fundamental attitude in the exercise of the right to review unconstitutionality, we probably cannot avoid violating the principle in exceptional instances when the third party's constitutional rights invoked by another are infringed yet the third party has no means to effectively preserve his rights by himself.

The majority opinion says that an accused who has suffered a declaration of confiscation may, as a matter of course, make a *jōkoku* appeal on the grounds of the unconstitutionality of the confiscation judgment since it is an additional penalty against the accused, even in cases concerning a third party's property. In the final analysis it only says something or other about the additional penalty (literally, "since it is an additional penalty . . .") and is completely a formalism. Does such a basis of argument have reasonable grounds as constitutional theory? The accused neither do nor attempt to allege or prove that they have suffered actual concrete detriment from the declaration of confiscation in this case. Even going so far as to concede that the *jōkoku* appeal is lawful on the grounds that the confiscation judgment in this case is unconstitutional as said in the majority opinion, I do not consider it necessary to make a constitutional judgment in this case in which the constitutionality of the judgment of confiscation is disputed by invoking only the constitutional rights of a third party who is an outsider to the lawsuit. My understanding is that a third party whose property is confiscated without being given notice or an opportunity of explanation and defense may be categorized as a person having rights under Article 497 (1) of the Code of Criminal Procedure, and so long as the owner of the thing confiscated alleges that the confiscation violates Article 31 of the Constitution he may institute an administrative lawsuit against the state claiming return of the confiscated thing. Consequently, since a third party owner may later assert his constitutional rights and validly argue the unconstitutionality of the confiscation, it is unnecessary to make a constitutional judgment in anticipation during the criminal proceedings at the stage in which it is not determined yet whether the third party will tolerate the infringement on his constitutional rights. Thus, I firmly believe that the decision in this case should embody the following judgment: Although the accused allege the unconstitutionality of the declaration of confiscation as their grounds for *jōkoku* appeal, the accused, merely invoking the constitutional rights of a third party owner of the thing confiscated, do not argue that their own constitutional rights were infringed. We should hold then that an attack on constitutionality by invoking only constitutional rights of another is allowed only in exceptional cases when it is impossible for the possessor of constitutional rights to allege existence of his rights himself later, or when there is no practical benefit if such allegation is made at a later date; in the ordinary case, an attack on constitutionality is not permissible when invoking only the constitutional rights of another. Since the present case falls under the category of a case in which it is possible and valid for the owner of the confiscated thing to dispute the matter of constitutionality himself later, we need not give a judgment on the unconstitutionality alleged by the accused in the present case. Consequently, the argument alleging unconstitutionality of the confiscation in this case is thus groundless and cannot be accepted.

Justices Kisaburō Yokota (presiding), Hachirō Fujita, Matasuke Kawamura, Toshio Irie, Katsu Ikeda, Katsumi Tarumi, Daisuke Kawamura, Masuo Shimoiizaka, Ken'ichi Okuno, Tsuneshichi Takagi, Shūichi Ishizaka, Sakunosuke Yamada, Kakiwa Gokijyō, and Masatoshi Yokota.

Case 8. Japan v. *Iida et al (1963).* The Irrigation Reservoir Case

17 *Keishū* 5 at p. 521; Supreme Court, Grand Bench, 26 June 1963; Katsuragi Summary Ct. (First Instance), Osaka High Ct. (Second Instance), [constitutionality of limiting without compensation traditional land-use rights].

EDITORIAL NOTE: The accused, whose families had been cultivating the bank of a small reservoir for generations, were charged with violating a Nara Prefectural Ordinance that prohibited farming on the banks of a reservoir. They were convicted in the Katsuragi Summary Court, but the Osaka High Court reversed, on grounds that restriction of property rights by means of an ordinance is contrary to Article 29, paragraph 2 of the Constitution, and that deprivation of such rights without due compensation violates Article 29, paragraph 3. On appeal to the Supreme Court, the prosecutor's office argued that the word "law" in Article 29 includes ordinances and that compensation is not required, since the present restriction of rights is a reasonable one inherent in the right to own a reservoir.

REFERENCES

Constitution of Japan [ARTICLES 29 and 94 were at issue in this case. See Appendix 3 for these provisions].

Regulation Concerning the Preservation of Reservoirs (Nara Prefectural Ordinance No. 38 of 24 September 1954), ARTICLE 1. The purpose of this ordinance is to set forth those matters that are necessary for the care of reservoirs in order to prevent disasters due to damaged or broken reservoirs.

ARTICLE 2, 1. The terms are defined in each item below.

(1) A reservoir is defined as an irrigation pond with banks more than three meters in height or whose benefiting agricultural land is more than one *chōbu* [one *chōbu* is 2.45 acres] in coverage.

(2) A caretaker is a person who has title to the management of a reservoir, or a representative of more than one titleholder to it.

ARTICLE 4, 1. No one may commit any of the acts listed in the items below.

(1) Any acts that would impair the flow of the excess water from a spillway of the reservoir.

(2) Any acts of planting trees, bamboo, or crops, or of setting up a building or any other structures (excluding those structures that are necessary for the safety of the reservoir on the bank of the reservoir).

(3) Acts other than those cited in the items above that would cause damage or breakage to the reservoir.

ARTICLE 9. Those who violate the provisions of Article 4 above shall be fined not more than 30,000 yen.

Local Autonomy Law (Law 67 of 1947), ARTICLE 2, 2. The ordinary local public entities shall dispose of such administrative matters that exist within their respective localities excluding those that belong to the state, in addition to their own public works and those which laws or ordinances based thereupon assign to the local entities.

3. The matters referred to in the above paragraph, in general, include the following, except where specially provided for in a law or an ordinance based thereupon.

(1) Maintaining both the public order, and the safety, health, and welfare of the residents and those who stay in a locality.

(2) Building and managing parks, playgrounds, squares, greens, roads, bridges, rivers, canals, docks, reservoirs, sewages, and dikes, as well as controlling the use thereof. . . .

(8) Preventing crimes and fires, and rescuing victims of disasters. . . .

(18) Regulating, in accordance with laws, the structure, facility site and density of constructions, as well as zoning of residential, commercial, industrial, and other occupational areas including vacant lots.

(19) Expropriating and using, in accordance with laws, the movables and the immovables for public purposes in a locality.

ARTICLE 14, 1. The ordinary local public entities may enact their own ordinances on matters stipulated in Article 2, paragraph 2 so long as they do not violate laws or ordinances based thereupon.

2. An ordinary public entity shall stipulate the disposition of administrative matters, by ordinance, except where especially provided for in a law or ordinance.

5. Unless especially provided for in a law or ordinance, the ordinary local public entities may set forth in their ordinances provisions to the effect that an offender under the ordinance shall be subject to a penalty not exceeding two years of imprisonment at hard labor, or confinement, and a fine not exceeding 100,000 yen, a small fine, confiscation, or detention.

FORMAL JUDGMENT

1. The judgment of the court below is quashed.

2. The present case is remanded to the Osaka High Court.

REASONS. With regard to the purport of the appeal presented by M. Tanabe, deputy prosecutor under the chief prosecutor, Osaka High Public Prosecutor's Office, first, we shall consider the intent of enacting this ordinance and also the legal meaning of the prohibition of the present ordinance, which is at issue in the present case. We can ascertain from the record that in Nara Prefecture there are some 13,000 reservoirs for the purpose of irrigation. The present ordinance was enacted and promulgated in light of disasters due to damaged or broken reservoirs both in that prefecture and in other prefectures, and on a scientific basis after investigation into the causes of damaged or broken reservoirs. Such a disaster tends to cause great damage not only to their owners, but also to the life and property of ordinary residents and those who stay there.

The present ordinance makes it an "objective to set forth those matters which are necessary to control the reservoir" (Article 1). In this ordinance, a reservoir is defined as "an irrigation pond with banks more than three meters in height or whose benefiting agricultural land is more than one *chōbu* in coverage" (Article 2, item 1). In order to achieve the objective of Article 1 above, with regard to the reservoir in Article 2 above, Article 4 in the present ordinance prohibits "any acts which would impair the flow of the excess water from a spillway of the reservoir" (item 1), "any acts of planting trees, bamboo, or crops, or of setting up a building or any other structures (excluding those structures that are necessary for the safety of the reservoir) on the banks of the reservoir" (item 2), or any "acts other than those that are cited in each item above, that would cause damage or breakage to the reservoir" (item 3). At the same time, the provision of Article 9 in the same ordinance stipulates that "those who violate the provisions of Article 4 above shall be fined not more than 30,000 yen." Thus, Article 4 of this ordinance aims at preventing any disaster due to damaged or broken reservoirs, and also at maintaining local public order as well as the safety of residents and visitors. For this purpose, the provision prohibits those acts that the same provision stipulates would cause any damage or breakage of the reservoirs. Punishment is provided in Article 9 for those who violate this ordinance.

In the final analysis, Nara Prefecture has enacted this ordinance on the basis of its own power to enact ordinances. Furthermore, Article 3 of the present ordinance renders Articles 5 and 7 in that ordinance inapplicable to those parts that are under the supervision of the state or the local government, and yet makes the present ordinance applicable widely to reservoirs that are otherwise managed; and thus the present ordinance pertains to those matters stipulated in Article 2, paragraph 3, items 1 and 2 of the Local Autonomy Law. The judgment below has ascertained that the reservoir named "Tōko-pond" in the instant case, along with six acres of bank surrounding it, has been registered under the ownership of Tomio Matsukawa and Takeo Kamishima in Nara Prefecture, but in reality should be held to be jointly and concurrently owned by the farmers residing in that larger section of that village; that the reservoir has been used for the irrigation of arable lands in that larger section of the village, benefiting more than thirty acres of agricultural land; that it has been managed by the deputy chief of that larger section; that its surrounding bank has been used continuously from the days of their ancestors by approximately twenty-seven residents of that larger section of the village, including the accused themselves, who have grown bamboo, food, tea, and other crops; and, however, that by the administration of the present ordinance, people other than the accused voluntarily stopped growing produce there. Since the reservoir in the present case is clearly not managed by the state or local government, the present ordinance deals with matters set forth in Article 2, paragraph 3, item 1 of the Local Autonomy Law. Also, since it aims at the prevention of disasters due to damaged or broken reservoirs, it deals with matters under Article 2, paragraph 3, item 8 of the same law. (The judgment below in this case erred in its assumption in holding the present ordinance unconstitutional and unlawful on the assumption that the present ordinance dealt with the matters prescribed in Article 2, paragraph 3, item 2 of the same law.) Furthermore, each item of Article 4 of the present ordinance which prohibits any acts prescribed therein orders forebearance in the immediate sense. However, because item 2 of the same Article restricts the use of the bank of the reservoir, it amounts to the almost complete prohibition of its use by those persons who possess a property right to use the bank of the reservoir. In the final analysis, the said provision must be held to impose a considerable restriction upon such property rights.

However, the effect of such a restriction is to prohibit any acts of growing trees, bamboo, or crops, or of constructing buildings and other structures (excluding those structures which are necessary for the safety of the reservoir) on such banks of a reservoir, which in the legislators' judgment would contribute to damaging and breaking down the reservoir. As shown in relation to Article 1 of the ordinance in question, a prohibition such as this has been prescribed as a preventative measure against disaster due to damaged or broken reservoirs. The prohibition in Article 4, item 2 of the present ordinance applies to everybody, even those with ownership rights to use the bank. However, to prevent disaster, it is necessary in the life of our society that a person who possesses a property right to use the bank of a reservoir should be almost completely prohibited from the exercise of the right, for the reason stipulated in Article 1 of the present ordinance. Everybody who possesses a property right to use the bank of a reservoir is naturally obliged to exercise the same for the public welfare. The use of the bank of a reservoir in such a manner as to cause the damage or breakdown of the reservoir is not guaranteed either in the Constitution or in the Civil Code as a lawful exercise of a property right. Such use deviates from the exercise of a property right guaranteed by the Constitution and the Civil Code.

Therefore, prohibition of and punishment for these acts by an ordinance cannot be said to conflict with or deviate from the Constitution and the law. Since no other regulation already provides for the matters stipulated in the above provisions, the ordinance that does deal with them cannot be held to violate the Constitution or the law. Furthermore, it was the opinion of this Court in another case (16 *Keishū* 577; Sup. Ct., G.B., 30 May 1962) that Article 9 of the present ordinance, despite its provision for a penalty, was not in violation of Article 31 of the Constitution.

Certain matters are uniformly prescribed by the state in a law only with difficulty or inadequately, due to special circumstances of one or more local public entities, and it would be easy and adequate to have each local public entity decide them by their own ordinances. The issue of maintaining a reservoir, as in the present case, is of this type.

Therefore, the present ordinance does not provide for matters that cannot be prescribed by ordinance without violation of Article 29, paragraph 2 of the Constitution. The judgment below to the contrary must be said to be unlawful by reason of erroneous interpretation of the provision in the Constitution.

Second, the judgment below was of the opinion that when the exercise of a right is compulsorily restricted or suspended by an ordinance, compensation should be granted for the loss of such a right. Since there is no evidence to indicate that any compensation was granted in the present case, the application of the present ordinance to the accused becomes all the more difficult.

However, as explained above, the present ordinance was designed to prevent disaster and to maintain the public welfare. Although Article 4, item 2 restricts considerably the exercise of a property right to use the bank of the reservoir, it is after all, vital in our social life for preventing disaster and maintaining the public welfare. Properly construed, such a restriction must naturally be borne as a matter of duty by a person who has a property right to use the bank of a reservoir and does not necessitate compensation for loss under Article 29, paragraph 3 of the Constitution. The judgment below on this point erred not only in its premises, but also in its interpretation of Article 29, paragraph 3 of the Constitution, and must be held unlawful.

Third, due to its misinterpretation of Article 29, paragraphs 2 and 3 of the Constitution, the judgment below held Articles 4 and 9 of the present ordinance inapplicable to the accused, thereby acquitting them. This was improper. Appellant contentions on these points are reasonable, and the decision below must be quashed and the present case remanded to the court below.

Accordingly, the decision of this Court is decided, as stated in the Formal Judgment, pursuant to Article 410, paragraph 1, the Main Provision, Article 405, item 1, and Article 413 of the Code of Criminal Procedure.

This judgment is made by the unanimous opinion of all justices except for the supplementary opinions of justices Toshio Irie, Katsumi Tarumi, and Ken'ichi Okuno, and the dissenting opinions of Justices Daisuke

Kawamura, Sakunosuke Yamada, and Masatoshi Yokota [all of whose opinions are here omitted.].

Justices Kisaburō Yokota (presiding), Matasuke Kawamura, Toshio Irie, Katsu Ikeda, Katsumi Tarumi, Daisuke Kawamura, Masuo Shimoiizaka, Ken'ichi Okuno, Tsuneshichi Takagi, Shūichi Ishizaka, Sakunosuke Yamada, Kakiwa Gokijyō, Masatoshi Yokota, and Kitarō Saitō.

Case 9. Yoshida v. *Japan (1965).* The Bribery Compensation Case

19 *Keishū* at p. 203; Supreme Court, Grand Bench, 28 April 1965; Tokyo Dist. Ct. (First Instance), Tokyo High Ct. (Second Instance), [unconstitutionality of an order to pay in lieu of confiscation of bribe money].

EDITORIAL NOTE: A third party to a crime of bribery was judged to have knowingly received a bribe. He was ordered by the lower court to pay the government a sum equal to the bribery money, when it was discovered that the bribe money itself could not be confiscated. An appeal was lodged with the Supreme Court on the grounds that the third party had not been given opportunity to defend his property rights under Articles 29 and 31 of the Constitution prior to the court order.

REFERENCES

Constitution of Japan [ARTICLES 29 and 31 were at issue in this case. See Appendix 3 for these provisions].

Criminal Code (*Law 45 of 1907*, as amended), ARTICLE 197-2. A public employee or mediator who, upon request of others, makes a third party pay or promise to pay a bribe, or demand such a bribe, shall be sentenced to not more than three years of imprisonment at hard labor.

ARTICLE 197-4 (prior to revision by Law 107 of 1958). A bribe shall be confiscated from an offender and/or a third party who knowingly received it. Remuneration equivalent to whole or part of a bribe which cannot be confiscated shall be required of them.

FORMAL JUDGMENT

1. The decision below is quashed.
2. The accused is sentenced to one year of imprisonment at forced labor, except that execution of this sentence is to be suspended for three years from the date this judgment becomes final.

REASONS.* According to the investigation conducted under our authority, the first instance court had ascertained that the accused made Mitsuo Hiraita pay Tsutomu Okiishi 3,183,000 yen, and made it possible for Okiishi to retain 488,000 yen as personal profit. The court below then

*Five sentences are omitted in which the Court dismisses the appellant's contention that lower courts erred in fact-findings and application of laws and ordinances.

construed this finding of facts as meaning that Okiishi had knowingly received 488,000 yen as a bribe, to which crime he thus became a third party. The court ordered Okiishi to pay the state a sum equivalent to the bribe under Article 2 of the Supplement to Law 107 of 1958 and also under Article 197 of the Criminal Code prior to the revision by the above law.

Article 29 of the Constitution provides that a property right is inviolable, and Article 31 stipulates that "no person shall be deprived of life or liberty, nor shall any other criminal penalty be imposed, except according to procedure established by law." At the same time as the sentencing of the accused, the third party in the present case was given a court order to pay back a certain amount of money as a substitute for confiscation of the bribe money. This sanction against the third party infringed on his property rights without due process inasmuch as he was not given the opportunity to defend his property right. The above constitutional provisions have veen violated. It is true that Article 197-4 of the Criminal Code allows the state to require of a third party to a crime, who has knowingly received a bribe, a sum equivalent to the whole or part of bribe money which can no longer be confiscated. However, nowhere in the Code of Criminal Procedure or any other statute can one find a procedure providing a third party with notice and a chance to defend himself. Tsutomu Okiishi, a third party to the present case, was questioned merely as a witness in both the first and second instance deliberations. Therefore, a decision to order him to pay a sum equal to the bribe following the above provisions of the Criminal Code is a violation of Articles 29 and 31 of the Constitution. The decision of the court below must be reversed on this point.

Consequently, this Court quashes the judgment below in accordance with Article 410, paragraph 1, the main provision, Article 405, item 1, and Article 413, Proviso of the Code of Criminal Procedure, and also passes further judgment on the case of the accused.

When law is applied by the court of the first instance to the facts ascertained and this application of law is sustained by the court below, the above-stated acts of the accused fall under Article 197-2 of the Criminal Code. This Court sentences the accused to one year of imprisonment at forced labor . . . and suspends execution of this sentence for three years from the date of this judgment, pursuant to Article 25, paragraph 1 of the same Code.

This judgment is unanimous except for the opinion of Justice Sakunosuke Yamada [which is omitted here].

Justices Kisaburō Yokota (presiding), Toshio Irie, Ken'ichi Okuno, Shūichi Ishizaka, Sakunosuke Yamada, Kakiwa Gokijyō, Masatoshi Yokota, Asanosuke Kusaka, Kingo Osabe, Yoshihiko Kido, Kazuto Ishida, Goroku Kashiwabara, Jirō Tanaka, Jirō Matsuda, and Makoto Iwata.

Case 10. Koizumi v. *Japan (1963).* The Gypsy Taxi Cab Case

17 *Keishū* 12 at p. 2434; Supreme Court, Grand Bench, 4 December 1963; Tokyo North Summary Ct. (First Instance), Tokyo High Ct. (Second Instance), [constitutionality of the taxi licensing system].

EDITORIAL NOTE: An unlicensed taxicab operator was charged with violation of the Road Transportation Law, which prohibits the use of private automobiles for commercial activities such as transporting passengers for profit. Upon conviction, the accused appealed to the Supreme Court, on grounds that Article 101, paragraph 1 of the law prevents free competition and unreasonably restricts the constitutional freedom of occupation. The defense maintained that the law thus serves the special private interests of those already in the taxi business and fails to recognize that taxi service such as that of the defendant comes into being in response to social needs and contributes to the welfare of society.

REFERENCES

Constitution of Japan [ARTICLE 22 was at issue in this case. See Appendix 3 for this provision].

Road Transportation Law (*Law 183 of 1951*), ARTICLE 4, 1. A person desirous of starting an automobile transportation business must secure a license from the Minister of Transportation.

2. Subject to licensing in automobile transportation business are road routes, geographical areas of business, and kinds of automobile transportation business listed in the items under paragraph 2 and in the items under paragraph 3 of the previous Article.

3. A license of an automobile transportation business can restrict the volume of transport, passengers, or freight to be transported, and other aspects of the transportation business.

ARTICLE 101, 1. Private automobiles shall not be used for paid transportation, but may be used in case of an emergency caused by disaster, or for the purposes of the public welfare and after securing a permit from the Minister of Transportation.

ARTICLE 128-3, 2. A person who falls under any item below shall be subject to not more than three months imprisonment or a fine of not more than 50,000 yen [approximately $139.00 at the time], or both.

(2) Violation of provision of Article 101, paragraph 1. . . .

FORMAL JUDGMENT

The *jōkoku* appeal in the present case is dismissed.

REASONS. Concerning point 1 of the argument for appeal by Attorney K. Shiihara.

It is contended that Article 101, paragraph 1 of the Road Transportation Law is in violation of Article 22 of the Constitution.

But the provision of Article 22, paragraph 1 of the Constitution clearly stipulates that the freedom of occupation therein is not without limit, but may be restricted by requirement of the public welfare. The objective of the Road Transportation Law is to promote the public welfare by insuring fair competition and the proper operation of the road transportation business, while establishing order in road transportation which will contribute to the comprehensive development of an improved road transportation system. The law, which grants under fixed standards a license to operate an automobile transportation business instead of allowing anybody to be engaged in the business, is in conformity with the objective of the law itself, in view of the existing state of traffic and road transportation in Japan. Leaving the paid transportation business unregulated by allowing the use of noncommercial automobiles would not only lead very likely to the development of unlicensed businesses, but would also render regulation less effective under the licensing system. Therefore, it is a necessary restriction for the public welfare for the provision of Article 101, paragraph 1 of the law to ban the use of noncommercial automobiles in the paid transportation business. Thus, the Road Transportation Law is not contrary to Article 22, paragraph 1 of the Constitution, and the judgment below upholding the constitutionality of the law is proper. The argument for defense is groundless.

Concerning point 2. The contention of the defense assumes that Article 101, paragraph 1 of the Road Transportation Law violates Article 22, paragraph 1 of the Constitution and argues that the judgment below was in violation of Article 31 of the Constitution. But the present Court has already made clear that regulation by the Road Transportation Law does not violate Article 22, paragraph 1 of the Constitution in reference to point 1 above. The defense argument has erred in its assumptions and cannot be accepted. Moreover, a close examination of the record rules out the application of Article 411 of the Code of Criminal Procedure to the present case. Consequently, the Court decides as in the Formal Judgment, by the unanimous decision of the justices in accordance with Article 408 of the Code of Criminal Procedure.

Justices Kisaburō Yokota (presiding), Matasuke Kawamura, Toshio Irie, Masuo Shimoiizaka, Ken'ichi Okuno, Shūichi Ishizaka, Sakunosuke Yamada, Masatoshi Yokota, Kitarō Saitō, Asanosuke Kusaka, Kingo Osabe, Yoshihiko Kido, and Kazuto Ishida.

Case 11. Japan v. *Ki et al (1970).* The Ki Alien Reentry Case

24 *Minshū* 11 at p. 1512; Supreme Court, Second Petty Bench, 16 October 1970; Tokyo Dist. Ct. (First Instance), Tokyo High Ct. (Second Instance), [constitutionality of denial of reentry permit to resident alien].*

*This translation is the authors' own, but they have consulted the translation in The International Law Association of Japan, ed., *Japanese Annual of International Law*, no. 16 (1972): 77–79. Thanks are extended to Professor Sueo Ikehara of the University of Tokyo for bringing this to our attention.

EDITORIAL NOTE: In 1968 twelve Koreans resident in Japan wished to travel to the Democratic People's Republic of Korea (North Korea) to join in celebration of its twentieth anniversary. They applied to the director of the Immigration Control Bureau, Ministry of Justice, for permits to reenter Japan after their trip, maintaining that the term "reentry" in Article 26, paragraph 1 of the Immigration Control Ordinance should apply to a temporary trip overseas by a resident alien. The permits were denied, and the journey was not taken, but the case was taken to court.

In the 1958 Supreme Court precedent on which the Tokyo District Court relied in this case, the Grand Bench ruled that the freedom to travel abroad under Article 22 in the Constitution includes a temporary overseas trip.* Thus, the Tokyo District Court overruled the administrative denial of reentry permits,† reasoning as follows. The plaintiffs reside in Japan on a permanent basis, and their request was indeed for purposes of temporary travel abroad. Article 22 should be construed to guarantee rights of temporary travel abroad to aliens residing in Japan and subject to Japan's sovereignty. An application for reentry should be denied only when an applicant is likely to impair the national interest and the security of Japan, and the plaintiffs in the present case are unlikely to cause such problems. The high court sustained the court of first instance, and the case was appealed to the Supreme Court.

REFERENCES

Constitution of Japan [ARTICLE 22 was at issue in this case. See Appendix 3 for this provision].

Administrative Litigation Law (*Law 139 of 16 May 1962*), ARTICLE 9. Suits for revocation of disposition and decision may be filed only by persons (including persons having legal interest still to be recovered by the revocation of disposition or decision, even after the effect of the disposition or decision has ceased due to the elapse of the period therefor or for any other reason) having the legal interest with respect to seeking the revocation of the said disposition or decision.

Immigration Control Ordinance (*Cabinet Order 319 of 1951*), ARTICLE 26, 1. The minister of justice may grant permission, in accordance with the procedure set forth by the Justice Ministry's Order, on application for reentry to be submitted by an alien living in Japan (excluding maritime employees and others who are qualified to stay in Japan under Article 4, paragraph 1, item 3) who intends to leave Japan prior to the expiration of permit to stay, with the intent of reentering Japan.

FORMAL JUDGMENT

1. The judgment below is quashed, and the judgment of the first instance court is vacated.
2. All claims in this case are dismissed.

REASONS. According to the investigation conducted under our authority, the respondents sought a judgment quashing the justice minister's decision to deny permission on the application for reentry which the re-

*12 *Minshū* 1969 (Sup. Ct., G.B., 10 September 1958).
†*Hanrei Jihō*, No. 531, p. 3 (Tokyo Dist. Ct., 11 October 1968).

spondents had submitted with the intention to depart Japan on 22 August 1968, and to reenter on 23 October 1968. Passing a judgment on the merits of the respondents' claim, the court below sustained as follows the facts found by the first instance court, based on statements of the respondents and in oral arguments. The respondents intended to visit their ancestral country on the occasion of the twentieth anniversary of the foundation of the Democratic People's Republic of Korea (hereinafter referred to as DPRK); although it might be desirable for the respondents to visit the DPRK during the period of time for which they applied, the purpose of their visit could be achieved even if they visited at any time during 1968 or sometime in that neighborhood. Therefore, the respondents had an interest in initiating a suit seeking a judicial decision to reverse the appellant's denial of reentry permission. However, judging from the respondents' application for reentry permission, this Court finds that the respondents' visit to their home country was to take part during the celebration, on 9 September 1968, of the twentieth anniversary of the foundation of the DPRK, as members of a celebration group representing Koreans living in Japan. The respondents contend that they were going to attend events connected with the celebration such as the main assemblies of the celebration held in P'yŏngyang and elsewhere from 8 September to 17 October 1968, and the national art exhibition commemorating the twentieth anniversary which lasted through 28 October of the same year. In light of this purpose, as found by the court, the visit to their ancestral country lost its purpose after the last celebration event, granted that the same conclusion might not necessarily be reached had they not had to visit at a time so close to 23 October 1968, the date of reentry for which application had been made. The appellant denied permission to the respondents only because of the above-mentioned purposes and travel itinerary contained in their application.

The appellant's denial of reentry permission does not necessarily affect a future application by the respondents for other purposes and another travel itinerary. Consequently, the respondents in this case lost their legal interest to bring a suit on 27 November 1968, when the oral proceedings in the court below were concluded. The judgment below, decided on the merits of the case based on contrary findings, must be quashed, and the judgment of the first instance court, ruling for the respondents, must be vacated.

This Court quashes the judgment below, vacates the judgment of the first instance court, and dismisses all claims in this case, in accordance with Article 7 of the Administrative Litigation Law and Articles 408, 396, and 386 of the Code of Civil Procedure.

This judgment is unanimous except for the dissenting opinion of Justice Kōtarō Irokawa.

* * *

The dissenting opinion of Justice Kōtarō Irokawa follows.

The majority opinion, in determining the purposes of respondents' visit, construes the statements in the respondents' application too strictly and decides that legal interests for instituting a suit to vacate the disposition denying permission were lost when it became impossible for the respondents to attend the celebration events as they had intended. I cannot approve of this line of thinking. Although the purpose of the respondents' visit, as the majority opinion pointed out, was to attend certain celebration events, the real intention of the respondents continues to be to celebrate the twentieth anniversary of the foundation of their home country with fellow countrymen there, acting as goodwill envoys representing Koreans resident abroad. If this is so, to attend certain celebration events does not necessarily in itself constitute a crucial element in the purposes of the proposed visit. Therefore, it is enough if they can present their congratulations at any time when they visit their ancestral country, the DPRK; so the judgment below must be upheld for recognizing the interests in presenting the claims on the grounds that the respondents' visit could promote their interests if they visited the country during 1968 or at some time close to that period. Furthermore, the existence of interests in instituting a suit to protect rights should be decided, in general, with reference to the time when the oral proceedings were in fact concluded. There is, therefore, need for judging on the merits in the present case. Nevertheless, since the majority opinion decided to dismiss all claims as moot, it is of no value to inquire further into the grounds for appeal, and further argument is omitted.

Justices Asanosuke Kusaka (presiding), Yoshihiko Kido, Kōtarō Irokawa, and Tomokazu Murakami.

Chapter 7

Rights Related to the Quality of Socioeconomic Life (Shakaiken)

In discussions of constitutional law in Japan, the rights to "minimum standards of wholesome and cultured living" (Article 25 of the Constitution of Japan; see Appendix 3 for the full text of this and the following provisions), to education (Article 26), to work (Article 27), as well as "the rights of workers to organize and to bargain and act collectively" (Article 28) are all subsumed under the category of socioeconomic rights or, more literally "social rights" (shakaiken). *Article 28 in particular, sometimes in conjunction with free speech guarantees (see also, Chapter 10, below), has been at issue in litigation arising out of the activities of Japan's quite vigorous union movement.*

Case 12. Toyama et al v. *Japan (1966)*. The Tokyo Central Post Office Case

20 *Keishū* 8 at p. 901; Supreme Court, Grand Bench, 26 October 1966; Tokyo Dist. Ct. (First Instance), Tokyo High Ct. (Second Instance), [constitutionality of special limitations of the rights of postal employees].*

EDITORIAL NOTE: Each year Japan's union movement launches what is called "the spring labor struggle," a highly institutionalized form of mass presentation of socioeconomic demands and, especially perhaps during the 1950s and 1960s, political petition and protest. During the labor offensive of 1958, the accused in this case, officials of the National Postal Service Union, urged employees of the Tokyo Central Post Office to leave work and hold a rally. On 20 March, thirty-eight people left their jobs for several hours, and their leaders were charged with inciting a disruption of the work of postal workers. The Tokyo District Court dismissed the charges as follows. Although Article 17 of the Public Enterprise Labor Relations Law (PELRL) prohibits dispute activities by public employees, certain of these acts are justifiable as part of a labor dispute under Article 1, paragraph 2 of the Labor Union Law. The act of failing to carry out postal work

*The translation of judicial opinions is the authors' own, but they have consulted the translation of the General Secretariat, Supreme Court, trans., *Judgment upon Case of Criminal Immunity Related to Dispute Tactics of Employees of Public Corporations Etc.: Series of Prominent Judgments of the Supreme Court upon Questions of Constitutionality*, no. 9 (1967).

is an offense against Article 79 of the Postal Law, but it is justifiable in this case as part of a labor dispute. However, the Tokyo High Court, relying on a 1963 Petty Bench decision,* reversed and held that Article 17 of the PELRL should govern. Appellants argued before the Supreme Court that Article 17, paragraph 1 violates Article 28 of the Constitution.

REFERENCES

Constitution of Japan [ARTICLE 28 was at issue in this case. See Appendix 3 for this provision].

National Public Employees Law (*Law 120 of 21 October 1947*), ARTICLE 98, 2. Personnel shall be permitted to form or refrain from forming or to join or refrain from joining associations or other organizations. Through such organizations, personnel may designate representatives of their own choice and negotiate with proper authorities, subject to the procedures of the National Personnel Authority, for conditions of work and for other lawful purposes including social and welfare activities, provided, however, that such negotiation does not include the right of collective agreement with the government. No employee shall be denied the freedom to express dissatisfaction or voice opinions by reason of his not belonging to an employee organization.

4. Personnel of the police forces and firemen (including personnel of the National Fire Prevention Board) and personnel of the Maritime Safety Board and penal institutions shall be denied the right to organize employee organizations or to join employee organizations as specified in paragraph 2.

5. Personnel shall not engage in strikes, delays, or other dispute activities against the public, which the government represents in its capacity as employer. Nor shall they resort to acts of delay that reduce the efficiency of governmental operations. No one shall plan, conspire to effect, instigate, or incite such illegal actions.

ARTICLE 110, 1. A person falling under one of the following items shall be sentenced to penal servitude not exceeding three years or fined in an amount not exceeding one hundred thousand yen. . . .

(16) A person who organizes an employee organization in violation of Article 98, paragraph 4.

(17) Any person who conspires to effect, instigates, or incites the illegal action defined in the first part of Article 98, paragraph 5, or attempts such action.

Local Public Employees Law (*Law 261, 13 December 1950*), ARTICLE 31, 1. Personnel must take an oath to perform their duties as provided in the bylaws.

ARTICLE 37, 1. Personnel must not engage in strikes, slowdowns, or other dispute activities against their employer, that is, the local people, which the agencies of the local public entity represent, or in such acts of

*161 *Saibanshū Keiji* 185 (Sup. Ct., Second P.B., 15 March 1963).

delay which reduce efficiency in the operations of the agencies of the local public entity. No one shall plan, conspire to effect, instigate, or incite such unlawful acts.

2. Any employee who has acted in violation of the provisions of the preceding paragraph, simultaneously with the commencement of such acts, may not assert rights derived from such appointment or employment against local public entity, that he enjoys under laws and orders, or bylaws, regulations of the local public entity, or rules fixed by agencies of the local public entity.

Article 61, paragraph 1. A person who falls under one of the following items shall be sentenced to penal servitude not exceeding three years or fined in an amount not exceeding one hundred thousand yen. . . .

(4) Any person who plans, conspires to effect, instigates, or incites the unlawful acts stipulated in the first part of Article 31, paragraph 1. . . .

Public Enterprise Labor Relations Law (*Law 257 of 20 December 1948*), Article 3. A labor union of the employees of a public enterprise and the like (hereinafter referred to as "a union"), and labor relations as well as their adjustment shall be treated by this law, and the matters not provided for by this law shall be dealt with under the provisions of the Labor Union Law (Law 174 of 1949) (except for Article 5, paragraph 2, item 8; Article 7, the proviso to item 1; Article 8; and Articles 18 through 32 of the said law).

Article 17. The employees and their unions shall not engage in a strike, slowdown or any other dispute activities interfering with the normal conduct of business, nor shall any employees conspire to effect, instigate, or incite such prohibited acts.

2. Public Enterprises shall not engage in lockouts.

Article 18. Any employee found to have engaged in conduct that violates the provisions of the preceding Article shall be subject to dismissal.

Labor Union Law (*Law 174 of 1 June 1949*), Article 1, 1. The purposes of the present law are to elevate the status of workers by putting them on an equal footing in negotiations with their employers; to protect the practice on the part of workers of autonomous organization and association in labor unions, so that they may act collectively, as in the designation of representatives of their own choosing for negotiation of the terms and conditions of work; and to encourage the practice and procedures of collective bargaining resulting in labor agreements governing relations between employers and workers.

2. The provisions of Article 35 of the Criminal Code (Law 45 of 1907) shall apply to collective bargaining and other justifiable acts of a labor union performed for the attainment of purposes in the preceding paragraph; provided that in no event shall acts of violence be construed as justifiable acts of labor unions.

ARTICLE 7, 1. The employer shall not be permitted the following practices:

(1) To discharge or discriminate against a worker for being a member of a labor union, for having tried to join or to organize a labor union, or for having performed appropriate acts of a labor union; or to make it a condition of employment that the worker must not join or must withdraw from a labor union. Provided that this shall not prevent an employer from concluding a labor agreement with a labor union which requires, as a condition of employment, that the workers must be members of the labor union if such labor union represents a majority of the workers in the particular plant or working place in which such workers are employed.

(2) To refuse to bargain collectively with the representative of the workers employed by the employer without fair and appropriate reasons.

(3) To control or to interfere with the formation or management of a labor union by workers, or to give financial support thereto to defray the labor union's operational costs. Provided that this shall not prevent the employer from permitting the workers to confer or negotiate with him during working hours without loss of time or pay; and that this excludes the employer's contributions to welfare, benefit, or similar funds that are actually used for payments to prevent or relieve economic misfortune or accident, as well as the furnishing of minimum office space.

(4) To discharge or discriminate against a worker for having filed a complaint with the Labor Relations Commission to the effect that the employer has violated the provisions of this Article, for having requested the Central Labor Relations Commission to review the order issued under the provisions of Article 27, paragraph 4, or for having presented evidence or testimony at the investigation or hearing conducted by the Labor Relations Commission in regard to such complaint or request, or at the adjustment of labor disputes provided for in the Labor Relations Adjustment Law (Law 25 of 1946).

ARTICLE 8. No employer shall claim indemnity from a labor union or its members for damages received from a strike or other dispute activities that are appropriate acts.

Cabinet Order concerning the Provisional Measures To Be Taken in Consequence of the Letter of the Supreme Commander for the Allied Powers to the Prime Minister, dated 22 July 1948 (Cabinet Order No. 201). The Cabinet hereby establishes the Cabinet Order concerning the provisional measures to be taken in consequence of the letter of the Supreme Commander for the Allied Powers to the Prime Minister, dated 22 July 1948, under Imperial Ordinance No. 542 of 1945 concerning Orders to be issued pursuant to the acceptance of the Potsdam Declaration.

ARTICLE 1, 1. No person in the position of an employee of the government or a local public entity, regardless of whether appointed or employed (hereinafter referred to as "public employees"; the Provisional Personnel Commission has the authority to determine whether certain positions are in a public service or not when there is doubt) shall possess the right of collective bargaining, with its usually understood coercive character supported by the threat of a strike, vis-à-vis the government or a local public entity. Public employees or their organizations, however, may not be denied the freedom, within the restrictions of the present Cabinet Order, to negotiate with the appropriate agency of the government or the local public entity, in the sense that they can freely present, individually or collectively through their representatives their complaints, opinions, desires, and grievances, and to support the same by adequate opportunity for discussion and for submission of evidence.

2. All acts heretofore taken by the government or by local public entities in personnel matters affecting public servants will be valid so long as they do not violate the spirit of the limitations imposed by the present Cabinet Order, or were not taken in contravention of such limitations.

3. All mediation proceedings now pending in which the government or local public entities are parties shall be suspended. The National Personnel Authority will hereafter be the agency charged with the protection of the interests of public servants.

ARTICLE 2, 1. Public employees shall not engage in strikes, delays, or other dispute activities that tend to reduce the efficiency of operations of the government or a local public entity.

2. Any employee who has acted in violation of the provisions of the preceding paragraph, regardless of status as a public employee, may not assert rights derived from such appointment or employment against the government or a local public entity.

ARTICLE 3. Those who act in violation of Article 2, paragraph 1 shall be liable to penal servitude not exceeding one year, or a fine not exceeding 5,000 yen.

Supplementary Provisions: 1. The present Cabinet Order shall come into force from the day of its promulgation.

2. The present Cabinet Order shall be effective until by legislation of the Diet the amendment of the National Public Employees Law mentioned in the letter of the Supreme Commander for the Allied Powers to the Prime Minister, dated 22 July 1948, and other measures that may be deemed necessary, have been undertaken and have come into force.

Postal Law (*Law 165 of 12 December 1947*), ARTICLE 1. The objective of this Law is to promote the welfare of the people by furnishing all of them with postal service impartially and at the lowest possible rates.

ARTICLE 79, 1. An employee of the Postal Service who shall wilfully and maliciously mishandle mail, or cause it to be delayed, shall be subject to penal servitude not exceeding one year, or a fine not exceeding twenty thousand yen.

Criminal Code (*Law 45 of 24 April 1907*), ARTICLE 35. An act done in accordance with the laws and ordinances, or a justifiable act performed in the course of appropriate business is not punishable.

FORMAL JUDGMENT

The judgment below is quashed. This case is remanded to the Tokyo High Court.

REASONS. Concerning the reasons for *jōkoku* appeal submitted by the accused and by Attorneys M. Tōjō and H. Yamamoto:

While the reasons given for *jōkoku* appeal are based on grounds of conflict with provisions of the Constitution, judicial precedents and numerous other grounds, the gist of the reasons, in effect, amounts to two contentions: First, that Article 17, paragraph 1 of the Public Enterprise Labor Relations Law (hereinafter referred to as PELRL) violates Article 28 of the Constitution; and second, that the provisions of Article 1, paragraph 2 of the Labor Union Law should be applicable to dispute activities resorted to in violation of Article 17, paragraph 1 of the PELRL. (Such violation is exempted from criminal liability pursuant to Article 1, paragraph 2 of the Labor Union Law.) The opinions of this Court on these two contentions are as follows:

1. Article 28 of the Constitution guarantees the fundamental rights of workers, that is, the right to organize and to bargain and act collectively. This guarantee derives from the fundamental idea of Article 25 of the Constitution which provided that "all people shall have the right to maintain the minimum standards of wholesome and cultured living." On the premise that a life worthy of human beings is to be guaranteed to workers, the Constitution guarantees, on the one hand, the right to work in Article 27 and, on the other hand, in Article 28 the rights of workers to organize, to bargain collectively, and to resort to dispute activities, as the means to secure substantive freedom and equality to workers standing in a disadvantageous economic position.

A statute curtailing the fundamental rights of workers should be construed reasonably in light of the Constitution, which provides for the guarantee of these fundamental rights so as to be in conformity with the spirit of the constitutional guarantee. Under the Constitution, which guarantees the right to maintain minimum standards of wholesome and cultured living as one of its fundamental concepts, and which, along with the guarantee of the right to own property, enumerates the guaranteed rights of workers to work, to organize, to bargain collectively, and to resort to dispute activities, a legal interpretation of the substantive law curtailing fundamental rights of workers must be both sound and reasonable when interpreting the statute so as to maintain harmony and balance between these two groups of rights.

The fundamental rights of workers are guaranteed not only to employees in private enterprises but also, as a rule, to employees of public corporations and for workers engaged in national or local public services; for these public employees are not different from the workers mentioned in Article 28 of the Constitution. So it is not permissible, in our opinion, to deny these fundamental rights to public employees by relying on the provision of Article 15, which states, "all public officials are servants of the whole community and not of any group thereof." As will be explained later, the fundamental rights of workers engaging in public services or in public enterprises involve restrictions different from that of private enterprises only according to the nature of their duties.

With respect to the right to resort to dispute activities as a union activity, since such acts, within reasonable limits, are an exercise of the rights guaranteed by the Constitution and based upon justifiable cause, they do not give rise to such problems as dismissal or indemnity for damages caused by nonperformance of contractual obligation. Furthermore, since they are not illegal, tort liability does not ensue. Article 7 of the Labor Union Law prohibits the employer from discharging or discriminating against any worker for performing acts proper for a labor union; Article 8 of the law which provides that "no employer shall claim indemnity from a labor union or its members for damages incurred from a strike or other appropriate dispute activities" clearly restates what is normal based on the explanation above. Considered from such a point of view, naturally a strike or other dispute activities that are properly conducted for the attainment of the purposes of the Labor Union Law cannot be a target of criminal punishment. Article 1, paragraph 2 of the Labor Union Law states, "the provision of Article 35 of the Criminal Code shall apply to collective bargaining and other acts of a labor union which are justified as performed for the attainment of the purposes of the preceding paragraph." This must be understood as providing a precautionary measure concerning what is obvious. A proviso of this paragraph provides that "in no event shall acts of violence be construed as legitimate acts of labor unions," which clearly indicates the proper limitations imposed on dispute activities, and that any act or conduct transgressing this limitation is no longer exempt from criminal liability.

2. The fundamental rights of workers, such as the right to organize, to bargain collectively, and to resort to dispute activities, are guaranteed for all classes of workers by Article 28 of the Constitution, which is based upon the concept that "all people shall have the right to maintain the minimum standards of wholesome and cultured living." However, even these rights themselves are not absolute but are subject to restriction. Such rights should be understood to be subject to an inherent restriction, justified from the standpoint that the interests of the nation as a whole have to be protected. However, the extent to which such restrictions can

be constitutionally imposed is a problem that must be carefully solved on the basis of various considerations and factors. These considerations and factors are as follows:

(1) The propriety of the restriction imposed upon the fundamental rights of workers must be judged by balancing the necessity of preserving the fundamental rights of workers with the necessity of protecting the interests of the nation as a whole. However, since the fundamental rights of workers are directly linked with the right of workers to maintain minimum standards of wholesome and cultured living, and as the former is one of the most important ways to realize the latter, restrictions must be confined to the necessary and reasonable minimum.

(2) Restriction of the fundamental rights of workers is justified only when the nature of the duties of the occupation or business engaged in by workers is strongly imbued with a public interest, and a resultant delay in carrying out duties or business would be inimical to the interest of the people's livelihood and would result in serious obstructions of community livelihood. Therefore, when a restriction is to be imposed upon the fundamental rights of workers, it should be considered in the light that it is necessary and unavoidable in order to forestall the above-mentioned inimical effect.

(3) The penalty against a violator of restriction of the fundamental rights of workers should not exceed necessary limitations. In particular, criminal sanctions are to be imposed for dispute activities only when it is deemed necessary and unavoidable. Circumspection is especially needed when simple inaction, as in a strike or slowdown, is made a subject of criminal sanction. It is a principle under the present legal system that only civil legal effects such as cancellation of a contract or claims to damages result from nonperformance of a contractual obligation, and as a rule no criminal sanction may be imposed in such cases. This naturally ensues from the civilized idea of respecting human rights and from the ideal in penal policy of confining criminal sanctions to strongly harmful antisocial conduct. This is the same whether the contractual obligation arises from a service contract or from a labor contract.

Generally speaking, no criminal sanction should be imposed on a worker when he simply refrains from supplying labor (i.e., in the case of a strike), or when he supplies labor sparingly (i.e., in the case of a slowdown).

(4) If the nature of the work necessitates restriction of the fundamental rights of workers, some compensatory measures should be taken to make up for such restriction.

What we have so far mentioned must be heeded, not only at the time of the enactment of a statute which curtails the fundamental rights of workers, but also at the time of construing an existing statute which on its face curtails the fundamental rights of workers.

3. Looking into the specifics of statutes curtailing the fundamental

rights of workers, the degree of curtailment differs depending on statutes. A good number of amendments have been made in the development of the statutes now in force. Before 31 July 1948, the day of the promulgation and enforcement of Cabinet Order 201, no restriction was imposed upon either national or local public employees (except workers in charge of some specific duty) with respect to the full enjoyment of the rights to organize, to bargain collectively, and to resort to dispute activities. They had not been prohibited from resorting to dispute activities. By the enforcement of Cabinet Order 201, public employees, regardless of whether they were employed by the national government or by local public entities, were prohibited from resorting to any type of dispute activities, including a strike or slowdown, which tended to reduce the efficiency of the operation of the government or local public entities. The Cabinet Order provided criminal penalties for those who violated the prohibition. However, while the amended National Public Employees Law (hereinafter referred to as NPEL) in force from 3 December 1948 also prohibited workers from resorting to any type of dispute activities, it did not provide criminal penalties for employees who merely participated in dispute activities. It only penalized those who planned or engaged in acts of conspiracy, instigation, or incitement of dispute activities (The NPEL in force before amendment by Law 69 of 1965, Article 98, paragraph 5, Article 110, paragraph 1, item 17; the Local Public Employees Law, Article 37, paragraph 1, Article 61, paragraph 4). Under the PELRL promulgated on 20 December 1948 and enforced from 1 June 1949, the National Railways Corporation and the Japan Monopoly Corporation were defined as Public Enterprises, and their employees were prohibited from resorting to any type of dispute activity. However, the law did not contain any provision penalizing conduct violative of the prohibition. No criminal sanction has ever been imposed for an act violating the prohibition. By amendment of the law on 31 July 1952, the application of the provisions of the NPEL was also excluded from dispute activities by employees of five government enterprises, including the accused in the postal service, and provisions of the amended PELRL became applicable to acts of such employees. Consequently, while Article 17, paragraph 1 of the PELRL clearly prohibited employees of the postal service from resorting to any dispute activities, no penal sanction was imposed for any conduct violating this prohibition solely on the basis of violating this prohibition, whether it was a conspiracy, an instigation, an incitement, or a plan to resort to dispute activities.

In light of the history of the above-mentioned statutes, it is conceivable that, without distinction between employees engaged in public corporations and employees of the so-called five government enterprises, the legislature has respected the fundamental rights of workers guaranteed by the Constitution and has gradually modified sanctions on violations of the prohibition against any type of dispute activities, with the view that only necessary and minimum restrictions may be imposed on fundamental rights. And under the present law, no criminal sanction is imposed for resorting to any type of dispute activities so long as they do not exceed the proper limits.

4. When the PELRL is reviewed against the above-stated historical process, Article 17, paragraph 1 of the law provides that employees of the so-called five government enterprises and the three public corporations, and their unions shall not engage in strikes, delays, or any other dispute activities that interfere with the normal conduct of business, nor shall any employee conspire to effect, instigate, or incite such prohibited acts. This means that acts of employees categorized simply as nonperformance of a contract, or as acts of instigating such nonperformance are illegal when they interfere with the normal conduct of business. Thus, it is clear that this provision restricts the worker's right to resort to dispute activities which is guaranteed by Article 28 of the Constitution.

Appellants contend that Article 17, paragraph 1 of the PELRL violates Articles 18 and 28 of the Constitution and is invalid. However, this Court has decided that the said paragraph does not violate either of these two Articles of the Constitution. (Concerning the former, cf. 9 *Keishū* 1189; Sup. Ct., G.B., 22 June 1955; concerning the latter, cf. 7 *Keishū* 775; Sup. Ct., G.B., 8 April 1953.) At the present moment, we do not think it necessary to alter the conclusion that this paragraph is not repugnant to the Constitution. The reasons shall be explained in detail.

As mentioned above, the fundamental rights of workers guaranteed in Article 28 of the Constitution are not absolute but are subject to restriction. These rights are to be understood to involve an inherent restriction justified from the standpoint that the livelihood of the nation as a whole should be protected. The work of employees in the five government enterprises and the three public corporations has a more or less direct or indirect relationship to the interests of community life. There is no doubt that stoppage or neglect of work is inimical to the interests of the people and tends to seriously obstruct community life. Without speaking of other types of work, suffice it to say that the work of the postal service involved in this case is a monopoly, has a close relationship to the people's livelihood, and its stoppage or neglect seriously obstructs the community's life and exerts immense influence upon the general public. Therefore, a provision prohibiting postal service employees from resorting to any dispute activities and imposing some disadvantage on those who violate the prohibition should not be held to be repugnant to the Constitution and thus invalid, so long as the disadvantage to be imposed is within necessary and proper limits and is reasonable in light of the above-mentioned standards.

Looking into sanctions to be imposed for acts violating the prohibition on dispute activities in Article 17, paragraph 1 of the PELRL, we find that Article 18 of the law provides that "any employee found to have engaged in conduct which violates the provisions of Article 17 shall be subject to dismissal." Although it states that "matters not provided for by this law shall be dealt with under the provisions of the Labor Union Law," Article 3 of the law clearly rules out application of Article 8 of the Labor Union Law which states "no employer shall claim indemnity from a labor union or its members for damages received from a strike or other dispute activities which are proper acts." Thus, an act violating the prohibition of Article 17 is subject to civil liabilities and is illegal only in this sense. Furthermore, to compensate for this prohibition or dispute activities, the PELRL provides a system of mediation, conciliation, and arbitration through the Public Enterprise Labor Relations Commission for dealing with disputes between a public corporation and its employees. An arbitration order made by the commission composed of PELR Commissioners is given the same effect as a labor agreement and is binding on both employees and employers. Therefore, the law leaves no doubt that the prohibition on any type of dispute activity imposed by Article 17, paragraph 1 without exempting violators from civil liabilities, is not repugnant to either Article 18 or Article 28 of the Constitution.

5. May criminal sanctions be imposed on one who resorts to any type of dispute activities in violation of Article 17, paragraph 1 of the PELRL? As we have stated in the legislative history, restrictions imposed upon dispute activities have been gradually modified, and the PELRL does not contain any special penal provision. This shows, in our view, that the legislators at the time of enactment of the law did not intend to impose criminal sanctions on any acts violating the provision that prohibits dispute activities. This view is supported by the fact that Article 3 of the law does not rule out the application of Article 1, paragraph 2 of the Labor Union Law, which provided an exemption from criminal liability that presupposes the application of that paragraph to dispute activities. This manifests the basic attitude of a legislator who takes the view that the legal sanctions for violating the prohibition on dispute activities must be kept to the necessary minimum in conformity with the basic spirit of the fundamental rights of workers guaranteed in Article 28 of the Constitution, and that civil liability alone, not criminal sanctions, may be imposed for illegal dispute activities.

It is worthwhile to compare, in terms of the sanctions imposed for dispute activities, those employees who are not employed in governmental enterprise activities and those governed by the NPEL or the Local Public Employees Law (hereafter referred to as LPEL). The NPEL and the LPEL only penalize those who conspire to effect, instigate, incite, or plan a strike, delay, or other acts of dispute (Article 98, paragraph 5 and Article 110, paragraph 1, item 17 of the NPEL in force before the amendment by Law 69 of 1965; Article 37, paragraph 1 and Article 61, item 4 of the LPEL). The purport of these laws is as follows; on the one hand, public employees are to be prohibited for the protection of the public welfare from resorting to dispute activities, and on the other hand, they, as workers, are guaranteed by the Constitution the fundamental rights of workers. In order to adjust and satisfy the demands of the public welfare and the Constitutional guarantee, these laws provide civil sanctions only for those who simply participate in dispute activities, and criminal sanctions only for those who actively assume the leadership in any dispute activities. Undoubtedly, the duties of public employees are of a stronger public nature than those of workers in the manual services to whom the PELRL is applicable. Even with respect to a public employee's dispute activities, criminal sanctions are imposed only upon those who actively assume the leadership and are not imposed on those who simply participate in such dispute activities. Therefore, it is quite natural that a lighter sanction, or none at all, would be imposed upon acts of workers in the manual services to whom the PELRL is applicable. Since the PELRL does not contain a provision concerning criminal sanctions, it should be understood that no criminal sanctions were intended.

When we take this view, it is proper to conclude that the dispute activities to which Article 1, paragraph 2 of the Labor Union Law is applicable by virtue of Article 3 of the PELRL, are for the achievement of purposes provided in Article 1, paragraph 1 of the Labor Union Law. Dispute activities for which no criminal sanctions are directed are limited to such inactions as a strike or slowdown which are not accompanied by acts of violence or other improper acts. Dispute activities are not made the object of criminal sanction only within the above-mentioned limit. In a case when dispute activities are resorted to not for attaining a purpose provided in Article 1, paragraph 1 of the Labor Union Law, but for the attainment of a political aim, or when they are accompanied by acts of violence, or when they seriously interfere with the life of the nation by extending over long periods not permissible in the light of common sense, then they exceed the permissible limits of dispute activities guaranteed by the Constitution and so are not exempt from criminal sanctions. We are of the opinion that the decision of the Second Petty Bench of this Court (17 *Keishū* 23, Sup. Ct., 2nd P.B., 15 March 1963) negating the application of Article 1, paragraph 2 of the Labor Union Law to any type of dispute activities engaged in by employees under the PELRL, and holding that there is no room to examine the question of whether the specific dispute activities are justifiable or not, must be overruled.

6. Article 79, paragraph 1 of the Postal Law provides that when a person engaged in the postal service intentionally refuses to handle mail or delays the mail, he shall be punished with imprisonment of up to one year or a fine of up to 20,000 yen. This provision is one of the exceptions to the general rule of not imposing criminal sanctions for not discharging contractual obligations. However, in light of the strong public nature

of the postal service, to provide for such a degree of punishment is reasonable and does not exceed necessary and proper limits (Article 21 of the Law concerning Mail Transportation). It is quite clear that this penal provision is not directed exclusively to the conduct of dispute activities. Since it is impossible to find any reason for ruling out application of the provision in a case where postal employees commit the offense as dispute activities, there is no alternative to interpreting the provision as applicable to such dispute activities. However, as Article 1, paragraph 2 of the Labor Union Law clearly states, the penal provision of the Postal Law is not applicable to a justifiable act, which includes any conduct related to dispute activities so long as they are for the attainment of a purpose provided in Article 1, paragraph 1 of the Labor Union Law, and are not accompanied by acts of violence or other improper acts. Conversely speaking, the penal provision is applicable if dispute activities are not for the attainment of a purpose provided in Article 1, paragraph 1 of the Labor Union Law or if dispute activities are accompanied by any acts of violence or other improper acts. Furthermore, one who instigates such illegal dispute activities is punishable as an accomplice according to the Criminal Code.

7. The judgment of the court of the first instance in this case found that the acts of thirty-eight persons, including Tamiji Ishizaki, constituted an offense under the first part of Article 79, paragraph 1 of the Postal Law. The judgment below following the above-mentioned decision of the Second Petty Bench of this Court, held that since employees of public corporations were prohibited from resorting to any type of dispute activities, Article 1, paragraph 2 of the Labor Union Law was not applicable to the acts of the thirty-eight persons found guilty by the judgment of the court of the first instance, and that the question of whether the specific dispute activities were justifiable was not open to discussion.

However, it is clear, by the finding of the court of the first instance, that the accused have committed the acts alleged in this case as dispute activities. Consequently, the determination of the criminal responsibility of Tamiji Ishizaki and others must be made under Article 79, paragraph 1 of the Postal Law, which of necessity, under Article 1, paragraph 2 of the Labor Union Law, involves an interpretation of whether or not the acts of Tamiji Ishizaki and others in question constituted justifiable acts. This judgment must be made on the basis of the concrete facts involved as well as in accordance with a reasonable interpretation of Article 28 of the Constitution and Article 17, paragraph 1 of the PELRL. The judgment below erred in the construction and application of law, and the mistake is material to the judgment. It is incompatible with justice not to quash the judgment of the court below.

In the light of what we have said, the appellants' contention that Article 17, paragraph 1 of the PELRL and the judgment below are repugnant to Articles 11, 14, 18, 25, 28, 31, and 98 of the Constitution, is not well founded. Therefore, according to Article 411, paragraph 1 and Article 430, main clause of the Code of Criminal Procedure, this Court reverses the judgment of the court below as pronounced in the Formal Judgment, without determining the correctness of other contentions, and remands the case to the Tokyo High Court for further proceedings.

This judgment is rendered by the unanimous opinion of all the justices except for the supplementary opinions of Justices Jirō Matsuda and Makoto Iwata, and the dissenting opinions of Justices Ken'ichi Okuno, Kakiwa Gokijyō, Asanosuke Kusaka and Kazuto Ishida. [All of the opinions except for the principal dissenting opinion have been omitted.]

* * *

The dissenting opinion of Justices Ken'ichi Okuno, Asanosuke Kusaka, and Kazuto Ishida follows.

Concerning the appellant contentions that Article 17, paragraph 1 of the PELRL violates Article 28 of the Constitution, and that Article 1, paragraph 2 of the Labor Union Law is applicable to conduct during dispute activities violating Article 17, paragraph 1 of the PELRL:

This Court has previously held that even the fundamental rights of workers guaranteed by Article 28 of the Constitution are not absolute and unrestricted rights. They are subject to reasonable restrictions if it is necessary for the public welfare (7 *Keishū* 775; Sup. Ct., G.B., 8 April 1953).

Article 1 of the PELRL provides that "this Law aims at securing the uninterrupted operation of public corporations and national enterprises at maximum efficiency for the promotion and protection of the public welfare. . . ." In order to attain this aim, Article 17 of the law states that "the employees or their union shall not engage in a strike, slowdown or any other dispute activities interfering with the normal conduct of business." Thus, these employees are prohibited from resorting to any dispute activities hampering the normal conduct of business. The law deems the employees of a public corporation to be public officials or quasi-public officials and, for the promotion and protection of public welfare, prohibits them from resorting to dispute activities. This derives from the facts that the activities of public corporations are highly public in nature in that they have an important relationship to the national economy, and the normal conduct of their business should not be hampered in the slightest; and that the work of the employees of public corporations is closely related to the interests of the people, and their functions differ greatly from those of private enterprise employees. The law, as compensation for depriving them of the right to resort to dispute activities, established the Public Enterprise Labor Relations Commission whose function is to mediate, conciliate, or arbitrate disputes between public corporations and their employees. An arbitration order made by the commission is given the same effect as a labor agreement and is final and binding upon both parties (Article 35 of the law).

That is to say, the law, taking into consideration the public nature of the functions of public corporations, on the one hand prohibits employees of public corporations from resorting to dispute activities, and on the other hand, protects the interests of the employees by establishing as compensatory measures this mediation, conciliation, and arbitration system. To restrict the rights of workers in that manner is permissible as a reasonable restriction for the promotion and protection of the public welfare. Therefore, the law is not violative of Article 28 of the Constitution. This Court has decided that Article 17 of the PELRL is not repugnant to the Constitution (9 *Keishū* 1189; Sup. Ct., G.B., 22 June 1955). We do not find any need to overrule it.

As stated above, employees of public corporations are prohibited by law from resorting to dispute activities that obstruct the normal conduct of business. Consequently, dispute activities that violate the prohibition are illegal and cannot be considered proper and justifiable. In other words, even when the content of dispute activities is simply a passive inaction, such as deserting their posts, if it is a strike or slowdown under Article 17 of the law, it is illegal and cannot be considered proper and justifiable.

When all types of dispute activities are prohibited, and dispute activities are held to be illegal in one law, to judge them not to be illegal under another law is not permissible, because a judgment that an act is illegal should be made independently of other laws. It is theoretically impossible to hold an act which is illegal under the PELRL to be free of illegality under the Criminal Code. A prohibited act is to be illegal and improper under other laws as well, whether or not a provision for sanctions attached to the prohibited acts is found in the same law; whether or not there exists a provision providing criminal sanctions for the prohibited act, such as Article 64, paragraph 2 and Article 119, paragraph 1, item 3 of the Self-Defense Force Law; and whether or not provision is made only for a civil sanction of dismissal, as in Articles 17 and 18 of the PELRL. Therefore, dispute activities in violation of the prohibition of Article 17 on which no criminal sanctions, but only civil sanctions, are imposed, cannot possibly be termed proper and justifiable under the Criminal Code, on grounds that it provides for no criminal sanctions for the violation, but only a civil sanction of dismissal. Accordingly, the said Article does not simply prohibit nonperformance of the contractual obligation of providing labor, but also prohibits absolutely all types of dispute activities, based on the fact that to hamper the normal conduct of business of public corporations exerts great influence on the national economy. Therefore, a prohibition on all types of dispute activities is necessary for the promotion and protection of the public welfare. It should also be concluded that resorting to such dispute activities is held illegal not only in the light of criminal law, but also in the light of legal order in general.

Since employees of public corporations are, as we have stated, prohibited from resorting to any type of dispute activity and are deprived of the right of dispute by law, there is no room for an application of Article 1, paragraph 2 of the Labor Union Law, which provides exemption from criminal liability for dispute activities engaged in contrary to the said prohibition. Article 1, paragraph 2 of the Labor Union Law, in providing for an exemption from criminal liability, is a provision that intends that even dispute activities which fulfill the constituent elements of an offense should be held lacking in illegality, so long as the conduct is performed by a labor union, whose right of dispute is recognized by law, and so long as it is properly performed for the attainment of a purpose provided in Article 1, paragraph 1 of the Labor Union Law. There is no room for the application of the exemption to illegal and improper conduct during illegal dispute activities of employees who have been deprived of the right of dispute. Furthermore, there is no room for examining whether the specific conduct during dispute activities is justifiable, for dispute activities are improper from the beginning. It is clear, in comparing the provisions of Article 17 of the PELRL with those of Article 1, paragraph 2 of the Labor Union Law, that dispute activities of employees of public corporations who have been deprived of the right of dispute, are not included in the terms "collective bargaining and other acts of labor unions" stated in Article 1, paragraph 2 of the Labor Union Law. (Assuming that paragraph 2 is applicable to dispute activities of employees of public corporations, these dispute activities are afforded protection under the Criminal Code different from that for activities of employees of private enterprises. So, this interpretation is not in conformity with the purport of Article 17 of the PELRL establishing a mediation, conciliation, and arbitration system for employees of public corporations as measures compensating for the deprivation of the right of dispute.)

It is true that Article 3 of the PELRL does not explicitly exclude the application of Article 1, paragraph 2 of the Labor Union Law. The employees of public corporations are deprived of the right of dispute, but they still maintain the right to organize and to bargain collectively, and there is ample opportunity to for applying Article 1, paragraph 2 of the Labor Union Law to acts engaged in during the process of collective bargaining. Therefore, complete exclusion of the application of the paragraph is not to be allowed. A special provision has not been established to exclude the application of the paragraph in relation to conduct during dispute activities. There is clearly no room for applying the said paragraph to dispute activities of those for whom the right of dispute is not recognized. The legislators must have thought that there was no need for clarification by means of deliberately establishing such a special provision. Conversely, Article 3 of the PELRL clearly excludes the application to a situation of Article 8 of the Labor Union Law, which only relates to dispute activities, because dispute activities of employees of public corporations are neither proper nor justifiable. Therefore, it is not proper to interpret Article 1, paragraph 2 of the Labor Union Law as applicable to dispute activities of employees of public corporations on grounds that the PELRL on the one hand specifically excludes by Article 3 the application of Article 8 of the Labor Union Law, and on the other hand does not exclude the application of Article 1, paragraph 2 of the Labor Union Law.

The appellants also contend that the exemption of dispute activities from criminal liability flows from Article 28 of the Constitution itself; that Article 1, paragraph 2 of the Labor Union Law, following the constitutional provision, provides for the exemption; and that the PELRL is a norm subordinate to the Supreme Law, the Constitution, and therefore cannot change the latter. To exclude the application of Article 1, paragraph 2 of the Labor Union Law on the grounds that Article 17 of the PELRL exists is not constitutionally permissible. But there is no room for contending that the dispute activities of employees whose functions are very strongly public in nature, such as police officers or firemen, are justifiable. Even Article 28 of the Constitution does not seem to guarantee these employees the right of dispute. It is a matter of legislative policy to review the degree of public nature of particular work, and to determine the extent to which the right of dispute should be restricted with regard to the personnel engaging in such work. If a law curtailing the right is a reasonable one, it does not violate the Constitution. Since Article 28 of the Constitution itself cannot be said to be guaranteeing exemption from criminal liability to all types of dispute activities, the appellant contention that Article 1, paragraph 2 of the Labor Union Law is applicable to dispute activities that violate Article 17 of the PELRL cannot be adopted.

To elaborate, the commissioners representing the government, at the time of the Diet discussion on the bill for the PELRL, repeatedly explained their view that Article 1, paragraph 2 of the Labor Union Law would cease to be applicable to dispute activities engaged in by employees of public corporations as the result of enactment of Article 17 of the PELRL . . . (Vol. 3, Report of the Labor Committee, the House of Councillors, Fourth Diet Session, 8 December 1948; Vol. 12, Report of the Labor Committee, the House of Representatives, Third Diet Session, 29 November 1948). After discussion, the bill was passed. So the intent of the legislature may be presumed to be the same as that of the commissioners. Due respect should be paid to such legislative intent.

Therefore, the appellant contentions that Article 17 of the PELRL violates Article 28 of the Constitution and that Article 1, paragraph 2 of the Labor Union Law is applicable to dispute activities in violation of Article 17 cannot be adopted.

Finally, we would like to offer our comments concerning the majority opinion.

The majority opinion, in its essence, states: (1) Since government and local entity employees, not to mention employees of public corporations, are workers under Article 28 of the Constitution, their right of dispute is as a rule guaranteed. If dispute activities do not exceed the proper limits, they are not subject to criminal sanctions. Article 1, paragraph 2 of the Labor Union Law is noteworthy in stating this as a matter of course. (2) Since Article 17 of the PELRL prohibits them from resorting to dispute activities, since no criminal sanctions are provided for violation of the prohibition, since Article 18 of the law only provides for the sanction of dismissal, and since Article 3 rules out the application of Article 8 of the Labor Union Law with respect to indemnity for damages, acts violating such a prohibition can be held illegal only in the sense that they are not exempted from civil liability. (3) Since the PELRL does not rule out the application of Article 1, paragraph 2 of the Labor Union Law, this paragraph naturally is applicable to dispute activities of employees of public corporations. If such acts do not exceed the proper limits, they are exempted from criminal sanction through the application of Article 1, paragraph 2 of the Labor Union Law.

However, (1) Article 28 of the Constitution guarantees the fundamental rights of workers as means for improving wages and other working conditions. In order not to disturb the balance between the legally protected interests of individuals and the interests of the people as a whole, it is unavoidable to curtail or to deny the right of dispute to meet the requirements of promoting the public welfare, if dispute activities seriously damage the interests of the people and notably interfere with the national economy. This view conforms to the intent of Article 13 of the Constitution and is not repugnant to the Constitution (of course, proper compensatory measures are in order). Article 17 of the PELRL is indeed a provision enacted to meet the requirement of promoting the public welfare (and the law, as compensatory measures, established for employees the Public Enterprise Labor Relations Commission whose function is to mediate, conciliate, or arbitrate disputes). Thus, employees of public corporations are prohibited from resorting to any type of dispute activity, and their right of dispute has been denied by law. In our view, an opinion that presupposes the existence of the right is weak in its premises. (2) As stated above, Article 17 of the PELRL prohibits any type of dispute activities. The fact that not a criminal sanction, but a civil sanction of dismissal is imposed for dispute activities makes no difference in the efficacy of the absolute prohibition on such acts. Therefore, it is not correct to conclude that acts violating the prohibition are illegal solely in civil law. (3) Since employees of public corporations, who are denied the right of dispute by law, cannot, of course, resort to "proper and justifiable dispute activities," it is clear that there is no room to apply Article 1, paragraph 2 of the Labor Union Law, which provides an exemption from criminal liability for "proper and justifiable dispute activities" in the case of employees of public corporations.

Justices Toshio Irie, Ken'ichi Okuno, Kakiwa Gokijyō, Masatoshi Yokota, Asanosuke Kusaka, Yoshihiko Kido, Kazuto Ishida, Goroku Kashiwabara, Jirō Tanaka, Jirō Matsuda, and Makoto Iwata. Presiding Justice Kisaburō Yokota did not sign due to his retirement.

Case 13. Japan v. *Sakane et al (1969).* The Court Worker Incitement Case

23 *Keishū* 5 at p. 685; Supreme Court, Grand Bench, 2 April 1969; Fukushima Dist. Ct. (First Instance), Sendai High Ct. (Second Instance), [constitutionality of restrictions on the rights of national public employees; constitutionality of the United States-Japan Security Treaty].

EDITORIAL NOTE: In the spring of 1960, the largest mass movement in Japanese history took place, in protest against the revised treaty with the United States, but primarily in opposition to the manner in which Prime Minister Nobusuke Kishi handled the controversial ratification of the Security Treaty. As part of this series of demonstrations held throughout Japan, a political meeting of court employees was held at the Sendai courthouse on 4 June 1960, sponsored by the Sendai branch of the National Judicial Employees' Union, and encouraged by members of other unions and by other participants in the national "joint struggle" movement.

The accused before the Supreme Court were a mixture of officials of both the court workers union and other unions who were charged with incitement of public employees to illegal acts and with illegal political acts by public employees. In urging the Sendai court employees to rally during business hours on the High Court's premises against the Security Treaty, they had allegedly engaged in political, and thus illegal, labor dispute activities unrelated to the workers' economic betterment, and had, moreover, illegally interfered with the normal functioning of the courts on behalf of the general public during the morning in question.

The first instance court acquitted three of the original eight accused and convicted five; both the prosecution and the defense appealed the result to the Sendai High Court. After conducting additional fact-finding of its own (a procedure itself unsuccessfully challenged later in the Supreme Court), the High Court in 1966 upheld two of the acquittals, reversed the lower court judgment in three cases, and dismissed the remaining appeals.

At issue before the Grand Bench were, *inter alia*, the constitutionality of certain restrictions on political activities of public employees under the National Public Employees Law (NPEL), the legal propriety of penalties for engaging in such activities, and the constitutionality of the 1960 Security Treaty under the pacifist clauses of Article 9 of the Constitution. In convicting union officials Sakane, Chiba, Tezuka, and Abe, the highest tribunal divided while providing, as in the Tokyo Teachers Union Case, guiding interpretations for the disposition of future cases involving "acts of incitement" by public employees. In addition, Justice Irokawa's dissenting opinion offers rare insight into the postwar history of labor rights in Japan. Finally, for the first time since 1959, the Grand Bench spoke to the meaning of Article 9 in upholding the new Security Treaty, which remains as the basis for Japan's defense posture and much of United States–Japan relations.

REFERENCES

Constitution of Japan [PREAMBLE, ARTICLES 9, 11, 18, 21, 28, 31, 97, and 98 were at issue in this case. See Appendix 3 for these provisions].

Treaty of Mutual Cooperation and Security between the United States and Japan (Treaty No. 6 of 23 June 1960).

The United States of America and Japan,

Desiring to strengthen the bonds of peace and friendship traditionally existing between them, and to uphold the principles of democracy, individual liberty, and the rule of law,

Desiring further to encourage closer economic cooperation between them and to promote conditions of economic stability and well-being in their countries,

Reaffirming their faith in the purposes and principles of the Charter of the United Nations, and their desire to live in peace with all peoples and all governments,

Recognizing that they have the inherent right of individual or collective self-defense as affirmed in the Charter of the United Nations,

Considering that they have a common concern in the maintenance of international peace and security in the Far East,

Having resolved to conclude a treaty of mutual cooperation and security,

Therefore agree as follows:

ARTICLE 1. The parties undertake, as set forth in the Charter of the United Nations, to settle any international disputes in which they may be involved by peaceful means in such a manner that international peace and security and justice are not endangered and to refrain in their international relations from the threat or use of force against the territorial integrity or political independence of any state, or in any other manner inconsistent with the purposes of the United Nations.

The parties will endeavor in concert with other peaceloving countries to strengthen the United Nations so that its mission of maintaining international peace and security may be discharged more effectively.

ARTICLE 2. The parties will contribute toward the further development of peaceful and friendly international relations by strengthening their free institutions, by bringing about a better understanding of the principles upon which these institutions are founded, and by promoting conditions of stability and well-being. They will seek to eliminate conflict in their international economic policies and will encourage economic collaboration between them.

ARTICLE 3. The parties, individually and in cooperation with each other, by means of continuous and effective self-help and mutual aid will maintain and develop, subject to their constitutional provisions, their capacities to resist armed attack.

ARTICLE 4. The parties will consult together from time to time regarding the implementation of this treaty, and, at the request of either party, whenever the security of Japan or international peace and security in the Far East is threatened.

The use of these facilities and areas as well as the status of the United States armed forces in Japan shall be governed by a separate agreement, replacing the administrative agreement under Article 3 of the Security Treaty between the United States of America and Japan, signed at Tokyo on 28 February 1952, as amended, and by such other arrangements as may be agreed upon.

ARTICLE 7. This treaty does not affect and shall not be interpreted as affecting in any way the rights and obligations of the parties under the Charter of the United Nations or the responsibility of the United Nations for the maintenance of international peace and security.

ARTICLE 8. This treaty shall be ratified by the United States of America and Japan in accordance with their respective constitutional processes and will enter into force on the date on which the instruments of ratification thereof have been exchanged by them in Tokyo.

ARTICLE 9. The Security Treaty between the United States of America and Japan, signed at the city of San Francisco on 8 September 1951, shall expire upon the entering into force of this treaty.

ARTICLE 10. This treaty shall remain in force until in the opinion of the governments of the United States of America and Japan there shall have come into force such United Nations arrangement as will satisfactorily provide for the maintenance of international peace and security in the Japan area.

However, after the treaty has been in force for ten years, either party may give notice to the other party of its intentions to terminate the treaty, in which case the treaty shall terminate one year after such notice has been given.

National Public Employees Law (*Law 120 of 1947*, as prior to revision by Law 69 of 1965), ARTICLE 98, 5. Personnel shall not engage in strikes, delays or other dispute activities against the public, which the government represents in its capacity as employer. Nor shall they resort to acts of delay that reduce the efficiency of governmental operations. No one shall plan, conspire to effect, instigate, or incite such illegal actions.

ARTICLE 110, 1. A person falling under one of the following items shall be sentenced to penal servitude not exceeding three years or fined in an amount not exceeding one hundred thousand yen [$277.77 at the time of this decision]. . . .

(17) Any person who plans, conspires to effect, instigates, or incites the illegal actions stipulated in the first part of Article 98, paragraph 5.

FORMAL JUDGMENT

Each *jōkoku* appeal in this case is dismissed.

REASONS. With respect to point 1 of the appeal presented by Counsel S. Ōkawa and six others:

The contention is that Article 98, paragraph 5, and Article 110, paragraph 1, item 17 of the National Public Employees Law (as prior to revision by Law 69 of 1965; hereafter referred to as the NPEL), are contrary to Articles 11, 18, 28, and 97 of the Constitution, and that the decision below that applied these provisions is unconstitutional.

Article 98, paragraph 5 stipulates: "Personnel shall not engage in strikes, delays, or other acts of dispute against the public, which the government represents in its capacity as employer. Nor shall they resort to acts of delay that reduce the efficiency of governmental operations. No one shall plan, conspire to effect, instigate, or incite such illegal actions."

Article 110, paragraph 1, item 17 of the same law provides for penalties of up to three years imprisonment or up to 100,000 yen in fines for "any person who plans, conspires to effect, instigates, or incites the illegal actions stipulated in the first part of Article 98, paragraph 5." If these provisions are interpreted literally to prohibit all dispute activities on the part of all national public employees, and to penalize anyone who conspires to effect, instigates or incites (hereafter, "an incitement") the same, then neither of these provisions could escape doubts about their constitutionality, as contrary to the intent of the guaranteed fundamental rights of public employees, as exceeding the bounds of unavoidable necessity in prohibiting dispute activities, and as imposing penalties in disregard for the requirement that they be confined to the minimum necessary. However, insofar as possible, the provisions of a law should be interpreted reasonably as conforming to and capable of harmony with the spirit of the Constitution. From this standpoint, we cannot take the position of adhering solely to the letter of these provisions and immediately concluding that they are unconstitutional.

As long as they are interpreted in the above qualified (*genteiteki ni*) manner, neither Article 98, paragraph 5, nor Article 110, paragraph 1, item 17 of the NPEL, cited above, can be said to violate Article 28 of the Constitution; nor can we call them contrary to the Preamble, Article 11 or Article 98 of the Constitution. Since this is clear in light of precedents of the Grand Bench of this Court (20 *Keishū* 901; Sup. Ct., G.B., 26 October 1966 and 71 *Saibanshū Keiji* 13; Sup. Ct., G.B., 2 April 1969)* the contention that these provisions are in themselves unconstitutional is unreasonable. Consequently, we cannot accept the argument taking issue with the decision below for applying the above Article 110, paragraph 1, item 17 of the NPEL.

**See* Case 12, Toyama et al v. Japan (1966), in this volume.

Concerning point 2 of the appeal, it is maintained that the provisions of Article 110, paragraph 1, item 17 of the NPEL violate Article 21 of the Constitution by punishing an incitement even in the absence of a clear and present danger.

However, not only has precedent of this Court (9 *Keishū* 2545; Sup. Ct., G.B., 30 November 1955) held that the above penal provisions are not contrary to Article 21 of the Constitution, but as explained above, the said penal provisions are clearly not in violation of Article 21 of the Constitution as long as they are interpreted and applied in a qualified manner. It is hard to accept counsel's contention of unconstitutionality, which is based on very subjective views.

With regard to point 3 of the appeal, as explained with reference to point 1 of the appeal, as long as Article 110, paragraph 1, item 17 of the NPEL does not penalize the dispute activities of public employees in themselves, and as long as an incitement, in the above provisions, is interpreted in the sense explained hereafter, the above provisions cannot be said to violate Article 18 of the Constitution. Therefore, the contention of appellants cannot be accepted.

Concerning point 4 of the appeal, defense counsel maintains that Article 110, paragraph 1, item 17 of the NPEL is contrary to Article 31 of the Constitution and that the decision below which applied these provisions is also unconstitutional. The contention is that those provisions are extremely unreasonable, because the content of the conditions constituting a violation which they establish is vague and because they ignore the realities of the labor movement and penalize a mere incitement, which is an activity preliminary to dispute activities.

However, it is appropriate to construe the relevant terms as respectively indicating the following: "conspiracy" in Article 110, paragraph 1, item 17 of the NPEL is to consult in the sense that more than two persons, based on a shared purpose, become one unit, making mutual use of each other's acts and directing their respective wills to action in order to carry out illegal acts stipulated in Article 98, paragraph 5 of the same law (12 *Keishū* 1718; Sup. Ct., G.B., 28 May 1958); "instigation" is to engage in acts of persuasion, with the intention of effecting illegal acts stipulated in Article 98, paragraph 5 of the same law, sufficient to give rise in another person to a new determination to carry out those acts, (8 *Keishū* 555; Sup. Ct., 3rd P.B., 27 April 1954); and an "incitement" is, with the above intention, to stir up other persons to a resolve to carry out those acts, or so as to heighten an already developed resolve (16 *Keishū* 107; Sup. Ct., G.B., 21 February 1962). Thus, it would be hard to say, as contended, that the conditions constituting a crime as provided in Article 110, paragraph 1, item 17 of the NPEL are vague in content; the defense contention of unconstitutionality is groundless.

Moreover, with respect to illegal dispute activities, it would be difficult to term necessarily unreasonable the punishment as a separate crime of a mere incitement, which is an act preliminary to those acts—whether it can be called suitable policy or not is a separate question; hence, neither can we accept the criticism on this point.

With respect to point 5 of the appeal, the defense contends that the judgment below erred in interpreting and applying "an incitement" under Article 110, paragraph 1, item 17 of the NPEL.

Now, as the appeal contends, the judgment below interpreted Article 110, paragraph 1, item 17 of the NPEL in a qualified manner, as did the court of first instance, and applied this method of interpretation to the facts in this case; but for the following reasons, the present Court considers it appropriate to uphold the conclusions of the judgment below, which applied the above provisions to the facts in the present case. For an incitement to be punishable, the dispute activities themselves must be strongly tainted with illegality, by deviating from the essential purposes of the employees' organization, by attendant violence or otherwise improper pressures similar in kind, or by seriously interfering with the daily life of the people by improper delays and other means contrary to the common sense of the community. In addition, the incitement would have to be construed as something not recognized as ordinarily attendant to dispute activities. That is to say, when an incitement is hastily made the object of penalties, even though dispute activities engaged in by employees are not themselves made an object of punishment, this willy-nilly penalizes many participants in dispute activities and contradicts the principle of not punishing those who engage in dispute activities, which is the cornerstone of the NPEL.

Consequently, according to the relations of fact in this case confirmed by the decision below, the defendants (with the exception of Kajiura) did engage in the acts mentioned as point 1 (excepting the latter part on so-called indirect incitement) and point 2 in the decision of the first instance judgment; namely, they urged the staff on the Sendai High Court, District Court, and Summary Court to participate in an on-the-job rally against the New Security Treaty, which would be held by crowding in front of the entranceway to the Sendai High Court during office hours for one hour between 8:30 A.M. and 9:30 A.M. on 4 June 1960. According to the above finding, the on-the-job rally in question was in effect an on-the-job meeting of the Sendai branch of the National Judicial Employees Union (*Zenshihō Rōso*), which is the organization of the above-mentioned court employees, and the walk-out by the court staff, for however short a time, constituted dispute activities on the part of judicial employees.

With respect to restriction of the dispute activities of court employees, in light of the facts that the whole judicial power is vested in the courts, and that the courts have the mission, based on this inherent state power, to protect the rights and liberties of the people and to maintain the social order of the state, the staff functions of those engaged in such judicial duties carried out by the courts are generally of a strongly public nature. We must say it is likely that an interruption of those functions will obstruct the achievement of that mission and, in turn, will seriously impair the daily life of the nation.

With regard to the on-the-job rally in this case, as the appeal maintains, the on-the-job rally in question might have taken place as one segment of a movement; a widespread campaign against the New Security Treaty did occur at that time as a people's movement to protect the Constitution. Labor unions and various other organizations were actively engaged in that campaign. However, in view of the essential purposes of a court employees' organization, as involvement in disputes for such political purposes cannot be said to be directly related to maintaining or improving economic status vis-à-vis the state as employer, it departs from the proper sphere of dispute activities and should not be permitted. Furthermore, even if short in duration and nonviolent, there is the danger that they will cause an interruption of the functions of court employees engaged in judicial duties and will seriously interfere with the daily life of the nation. Such dispute activities must be held patently illegal.

According to the facts confirmed by the decision below, at the time of the incident in question:

(a) The accused Sakane held a position on the Central Executive Committee of the National Tax Agency Labor Union and was sent to Sendai as an organizer by the National Public Employees Joint Struggle Council. The accused Chiba was employed at the Ishimaki Agency, Miyagi Farm Product Information Office, Ministry of Agriculture and Forestry, and held the position of vice-chairman of the Executive Committee at the Miyagi Prefecture headquarters of the National Labor Union for the Ministry of Agriculture and Forestry. The accused Tezuka was employed at the North Sendai Tax Office and held the positions of member of the Executive Committee, Tōhoku District Federation, National Tax Agency Labor Union, and vice-chairman for Miyagi Prefecture of the National and Local Public Employees Joint Struggle Council. The accused Abe was employed in the Sendai District Court as an assistant court secretary and occupied the position of chairman, Executive Committee, Sendai branch, National Judicial Employees Union.

(b) The acts cited in point 1 of the opinion of the first instance judgment (excepting the latter passage concerning so-called indirect incitement) were carried out by a conspiracy of the accused Abe, Sakane, and others; the acts mentioned in point 2 of the opinion were perpetrated by a conspiracy of the accused Sakane, Abe, Chiba, Tezuka, and others.

Upon examining the question of whether or not the above acts of the accused should be found to be of a kind ordinarily attendant to dispute activities engaged in by judicial employees, it is clear that we cannot recognize as ordinarily attendant to the dispute activities of judicial employees the acts that were carried out by the accused Sakane, Chiba, and Tezuka, who, among the accused, are not judicial employees, and who are third parties without a relationship to the judicial employees' organization. Moreover, since the accused Abe is a court employee and in the position of chairman of the Executive Committee, Sendai branch, National Judicial Employees Union, which is his organization, we could regard his incitement as something ordinarily attendant to dispute activities, as long as its manner involved nothing out of the ordinary. However, in this case, since the accused Abe carried out the acts referred to above in (b) in conspiracy with the above-mentioned third-party defendants, we must say on the basis of the above relations of fact that the acts of accused Abe as well cannot be regarded as acts ordinarily attendant to dispute activities.

Thus, the application by the court below of Article 110, paragraph 1, item 17 of the NPEL to the above-cited acts of the defendants differs in places in its reasoning from the views of the present Court, but in the final analysis it is correct in result, and we cannot accept the argument that there is statutory illegality in the judgment below based on the above difference of views.

Regarding point 6 of the appeal, the defense contends that the decision below, in its interpretation of "an incitement" under Article 110, paragraph 1, item 17, judges at variance with precedent of the present Court cited in the appeal (20 *Keishū* 901; Sup. Ct., G.B., 26 October 1966).

However, the cited decision was made after a judgment was rendered in the judgment below, and for this reason it cannot be construed as precedent under Article 405, item 2 of the Code of Criminal Procedure; the argument does not correspond to the legal grounds for a *jōkoku* appeal.

Concerning point 7 of the appeal, the defense claims unconstitutionality (under Article 31), but since Article 110, paragraph 1, item 17 of the NPEL makes acts of "incitement" stipulated therein the object of penalties as separately punishable acts* in applying the theory of so-called conspiracy-as-sharing-in-the-principal-offense†, this provision should be interpreted as in no way different from cases of other separate crimes. Thus construed, this provision is not contrary to Article 31 of the Constitution, and the decision below to the same effect is correct. The defense contention of unconstitutionality is without grounds.

With respect to point 8 of the appeal, the defense claims that the decision below is illegal in that it erred in interpreting the Treaty of Mutual Cooperation and Security between the United States and Japan (Treaty No. 6 of 23 June 1960; hereinafter referred to as the New

**Hanzai ruikei: "Delikatstypus;"* analogous to, but separate from the crime itself.
†*Kyōdōseihan: "Mittaterschaft"*, in German law.

Security Treaty) and in interpreting Articles 9, 98 (paragraph 1), and 81 of the Constitution.

However, in rendering legal judgment as to the unconstitutionality of such matters as the New Security Treaty, which are of highly political nature with an important relationship to the basis of our country's existence as a sovereign nation, the judicial courts have need of circumspection; so long as that treaty is not deemed to be clearly contrary to provisions of the Constitution, it should not unnecessarily be held unconstitutional and invalid. Furthermore, it is clear in light of the intent of precedent of the Grand Bench of the present Court (13 *Keishū* 3225; Sup. Ct., G.B., 16 December 1959)* that the New Security Treaty is not deemed to be clearly unconstitutional as violating the intent of Article 9, Article 98, paragraph 2, and the Preamble of the Constitution. Accordingly, the decision below to the same effect is correct, and the defense contention of unconstitutionality is without grounds. . . .

[Points 9 and 10: technically deficient grounds for *jōkoku* appeal.]

Concerning point 11 of the appeal, the defense contends that the decision below is contrary to precedent cited by counsel (4 *Keishū* 1783; Sup. Ct., G.B., 27 September 1950) in holding that the premises of the Sendai High Court correspond to the environs of a building as referred to in Article 130 of the Criminal Code.

However, the precedent cited above mentioned the placing of a guard or patrol only as an illustration of ways to prohibit unauthorized passage in and out by outsiders. Since this clearly is not made a condition for constituting the environs of a building under the same provision, the argument of defense for a violation of precedent is weak in its premises and does not constitute proper grounds for *jōkoku* appeal.

With respect to points 12 and 13 of the appeal, concerning the points in the appeal alleging unconstitutionality (under Articles 31, 32, 37 [paragraph 2], 76 [paragraphs 1 and 3], 81, and 14), the intent of precedents of the Grand Bench of the present court (10 *Keishū* 1147; Sup. Ct., G.B., 18 July 1956; 10 *Keishū* 1391; Sup. Ct., G.B., 26 September 1956; 2 *Keishū* 175; Sup. Ct., G.B., 10 March 1948) has been as follows. With regard to defendants acquitted in a court of first instance, it is not unconstitutional for the court below to quash and reverse the acquittal by the court of first instance as a result of its own fact-finding. Moreover, the inquiry into facts may not go beyond the second instance court and the grounds for *jōkoku* appeal are restricted under Article 405 of the Code of Criminal Procedure; it is not unconstitutional if the way is thus closed to arguing an error in fact-finding on appeal, when the second instance judgment quashes an acquittal by the court of first instance and hands down a conviction. Thus, the contentions of unconstitutionality are without grounds, and the remainder merely alleges violation of procedural law, which does not constitute proper grounds for *jōkoku* appeal.

*The *Sunagawa* Decision. For a translation, *see* J. M. Maki, *op. cit.*, p. 298.

[Point 14: technically improper procedural grounds for *jōkoku* appeal.]

Concerning the reasons for jokoku appeal presented by defendants S. Sakane and T. Abe:

With regard to the point in the appeal alleging the unconstitutionality (under the Preamble and Article 9) of the New Security Treaty, this Court's view is expounded with respect to point 8 of the *jōkoku* appeal presented by Counsel S. Ōkawa and six others; and on the point alleging the unconstitutionality (under Article 28) of Article 98, paragraph 5, and Article 110, paragraph 1, item 17 of the NPEL, our view is that set forth concerning point 1 of the above *jōkoku* appeal. All of the above contentions are without grounds, and the rest simply claim violations of statutes and errors in fact-finding that do not constitute proper grounds for *jōkoku* appeal. . . .

[The appeal of the accused N. Chiba and S. Tezuka contests the constitutionality of the New Security Treaty. It is dismissed with a reference to the Court's holding on point 8 of the Ōkawa brief.]

Concerning the prosecutor's reasons for *jōkoku* appeal:

The contention is that the judgment of the decision below on interpreting Article 110, paragraph 1, item 17 of the NPEL is at variance with a cited judgment of the Tokyo High Court of 16 November 1965 (7 *Kakyū Keishū* 1955).

According to the decision below, the provision in question does not consider punishable all acts listed therein; rather, the imposition of penalties as appropriate from the standpoint of the public interest is limited to those acts that, judging from their nature, method, and manner, are very likely to be so strongly tainted with illegality as to affect the carrying out of the dispute activities. This is the thrust of the decision below on the proper interpretation of the object of penalties; but the above-cited judgment of the Tokyo High Court takes the view that the provision in question should not be construed as intending to punish only "an incitement" that is strongly tainted with illegality due to the manner and so on of the act or the one acting. Since this judgment was handed down before the decision below, we must hold that the decision below judged at variance with precedent of the above High Court, which was a *kōso* appellate court in the absence of Supreme Court precedent, as stipulated in the latter part of item 3, Article 405 of the Code of Criminal Procedure.

The views of the present Court concerning interpretation of Article 110, paragraph 1, item 17 of the NPEL are set forth above, and we cannot uphold the views on this point of either the above High Court precedent or the decision below. However, as explained before, the decision below was correct, in the final analysis, in its application of the provision in question to the activities of the accused under point 1 judged in the first instance decision (excluding the latter part on so-called indirect incitement), and to the activities under point 2. Furthermore, regarding the latter part of the point 1 activities of the accused in the first instance judgment (the so-called indirect incitement), based on the relations of fact confirmed by the court below, it would be hard to find that they so strongly stimulated the court employees as to make them resolve to carry out the dispute activities in this case or to strengthen such a resolve that has already developed. It was appropriate to find that this did not correspond to an incitement under the provision in question. Consequently, the decision below was correct in its conclusion that there is not proof of a crime in the above facts and that acquittal is called for. Therefore, although there is a violation of precedent in the decision below, this does not become grounds for quashing the decision below, because the circumstances of this violation of precedent make this clearly a case, coming under the proviso in Article 410, paragraph 1 of the Code of Criminal Procedure, in which the judgment has not been affected.

Accordingly, the Court dismisses each *jōkoku* appeal in this case, pursuant to Articles 414 and 396 of the Code of Criminal Procedure and decides as stated in the Formal Judgment.

This judgment is the opinion of all the justices except for the opinions of Justices Toshio Irie and Makoto Iwata, the opinion of Justices Ken'ichi Okuno, Asanosuke Kusaka, Kazuto Ishida, Kazuo Shimomura and Masao Matsumoto, and the dissenting opinion of Kōtarō Irokawa.

* * *

The opinion of Justice Toshio Irie follows.

1. I come to the same conclusions as the majority opinion, and for the most part I agree with its reasoning; on one point only my way of thinking differs fundamentally from that of the majority opinion. This point is of such a nature as to have no effect on the result of the judgment in this case; but since it is a problem which may well control the result in a judgment of a case at another time, where the facts at issue are differnt but similar, I would first set forth my opinion on this point on this occasion.

(1) The fundamental rights of workers under Article 28 of the Constitution are not absolute and without limits, and it is not unconstitutional to impose reasonable limitations on these rights in accordance with requirements of the public welfare. But in light of the legal intent of Article 28 of the Constitution, such limitations on the fundamental rights of workers should be determined by means of comparative consideration, with the object of maintaining a proper balance between the need to protect and respect the fundamental rights of workers, and the need to uphold and promote the interests of the nation's life as a whole. This has already been held in precedent of this Court (20 *Keishū* 901; Sup. Ct., G.B., 26 October 1966), which held that, in keeping with the concrete contents of their duties, the restriction of public employees in a manner different from workers in private enterprise must be termed

unavoidable. . . . Although Article 98, paragraph 5 of the NPEL . . . at issue in this case, prohibits dispute activities among public employees, it does not uniformly prohibit as illegal all dispute activities of all public employees. Rather, we should judge whether or not they correspond to the dispute activities forbidden by the said legal provision upon due consideration of the requirements of the public welfare, based upon the concrete case. If we forbid as illegal all dispute activities of national public employees without paying any heed to such considerations, that in itself is contrary to Article 28 of the Constitution, according to the intent of the above-cited precedent of this Court. The cited provision of the NPEL stops at simply referring to "dispute activities." Provisions covering disciplinary action are placed in Article 82 of the same law. If we merely interpret the text of the law literally, then all dispute activities of national public employees are prohibited, and all dispute activities carried out in violation of this legal provision will be subject to disciplinary action. However, we should naturally apply an appropriate interpretation to these legal provisions, based on the legal intent of Article 28 of the Constitution; and it must be said that dispute activities are forbidden to the extent of that intent, and that we are justified in imposing sanctions only on dispute activities thus forbidden. Up to this point, my opinion does not differ from the majority opinion.

(2) However, the problem in this case is not whether or not to penalize the dispute activities of national public employees in themselves, but whether or not to penalize an incitement to those dispute activities. Article 110, paragraph 1, item 17 of the NPEL makes an incitement, as stipulated in the same item, a separate criminal act and is a provision that establishes penalties to be imposed for such. Now if dispute activities are such that in light of the legal intent of Article 28 of the Constitution, they are not found to be forbidden by the NPEL and are consequently not the object of disciplinary action from the standpoint of the NPEL, then from the standpoint of the Constitution, those are not properly dispute activities; and since they are constitutionally protected actions, there is clearly no room for the application of the penal provisions in the NPEL simply on the grounds that an incitement to these activities has taken place. But we must say that it is proper to apply the above cited penal provisions in the case of an incitement to dispute activities that are deemed illegal from the standpoint of the NPEL. Among dispute activities that are the object of an incitement and that are illegal under the NPEL, the majority opinion sets up distinctions regarding degrees of illegality in dispute activities and degrees of antisociality; but such an interpretation, illustrated by the majority opinion—whereby an incitement to acts greater in degree can be subject to application of the above-mentioned penal provisions of the NPEL, while an incitement to acts lesser in degree falls outside their application—is fundamentally weak and cannot receive my complete support, in light of the legal intent

of Articles 28 and 31 of the Constitution, and as interpretation of the NPEL. Obviously, in theory, if improperly severe penalties are imposed for an incitement to acts with a slight degree of illegality or antisociality, among such dispute activities as are deemed illegal under the NPEL, and if as a result the dispute activities of public employees are themselves in the end improperly restricted, then we must say this gives rise to a problem of unconstitutionality in light of the legal intent of Articles 28 and 31 of the Constitution. However, so far as the present case is concerned, I do not think that the above-cited penal provision of the NPEL presents us with that kind of situation. . . . Moreover, from the standpoint of legislative policy I cannot conclude that the above penal provision departs from the sphere of legislative discretion possessed by the legislative branch. . . .

(3) The dispute activities in this case were of course quite illegal. . . . But I consider it quite unnecessary to make an issue out of the greater or lesser degree of that illegality in applying to this case Article 110, paragraph 1, item 17 of the NPEL, and there is nothing in my interpretation contrary to Articles 28 and 31 of the Constitution.

(4) Furthermore, in the so-called Tokyo Central Post Office Decision cited above, this Court presents a judgment, in a case where penalties are imposed under the Postal Law for dispute activities of postal workers, concerning the interpretation of Article 79, paragraph 1 of the Postal Law and Article 17 of the Public Enterprise Labor Relations Law (hereinafter abbreviated as the PELRL). According to that judgment, it is clear that the above legal provision of the Postal Law is not exclusively concerned with dispute activities; but on the other hand, there is no reason to foreclose its application where postal employees carry out acts designated dispute activities in the said provision, and there is no alternative to construing it to apply also in cases where dispute activities have actually been carried out. With respect to the PELRL, it stops at affirming the way of taking disciplinary action under Article 18 of the said law for illegal dispute activities carried out in violation of Article 17, paragraph 1 of the same law. Although there is absolutely no provision imposing criminal penalties, in the PELRL, criminal penalties are imposed, as a matter of exception, for illegal dispute activities of postal employees under the legal provisions of the above-cited Postal Law. Considering this point, and in view of the fact that among the dispute activities of employees under the PELRL some are subject to criminal penalties and some are not, the above dispute activities of postal employees which are liable to criminal penalties are properly understood as confined to activities especially strong in illegality and antisociality, such as those on which judgment was passed in the above-mentioned Central Post Office Decision. Such an interpretation provides a rationale in line with a reasonable construction of Article 28 of the Constitution and Article 17, paragraph 1 of the PELRL. However, in this case the

imposition of criminal penalties for the dispute activities themselves is not the issue, and the problem is the imposition of criminal penalties for an incitement to dispute activities that are considered illegal. As far as this point is concerned, the Central Post Office Decision differs from the present case and is not pertinent to the case at issue. In relation to the above-noted part of the majority opinion that I opposed on the provision of criminal penalties for an incitement, I would like to add that it is my understanding that the Tokyo Central Post Office Decision included no judgment on that at all.

2. Next, the majority opinion made it a condition for the liability of an incitement that the incitement not be deemed something ordinarily accompanying the dispute activities that are its object. On this point I am in agreement, but I would present some supplementary views.

My personal opinion regarding the rationale on which the above interpretation of the majority opinion rests is as follows: . . . Since an incitement ordinarily has the character of something secondary and incidental to the dispute activities that are its object, if we find criminal liability in such secondary and incidental acts while saying that criminal penalties cannot be imposed where workers engage in dispute activities on their own accord, then that in result, is to pick out and punish one part of the acts that are understood as actually included in those dispute activities carried out by workers of their own accord. I consider that unreasonable in the extreme and contradictory to the premise that dispute activities per se are not charged with criminal liability, and thus that view can only lead to concern about violating the legal intent of Article 28 of the Constitution which recognizes the fundamental rights of workers. For that reason, what is here referred to as "something recognized as not ordinarily accompanying" is properly understood to mean cases in which an incitement or the like occurring in connection with dispute activities is found to be notably wrongful from the standpoint of the prevailing ideas of the community: for example, an instigation to carry on dispute activities without a basis in the collective intention of a union to engage in dispute activities, or inflammatory actions that in manner, method, and degree go beyond what ordinarily occurs on the occasion of dispute activities, or again, the presentation of intentionally erroneous reports and the use of the methods and means of deception, force, violence, and so on. In consequence, there is a problem with respect to the restriction of such acts when those who carry out an incitement are such workers or people in an equivalent position who are essentially under the guarantees of Article 28 of the Constitution and who are free from criminal penalties for their dispute activities. However, there is no problem about such restriction with respect to those who are unmistakably third parties to a dispute and who are entirely outside the guarantees of Article 28 of the Constitution. In other words, there is neither room nor need for considering whether an incitement carried out by third parties was something ordinarily accompanying dispute activities and the matter is unrelated to the requirements of Article 28 of the Constitution. Based on the stipulations of the law as well, we should say that obviously all such incitements by third parties are subject to application of the above-mentioned penal provisions of the NPEL. Moreover, even if those who conspire with such third parties are workers, since they are partners in crime to the third parties as independent offenders, the acts of that incitement present a situation in which there is neither room nor need to construe what ordinarily accompanies dispute activities, and in which there is no relationship with the requirements of Article 28 of the Constitution. . . . The conclusion of the decision below imposing criminal liability on the accused in this case was correct. (. . . When a political movement for the achievement of a highly political goal is carried out in the form of dispute activities, such dispute activities are unrelated to the constitutional guarantees of Article 28. However, I think that such dispute activities should also be included as a matter of positive law among dispute activities under the NPEL. Even in such cases, if those who carried out that incitement are themselves workers, and if we hold to the principle that the current NPEL does not impose criminal penalties for dispute activities such as the above per se, then to balance with that, is it not a correct construction to consider it impermissible, under the requirements of Article 31 of the Constitution and under an appropriate interpretation of the current NPEL, to impose criminal penalties on the above incitement alone, as long as it is found to be something that ordinarily accompanies the above dispute activities? Here . . . we have a case concerning an incitement to a labor dispute for the purpose of opposing the New Security Treaty; but in the present case, the above point has no effect on the result of the judgment, because the accused carried out the incitement in question in conspiracy with third parties. . . .)

* * *

The opinion of Justice Makoto Iwata follows.

1. When a literal interpretation of a provision of law leaves doubts about its constitutionality, insofar as possible we should apply to this provision a reasonable, qualified interpretation and construe it to be in harmony with the intent of the Constitution. . . .

2. Article 110, paragraph 1, item 17 of the NPEL purports not to penalize a person for having carried out dispute activities per se, but to punish one who conspires to effect dispute activities by instigating, inciting, or planning these acts. However, dispute activities engaged in by employees' unions are understood to be ordinarily proposed by union officials or union members, decided upon by their established decision-making machinery, and carried out in practice accordingly. When acts such as an incitement . . . are carried out in that union in the process of proposing, planning, and carrying through dispute ac-

tivities autonomously engaged in for the basic purposes of maintaining and improving working conditions, to enhance economic status, and for related purposes, then to penalize this as criminally liable is, in the final analysis, to inhibit any and all dispute activities of all public employees with criminal sanctions and to give rise to the suspicion that it violates Article 28 of the Constitution. Therefore, "an incitement" (with union officials and union members taking part of course, but even if others are involved such as union officials at a higher level or from the federation of that union) that occurs in the process of proposing, planning, and carrying out dispute activities, engaged in autonomously by an employees' union of national public employees recognized under the NPEL to achieve its basic purposes, should be construed as not liable to penalties . . . under Article 110, paragraph 1, item 17 of the NPEL, as long as it is not accompanied by violence and the like.

In short, I interpret as punishable under the provisions of this Article "an incitement" of national public employees to dispute activities found to be so carried out as to go beyond the primary purposes of the union, and all "incitements" that are not undertaken in the process of proposing, planning, and carrying out dispute activities autonomously engaged in by the union. None of the contrary aforementioned acts can be termed an exercise of the fundamental rights of workers guaranteed to workers under Article 28 of the Constitution.

3. . . . I cannot readily agree with the intent of the majority opinion in the standard it takes for qualified interpretation in order to make Article 110, paragraph 1, item 17 of the NPEL concur with the Constitution, if they look for the standard in the relative illegality of the dispute activities engaged in by national public employees that are the object of "an incitement," and consider "an incitement" punishable under Article 110, paragraph 1, item 17 to the extent that these dispute activities are strong in illegality. I do not think that the relative strength of illegality of the dispute activities intended by "an incitement" should determine the applicability of Article 110, paragraph 1, item 17 of the NPEL (Since Article 98, paragraph 5 of the NPEL prohibits dispute activities by national public employees, the dispute activities of national public employees are in principle unlawful from the standpoint of the NPEL. [That does not mean this illegality should be dealt with by criminal penalties.]. . . .) If the dispute activities are for a political purpose rather than for economic goals of the union . . . then whether or not it is something that ordinarily accompanies dispute activities, "an incitement" cannot be termed an exercise of the fundamental rights of workers guaranteed under Article 28 of the Constitution. Moreover, with respect to "an incitement" as well, I cannot agree that acts which ordinarily accompany dispute activities cannot be punished because they are weak in illegality.

Rather, since such acts are recognized as an exercise of the fundamental rights of workers, particularly of the right to act collectively, guaranteed to workers under Article 28 of the Constitution, such acts do not correspond to "an incitement" under Article 110, paragraph 1, item 17 of the NPEL, and thus cannot be penalized, as long as the dispute activities intended are for the achievement of the primary goals of the union.

4. Since the acts in the present case were for political, not economic purposes, the accused are clearly guilty. . . . . I agree with the majority opinion on points other than those discussed above.

* * *

The opinion of Justices Ken'ichi Okuno, Asanosuke Kusaka, Kazuto Ishida, Kazuo Shimomura, and Masao Matsumoto follows.

1. National public employees participate in government as the servants of all, based on the people's trust. Article 98, paragraph 5 of the NPEL . . . prohibits them from engaging in strikes, delays, or other dispute activities against the people at large who are their employers, as unlawful acts contrary to the public welfare, seriously interfering with the daily life of the nation, disrupting the operations of government, and betraying the people's trust. Similarly, Article 37, paragraph 1 of the Local Public Employees Law (hereinafter referred to as the LPEL) prohibits as unlawful dispute activities on the part of public employees of local autonomy units. These prohibitions on the dispute activities of public employees are based upon the requirements of the public welfare, and thus cannot be said to violate Article 28 of the Constitution.

These laws, while prohibiting dispute activities of public employees as unlawful, do not punish each public employee actually involved, and go no further than possibly depriving these public employees of rights acquired through their commissions or employment. However . . . based on the assumption that those who provide the motive force for unlawful dispute activities are more notably in violation of society's interests than those who only participate in the dispute activities, and should accordingly be subject to special penalties, these laws purport to prevent unlawful dispute activities by punishing only instigators and others who exercise leadership functions with respect to a dispute. In similar fashion, it is quite reasonable to view with special seriousness the illegality of instigation and other acts that provide the motive force for unlawful acts involved in collective activities. This is exemplified by penal policies with respect to insurrection and riot; it is not at all unreasonable legislation, it is well within the purview of legislative policy, and it would be difficult to consider it unconstitutional.

Regarding "an incitement" which the law punishes as the motive force . . . for illegal dispute activities, the concept of "an incitement" is not vague in its constituent elements and is appropriately construed to mean "with the intention of causing unlawful acts, to stir up other persons to a resolve to carry out those acts, or so as to heighten an already developed resolve". . . . In the absence of a statutory definition of "an incitement," acts of "incitement" as defined above become liable to punishment as unlawful acts. Under the law, there is no room for distinguishing between these acts on the basis of the relative strength of their illegality and for holding criminallly liable only those acts that are strong in illegality.

We cannot agree at all with the construction that "an incitement" becomes subject to punishment only when dispute activities deriving from such an incitement are either of a strongly illegal nature or of such a nature as to be held criminally liable. Since there is provision for punishment of those who incite while the dispute activities themselves are not punished, to interpret the law as intending to punish only acts of incitement to such dispute activities is patently contrary to the provisions of the law.

For that reason, when establishing the criminality of "an incitement," there is no room for discussing the propriety of the dispute activities themselves intended by that "incitement." Consequently, the determination on the said crime should not be influenced at all by the question of whether or not those dispute activities were, for instance, carried out for political purposes. Furthermore, since public employees whose right to dispute has been denied under the law are naturally unable to engage in "justifiable dispute activities," there is obviously no room for applying to the dispute activities of public employees the provisions of Article 1, paragraph 2 of the Labor Union Law, which establishes immunity from criminal liability for dispute activities which are "justifiable"—let alone for resorting to the supplementary provisions of Article 16 of the NPEL and Article 58 of the LPEL. We must say that on this score there are no grounds for arguing the propriety of the dispute activities themselves intended by the "incitement," or for discussing whether or not the illegality is liable to criminal penalties.

Moreover, we cannot accept a construction that would exempt from punishment acts of "incitement" of the constituents of a union on grounds that such acts as planning . . . a dispute are inseparably related to the dispute with the constituents of the union naturally involved, so that punishing this amounts to punishing dispute activities. The provisions of Article 98, paragraph 5, latter section, and Article 110, paragraph 1, item 17 of the NPEL, and of Article 37, paragraph 1, the latter section, and Article 61, item 4 of the LPEL, clearly intend to punish "anyone" and "everyone" who commits acts of incitement, because they clearly intend to punish equally, whether those involved are union members, or third-parties who are not constituent members of a union, or both in collaboration, and regardless of whether or not they are people inseparably related to and naturally involved with the dispute.

In short, to confine the concept of "an incitement" to that which is tainted with a high degree of illegality, to construe the law as distinguishing between union members and non-union members . . . and as punishing only the acts of outsiders or those in conspiracy with them, or to interpret the law restrictively as intending to taint with liability to punishment acts of "incitement" only when the intended dispute activities are strong in illegality or of such an illegality as to be subject to criminal penalties, all of these interpretations are a kind of legislation that is contrary to the provisions of the law and that exceed the bounds of justifiable interpretation of the law.

2. Viewing the present case from the above standpoint, it is clear that the acts (except for the so-called "indirect incitement" . . .) of the accused in this case (except for Kajiura) come under acts of "incitement" in Article 110, paragraph 1, item 17 of the NPEL, and the judgment below which applied the said provision to the aforementioned acts of the accused is correct in its conclusion.

* * *

The dissenting opinion of Justice Kōtarō Irokawa follows.

1. At issue in the present case is an incitement to carrying out "dispute activities." The judgment below defines "dispute activities" as "organized acts of public employees, contrary to the wishes of the government authorities concerned, which obstruct the normal conduct of the business of the nation." While acknowledging that the on-the-job meeting in the present case was a protest rally that was part of a movement opposing the revision of the Security Treaty, the court held that "disputes referred to as so-called political strikes" are also prohibited under Article 98, paragraph 5 of the NPEL. . . . The court reasoned that the said provision purports "to prevent the danger of national public employees, who are servants of the whole community, neglecting their duties and betraying the people's trust." If that is so, it is hard to understand why something is not prohibited when it is not an organized action. Be that as it may, relying upon the definition of the judgment below, "dispute activities" must be taken to include collective walk-out for purposes of pleasure and so on, that is, forsaking of duties for the sake of forsaking itself, which is not a means to fulfilling any particular needs. (Indeed, this may be the worst form of neglect of duty and betrayal of the trust of the people.) I do not think that a definition so vague and so lacking in clarity as the above would be permitted as interpretation of any penal provision; in any event, the reasons why one cannot accept such an interpretation will become clear from what is stated below. I cannot agree at all with the majority opinion, which, by accepting such a definition, includes activities for political purpose under "dispute activities" in Article 98, paragraph 5 of the NPEL, thus approving the application of Article 110, paragraph 1, item 17 of the said law to the conduct of the accused.

2. The NPEL nowhere provides the meaning of "dispute activities," but I think it should be sought in Article 7 of the Labor Relations Adjustment Law (hereafter referred to as the LRAL). The term "dispute activities," unlike such terms as "a strike" and "a slowdown," was first used in legislation after the war; it was not an everyday word in common use before that, and is a purely technical term in law. Consequently, its meaning should be sought first of all on the basis of interpreting legal provisions. Among the current laws that employ the term "dispute activities," there are, in addition to the aforementioned NPEL and LRAL, the Maritime Employees Law (Article 30), the Public Enterprise Labor Relations Law (Article 17), the Labor Union Law (Article 8), the Local Public Employees Law (Article 37), the Law Regulating the Methods of Dispute Activities in the Electrical, Coal and Mining Industries (Articles 2 and 3), and the Self-Defense Forces Law (Article 64). In spite of the fact that more than half of those laws, and excepting the LRAL, prohibit dispute activities and hold them criminally liable, they are completely lacking in provisions that define what "dispute activities" are. This is a fact we should not overlook. (Only the Maritime Employees Law is clear in giving a framework for discussing "dispute activities" by providing that they are "dispute activities which involve labor relations." This may have been taken from Article 60 in the Old Maritime Employees Law, Law 79 of 1937, which provided: "In cases corresponding to any one of the following items above, when a maritime employee engages in a work stoppage or obstructs the progress of work in connection with a labor dispute, he will be subject to imprisonment for no more than one year or a fine of no more than 500 yen." Except for the Maritime Employees Law, the laws mentioned above contain no qualification such as the above concerning "dispute activities." In light of the intent of these laws, and in consideration of their common object, they are properly construed as calling strongly for analogical interpretation and as not allowing mutually opposed interpretations.) The LRAL was promulgated on 27 September 1946, and the establishment and promulgation of all the rest of the laws mentioned above came later. (The above listing of laws is in the order of their promulgation. The Maritime Employees Law was promulgated on 1 September 1947.) One can make an issue of whether or not to call the LRAL one of the "Three Labor Laws," but it is unquestionably a fundamental law which, like the Labor Union Law, is intended to regulate collective labor relations; therefore, the significance of the term "dispute activities" in later legislation must be construed, in a broad sense, as following the definition given in the LRAL.

Some might argue that Article 7 of the LRAL does nothing more than prescribe prerequisites under which a Labor Relations Commission initiates an adjustment of a labor dispute, and that its definition is not appropriate for other laws unrelated to adjustment, and so should not be used to construe in a qualified manner "dispute activities" in other kinds of laws such as the NPEL. As they argue, the settlement of disputes with workers is to be based primarily upon the autonomous action of the parties; and since hasty intervention by a Labor Relations Commission is not proper, there must be some kind of brake to control the kind of cases in which these organs should initiate adjustment actions. Consequently, perhaps no one would dispute the point that one of the legislative purposes of Article 7 is to require, for an adjustment to take place, that the grievances of workers have developed into a labor-management dispute situation. However, this is just one side of the coin. An examination of the structuring of the LRAL at the time of its enactment clearly reveals that in spite of its title, the Labor Relations Adjustment Law is not merely a law concerning the adjustment of labor disputes. The LRAL started out with three functions: (1) establishment of adjustment procedures for labor disputes (Chapters 2 to 4), and of the duty to report attendant dispute activities (Article 9); (2) a guarantee of the right to engage in dispute activities (Article 41 in the former law); and (3) a prohibition on restricting dispute activities (Articles 36 and 37; Articles 38 and 39 in the former law). Article 38 of the former law should be particularly noted:

"ARTICLE 38. Police officers, firemen, persons employed in a prison, and administrative, judicial, and other officials, excepting those engaged in manual services for the state or for public entities, shall not engage in dispute activities."

A total fine of 10,000 yen was to be imposed on an organization and its officials for violation of the above provision (the former Article 39). Thus it happened that, except for those in the manual services, public officials, who had had freedom to engage in dispute activities till then, had those activities broadly restricted.

Under circumstances described later, the above-quoted legal provision was deleted by Law 175 of 1949, and after a time Article 38 of the same law became blank. When the Emergency Adjustment System was established by Law 288 of 1952, what we now see was added on, and nothing now remains of the former state of affairs. Nevertheless, even the structure of the present law not only provides adjustment procedures for labor disputes, but also now establishes in Chapter 5 a prohibition on restricting dispute activities. The definition of "dispute activities" in Article 7 of the said law has provided clarification from the beginning till now of the meaning of the underlying idea of a "labor dispute" (precisely this is stipulated as the prerequisite for an adjustment to take place) in Article 6, while delineating the parameters of the acts that are restricted or prohibited.

3. To know what kind of relationship there might be between the definition in Article 7 of the LRAL and "dispute activities" under Article 98 of the NPEL, we must inquire into legislative history and change.

As noted above, the LRAL was the first postwar legislation banning dispute activities on the part of public employees. However, the penalties provided for violations of Article 39 of the old law were nominal. Not only that, but an enormous number of public employees engaged in manual services for the National Railways and the Postal Service and other agencies (their organized unions constituted the very core of the Japanese labor movement) were all beyond the bounds of regulation under Article 38 of the old law. Moreover, originally the NPEL (Law 120 of 1947) nowhere touched upon dispute activities. Looking back at various objective circumstances of the time, the destructive evils of inflation were incessantly accelerating, and goaded by that, the labor movement became increasingly stormy; in July 1948 a confrontation took place between the government and the National Government and Public Enterprise Employees Union over the issue of a base salary of 5,200 yen, and in the tense situation, a strike of unprecedented scale centered around government workers and public employees at the beginning of August seemed to be unavoidable. A letter dated 22 July 1948 was sent by General MacArthur of the Supreme Command, Allied Powers, hereafter referred to as SCAP, to Prime Minister Ashida in order to prevent these unprecedented dispute activities.* In this letter, the part that is related to the present case (and this makes it an important part of the letter), in sum, discusses the nature of public employees and points out the sharp difference between them and the employees of private enterprises. For that reason, the letter stated, public employees cannot adopt such methods as collective bargaining, which is allowed in private enterprise; and furthermore, since public employees have a duty of unconditional loyalty to the public trust, public employees are not at all permitted to press their demands with such dispute activities as manifestation of an intention to obstruct governmental operations. After making such a verdict, the letter advised the Japanese government that a comprehensive revision of the NPEL was needed in the direction of conforming with this way of thinking, and that it should begin that task immediately. Following this advice, as a first step toward the complete revision of the NPEL, the government promulgated and put into effect on 31 July 1948 with Cabinet Order 201, "The Cabinet Order concerning Provisional Measures to be taken in consequence of the Letter of the Supreme Commander for the Allied Powers to the Prime Minister, dated 22 July 1948" (hereafter referred to as Cabinet Order 201). It contained three Articles. Article 1 stipulates that no public employee who is in the position of an employee of a national or local public entity possesses the right of collective bargaining backed up by dispute activities, that existing agreements are not in force, that the Labor Relations Commission is deprived of its jurisdiction to deal with labor disputes between public

*The English version of this letter can be found in Government Section, SCAP, *Political Reorientation of Japan* (Washington D.C.: Government Printing Office, 1948), Appendix B: 8c, p. 581.

employees and the state and so on, and that henceforth the Provisional Personnel Commission shall be the sole agency charged with safeguarding the interests of public employees. Article 2 completely negates the right to dispute, and Article 3 provides penalties for violation of the previous Articles. Thus, it will be noticed, the denial of the right to dispute in this Cabinet Order is inseparably interwoven with a denial of the right to collective bargaining (with administrators as the other party, of course). In short, both the demand for a ban in the MacArthur letter and the prohibition in Cabinet Order 201 stick very closely to the subject of collective bargaining; that is, they rule out dispute activities in the relations between employers and employees; and we can interpret them as not aimed generally at acts obstructing work which are unrelated to collective bargaining. In other words, there was a sweeping reduction in the guarantees under Article 28 of the Constitution with respect to public employees. This is not difficult to infer also from the fact that the Provisional Personnel Commission was presented as compensation for a restriction on fundamental rights. That organ is later the National Personnel Authority, and like the present National Personnel Authority, its purposes were to improve salaries and other working conditions, to secure fairness in personnel administration, and to protect the interests of employees. It was not charged with such tasks as adjusting their political demands or dissolving the complaints and dissatisfaction found in social action.

In November of the same year, a bill for revision of the NPEL, prepared under the strong advice of SCAP, was presented to the Diet and was enacted into law in December. The part concerning the prohibition of dispute activities was not given full debate in related committee meetings, it passed in the Diet without amendment and was established as Article 98 and Article 110, paragraph 1, item 17 of the NPEL, which was later revised by Law 69 of 1965. At the same time, the former Article 38 of the LRAL became inapplicable to national public employees. Subsequently, this Article was deleted on the occasion of the first revision of the LRAL (10 June 1949), and the former Article 38 was reborn as Article 98 and Article 110, paragraph 1, item 17 of the NPEL.

Judging from the developments analyzed above, I think we should construe the significance of "dispute activities" under Article 98 of the NPEL as in no way different from that established under Article 7 of the LRAL.

4. Article 7 of the LRAL stipulates: "In this law, dispute activities refer to strikes, slowdowns, lockouts, and other acts and counteractions carried out by parties in labor relations to achieve their objectives, which obstruct the normal conduct of business." In this provision, what is called "dispute activities" must include the following three elements: (1) a party in labor relations; (2) an act which intends to achieve the party's objec-

tives; (3) its mode must be such as to obstruct the normal conduct of business. Now each of these elements will next be examined with reference to the present case.

First, "dispute activities" are acts taken in one's position as a party in labor relations. Judging from the legislative intent of the LRAL, a party refers to a party in collective labor relations, and does not mean a party in individual worker relations. Acts obstructing business carried out by workers as individuals are not treated exclusively as dispute activities. Moreover, while a worker may be an employee in his relationship with administrators, he is also an individual citizen, or one of the people. Since their organization, in one respect, is a collective body of citizens and of the people, they are naturally not precluded from taking action (social action or political activities) in their capacity as citizens and the people, unrelated to a conflict or contention with administrators, and as a matter of fact this often happens. However, these are not actions as a party in labor relations. This is exactly the same with respect to public employees and their organizations. Under one aspect, they are parties in labor relations, but under another aspect they are citizens or the people, and a collective body of the same. By the same token, in one respect the government is the employer from the standpoint of labor relations, while under another aspect it appears as an organ of the state which exercises sovereignty. Since the government in its capacity as employer does not differ essentially from an employer in private enterprise, it is required to acknowledge opposition from the organizations of public employees and to negotiate with them on a footing of equality. There is no room for doubting this duality of the government, which has long been pointed out. In their capacity as employees, public employees view the government as their employer, and this is not a relationship between the governing and the governed. Public employees as a group can conceivably take actions in confrontation with the government of three principal types: (1) actions to achieve demands based on their involvement in labor relations; (2) actions taken in their capacity as the people to press for changes in policy or to oppose policies; (3) walk-outs and other acts engaged in, not to present demands, but out of disregard for their duties. Among the above, "dispute activities" as a legal term under Article 98, paragraph 5 of the NPEL are limited to (1). (Article 98, paragraph 5 prohibits "acts of delay which reduce the efficiency of governmental operations," as well as "dispute activities." Judging only from the words in the provision, it might seem to set up acts of delay as an analogous classification distinct from dispute activities; but if we ponder the reasons behind the legislation, or check it against its actual basis, the MacArthur letter, we shall interpret this provision as established only as a precaution, to force out the apparently legal tactics of so-called "law-abiding struggle" employed at the time by the National Government and Public Enterprise Employees Union, such as not working overtime or taking vacations all at the same time. This was nothing more than one type of dispute activities belonging to category (1) above.)

5. Second, dispute activities are acts that intend to achieve objectives. (Broadly speaking, "counteractions" in Article 7 of the LRAL may also be included under achievement of objectives here.) Since the question of the possibility of achieving the objectives is not raised, even a simple protest demonstration is not precluded from dispute activities, as long as it is something that obstructs the normal conduct of business as an act carried out for the achievement of objectives. Next, there is the problem of whether those objectives need be in the area of labor relations, or are in no way limited in nature. There is the view that the latter is more in line with Article 6 of the same law; but as related above, Article 7 also serves as a defining provision for the purpose of clarifying what that "labor dispute" is which is a prerequisite for an adjustment of the dispute to take place. Moreover, taking into consideration also the fact that "dispute activities" must be acts of those in the position of a party in labor relations, and so on, we might best interpret this use of the term *objectives* as limited to demands made in labor relations. If that is so, a so-called political strike engaged in in their capacity as the people to oppose policies of the government or to compel a change in its policy, must not be included in "dispute activities" as a legal term in Article 98, paragraph 5 of the NPEL.

Since the on-the-job rally in the present case was held with as many as seventy court employees participating and cut into office hours from 8:30 A.M. to 9:30 A.M., it undeniably obstructed the normal conduct of the business of the courts. However, what it stood for was an expression of will in opposition to the New Security Treaty, it was action directed toward the government as one exercising sovereignty, and it was not something addressed to the government as their employer. Furthermore, since there is not the slightest doubt that their objective was not something concerning labor relations, for example, working conditions and the like, there is no need to belabor the fact that, in accordance with what was stated before, this meeting does not fall under "dispute activities." Regulation of such acts may be possible under other legal provisions, and should not be suspect on account of Article 110, paragraph 5, item 17 of the NPEL.

6. Essentially, public employees are "workers" under Article 28 of the Constitution and as a rule enjoy the protections of that Article (20 *Keishū* 901; Sup. Ct., G.B., 26 October 1966; hereafter referred to as the Central Post Office Decision). The legal intent of Article 28 of the Constitution is "to guarantee the right to organize and to act collectively to workers who are in an economically weak position in their relationships as workers with leaders of an enterprise, in other words, as employees with employers" (3 *Keishū* 772; Sup. Ct., G.B., 18 May 1949). "The aim of this provision, deriving from the fundamental idea of guaranteeing the so-

called right to livelihood established in Article 25 of the Constitution and from the premise that a life worthy of human beings is to be guaranteed to workers . . . is to guarantee the rights of workers to organize, to bargain collectively, and to resort to dispute tactics, as the means to secure substantive freedom and equality to workers standing in a disadvantageous economic position" (Central Post Office Decision, in Case 12). The constitutional guarantee of the fundamental rights of workers is concretized in the Labor Union Law. The purposes of that law are to protect associations and to maintain and support collective activities and collective bargaining so that workers may negotiate with their employers on a footing of equality (Article 1, paragraph 1). This is not to confer upon workers and their organizations any privileges vis-à-vis society and the state, abstracted from their relations with employers, which are not accorded the people in general and their organizations. The right to organize protected by the Labor Union Law is found in Article 1, paragraph 1, and the collective activities protected therein are confined to that which is prescribed in paragraph 1. Of course labor unions have the freedom to engage in political activities (*Saibansho Jihō*, No. 511, p. 2; Sup. Ct., G.B., 4 December 1968), and there is no good reason for considering the political activities of labor unions naturally illegal under criminal law; but the Labor Union Law neither protects nor prohibits general political activities of labor unions insofar as they are irrelevant to the economic bargaining of workers; rather, it is silent on the subject. (Article 2, item 4 merely provides for the conditions an organization must meet under that law to be treated as a labor union.)

In spite of the provisions of the former Labor Union Law (which, in principle, safeguarded for public employees the fundamental rights of workers), the former Article 38 of the LRAL imposed severe restrictions on the right of dispute of government and public enterprise employees other than manual service employees, so that legal provision has the character of a special law related to the old Labor Union Law. First, these public employees were guaranteed the right to organize, the right to bargain collectively, and the right of dispute in their relations with their employers, but the right of dispute was later suppressed. This right of dispute which is the object of suppression corresponds with what Article 28 of the Constitution calls the "right of dispute"; in other words, it should be self-evident that it is a matter of right to engage in dispute activities in relations with employers. In short, we must hold that in no other respect does it regulate collective activities in any sense. By an examination of the history related above, we should easily be able to understand that since Article 98 of the NPEL should be termed an adaptation of the former Article 38 of the LRAL, Article 98 is a special law related to the Labor Union Law and does not purport to restrict political activities.

7. Judging from the wording of the said legal provision, that Article states in part: "Personnel shall not engage in delays . . . or acts of

dispute . . . against the public, which the government represents in its capacity as employer." Whether or not the public is an employer in the basic sense of the term, this Article is sufficient for seeing that "dispute activities" are something directed at an employer. Since "the public" by nature is not something organized, there is no reason for establishing a relationship in law between "the public" and public employees. Labor relations arise with the government, acting through its authorities; "the public" as employer may only refer symbolically to the facts that sovereignty resides in the people and that all public power derives from the people. Thus, "dispute activities" in the said Article should be regarded as directed at the government as employer, and as in perfect agreement on that point with Article 7 of the LRAL. Needless to say, "an employer" is one who is in a position to employ workers as a party to a labor contract, a concept completely different from that of the government as one exercising sovereignty. Coordinated actions unrelated to labor relations, such as those presenting political demands, are nothing but a defiance of the government in its latter capacity, even when they interfere with the normal conduct of business. I believe that Article 98 of the NPEL quite clearly has nothing to do with that whole matter.

8. The on-the-job rally in the present case was a purely political activity in opposition to the New Security Treaty. Since the word "strike" is a common, everyday term, we are free to call this rally a political strike. That usage does not differ much from terming a strike a school boycott by students opposing the Security Treaty, and it must be precisely distinguished from "a strike" under Article 98 of the NPEL. However, "a strike" in that Article is a concept included in "dispute activities" in the same Article, since the definition of "dispute activities" explicated above must be applied to all "strikes."

According to the judgment in the above-mentioned Central Post Office Case, dispute activities contrary to Article 17, paragraph 1 of the PELRL are not criminally liable, when they are for the purpose of achieving goals under Article 1, paragraph 1 of the Labor Union Law, are limited to forbearance of delay or a strike, and are not attended by acts of violence or other wrongful acts. However, the court explains: "When dispute activities are resorted to, not to attain the purposes provided in Article 1, paragraph 1 of the Labor Union Law, but for the attainment of political aims" and so on, "they exceed the permissible limits of dispute activities and so are not exempt from criminal sanctions." Perhaps some would say that Court was acknowledging the criminal liability of so-called political strikes by public employees in general. But the Central Post Office Case dealt with nothing more than the question of whether or not to apply penal provisions in Article 79, paragraph 1 of the Postal Law to postal employees under an application of the PELRL. (This, of course, contains no penal provisions for dispute activities.) What is more, that case is completely irrelevant to the question of whether or not so-called political strikes by employees of public corporations and the like are in general liable to criminal sanction. Not only that. Since so-called political strikes are not "dispute activities" under Article 98 of the NPEL, as we have already argued, the question of whether or not the acts in the present case by national public employees for political purposes are punishable does not arise at all in the present case, which involves an indictment for violation of Article 110, paragraph 1, item 17 of the NPEL. (Concerning this point, the constitutionality and the extent of applicability of Article 102 and Article 110, paragraph 1, item 19 of the NPEL and of Regulations 14 through 17 of the National Personnel Authority must be judged upon in connection with the relationship between the neutrality of public employees established in Article 15, paragraph 2 of the Constitution and the freedom of expression guaranteed them as citizens under Article 21 of the Constitution. But that should be inquired into elsewhere. . . .)

In summary, the judgment below is tainted with illegality for erroneously interpreting the law and should be quashed, for approving application of Article 110, paragraph 1, item 17 of the NPEL to the incitement to an on-the-job rally in the present case which does not belong in the category of "dispute activities" under Article 98 of the same law.

Justices Masatoshi Yokota (presiding), Toshio Irie, Ken'ichi Okuno, Asanosuke Kusaka, Yoshihiko Kido, Kazuto Ishida, Jirō Tanaka, Jirō Matsuda, Makoto Iwata, Kazuo Shimomura, Kōtarō Irokawa, Ken'ichirō Ōsumi, Masao Matsumoto, and Yoshimi Iimura. Chief Justice Masatoshi Yokota and Justice Ken'ichi Okuno did not sign due to their retirement.

Case 14. Asahi v. *Japan (1967)*. The Asahi Tuberculosis Case

21 *Minshū* 5 at p. 1043; Supreme Court, Grand Bench, 24 May 1967; Tokyo Dist. Ct. (First Instance), Tokyo High Ct. (Second Instance), [constitutionality of welfare payment levels].*

EDITORIAL NOTE: Shigeru Asahi was a tuberculosis patient at the Okayama National Sanitarium where he was receiving 600 yen (ca. $1.75) from the government, the highest monthly allowance set by the Minister of Welfare, in addition to free meals and free medical treatment. However, when his brother began to send him 1,500 yen each month, the director of the Social Welfare Office not only stopped payment of the 600 yen, but also ordered Asahi to pay 900 yen out of the amount sent by his brother to cover part of his medical expenses. Asahi sought and received a court order restoring the 600 yen payments in full, on grounds that the allowance was unreasonably inadequate for a patient to maintain the minimum standards of healthy and cultured living guaranteed by the Livelihood Protection Law (Article 3 and Article 8, paragraph 2) and Article 25

*The translation of judicial opinions is the authors' own, but they have consulted General Secretariat, Supreme Court, trans., JUDGMENT UPON CASE OF THE SO-CALLED "ASAHI CASE": SERIES OF PROMINENT JUDGMENTS OF THE SUPREME COURT UPON QUESTIONS OF CONSTITUTIONALITY, no. 10 (1968).

of the Constitution. However, the Tokyo High Court* overturned the first instance decision and held that the minister has the discretionary power under the law to determine the level of payment necessary pursuant to Article 3 of the Livelihood Protection Law. The monthly allowance was found to be low, but not unlawfully low; the monthly cost of daily necessities was computed to be 670 yen for such a patient at that time. The plaintiff's executors appealed the case to the Supreme Court.

REFERENCES

Constitution of Japan [ARTICLE 25 was at issue in this case. See Appendix 3 for this provision].

Livelihood Protection Law (*Law 144 of 1950*), ARTICLE 2. All citizens, insofar as they satisfy the requirements under this law, are entitled to receive assistance under this law (hereinafter to be referred to as "assistance"), without discrimination or preference.

ARTICLE 3. The minimum living guaranteed by this law shall be of such an extent as to enable maintenance of standards of wholesome and cultured living.

ARTICLE 8, 1. Assistance shall be provided on the basis of the total needs of the person requiring assistance, as measured by standards established by the Minister of Welfare, and to the extent that the said total needs cannot be met by the person's money or goods.

2. The standard under the preceding paragraph shall be sufficient to meet, but not in excess of the needs for a minimum standard of living, taking into consideration differences in age, sex, family composition, and location and other necessary factors affecting the beneficiary, and depending on the kind of assistance involved.

ARTICLE 9. Assistance shall be provided effectively and adequately, taking into consideration, among other factors, actual variations in individual and family requirements, such as differences in age and sex, and the condition of health of the person requiring assistance.

ARTICLE 24, 1. The mayor of the city, town or village shall, when he receives an application for the initiation of assistance, determine the necessity, kind, extent, and method of the assistance and notify the applicant of these in writing.

3. The notification under paragraph 1 shall be made within fourteen days after the day when the submission of the application was made; provided, however, that in a case where there is a particular reason, such as that time is required for making investigations regarding the financial situation of a person who is under an obligation to furnish support, the above-mentioned period may be extended up to thirty days. In this case the reasons for this shall be clearly stated in the written document under the same paragraph.

4. In case no notification has been made under paragraph 1 within

*HANREI JIHŌ, no. 351, p. 11 (Tokyo High Ct., 14 January 1963).

thirty days of submission of an application for assistance, the applicant may regard his application as having been rejected by the mayor of the city, town, or village.

ARTICLE 59. The recipient is not authorized to transfer the right to receive assistance.

ARTICLE 64, 1. In case any recipient or person who has made an application for commencement or modification of assistance, is dissatisfied with the disposition made by the mayor of the city, town or village regarding his assistance, he may appeal in writing through the mayor of city, town, or village concerned to the governor of the metropolis, Hokkaidō, or the urban or rural prefecture within thirty days after the day when the decision was made.

2. In case an appeal has been filed in accordance with the provisions of the preceding paragraph, the mayor of the city, town, or village shall forward the appeal, attaching his written opinion thereon and other related documents, to the governor of the metropolis, Hokkaidō, or the urban or rural prefecture within ten days after the day when he received the appeal.

3. In case the governor of the metropolis, Hokkaidō, or the urban or rural prefecture has deemed an appeal to have been made for compelling reasons, he may accept it even after the time limit for appeal mentioned in paragraph 1 has expired.

ARTICLE 65, 1. In case the governor of the metropolis, Hokkaidō, or the urban or rural prefecture has received an appeal forwarded in accordance with the provisions of paragraph 2 of the preceding Article, he shall make the necessary review of it, and if he deems the appeal unjustifiable, he shall reject it by his decision, cancel or change the disposition made by the mayor of the city, town or village, or order the mayor of the city, town, or village to make the necessary decision on assistance within a fixed period of time.

2. The decision made by the governor of the metropolis, Hokkaidō, or the urban or rural prefecture mentioned in the preceding paragraph shall be communicated in writing to the appellant and to the mayor of the city, town, or village concerned within forty days after the day of receipt of the appeal forwarded.

3. The provisions of Article 24, paragraph 4 shall apply *mutatis mutandis* to cases where the notification of the decision has not been effected within the fixed period of time mentioned in the preceding paragraph.

Administrative Litigation Law (*Law 139 of 1962*), ARTICLE 9. Suits for revocation of disposition and of decision may be filed only by persons (including persons having legal interest still to be recovered by the revocation of disposition or decision even after the effect of the disposition or decision has ceased due to the elapse of the period therefor or any other reason) having the legal interest with respect to seeking the revocation of the said disposition or decision.

Code of Civil Procedure (*Law 29 of 1890*), ARTICLE 89. The costs of the suit shall be borne by the losing party.

ARTICLE 95. The court shall, in a decision closing a case, render decision, upon its own authority, with respect to the whole court costs in the particular instance. Provided, that it may, according to the circumstances, in a decision relating to a part of the case or an interlocutory dispute, render decision on the costs thereof.

ARTICLE 208, 1. Proceedings are interrupted on the death of a party. In such cases, proceedings must be taken over by his heir, the administrator of the estate, or any other person who is bound by laws and ordinances to continue the action.

2. During such time as he is entitled to waive the succession, the heir shall not take over the proceedings.

FORMAL JUDGMENT

1. The suit terminated on 14 February 1964, upon the death of the appellant.

2. The costs of the Court incurred in the course of the *ad interim* dispute shall be borne by Kenji and Kimiko Asahi, successors to the appellant.

REASONS. In conducting examination *ex officio*, it is apparent from the documents that the appellant who filed this appeal with the Court on 20 November 1963, died on 14 February 1964.

The appellant was hospitalized for more than ten years in the National Okayama Sanitarium as a tuberculous patient with no kith and kin, was receiving 600 yen a month as an incidental expense allowance as well as medical benefits and meals, which items were stipulated as the maximum aid in the livelihood assistance schedule set by the Minister of Health and Welfare. Meanwhile, it was found that his own brother, Keiichi, was alive, and as the appellant began receiving monthly support of 1,500 yen from this brother, the director of the Tsuyama Welfare Office issued an order to terminate the aforesaid allowance of 600 yen a month, and to assess against him, as a part of the medical expenses, 900 yen a month which was derived from the difference between the amount of support sent him from his brother and the stipulated amount for living expenses. This order was sustained both in the remedial proceedings before the governor of Okayama Prefecture and in the remedial proceedings before the minister of Health and Welfare. The appellant filed this suit against the minister of Health and Welfare, alleging that the determination made by the minister to dismiss the claim for administrative remedy should be overruled on the grounds that the amount of 600 yen a month allowed under the schedule was too low to maintain minimum standards of healthy and cultured living prescribed by the Livelihood Protection Law and therefore is illegal.

It must be noted here that the benefits the needy person receives or is receiving under the provisions of the Livelihood Protection Law are not benefits given merely as a benefice of the state or as a reflection of social policy. It should be interpreted as a right under the law which may be termed the right to receive a livelihood. This right, however, is a personal right to be secured exclusively to beneficiary, and is not transferable (Article 59) or inheritable. Moreover, the right to receive benefits whose payment has been delayed during the lifetime of the beneficiary ceases at his death and cannot be inherited, even if such benefits are living expense benefits given in cash, as well as medical benefits; because such benefits are aimed at satisfying the need of the one protected for a minimum standard of living. They are intended only for objectives contemplated by the law. As for the claim submitted for the return of funds unjustly exacted by the government, such a claim cannot be established without the existence of a claimant's right to receive livelihood assistance itself. Since this right is secured personally to the individual protected, as mentioned above, it is proper to hold that this kind of right cannot become an object of inheritance.

Consequently, it must be concluded that this suit terminated upon the death of the appellant, and that there is no room for his heirs, Kenji and Kimiko Asahi, to succeed to his suit in his place.

(For reference, the following opinion is given concerning the propriety of the livelihood aid schedule at issue.)

1. Article 25, paragraph 1 of the Constitution provides that "All the people shall enjoy the right to maintain the minimum standards of wholesome and cultured living." This provision merely proclaims that it is a duty of the state to administer national policy in such a manner as to enable all the people to enjoy at least the minimum standards of wholesome and cultured living, and it does not grant the people as individuals any concrete rights (2 *Keishū* 1235; Sup. Ct., G.B., 29 September 1948). A concrete right is secured only through the provisions of the Livelihood Protection Law enacted to realize the objectives prescribed in the provisions of the Constitution. The Livelihood Protection Law provides that any person who satisfies "the requirements under this law" is entitled to "receive assistance under this law" (Article 2), and such protection is to be given according to the schedule set by the Minister of Health and Welfare (Article 8, paragraph 1). Therefore, the concrete right consists of a right to receive such assistance as is stipulated in the schedule that the minister of Health and Welfare establishes on the belief that the schedule is sufficient to maintain minimum standards of living. Such standards should be set in accordance with the requirements enumerated in Article 8, paragraph 2 of the law and thereby be appropriate to maintain the minimum standards of wholesome and cultured living guaranteed by the Constitution. The concept of minimum standards of wholesome and cultured living, however, is rather abstract and relative. Its substance changes in relation to the development of culture and the

national economy and can be determined only after taking into consideration all these and other uncertain factors. Consequently, the authority to determine what constitutes the minimum standards of wholesome and cultured living is usually vested in the discretionary power of the minister of Health and Welfare. His decision may not directly create an issue of illegality, although it might lead to political debate on an issue of propriety and governmental responsibility. Only in cases where such a decision is so made as to exceed or abuse the power bestowed by the law in violation of the objectives of the Constitution and the Livelihood Protection Law, by ignoring the real conditions of life and establishing extremely low standards for the schedule, would such a decision be subject to judicial review as an illegal action.

The judgment below interpreted the act of establishing the standards for aid as a limited administrative action. It was also of the opinion that it is left to the expert discretion of the minister of Health and Welfare to determine what are the minimum standards of wholesome and cultured living and that a mistake made in such judgment is merely a question of propriety as long as it does not deviate from the aims and purposes of the law. Even restricted discretionary action undeniably allows some room for the administrative office to exercise its discretionary power. The judgment below, therefore, was not involved in any illegal contradictory reasoning when regarding the act of establishing standards for aid as an exercise of limited discretion on the one hand, and on the other hand admitting some room for expert discretion of the minister of Health and Welfare. Moreover, the judgment below allegedly took into consideration elements not directly involved in life maintenance when judging the propriety of the aid schedule in this case. These elements would include such factors as the existing national income or the national financial condition as reflected by such income, general standards of living, differences in urban and rural living standards, living standards of the lower income bracket, and the percentage of the population belonging to this class, sentiment among some people that it is unjust to allow better living conditions to those who receive livelihood protection than to the mass of people who do not receive protection, and the priorities of the national budget. It falls within the discretionary power of the minister of Health and Welfare to take these elements into consideration, so his decision does not raise any issues of illegality, but of propriety, as long as it does not deviate from the aims and purposes of the law.

2. As for the livelihood aid schedule under consideration in the present case, the standard was established in July 1953, and the items, quantities, and unit costs that were used as bases for the calculation of 600 yen a month are, as shown in the appendix, attached to the first instance judgment.

The minimum standard of living guaranteed by the Livelihood Protection Law should be of such a level as to make it possible to maintain standards of wholesome and cultured living (Article 3), and the substance of the assistance offered should be determined efficiently and properly with due consideration given to the actual needs of the beneficiary himself and of his family (Article 9); but at the same time, it should not be more than what is required to satisfy the minimum requirements of living (Article 8, paragraph 2). Concerning a beneficiary who is an in-patient like the appellant in this case, there are certain restrictions arising from special factors, such as long-term hospitalization and other medical reasons. In such instances, there is undeniably a certain relationship between the cost of commodities and the effective cure of a disease; and a shortage may have a grave bearing upon the patient. As a means to satisfy the minimum needs of patients, the law prescribes the kind and scope of aid for meeting their needs as well as for providing appropriate aid; the law divides the protective scheme into single and double benefits, and enables in-patients to receive medical aid, including meals, in addition to general livelihood assistance. There is, of course, a difference between the medical and livelihood benefits, both in nature and in manner of disbursal; there is also a system for rehabilitation aid. Therefore, attacks on the livelihood aid schedule as illegal must not be allowed on grounds that no expenditures are made for daily expenses to effect cures or to fill gaps in the present medical and nursing systems, or that it is necessary to maintain one's livelihood after he has left the hospital.

The quantity of daily necessities used by patients naturally depends on the degrees of their individual frugality and the quality of articles concerned. The type of articles needed also differs from patient to patient depending upon the seriousness of the illness; and among certain categories of patients, articles may be used interchangeably. Consequently, in examining whether or not the general and abstract yardstick, called the livelihood aid schedule, for measuring the degree of daily needs of patients is appropriate in actual practice, the answer cannot be determined by analyzing the quantity or unit cost of each individual item. It must be determined with a grasp of the overall picture. Furthermore, daily articles for in-patients can be divided into those for ordinary needs and those for extraordinary need; it is left to the discretion of the minister of Health and Welfare to determine whether to put such an expenditure under the ordinary schedule, a special schedule, contingency benefits, or a loan system.

Thus construed, the livelihood aid schedule that was determined by the minister of Health and Welfare to be sufficient to meet the minimum daily needs of the in-patient under the facts found by the court below, cannot be said to have exceeded the discretionary power granted him under the law, or to be an abuse of such power, and therefore illegal.

Therefore, this Court, by the opinion of all the justices on the bench,

except for the supplementary opinion of Justice Ken'ichi Okuno and the dissenting opinions of Justices Asanosuke Kusaka, Jirō Tanaka, Jirō Matsuda and Makoto Iwata, renders judgment as stated in the Formal Judgment in accordance with the provisions of Articles 95 and 89 of the Code of Civil Procedure.
[All other opinions except the dissenting opinion of Justice Tanaka have been omitted.]

* * *

The dissenting opinion of Justice Jirō Tanaka follows.

1. The majority opinion stated: "It must be concluded that this suit was terminated upon the death of the appellant, and that there is no room for his heirs, Kenji and Kimiko Asahi, to succeed to this suit in his place," and gave a judgment of termination of the suit on a premise which had no bearing upon the grounds of appeal. I disagree with this view.

There is a room for argument as to whether or not the litigation in question is capable of succession. There is an increasing tendency in many countries to interpret an administrative litigation as flexibly as possible and to open the door for judicial relief as widely as possible. There is ample reason for this trend inasmuch as administrative litigation, especially that involving personal complaints, was basically designed to permit people to have recourse against administrative power. In our country, too, we should try to render judgment on the merits and avoid a type of trial which would give the appearance of turning away the caller at the door. I believe that this is the basic attitude to be taken by the Court in serving the people.

When we review the case at hand from such an angle, it is theoretically possible to recognize the right of succession to this suit; and I think it would show a proper attitude for the Court to reconsider the merits of the case and to declare a judgment accordingly.

Based on such a premise, I am opposed to the majority opinion and would like to clarify the reasons for recognition of the right of succession to this suit. I would also like to state my opinions about the grounds of appeal alleged by the appellant, while granting that it would be of little significance to respond on each ground of appeal in detail, since this case has already been terminated by the majority opinion. I would not go further than to give my basic view about main points at issue in this suit; that is, problems surrounding the guarantee of the right of survival provided for in Article 25 of the Constitution, which has attracted such great concern among the people.

2. The reasons why I approve the succession of this suit are as follows:

The majority opinion states that the benefits the person in need receives or is receiving under the provisions of the Livelihood Protection Law are not benefits given merely as a benefice of the state or as a reflection of social policy. It should be interpreted as a legal right that may be termed the right to receive a livelihood. It further states that this right, however, is a personal right secured exclusively to the individual to be protected or being protected and is not transferable or inheritable. The basic point made is correct, and there can be no objection to it. However, the majority opinion goes on to state that not only the right to receive aid, but also the right to receive the benefits that should have been given and have been held in arrears during the lifetime of the beneficiary, cease and cannot be inherited, as these rights were granted to meet the minimum needs of the beneficiary's livelihood. It also states that a claim to the return of funds unjustly exacted by the government to be mentioned below is not inheritable, because such a claim is established only on the premise of the right to receive protection, which is secured exclusively to the individual to be protected. Thus, the majority opinion concludes that there is no room for succession to this suit.

However, I would contend that it is still a matter for debate whether or not the right to receive livelihood benefits that have fallen in arrears is restricted by the purpose of consumption for which the allowance is given, in the same manner as the right to receive protection itself. Even if I should follow the majority opinion on this point, this does not immediately constitute a basis for the denial of succession to this suit. Originally, this was a suit to demand the overruling of a decision that approved a change in the status of aid, according to the principle of supplementary protection. Under that order, Shigeru Asahi was denied the benefit of 600 yen for monthly incidental expenses and was required, in partial payment of his medical expenses, to pay 900 yen a month out of the 1,500 yen a month his brother, Keiichi had sent him. (This remittance was reduced to 600 yen and later to nothing.) Therefore, more crucial to solving the issue of recognition of the right of succession to this suit than the right to a livelihood provided for by the Livelihood Protection Law, or the claim for payment which is in arrears, is the claim for the return of unjustly exacted funds, the difference between the amount due under the livelihood aid schedule set by the minister and a proper amount up to 900 yen which Asahi paid for medical expenses after the order changing the assistance he received.

To be more specific about this point, before the order was issued by the director of Tsuyama Welfare Office, Shigeru Asahi had the right to receive 600 yen monthly in livelihood aid and allowance in kind, as free as his medical aid; but under the order issued by the director, his 600 yen in monthly livelihood aid was terminated. Furthermore, he was ordered to pay 900 yen to cover medical expenses (though this was later reduced to 400 yen). Thus, should that decision be nullified, it would imply that the government unjustly suspended the monthly payment of 600 yen in livelihood support, and Asahi improperly turned over to the hospital for medical expenses up to 900 yen, the difference between that amount and the amount received from his brother. Of course, the beneficiary Shigeru Asahi cannot *ipso facto* be said to have the right to demand protection under a proper livelihood aid schedule. Should this decision be overruled, the minister of Health and Welfare would be bound to set a proper standard according to the aim of the provisions of the Constitution and the Livelihood Protection Law, and the government would be required to return what it had received under the voided order to Shigeru Asahi to the extent mentioned above. Shigeru Asahi should be allowed to lodge a claim against the government for the return of unjustly exacted funds within the same limits. (However, according to the facts established by the judgment below, it is not clear whether the whole amount of the above mentioned 900 yen was paid to the National Okayama Sanitarium and turned over to the National Treasury; but even if a certain portion of it was not paid to the Treasury, Shigeru Asahi could have asked for an affirmation that he had owed nothing. No difference can be found between that case and one in which a claim lodged for the return of unjustly exacted funds is approved.) The claim against the government for the return of unjustly exacted funds is not a claim for assistance itself, nor is it a demand for the payment of livelihood aid allowances in arrears. It is a demand for the return of money that Shigeru Asahi could have used freely as he saw fit; and therefore, in my opinion reasonable grounds cannot be found for denying that such a right is transferable or inheritable.

If the demand for return of unjustly exacted funds in the above sense is to be admitted, it is a prerequisite for the exercise of appellant's claim that the object of this case be the voiding of the order. It is, then, reasonable to interpret Kenji and Kimiko Asahi, who succeeded to the right, as having the legal interest that they would have regained upon an overruling of the order.

The object of the suit in the present case was not to seek the return of unjustly exacted funds; it was brought primarily to seek annulment of the above-mentioned order. Generally speaking, the aim of a suit seeking nullification of an administrative action or decision is to restore the original state of affairs that would have maintained but for the action or decision and to remove harmful conditions resulting from such an action and decision. In deciding on the standing of a person as plaintiff in a suit seeking nullification of an action or decision, Article 9 of the Administrative Litigation Law defines the person to include "those who have a legal interest to be recovered upon nullification of an action or decision even after such an action or decision becomes ineffective with the lapse of time or for other reasons." It must be understood that this provision of the law was specifically designed to establish the standing of a plaintiff in suits such as the one at hand. A decision of the Grand Bench of this Court overrules past precedents and declares that if there is a legal interest to be recovered by nullifying an action, then a person is qualified as a plaintiff to institute a suit (19 *Minshū* 721; Sup. Ct., G.B., 28 April 1965).

In a case where a party loses the right to continue a suit in the course of proceedings, by his death, by loss of standing, by transfer of the right or legal relations that constituted the object of the suit, or for other reasons, the suit will become subject to rejection by the court on the grounds that there is no longer a basis for litigation. If however, the dispute is not settled for such objective reasons, it would be against economy of procedure to require a suit to be reinstituted by or against the successor. Therein lies the basic purpose of the rule of succession to suit which permits the successor to continue the suit in place of the former party. Thus even in a case where a right and other legal interests are not the object of a pending suit, as in the present case, if a remaining legal interest is recognized in the successor to continue the suit for the purpose of exercising the right and other legal interests evolving from such succession, then the successor should be permitted to continue the pending litigation established by the former party.

On the grounds stated so far, I would hold that in this case Kenji and Kimiko properly succeeded to the right to continue the litigation upon the death of Shigeru Asahi.

3. Inasmuch as it is my belief that this suit is subject to succession, I will present my opinion about the principal issue involved.

Stating the conclusion first, I think this appeal cannot avoid dismissal. The reasons for this may be briefly stated as follows:

(1) Regarding the first and the second grounds of appeal presented by S. Unno and fourteen others representing the appellant (including the first supplemental ground presented by S. Unno and seventeen others):

I would hold that it is not by a benefice of the state nor as a reflection of social policy, but by legal right that a person in need of assistance receives protection in sufficient amount to maintain minimum standards of wholesome and cultured living. As stated above, such is the epoch-making nature of the present Livelihood Protection Law. The question is, what is the legal basis of such a right, and what does it contain?

Article 25, paragraph 1 of the Constitution provides: "All the people shall enjoy the right to maintain minimum standards of wholesome and cultured living," but as stated in the precedents of the Court, this provision merely declares it is a duty of the government to administer its policies in such a way as to assure all the people . . . minimum standards of living. It does not itself grant any concrete right to individuals as obligatory claims for assistance (2 *Keishū* 1235; Sup. Ct., G.B., 29 September 1948). A concrete right to such a protection is granted by the Livelihood Protection Law enacted to implement the purport of the Constitutional provision. . . . Thus, this law guarantees the right to receive protection according to the schedule that the minister of Health and Welfare sets up and recognizes as sufficient to maintain a minimum standard of living. . . . The protection schedule set by the minister must of course be in close compliance with the points prescribed in Article 8, paragraph 2 and must be such that it provides enough to maintain minimum standards of wholesome and cultured living, as stated in Article 25, paragraph 1 of the Constitution. However, these minimum standards of living are not a fixed or definite idea but an abstract and relative concept the substance of which improves constantly with the development of the culture and economy of the nation. This can be fixed only after taking many factors into consideration and is hardly definable in terms of a certain point of time with mathematical accuracy. The Constitution itself does not intend to guarantee the right to maintain minimum standards of living that are assumed on an objective basis without any argument. We cannot consider the Livelihood Protection Law unconstitutional simply because it does not provide for a right to what is actually sufficient to maintain the above-mentioned standards of living.

From this standpoint, it is fair to conclude that the determination with regard to what constitutes minimum standards of wholesome and cultured living is provisionally left to the reasonable and technical discretion of the minister of Health and Welfare. Misjudgment on his part may raise a question of political responsibility for the government as a matter of propriety, but does not in itself constitute a question of illegality. An established schedule may become the object of judicial review as an illegal act only when it exceeds or abuses the power of discretion entrusted by the law, thus violating the aims and purposes of the Constitution and the Livelihood Protection Law; for example, by fixing a low standard that ignores the conditions of real life. The Livelihood Protection Law limits the object of complaints to dispositions with respect to decisions on assistance and actual provision of assistance (Article 65, paragraph 1) and does not refer at all to the process of fixing a support assistance schedule itself.

Article 8, paragraph 2 of Livelihood Protection Law states in fact that "the standard under the preceding paragraph shall be sufficient, but not in excess of the needs for a minimum standard of living, taking into consideration differences in age, sex, family composition, and location and other necessary factors affecting the beneficiary." The minister of Health and Welfare must try to meet the above-mentioned requirements in setting a schedule by adopting a method such as the calculation of actual living expenses. In adopting such a method, he must determine which data concerning a livelihood are to be considered. Since, as stated above, minimum standards of wholesome and cultured living is an abstract and relative concept the substance of which improves as the culture and economy of the nation develop, and since they cannot be fixed without taking many factors into consideration, it is difficult to determine what data should be taken into account in calculating minimum expenses of a healthy and cultured life, without considering factors not directly related. Therefore, it does not immediately constitute illegality to take these factors into consideration in setting up an aid schedule.

While the judgment below takes the view that the act of fixing an aid schedule falls within the realm of the limited discretionary acts of the minister, it states that the determination of what constitutes minimum standards of wholesome and cultured living is left to the technical discretion of the minister, and that misjudgment on his part raises only questions of propriety, so long as it does not violate the aims and purposes of the law. According to generally accepted theory, misjudgment in the exercise of limited discretion raises questions not only of propriety, but also of illegality, which is subject to judicial review. The terminology used in the judgment below, therefore, is not appropriate from this standpoint. The significance of the judgment below is in showing that the provisions in the Livelihood Protection Law never deny that the administration may exercise discretionary power concerning the aid schedule and do allow the minister of Health and Welfare some room for exercising technical discretion. Therefore, the conclusion reached by the judgment below must be accepted to that extent.

Proceeding to the factors not directly related to life support, the judgment below took into consideration many factors in judging the propriety of the aid schedule in the present case such as budget priorities. (As to the budget in particular, the judgment below mentions that the minister of Health and Welfare had not kept the aid schedule too low because, although the budget recognized to some extent the need for social security expenditures, there were insufficient funds in the budget; but that the minister justly managed a proper budget as necessary to maintain a balance between social security expenditures and various other financial expenditures.) Consideration of these factors in setting an assistance schedule should be left to the discretion of the minister of Health and Welfare. His judgment does not raise questions of illegality, unless it runs counter to the aims and purposes of the law. There may be some unfortunate phraseology in the judgment below in viewing the act of setting up an aid schedule as an act of limited discretion, while accepting the above-mentioned factors as a basis for deciding the propriety of the aid schedule. Such defects, however, have no influence upon the result of the judgment. The ground of appeal in this point has no validity and therefore should be rejected.

(2) Regarding the third and fifth grounds of appeal, including the second supplemental reason for appeal:

The judgment below states that the adoption by the minister of Health and Welfare of the so-called market-basket method* of calculating standard amounts for the livelihood assistance schedule may not be unreasonable. This is understandable in light of the evidence produced before the court. Furthermore, there is no violation of laws or ordinances in the judgment below, inasmuch as the lower court, in making its decision, exercised its judgment within the necessary limits and held appropriate for the present case the process and results of calculations made in determining the livelihood assistance schedule. The grounds for appeal on this point . . . contain a claim of unconstitutionality which is in substance nothing more than an alleged violation of statutes and cannot be upheld.

Next, based upon the facts of this case, I shall explain my point of view more concretely, in reference to the alleged illegality and unconstitutionality of the judgment below, which held that the livelihood assistance schedule in this case was not so low as to be illegal.

The livelihood aid schedule in the present case was established in July 1953; since social conditions changed considerably due to a rise in commodity prices, an order was issued to raise the level of aid around August 1956. The schedule was revised in April 1957, eight months after the order was issued. When all these things are taken into consideration, we must admit that the schedule in August 1956 was too low for that time, but that this fact alone does not immediately render illegal the livelihood aid schedule at issue.

In the first place, the minimum standard of living guaranteed by the Livelihood Protection Law means not only the minimum standard of living to maintain existence as human beings; it also requires that such a standard be such as to maintain standards of wholesome and cultured living (Article 3), and that the content of the assistance be determined effectively and appropriately by taking into consideration the practical needs of the individual concerned and his family (Article 9). The standard must be such as to satisfy these needs; but at the same time, it should not be more than that (Article 8, paragraph 2). The degree of assistance guaranteed by the Livelihood Protection Law cannot be so great as not to make the beneficiary feel inferior to his neighbors. Particularly when the beneficiary is an in-patient, as in this case, we must also pay attention to certain limitations arising from special conditions of his life, such as long-term hospitalization and medical purposes. In such cases, it cannot be denied that the amount of allowance for incidentals has something to do with an effective cure of the disease and that a shortage in the amount, even a little, may sometimes adversely affect the patient. In order to satisfy needs and make the assistance level appropriate, the Livelihood Protection Law establishes the types and limits of aid, divides the scheme of protection into cases of single and multiple allow-

*According to this formula, necessary living expenses are the total market price of all necessary items taken together.

ance, provides for medical aid, including meal service and livelihood aid for in-patients, and also establishes rehabilitation aid under a separate category. One cannot arbitrarily claim that additional expenditures are required to effectuate medical cure, to supplement the shortcomings of the present medical and nursing systems, or to secure a person's livelihood after he leaves the hospital. Neither can it be said that these additional expenses are necessary daily expenses, and that failure to include them in the computation of the livelihood aid schedule rendered the law invalid. Furthermore, the so-called "costs for extra meals" are not a matter of livelihood aid (allowance for incidentals), but of medical aid, for meal services are provided within the program of medical care. Therefore, we cannot hastily agree with the view that "costs for extra meals" should be included within the livelihood aid schedule in the form of a cash allowance. . . . The propriety as a general scale of the livelihood aid schedule debated in this case can be decided only by a consideration of ordinary articles of daily use excluding articles that might be provided under special schedules and so on.

When these considerations are kept in mind, we cannot conclude at all that, in the factual situation ascertained by the judgment below, the determination made by the minister of Health and Welfare in finding the livelihood aid schedule sufficient to meet the minimum cost of daily articles for hospitalized patients exceeded or abused the discretionary power entrusted to him by the law. As pointed out before, the above schedule was revised in April 1957, only eight months after August 1956, when the order changing the level of aid was issued. It is apparent from a comparison of the revised schedule with that in this case that the revised schedule included some new items, improved the quality of some common items, and increased the unit costs of other items. As the aid schedule improved, keeping pace with the development of the cultural and economic situation of the nation, it would not be fair to conclude on the basis of the revised schedule that the livelihood aid schedule at issue, which was set up three years earlier, was established arbitrarily by the minister of Health and Welfare.

Furthermore, according to the facts established in the judgment below, our national economy did not show any significant change between the period July 1953 and the end of 1954; but it grew rapidly in the 1955 fiscal year, and attained a higher level of growth than anyone had imagined possible in the 1956 fiscal year, especially in the latter half of the same year. This caused a natural increase in the nation's tax income, higher levels of consumption, and a rise in the commodity prices. In August 1956 when the order at issue was given, the content of the livelihood aid schedule in this case was already insufficient to maintain minimum standards of wholesome and cultured living under the improved social conditions. The schedule had to be revised sooner or later.

The judgment below, however, has justly confirmed that the degree of inadequacy in the aid was not so great as to be ineffective in protecting the livelihood of the in-patients. We must also note the facts that it takes a considerable length of time to conduct investigation for a revision of a schedule and that the actual change in business trends then could not be grasped accurately until the next fiscal year. When these facts are taken into consideration, the task of constantly adjusting an assistance schedule set up at a certain time to later changes in living conditions is an extremely difficult one. The gap between the schedule stated above and realities of life must be accepted as "an unavoidable evil" by law, as long as the adoption of a schedule system is accepted as a reasonable means of administration.

As stated before, the establishment of the lifelihood aid schedule in this case followed a theoretical means of calculation called the "market-basket method," which cannot be called unreasonable, Insofar as the gap between the above-mentioned schedule and the reality of life is to the extent examined above, although 600 yen monthly livelihood allowance may be criticized as being too low to cover daily incidental expenses, it is a matter of propriety which can be remedied by administrative actions. Consequently, we can only approve the conclusion of the judgment below that there is no illegality involved in this instance which is worthy of receiving judicial relief, even though we admit that there are certain imperfections in the market-basket method, and that even a small shortage in the allowance for incidentals may have adverse effects upon patients. Thus, I find no misinterpretation of the Constitution or statutes and no violation of the statutes in the process of judgment, as alleged. The complaint cannot be sustained because it argues illegality of the judgment below from a point of view that contradicts the reasons stated above and criticizes the selection of evidence and finding of facts, both of which are exclusively the function of the court below.

(3) Concerning the fourth reason in the appeal:

The judgment below finds that the livelihood aid schedule in the case at hand was designed primarily for the protection of patients with slight and moderate illnesses. With respect to these patients, the schedule, which does not include the cost of extra meals for seriously ill patients, cannot be said to be too low. In the case of the appellant himself, the lower court admitted that in August 1956, when the order under attack was issued, Shigeru Asahi was suffering from tuberculosis complications . . . and malnutrition and needed extra pajamas and such due to a perspiration problem. Yet, he was generally forced to suffer from a shortage of clothing. But the lower court also found that the hospital operated under a system of maintaining a short-term supply and of loaning pajamas and such; that the night clothes he actually obtained on loan were uncomfortably thick, but could be worn; and that between June 1955 and May

1958 he was not in need of any special outlays for special incidentals. Checking the evidence admitted in the court below, it is possible to agree with its finding, which is without illegality. . . .

Furthermore, the judgment below found that after the issuance of the order changing the status of aid, the Okayama Sanitarium reduced the amount Asahi paid for medical expenses from 900 yen to 500 yen a month, on the grounds that there was increased need for incidentals and for special foods suitable to his tastes; that for three years between July 1955 and May 1958, Shigeru Asahi's own expenses for incidentals averaged as high as 1,040 yen a month, because of the above-mentioned reduction in his allowance, and because of the extra financial aid he received from other sources; and that as alleged in the grounds for complaint against the decision changing the status of aid, he asked the authority to appropriate an additional 400 yen as monthly expenses for food he liked because his illness was serious, although he did not especially complain about the lack of an allowance for incidental expenses itself. It is clear from the reasoning of the judgment below that these findings contributed to the conclusion of the court below. . . . The reasoning in the complaint is nothing more than a description of the circumstances and does not influence the conclusion of the judgment below, which is proper. There is no violation of the Constitution or statutes, and the appeal on this point cannot be sustained.

4. As stated above, the livelihood aid schedule and the decision to change the status of aid in this case cannot be hastily called unconstitutional or illegal, nor is it possible to declare them to be null and void. The appeal is to be dismissed. As a judicial argument, such is the only possible conclusion that can be accepted. Assuming that the Livelihood Protection Law concerns itself with the administration of a great number of beneficiaries, it is inevitable that a certain "livelihood aid schedule" be set up to aid in the administration of its program, and it requires much time to conduct investigation for revision of the schedule. In order to implement the spirit of Article 25 of the Constitution, however, the government must conduct constant investigations and take special care that the protection offered keeps pace with the realities of life appropriately and promptly. Admitting that the adoption of a livelihood aid schedule is unavoidable, the authorities are expected to apply it in a way that allows some room for practical discretion in its operation so that the gap between the schedule and the real conditions of life can be filled properly and promptly. Livelihood assistance is not a system granted as a benefice but is guaranteed as a right. However, if the officer in charge of the administration of this scheme considers it only as a matter of right and duty and fails in the humane consideration of beneficiaries, the aims and purposes of the system cannot be realized. After all, the appellant fails in this suit and the government as the respondent wins, not because the measures at issue were appropriate, but because they were not illegal.

The government should take this situation seriously; and I do hope that the authorities and the officials in charge of administering livelihood assistance will give serious thought to a more effective administration of medical care and take necessary measures to meet the strong desires of the nation as a whole.

Justices Toshio Irie, Ken'ichi Okuno, Asanosuke Kusaka, Kingo Osabe, Yoshihiko Kido, Kazuto Ishida, Goroku Kashiwabara, Jirō Tanaka, Jirō Matsuda, Makoto Iwata, and Kazuo Shimomura. Chief Justice Kisaburō Yokota and Justice Kakiwa Gokijyō did not sign due to their retirement.

Case 15. Katō v. *Japan (1964).* The Textbook Fee Case

18 *Minshū* 2 at p. 343; Supreme Court, Grand Bench, 26 February 1964; Tokyo Dist. Ct. (First Instance), Tokyo High Ct. (Second Instance), [constitutionality of fees charged for textbooks in compulsory education system].

EDITORIAL NOTE: In the 1960s Japan's young people were required to attend six years of elementary school and three years of junior high school, but most were also attending senior high school by the 1970s. The guardian of a public elementary school pupil paid 865 yen (ca. $2.50) in textbook fees over a two-year period. The guardian sued the state in court for reimbursement of the 865 yen, arguing that since Article 26, paragraph 2 of the Constitution requires establishment of a free compulsory education system, the government should also pay for all textbooks necessary in the course of the years of compulsory education. He also sought a court order to prevent the government from collecting an additional 5,836 yen, the estimated textbook fees he would have to pay on behalf of his charge during the remainder of his years of compulsory education. Following an adverse judgment by the Tokyo High Court, the plaintiff appealed to the Supreme Court.

REFERENCES

Constitution of Japan, [ARTICLE 26 was at issue in this case. See Appendix 3 for this provision].

FORMAL JUDGMENT

The appeal in the present case is dismissed.

REASONS. Regarding the reasons for appeal by the appellant, the Court holds as follows:

Article 26 of the Constitution guarantees all the people the right to receive an equal education. At the same time, it prescribes a free, compulsory education under which all are obliged to have all boys and girls under their protection receive the minimum, ordinary education. However, one may not judge hastily that the system of compulsory education necessarily implies payment of all expenses required to educate children. The Constitution imposes the responsibility upon guardians to educate children not simply because a good education is necessary for the existence and prosperity of a democratic nation; the imposition of this duty also intends the carrying out of the guardians' responsibility to educate their own children, because it is necessary and indispensable for the children's maturation and character development. Therefore, it cannot be said that the state should naturally bear all the expenses necessary for such a compulsory education.

The statement that "such compulsory education shall be free" in Article 26, paragraph 2 of the Constitution means that the state should not charge money for compulsory education; in other words, no monetary compensation is to be collected from the children's guardians for them to receive the ordinary education. Since monetary compensation for education means tuition, it is proper to construe nonremuneration in the said Article as forbidding the collection of tuition. This construction also conforms to developments in the past, in that compulsory education is generally provided without monthly remuneration at schools established by the state and publicly financed. Moreover, Article 4, paragraph 2 of the Fundamental Law of Education, and Article 6, the proviso of the School Education Law both provide that no tuition shall be charged for compulsory education and can be construed to conform to the above intent of the Constitution. The constitutional provision that compulsory education shall be free cannot be interpreted to provide that in addition to the absence of tuition, all expenses including textbooks, school supplies, and other things necessary for education must be free of charge.

Since the Constitution makes it a duty of all the people to have the boys and girls under their protection receive the ordinary education, it is desirable that the state should try to decrease as much as possible the cost of buying textbooks to be borne by guardians. However, this kind of matter should be viewed as a problem of legislative policy, which must take into account the condition of national finance and should not be prescribed in a legal provision such as the above-mentioned provision of the Constitution.

The judgment below that adopted the same opinion as the above was appropriate. The appellant's contentions are only one man's view and cannot be accepted. Consequently, this Court decides as stated in the Formal Judgment, in accordance with Articles 401, 95, and 89 of the Code of Civil Procedure. This judgment is the unanimous opinion of all the justices.

Justices Kisaburō Yokota (presiding), Toshio Irie, Ken'ichi Okuno, Shūichi Ishizaka, Sakunosuke Yamada, Kakiwa Gokijyō, Masatoshi Yokota, Kitarō Saitō, Asanosuke Kusaka, Kingo Osabe, Yoshihiko Kido, Kazuto Ishida, and Goroku Kashiwabara.

Chapter 8

The Right to Participate in Election Politics (Sanseiken)

The right to participate in election politics (sanseiken), *as a category of constitutional law cases, includes much more than the right to vote. Among the other matters encompassed by this Japanese category are the prohibition of election canvassing, restrictions on the campaign activities of public employees, the freedom of candidacy, the regulation of corporate campaign contributions, and standing in an election suit.*

Case 16. Taniguchi v. *Japan (1967).* The Taniguchi Canvassing Case

21 *Keishū* 9 at p. 1245; Supreme Court, Third Petty Bench, 21 November 1967; Nagoya Dist. Ct. (First Instance), Nagoya High Ct. (Second Instance), [constitutionality of a law prohibiting door-to-door election canvassing].

EDITORIAL NOTE: The accused had visited the homes of fourteen voters in June 1965 to solicit votes for two Communist Party candidates prior to a House of Councillors election. He was charged with violating the Public Office Election Law, which prohibits door-to-door election canvassing, and he responded by contesting the constitutionality of the prohibition.

Both the Nagoya District Court (28 April 1966) and the Nagoya High Court (4 May 1967) found the accused guilty. The first instance court noted that freedom of speech under Article 21 of the Constitution is not absolute, and that the time, place, and manner of speech can be justifiably restricted for the public welfare (*kōkyō no fukushi*). Door-to-door canvassing is prohibited in the law partly because it tends to encourage such unfair practices as bribery and inducement to vote for vested interests, and partly because it disturbs the voters' peace. The accused filed an unsuccessful appeal, acted on by a Petty Bench of the Supreme Court, but sentiment and judicial decisions against the prohibition continued.

REFERENCES

Constitution of Japan [ARTICLES 15, 21, 37, and 38 were at issue in this case. See Appendix 3 for these provisions].

Public Office Election Law (Law 100 of 15 April 1950), ARTICLE 138, 1. No one shall conduct a door-to-door canvass with the intention of soliciting a vote for oneself or another person or to prevent the voter from voting for another person.

ARTICLE 239. A person who violates the provision of any one of the items below shall be imprisoned not longer than one year or fined no more than 15,000 yen [approximately $41.66 at the time].

(3) A person who conducts a door-to-door canvass in violation of Article 138 (on a door-to-door canvass). . . .

FORMAL JUDGMENT

The *jōkoku* appeal in the present case is dismissed.

REASONS. Concerning point 1 of the argument for appeal by attorneys N. Sakurai, N. Amano, K. Ōya, K. Hanada, I. Andō, Y. Itō, T. Sakamoto, M. Gō, T. Ozeki, G. Harayama (formerly G. Maejima), Y. Ishikawa, S. Fujii, and K. Harayama:

The defense counsels contend that the provisions of Article 138, paragraph 1 of the Public Office Election Law violates Article 21 of the Constitution. However, since door-to-door election canvassing may encourage various evils and impair fair elections, the said provision of the Public Office Election Law has prohibited all kinds of door-to-door canvassing carried out with an intention stipulated therein. The law, therefore, should not be construed to ban only door-to-door canvassing involving practices that substantively violate the spirit of fair elections, such as bribery, threats, or inducements to vote for special interests, or that which poses a clear and present danger to fair elections. The present Court in a Grand Bench decision (4 *Keishū* 1799; 27 September 1950) has already ruled that the measure of insuring fair elections by banning door-to-door canvassing may result in a certain degree of restriction on the freedom of speech, but does not violate Article 21 of the Constitution. Consequently, both this portion of the defense argument and the rest of point 1, which merely contends error in fact-finding and rule-application, lack proper grounds for *jōkoku* appeal.

Concerning point 2 of the argument, the contention of the defense to the contrary notwithstanding, a previous decision by the Grand Bench of this Court has ruled that Article 252 of the Public Office Election Law does not violate Article 15, paragraph 1 of the Constitution (9 *Keishū* 217; 9 February 1955). Consequently, neither this point nor the rest of the argument, which merely alleges error in rule-application, can be accepted as proper grounds for *jōkoku* appeal.

Concerning point 3 of the defense argument, the assertion that the weighing of the offense is improper does not constitute a reason for appeal.

Concerning point 4, the defense contends the said Election Law (in light of Articles 37 and 38 of the Constitution) is unconstitutional, but the present Court in a Grand Bench decision (11 *Keishū* 802; 20 February 1957) has ruled that the defendant does not have the right not to disclose his own name. The selection by the defendant of his counsel should be held invalid for failing without proper reason to sign the form prepared for requesting the assignment of defense counsel (19 *Keishū* 591; Sup. Ct., 3rd. P.B., 20 July 1965). Thus, point 4 is groundless.

Also, a close examination of the record does not provide grounds for applying Article 411 of the Code of Criminal Procedure to the present case. Consequently, the present Court, by the unanimous decision of the justices, decides as in the Formal Judgment, in accordance with Article 408 of the Code of Criminal Procedure.

Justices Masao Matsumoto (presiding), Jirō Tanaka, and Kazuo Shimomura.

Case 17. Iwasaki v. *Japan (1962).* The Election Invalidation Case

16 *Minshū* 3 at p. 537; Supreme Court, Grand Bench, 14 March 1962; Hiroshima High Ct. (First Instance), [constitutionality of a law invalidating an election by reason of campaign manager's crime].

EDITORIAL NOTE: The election campaign manager of a successful candidate in the Hiroshima Prefecture Assembly election of 23 April 1959 was convicted of violating the election law and sentenced to a year of imprisonment, with a three-year stay of execution. The defendant, the assemblyman-elect, challenged a suit filed by two voters in his district who contended that his election should be invalidated since his campaign manager had been found guilty of violating the Public Office Election Law. The Hiroshima High Court sustained their position, and the defendant appealed to the Supreme Court. He maintained that the relevant provisions of the election law are contrary to due process and to Articles 13 and 15 of the Constitution, and he stated that he did not know of the criminal act of his campaign manager, that his status as an assembly-man elect should be recognized absent grave reason, that his status can better be invalidated, if need be, by a new election than by other means, and finally, that the law deviates from the proper objectives of an election suit in invalidating a trust established by the voters because of a violation by a campaign manager.

REFERENCES

Constitution of Japan [ARTICLES 13, 15, and 31 were at issue in this case. See Appendix 3 for these provisions].

Public Office Election Law (*Law 100 of 1950*), ARTICLE 211, 1. Electors or candidates may initiate a suit against a successful candidate for a public office within thirty days from the election at a High Court, seeking a court decision to invalidate the latter's victory on grounds of Article 251-2, paragraph 1 (disqualification of a successful candidate due to an election law violation by his manager or treasurer), when an election campaign manager or treasurer of the successful candidate has been convicted of having committed a crime under Article 221 (bribery and inducement for special interests); Article 222 (bribing for the interests of a plurality of people); Article 223 (bribing for the interests of candidates, both successful and unsuccessful); or Article 223-2 (an unlawful use of newspapers and magazines).

2. Electors or candidates may initiate a suit against a successful candidate for a public office within thirty days from the election at a High Court, seeking a court decision to invalidate his victory on grounds of provisions of Article 251-2, paragraph 2 (disqualification due to a violation by a campaign treasurer of the legally-fixed election expenditures), when a campaign treasurer has been convicted of the offense of spending in excess of the amount allowed by law, as stipulated in Article 247 herein.

ARTICLE 251-2, 1. A successful candidate shall be disqualified when his election manager or treasurer has been indicted and convicted of having committed a crime under Article 221 (bribery and inducement for special interests); Article 222 (bribing for the interests of a plurality of people); Article 223 (bribing for the interests of candidates, both successful and unsuccessful); or Article 223-2 (an unlawful use of newspapers and magazines). But in case an act falls under the provisions of any one of the items below, it will be decided otherwise, as long as the alleged offense is concerned.

(1) When a person other than an election campaign manager or treasurer instigates acts stipulated herein with the intention of defeating his own candidate in collaboration with an opposing candidate or his campaign workers.

(2) When the manager or treasurer commits the crime stipulated herein in collaboration with opposing candidates or their campaign workers with the objective of defeating the opponent(s).

2. A successful candidate shall be disqualified when his campaign treasurer is charged and convicted with violating Article 247 (the lawful limit of campaign expenditures). The proviso in the preceding paragraph shall be applicable hereto.

FORMAL JUDGMENT

The *jōkoku* appeal in the present case is dismissed.

REASONS. Concerning points 1 and 2 of the argument for appeal by Attorney Y. Hayakawa:

It is contended that Article 251-2 and Article 211 of the Public Office Election Law are invalid as in contravention of the provisions of Articles 13, 15, and 31 of the Constitution.

As contended, the revision of the Public Office Election Law, effected by Law 207 of December 1954, strengthened the provision concerning guilt by association by removing the following reason from the so-called "escape clause": "When a successful candidate has paid proper attention to the selection and supervision of his election campaign manager." The intention behind the strengthened regulations concerning guilt by association was to insure a fair election of public officials by a free expression of voters' decisions. Since a manager in an election campaign acts as a principal promoter for a given candidate and exercises supervisory authority over every aspect of the election campaign, a manager who had violated the provisions of Article 251-2 of the Public Office Election Law would probably affect not only the election of his candidate, but also the free nature of the votes cast for the particular candidate. Since such a candidate would not have been elected in a fair election, making his victory void would conform to the spirit of the election system, even without reference to his negligence in selecting and supervising his campaign manager. Arguments to the contrary . . . alleging the unconstitutionality of Articles 251-2 and 211 of the Public Office Election Law cannot be accepted.

Regarding point 3, a contention that merely challenges the decision by the court below on the election manager does not constitute proper grounds for *jōkoku* appeal.

Consequently, the Court, by the unanimous decision of the justices, decides as in the Formal Judgment, in accordance with Articles 401, 95, and 89 of the Code of Criminal Procedure.

Justices Kisaburō Yokota (presiding), Kitarō Saitō, Hachirō Fujita, Matasuke Kawamura, Toshio Irie, Katsu Ikeda, Katsumi Tarumi, Daisuke Kawamura, Ken'ichi Okuno, Tsuneshichi Takagi, Shūichi Ishizaka, Sakunosuke Yamada, and Kakiwa Gokijyō.

Chapter 9

Procedural Questions

Articles 31 to 40 of the Constitution of Japan (See Appendix 3 for these provisions) provide the basis for Japan's system of procedural justice. See also the Introduction.

Case 18. Kojima v. *Japan (1966).* The Kojima Double Jeopardy Case

20 *Keishū* 6 at p. 609; Supreme Court, Grand Bench, 13 July 1966; Tokyo Dist. Ct. (First Instance), Tokyo High Ct. (Second Instance), [constitutionality of using criminal record in assessing penalties for a later crime].

EDITORIAL NOTE: In Japan it is very common to send cash by a special form of registered mail called *kakitome*; the use of personal checking accounts is not as widespread as in the United States. Thus, theft of funds by postal workers under such a system is an especially serious matter.

In this case a postal worker was convicted of stealing three pieces of mail containing cash and was sentenced to a year-and-a-half imprisonment, but with a five-year stay of execution. The prosecutor appealed the light sentence, citing the past criminal record of the accused. The Tokyo High Court imposed a sentence of ten months in prison without a stay of execution, noting that the motives of the accused left no room for compassion, since the crime was vicious and had serious repercussions on society as well as on the victims. In his appeal to the Supreme Court, the accused claimed double jeopardy (Article 39 of the Constitution) and violation of constitutional due process by reference to past offenses in the determination of a sentence.

REFERENCES

Constitution of Japan [ARTICLES 31, 38, and 39 were at issue in this case. See Appendix 3 for these provisions.

Code of Criminal Procedure (*Law 131 of 1948*), ARTICLE 317, 1. The ascertaining of facts shall be based on evidence.

ARTICLE 319, 2. No person shall be convicted in a case where the only proof against him is his own confession made during or outside of public trial.

FORMAL JUDGMENT

The *jōkoku* appeal in the present case is dismissed.

REASONS. Concerning point 1 of the argument for appeal by attorney M. Suzuki:

To ascertain facts on an unindicted crime is prohibited in a criminal trial, as is their use in weighing an indicted crime of an accused, thereby punishing the accused more heavily than would have been the case had only the indicted crime been weighed. Finding and using facts of crime not formally prosecuted with the above-mentioned intention violates not only the basic principle of "no indictment, no trial" of the Code of Criminal Procedure, but also the provision of Article 31 of the Constitution which guarantees that "no person shall be subject to any criminal penalty, except according to procedure established by law." Furthermore, it would violate the provision of Article 317 of the Code of Criminal Procedure setting forth the principle of a trial on the basis of evidence, and it may violate the restriction imposed on the use of confession and supporting evidence in Article 38, paragraph 3 of the Constitution and Article 319, paragraphs 2 and 3 of the Code of Criminal Procedure. Since there is no legal guarantee that an accused may not be prosecuted on other crimes later, to indict and convict an accused party on these other charges later would be to hold the defendant criminally liable for an act that had already been used in weighing the conviction of the defendant, and would thereby violate the provisions of Article 39 of the Constitution.

On the other hand, a court should decide a criminal case as it sees best by weighing all factors, including the character and background of the accused and his motive, objective, and method of crime. Therefore, a court is not necessarily prohibited from taking into account unindicted crimes as an additional factor in examining indicted crimes. (Of course, an examination of evidence of those charges that are not indicted should be confined to a reasonable minimum in each case and should not by indiscretion exceed the reasonable limits of the court's discretion.) A public indictment is not required in order to take into consideration unindicted crimes as an additional factor in examining an offense, because such consideration is not to ascertain and punish an unprosecuted crime. Using unindicted crimes as material with which to determine such additional elements as the character and background of the accused and his motives, objective, and method in crime differs from the finding and using of unindicted crimes to increase the punishment to be imposed upon the indicted crimes. A court of fact-finding should, therefore, be careful not to confuse the difference between the two.

As the defense contends, the court below stated that "judging from the fact that the accused had committed similar crimes many times during the six-month period prior to the present crime, and used the money for drinking, living expenses, and other personal use. . . ." However, this quoted passage from the decision below does not refer to such unindicted facts as the time of theft and the amount of stolen money but describes in detail the way the stolen money was spent, a fact that is not related to the existence of the crime. A close reading of other sentences therein would lead us to construe the above-quoted statement to have been used by the court as an additional element in determining the character of the accused and his motive and objective in the charged offense of theft, rather than as a basis for punishing the indicted offense heavily with the intention of punishing unindicted crimes as well. Thus, the argument for unconstitutionality is weak in its premises and cannot be accepted.

Concerning point 2, the contention . . . is a mere insistence that there has been an unreasonable weighing of the offense (though it may seem to be a constitutional issue) and does not constitute a proper ground for *jōkoku* appeal.

Neither does a close examination of the record justify the application of the provision of Article 411 of the Code of Criminal Procedure.

Consequently, in accordance with the provisions of Articles 414 and 396 of the Code of Criminal Procedure, the Court decides as in the Formal Judgment.

This judgment is the opinion of all the justices except for the opinion of Justices Kisaburō Yokota, Ken'ichi Okuno, Masatoshi Yokota, Asanosuke Kusaka, Yoshihiko Kido, and Jirō Tanaka.

* * *

The opinion of Justices Kisaburō Yokota, Ken'ichi Okuno, Masatoshi Yokota, Asanosuke Kusaka, Yoshihiko Kido, and Jirō Tanaka follows.

[Some eight sentences from the majority opinion are omitted here.]

In response to a prosecutor's brief for *kōso* appeal concerning other crimes of the accused not prosecuted, the court below stated that "in judging from such additional elements as the nature, manner, and motive of the present crime, the age, character and conduct, family and other background of the accused, circumstances after the crime, and the social effects of the present crime, as they are revealed in the court's record of facts, . . . the present, extremely vicious crime will have a grave impact on injured parties and society, as argued by the prosecuting attorney, and. . . ." This is followed by another statement that "judging from the fact that the accused had committed similar crimes many times during the six-month period prior to the present crime, and used the money for drinking, living expenses, and other personal use." This quoted statement, which was made after the overall judgment on additional factors in weighing the indicted offense, should be construed to describe those crimes that are not prosecuted. Furthermore, judging from the opinion of the court below, which concluded that the accused had repeatedly committed similar crimes, the quoted remark was, in fact, to ascertain the unindicted crimes and punish the accused more heavily than would have been the case had they examined only the crime indicted in the instant case. Convicting the accused on unindicted crimes would violate the provisions of Article 31 of the Constitution. It would also violate the provision of Article 38, paragraph 3 of the Constitution since it is obvious from a reading of the record that some facts of the unindicted crimes have been ascertained only from a confession of the accused. (Moreover, Article 39 of the Constitution would be violated should the accused be indicted at a later date on those crimes that were not prosecuted in the present case.)

However, even if the unprosecuted crimes have been discounted, still the court below was proper in weighing the offense in the light of the magnitude of the crime in the present case. The decision below is not affected by the suspected unconstitutionality on this point and should not be reversed.

Justices Kisaburō Yokota (presiding), Toshio Irie, Ken'ichi Okuno, Kakiwa Gokijyō, Masatoshi Yokota, Asanosuke Kusaka, Kingo Osabe, Yoshihiko Kido, Kazuto Ishida, Goroku Kashiwabara, Jirō Tanaka, Jirō Matsuda, Makoto Iwata, and Saburō Shimomura.

Case 19. Japan v. *Arima (1961)*. The Arima Narcotics Seizure Case

15 *Keishū* 6 at p. 915; Supreme Court, Grand Bench, 7 June 1961; Osaka Dist. Ct. (First Instance), Osaka High Ct. (Second Instance), [constitutionality of a narcotics search and seizure attendant to an arrest under conditions of urgency].

EDITORIAL NOTE: One fall evening in 1955 following the arrest of an individual for unlawful possession of drugs, four drug control officers went to the home of the accused, who had delivered the drugs to the person just arrested. The accused was not home, but with the consent of his seventeen-year-old daughter, the officers searched the house and discovered additional narcotics and related evidence, but prior to the issuance of a search warrant. Upon the return of the accused, the drugs were seized and he was arrested.

The Osaka District Court convicted the accused of unlawful possession and delivery of drugs, but the Osaka High Court acquitted him of the possession charge, on the grounds that the search was without true consent, since the daughter did not understand the meaning of search and seizure, and that the search and seizure was illegal, thus rendering the resulting evidence inadmissible in court. The Prosecutor's Office appealed the case to the Supreme Court.

References

Constitution of Japan [ARTICLES 33 and 35 were at issue in this case. See Appendix 3 for these provisions].

Code of Criminal Procedure (*Law 131 of 1948*), Article 210. A public prosecutor, public prosecutor's assistant official, or judicial police official may arrest a suspect after informing him or her of the reason for arrest, if there is sufficient reason to believe that the suspect has committed an offense that will result in capital punishment, imprisonment for life, or more than three years with or without hard labor, and if a warrant for arrest cannot be obtained from a judge because of the urgency of such an arrest. They shall immediately proceed to secure a warrant from a judge, following such an arrest. In case a warrant is not forthcoming, the suspect shall be immediately released.

Article 220, 1. A public prosecutor, public prosecutor's assistant official, or judicial police official may take the following action, if necessary, in arresting a suspect or an offender at the scene of crime, by provision of Article 199. The same shall apply when arresting a suspect under the provisions of Article 210.

(1) To search a suspect by entering a home, building or vessel in which people live or watch.

(2) To search, seize or inspect at the site of arrest.

2. In case a warrant is unobtainable, as stated in the latter part of the preceding paragraph, an object seized shall be immediately returned.

3. No warrant is necessary in disposing of matters in paragraph 1.

4. The provisions of paragraph 1, item 2 and the preceding paragraph shall be applicable where a member of the staff of the prosecutor's office or a judicial police official carries out a warrant for arrest or detention. Paragraph 1, item 1 shall also be applicable in carrying out a warrant issued to arrest or detain a suspect.

Article 309, 1. A prosecutor, an accused, or his attorney may lodge an objection to a taking of evidence.

2. In addition to the preceding paragraph, they may lodge an objection to a disposition by a presiding judge.

3. A court shall decide on an objection lodged under the preceding two paragraphs.

Article 326, 1. Written or oral statements that a prosecutor and an accused agree to use as evidence may be used as evidence in spite of Article 321 and the preceding Article as long as they are reasonable after considering the circumstances under which the written or oral statements were made.

2. Where the taking of evidence in the absence of an accused is permissible, his absence may be construed to be his consent, as required in the preceding paragraph. This is not the case where a representative or attorney of the accused is present.

Formal Judgment

1. The judgment below is quashed.
2. This case is remanded to the Osaka High Court.

REASONS. With regard to the purport of the appeal presented by Y. Yoneda, Deputy Prosecutor under the Chief Prosecutor, Osaka High Public Prosecutor's Office:

It is contended that the court below erred in applying a court precedent. But a decision of the Supreme Court Third Petty Bench, cited by the appellant, deals with the issue of whether or not goods seized can be used as evidence and is not applicable to the present case. Furthermore, it is clear from a reading of the decision below that the court below did not contradict a decision of the Tokyo High Court, cited in its opinion. Thus, the appellant's contentions do not follow the decision below and cannot become proper grounds for appeal.

According to our investigations, whereas Article 35 of the Constitution allows search and seizure without the search warrant required in Article 33 therein, this Court held in its 14 December 1955 decision that Article 210 of the Code of Criminal Procedure, which recognizes arrest under conditions of urgency, is not in violation of Article 33 of the Constitution (19 *Keishū* 2760, G.B., 14 December 1955).

Article 35 of the Constitution should be construed to constitute an exception to the principle of search and seizure with a search warrant, so long as the search and seizure without a search warrant is conducted incidental to an arrest and can be carried out without an unreasonable infringement upon human rights. The provision in Article 220 in the Code of Criminal Procedure which does not require a search warrant for search and seizure at the time of an arrest under urgent conditions fulfills the intent of Article 35 of the Constitution.

The phrases "in a case of apprehension" and "at the time of arrest" in the Code of Criminal Procedure need clarification. The former phrase should be construed to refer to the broad context of arrest rather than to any specific time, and the latter phrase should designate the same place as an arrest. Furthermore, the former requires a connection, in time, between search and seizure on the one hand and the arrest on the other. But which comes first, the search and seizure or the arrest, is not relevant; this construction is also derived from paragraph 1, item 1 of the same provision. For example, drug control officers who attempt an arrest of a suspect under conditions of urgency at his place, and who find him absent, may commence a search and seizure under such circumstances to prepare for his arrest immediately upon his return or incidental to an intended arrest. Under these circumstances, there is nothing to prevent us from interpreting such a search and seizure as conducted incidental to an arrest under conditions of urgency.

The search and seizure incidental to such an arrest, when conducted to secure evidence of a suspected crime that is the reason for the arrest, and when judged to be within the scope of such an objective, should be construed as conforming to the requirements of paragraph 1, the latter section of Article 220 of the Code of Criminal Procedure which states "if necessary in arresting a suspect."

A review of the search and seizure conducted in the instant case shows that about 8:30 P.M. on 11 October 1955, four drug control officers questioned and arrested on the street Miss Mitsue Segami on a charge of possessing drugs. Around 9:30 P.M. they took her to Mr. Ki'ichi Arima's home with the intent of arresting him on suspicion of selling drugs to Miss Segami. When they found him absent, they began to search his home and confiscated the magazine apparently used for wrapping the drugs (Exhibits 1 [1] and 1 [2] in the first instance trial). The search was nearly completed when the suspect arrived home around 9:50 P.M., when he was promptly arrested. A search warrant was immediately issued by a judge upon request.

Thus, the present case falls into the category of an apprehension under conditions of urgency. The search and seizure and the arrest took place at the same place and almost simultaneously, although the former preceded the latter. This can be interpreted as a search and seizure made at the place and time of arrest, and we find it to be within the limits incidental to an arrest in conditions of urgency. Consequently, there is no reason to hold it unconstitutional and unlawful.

However, the judgment below held that search and seizure conducted in accordance with Article 220, paragraph 1, the Latter Section of the Code of Criminal Procedure must follow and not precede such an arrest; that a search and seizure incident to such an arrest should be limited to evidence directed to the facts of the suspected crime that is the basis of the arrest and should not be extended to evidence related to other crimes; that drug control officers went to Mr. Ki'ichi Arima's home to arrest him, and when they found him absent started searching his place and confiscated the drugs (Exhibit 1 [2] at the first instance trial) before he returned home to be arrested; and that the search and seizure in the present case must be held unlawful not only because it preceded the arrest, but also for the reason that it was conducted to secure evidence for the separate crime of possessing drugs. The judgment below held that the present search and seizure was without warrant and conforms neither with the provision of Article 220, paragraph 1, Latter Section of the Code of Criminal Procedure, nor with Article 35 of the Constitution; and that the said drugs, which were unlawfully seized, and the drug control officers' report on the present search and seizure should not be admitted to the court as evidence. However, the court below erred in its interpretation of the Constitution and the Code of Criminal Procedure, with effect on the judgment; consequently, the judgment below must be quashed.

Furthermore, it is clear from the record of the trial that the report on search and seizure dated 11 October 1955, prepared by the drug control officers, which was used as supporting evidence following the confession of the accused concerning the Exhibit 1 (2) of the first instance court (i.e., the crime of possessing drugs at the home of the accused on 11 October 1955), and also an opinion dated 17 October 1955, prepared by Mr. Yūzō Nakagawa, a welfare technical officer who examined the drug, were both used as evidence with the consent of the accused and his counsel and met a lawful screening of evidence without objection. Both the report and the expert opinion are permissible as evidence despite the unlawful search and seizure, and there is nothing unlawful in the judgment of the first instance court, which used them as evidence. Therefore, the judgment below is unlawful in this respect and must be quashed.

Consequently, the Court decides, as stated in the Formal Judgment, that the decision below be quashed in accordance with Article 410, the main text, Article 405, item 1 and Article 411, item 1 of the Code of Criminal Procedure, and that this case be remanded to the Osaka High Court in accordance with Article 413, the main text of the same Code.

This judgment is the unanimous opinion of all the justices except for the supplementary opinions of Toshio Irie, Katsu Ikeda, and Katsumi Tarumi, the opinions of Justices Kisaburō Yokota, Hachirō Fujita, and Ken'ichi Okuno, and the dissenting opinions of Justices Katsushige Kotani and Daisuke Kawamura [all of which opinions are here omitted.]

Justices Kisaburō Yokota (presiding), Katsushige Kotani, Tamotsu Shima, Yūsuke Saitō, Hachirō Fujita, Matasuke Kawamura, Toshio Irie, Katsu Ikeda, Katsumi Tarumi, Daisuke Kawamura, Masuo Shimomura, Ken'ichi Okuno, Kiyoshi Takahashi, and Shūichi Ishizaka.

Case 20. Ichikawa et al v. *Japan (1961).* The Ichikawa Hanging Case

15 *Keishū* 7 at p. 1106; Supreme Court, Grand Bench, 19 July 1961; Nagoya Dist. Ct. (First Instance), Nagoya High Ct. (Second Instance), [constitutionality of the method used for capital punishment].

EDITORIAL NOTE: The accused in this case, convicted of burglary and murder, challenged the constitutionality of the method presently used in imposing the death penalty. Japan's Criminal Code, Code of Criminal Procedure, and Prison Law provide for capital punishment and empower persons to authorize the execution of the death penalty whose duties include setting the time and place of the execution, as well as witnessing and recording it. But these Codes do not specify the manner of imposing capital punishment; i.e., the type of equipment, the way to use it, and other details. In these matters, Japan still relies on the 20 February 1873 Cabinet Order No. 65, "A Revised Chart of Hanging Equipment."

In appealing to the Supreme Court, defense counsel maintained:

1. The method prescribed by Cabinet Order No. 65 inflicts cruel punishment, in violation of Article 36 of the Constitution.

2. The Cabinet Ordinance lost its force under the 1947 law concerning ordi-

nances effective when the 1947 Constitution of Japan went into force, and the Diet has not approved the ordinance. Moreover, the present method of underground hanging differs from the method stipulated in the Ordinance, which calls for aboveground gallows.

3. The Nagoya High Court sentenced the accused without specifying under a provision of a law the method of execution, thus contravening Articles 31 and 36 of the Constitution.

REFERENCES

Constitution of Japan [ARTICLES 31 and 36 were at issue in this case. See Appendix 3 for these provisions].

Criminal Code (*Law 45 of 1907*), ARTICLE 11. The death sentence shall be executed by a hanging inside a jail.

FORMAL JUDGMENT

Each appeal in the present case is dismissed.

REASONS. Concerning point 6 in the appeal brief submitted by K. Amano, counsel to the accused, Tetsuo Ichikawa:

It is contended that since there is no legal prescription for the method of executing a death sentence, sentencing to capital punishment by hanging without specifying the method would violate Articles 31 and 36 of the Constitution.

However, there exists no legal ground for acknowledging that Cabinet Order No. 65 of 1873 has been abolished or has become ineffective from its proclamation to the present. All matters concerning the method of executing the death sentence prescribed in the said Order cannot be called legal matters requiring prescription by law, under the old or new Constitution; but the said Order sets forth important matters with regard to the execution of capital punishment (for example, "in carrying out the capital punishment by hanging . . . tie both hands behind the back . . . blindfold the face . . . bring the person up onto the platform and make him stand on the centerboard . . . put the rope around his neck . . . open the trap door . . . let the convicted hang in the air," and so on). These are basic matters concerning the execution of capital punishment. It is proper to construe basic matters concerning the method of execution for grave crimes such as capital punishment as legal matters even under the Meiji Constitution (Article 23 of the Meiji Constitution), and the said Order as already effective as law under the Meiji Constitution, since among regulations that existed prior to the Meiji Constitution, those that stipulated matters to be set forth by law under the old Constitution continued in force by whatever names they might have been called (Article 76, paragraph 1 of the Meiji Constitution). (This reasoning would not make any difference even if there was not a basis under the Meiji Constitution for revision of the said Order.)

Furthermore, even under the new Constitution such basic details concerning the execution of the death sentence as are prescribed in the said

Order should be said to fall under legal matters (Article 31 of the Constitution). Prosecuting attorneys reply that the Order in its content is not a legal matter but merely a standing rule for the executioner of capital punishment, and that under the existing legal system such matters can be stipulated by an order from the Ministry of Justice. However, this Court cannot agree with this opinion. It must take a future law to change or abolish those portions of the Order that pertain to basic matters. Furthermore, Law 72 of 1947, entitled "Law Concerning the Effectiveness of Provisions of Orders that are Enforced at the Time the Constitution of Japan Comes into Effect," provided for its effectiveness under the new Constitution in conformity with the provisions of the ordinance, which stipulated those matters that must be set forth by law under the new Constitution. It does not touch upon regulations whose effectiveness was already recognized under the Meiji Constitution (for example, Cabinet Order No. 65 of 1873 in the present instance, which is construed to have been effective as a law under Article 76 of the old Constitution, or as an emergency Imperial Ordinance by Article 8 of the old Constitution which secured the approval of the Imperial Diet). Therefore, there is no room for the interpretation that the said Order lost its force after 31 December 1947, and even under the new Constitution it retains its same effectiveness as law. A decision by the present Court (9 *Keishū* 663; Sup. Ct., G.B., 6 April 1955) cited in the explanation of point 1 above has already shown that the existing method of executing the capital punishment does not correspond to "cruel punishments" in Article 36 of the Constitution. Therefore, the Order must be said to retain its same effectiveness as a law (Article 98, paragraph 1 of the Constitution).

Under the existing legal system, concerning capital punishment are Article 11 of the Criminal Code, Article 71, paragraph 1 and Article 72 of the Prison Law, and Articles 475 and 478 of the Code of Criminal Procedure. In addition, there is Cabinet Order No. 65 of 1873, which constitutionally has the same kind of force as a law that is still effective. The sentence of capital punishment in the present case, which was based upon these provisions, is clearly according to procedures established by law under Article 31 of the Constitution.

It has been contended that the method of executing capital punishment at present may not always be in conformity with the provisions of the Cabinet Order. Yet no violation has been found concerning the basic details of executing the death sentence as prescribed in the Order; so this alone cannot be said to invalidate the existing method of capital punishment as in contravention of Article 31 of the Constitution. Therefore, the contentions that the Order has already lost its force, and that the present method of carrying out the death sentence based on the Order violates Articles 31 and 36 of the Constitution cannot be accepted.

Consequently, the Court decides as stated in the Formal Judgment in accordance with Article 414, Article 396, and Article 181, paragraph 1, the proviso. This judgment is made unanimously by all the justices, except for the supplementary opinions of Justices Yūsuke Saitō, Hachirō Fujita, and Ken'ichi Okuno, and the opinion of Justices Tamotsu Shima, Matasuke Kawamura, Katsu Ikeda, and Shūichi Ishizaka, all concerning point 6 in the appeal brief submitted by K. Amano, counsel to the accused, T. Ichikawa. [All but the majority opinion are omitted here.]

Justices Kisaburō Yokota (presiding), Tamotsu Shima, Yūsuke Saitō, Hachirō Fujita, Matasuke Kawamura, Toshio Irie, Katsu Ikeda, Katsumi Tarumi, Daisuke Kawamura, Masuo Shimoiizaka, Ken'ichi Okuno, Kiyoshi Takahashi, Tsuneshichi Takagi, and Shūichi Ishizaka.

Case 21. Saitō v. *Japan (1962).* The Saitō Accident Report Case

16 *Keishū* 5 at p. 495; Supreme Court, Grand Bench, 2 May 1962; Tokyo Dist. Ct. (First Instance), Tokyo High Ct. (Second Instance), [constitutionality of accident report requirements despite guarantees against self-incrimination].

EDITORIAL NOTE: The accused had been driving a car while intoxicated, without a driver's license, and in excess of the Tokyo speed limit. His car hit a man, inflicting serious injuries, but the accused drove away without rendering assistance or notifying the police. The injured man died within hours at a hospital.

The accused was convicted by the Tokyo District Court of, among other crimes, leaving the scene of an accident, failing to report the accident to the police, and serious negligence leading to a death. He was sentenced to ten months in prison, and his appeal to the Tokyo High Court was dismissed. In arguing for reversal by the Supreme Court, defense counsel contended that accident report requirements in the Road Traffic Control Law (Article 72, paragraph 1, latter part) violated Article 38 protections against self-incrimination.

REFERENCES

Constitution of Japan [ARTICLE 38, paragraph 1 was at issue in this case. See Appendix 3 for this provision].

Road Traffic Control Law (*Law 105 of 1956*), ARTICLE 24, 1. In case a horse, motor vehicle, or streetcar causes an injury or death to a person, or damage to property, its driver, conductor, or other personnel shall rescue the injured and take other necessary measures in accordance with orders.

ARTICLE 28. A person who falls under any one of the items below shall be subject to not more than three months of imprisonment at hard labor and a fine of not more than five thousand yen.

(1) A person who violates Article 7, paragraph 1 or Article 24, paragraph 1.

Road Traffic Control Law Enforcement Ordinance (*Cabinet Order 270 of 11 October 1960*), ARTICLE 67, 1. In case a horse, motor vehicle, or streetcar causes an injury or death to a person or damage to property, its driver, conductor, or other personnel shall immediately rescue the injured, or take necessary measures to prevent danger or to ensure safety for other traffic on the road. They shall also receive instructions from any police officer who may be at the scene of the accident.

2. A driver (or conductor or other personnel in case a driver is injured) of a horse, motor vehicle, or streetcar in the above paragraph, upon completion of the measures provided for in the above paragraph, and in the absence of a police officer at the scene of the accident, shall immediately report the accident and the measures taken in accordance with the above provisions to the police station with jurisdiction over the site of the accident, and receive a police officer's instructions on whether or not he may resume driving the horse, motor vehicle, or streetcar and leave the scene of the accident.

FORMAL JUDGMENT

Neither point 1 nor 2 in the appeal brief in the present case is well grounded.

REASONS. Regarding points 1 and 2 in the appeal brief submitted by defense counsel T. Ishiguro:

It is contended that the judgment below found the accused guilty on grounds of failure to report an accident he caused while driving an automobile and failure to receive instructions from the police with jurisdiction over the accident in question. The judgment below upheld the first instance conviction of the accused, which had applied Article 24, paragraph 1 and Article 28, item 1 of the Road Traffic Control Law, and Article 67, paragraph 2 of the Road Traffic Control Enforcement Ordinance. Since the "nature of an accident" in Article 67, paragraph 2 of the Enforcement Ordinance includes, among others, those accidents that may render a person criminally responsible, the stipulation in the said Article requiring the reporting of an accident would result in self-incrimination contrary to Article 38, paragraph 1 of the Constitution. Thus, that portion of the judgment below that upheld his conviction should be quashed.

The Road Traffic Control Law (hereinafter referred to as the Law) is designed to prevent road danger and to ensure the safety of other traffic; Article 24, paragraph 1 of the Law calls for an ordinance that will prescribe necessary measures to be taken by a driver and other users of motor vehicles in case of an accident involving an injury or death arising from traffic of horses, motor vehicles, streetcars, or trains. Article 67, paragraph 1 of the Road Traffic Control Enforcement Ordinance (hereinafter referred to as the Ordinance) requires a driver or other users of motor vehicles to take measures necessary to rescue the injured or to prevent road danger and to ensure the safety of other traffic. It also requires them to receive instructions from the policeman at the site of the accident. Paragraph 2 requires that the nature of the accident and measures taken be immediately reported to the police station with jurisdiction over the site of the accident. In short, it prescribes emergency measures to be taken by a driver and other vehicle users in case of a traffic accident.

Article 67 of the Ordinance must be judged to be in accordance with the objective of the Law and must be upheld as a necessary and reasonable provision. This provision enables the police to be speedily informed of a traffic accident and also enables the police to take proper measures in rescuing the injured and restoring orderly traffic, thereby reducing further road danger and damage, and thus attempting to maintain traffic safety. Furthermore, the "nature of an accident" in Article 67, paragraph 2 should be construed to designate matters concerning the condition of the traffic accident, including the date, time, and place of the accident, the number of casualties, the degree of any injury, and damage. Therefore, drivers and other transportation employees are required to make a report to the extent necessary for a policeman to carry out his duties concerning the traffic accident. This is the extent of his responsibility, and, despite the contention of the accused to the contrary, information that must be reported to the police does not include the cause of an accident and other information for which a person may be held criminally responsible.

This Court has already ruled in another case (11 *Keishū* 802; Sup. Ct., G.B., 20 February 1957) that the legal intent of Article 38, paragraph 1 of the Constitution which provides for the right to remain silent should be construed to guarantee a person from testifying against himself on matters for which he may be held criminally responsible.

Therefore, Article 67, paragraph 2 of the Ordinance which requires reporting does not fall under self-incrimination in Article 38, paragraph 1 of the Constitution.

Therefore, there is nothing unconstitutional about Article 67, paragraph 2 of the Ordinance as the accused contends. Such a contention cannot be accepted.

Consequently, the Court decides as stated in the Formal Judgment, by the unanimous opinion of all the justices except for the concurring opinions of Justices Ken'ichi Okuno and Sakunosuke Yamada [which are here omitted].

Justices Kisaburō Yokota (presiding), Yūsuke Saitō, Hachirō Fujita, Matasuke Kawamura, Toshio Irie, Katsu Ikeda, Katsumi Tarumi, Daisuke Kawamura, Masuo Shimoiizaka, Ken'ichi Okuno, Tsuneshichi Takagi, Shūichi Ishizaka, Sakunosuke Yamada, Kakiwa Gokijyō, and Masatoshi Yokota.

Case 22. Abe v. *Japan (1966).* The Abe Confession Case

20 *Keishū* 6 at p. 537; Supreme Court, Second Petty Bench, 1 July 1966; Okayama Dist. Ct. (First Instance), Hiroshima High Ct. (Second Instance), [unconstitutionality of evidentiary use of a confession that is not clearly voluntary].

EDITORIAL NOTE: In 1964 the accused confessed to his receipt of a bribe following the prosecutor's offer to suspend prosecution in his regard if he would confess. In later appealing his conviction to the Supreme Court, the accused challenged the admissibility of evidence resulting from his confession, on grounds that it was not a voluntary confession.

REFERENCES

Constitution of Japan [ARTICLE 28, paragraph 2 was at issue in this case. See Appendix 3 for this provision].

Code of Criminal Procedure (*Law 131 of 1948*, as amended), ARTICLE 319, 1. Confession made under compulsion, torture, or threat, or after prolonged arrest or detention, or confession that is suspected not to be voluntary shall not be admitted as evidence.

FORMAL JUDGMENT

The *jōkoku* appeal in the present case is dismissed.

REASONS. Concerning that portion of point 1 of the argument for appeal presented by Counsel M. Shiba, which contends a violation of judicial precedent:

According to the defense contention, when Kōzō Okazaki, attorney for Ki'ichirō Kunitomi, who allegedly bribed the accused in the present case, visited and spoke in behalf of the accused to Mikasa, a prosecuting attorney, on 28 August 1964 at the Okayama District Prosecutor's Office, the prosecuting attorney told him informally, in effect, that if the accused gave up his false pretenses, confessed to an intention to receive money and other goods, and showed remorse, he might be inclined to suspend the sentence of the accused, inasmuch as the accused had returned the bribe before his arrest. The prosecutor suggested that the attorney urge the accused to stop his useless denials and to confess the truth. Then, in the company of Kusunoki, an attorney for the accused, Attorney Okazaki visited the accused, who was held in custody at Kojima police station, and advised him: "The prosecutor thinks that you are telling a plain lie. He is saying that if you show remorse he will suspend your prosecution. So if you have indeed received the bribe, you should admit it. You will be much better off to admit it quickly than to hurt yourself by continuing to talk foolishness." The accused, believing what attorney Okazaki told him and hoping for a suspension of his prosecution, gradually began confessing from the second questioning of his intention to receive money and other bribes, and also of the ways he had spent the money.

After ascertaining the above-mentioned facts, which involve the question of the voluntariness of the confessions of the accused both to the judicial police officer and to a prosecuting attorney, the contention continues, the court below ruled that "since there is nothing unlawful in the investigator's conduct in the present case, confessions of the accused and his motive behind them, which might have been the above-mentioned factor, cannot be said to be less than voluntary." It is contended that the judgment below is in contravention of the precedent established by the Fukuoka High Court on 10 March 1954 (*The High Court Criminal Decisions Special Report*, No. 26, p. 71), as quoted by defense counsel.

Concerning this point of the argument, the Fukuoka High Court in the case quoted above ruled that "a confession made on the premise that a prosecuting attorney will suspend a prosecution should be construed to constitute a confession that is not entirely voluntary, and that using such a confession as evidence of crime would violate the principle of evidence." Since the provisions of Article 405, item 3, latter paragraph of the Code of Criminal Procedure require the application of precedent established by a High Court that is an appellate court, in the absence of Supreme Court precedent, the decision below in the present case should be held to contradict the ruling of the Fukuoka High Court as quoted. Since the accused believed true the words of a prosecuting attorney who was empowered to suspend his prosecution, it is doubtful that he made a voluntary confession since he did it in the expectation of a suspended prosecution. Such a confession with doubtful voluntariness cannot stand as evidence.

But even after the confession of the accused both to a judicial police officer and to a prosecuting attorney has been denied as evidence, still other evidence listed in the judgment of the court of first instance is sufficient to ascertain the fact of crime stated in the opinion of the same court. Therefore, the judgment of the court below, which erred in applying a judicial precedent, constitutes what the provision of Article 14, paragraph 1, the proviso of the Code of Criminal Procedure calls an act that clearly does not affect the judgment.

Neither the rest of point 1 of the argument charging violation of statutes, nor points 2 and 3 insisting on an error of fact-finding and rule-application, constitute proper grounds for *jōkoku* appeal.

Moreover, a close examination of the record does not justify application of Article 411 of the Code of Criminal Procedure to the present case.

Therefore, the Court, by the unanimous decision of the justices, decides as in the Formal Judgment in accordance with the provision of Article 408 of the Code of Criminal Procedure.

Justices Ken'ichi Okuno (presiding), Asanosuke Kusaka, Yoshihiko Kido, and Kazuto Ishida.

Case 23. Yoshimura v. *Yoshimura (1965).* The Nonlitigious Trial Case

19 *Minshū* 4 at p. 1089; Supreme Court, Grand Bench, 30 June 1965; Fukuoka Family Ct. (First Instance), Fukuoka High Ct. (Second Instance), [constitutionality of nonlitigious trial methods in domestic relations cases].

EDITORIAL NOTE: The Domestic Relations Adjustment Law of Japan attempts to deal with various family problems without recourse to a litigious trial situation involving confrontation of witnesses in open court.

The present case involved a dispute concerning the mutual obligations of a married couple with respect to cohabitation, cooperation, and support, in which the constitutionality of the nonlitigious procedures was challenged in the Supreme Court.

REFERENCES

Constitution of Japan [ARTICLES 32 and 82 were at issue in this case. See Appendix 3 for these provisions].

Civil Code (*Law 89 of 1896*), ARTICLE 752. Spouses shall cohabit, cooperate, and support each other.

Domestic Relations Adjustment Law (*Law 152 of 1947*), Article 7. An adjustment (*shimpan*) and conciliation (*chōtei*) shall be conducted by applying the provisions of Chapter 1 of the Code of Procedures for Nonlitigious Cases, except as otherwise stipulated, or as contrary to the nature of an adjustment and conciliation. The provision of Article 15 of the Domestic Relations Adjustment Law is not necessarily of that type.

ARTICLE 9, 1. The family court shall conduct an adjustment (*shimpan*) on the following matters.

(B), (1) Disposition regarding cohabitation, cooperation, and mutual support between husband and wife, as stipulated in Article 752 of the Civil Code.

ARTICLE 15. An adjustment ordering payment of money, delivery of goods, execution of the duty to register, and other services shall have the same effect as an enforceable title of debt.

FORMAL JUDGMENT

The present appeal is dismissed.

REASONS. The Constitution, in Article 82, stipulates that "trials shall be conducted and judgment declared publicly." The Constitution is silent about what areas are subject to this stipulation. However, it should be construed as requiring that a trial of a dispute involving substantive legal rights or duty be conducted and its judgment declared publicly. Since it is the inherent function of the judicial power to adjudicate a dispute involving substantive legal right or duty, no legislation is allowed to evade the aforementioned constitutional prescription by dissolving such a conflict in the form of a nonlitigious or adjustment (*shimpan*) procedure.

The provision of Article 9, paragraph 1 (B) of the Domestic Relations Adjustment Law stipulates that a case involving cohabitation of husband and wife, or other issues related to mutual assistance between the two should be tried in the form of and by the procedure of adjustment, like disputes involving the question of the sharing of marriage expenses and support, or of dividing the property and inheritance. Its underlying principle seems to be that the obligation of cohabitation between husband and wife, and other rights and duties stipulated in the Domestic Relations Law and in the Inheritance Law involve a great deal of ethical and moral content and the status relations of the parties, and could be better disposed of, first, by avoiding the oral argument of a litigious method that takes the form of a confrontation between the two parties; second, by seeking a conciliation (*chōtei*) based on an agreement between the parties; and third, by the use of an adjustment (*shimpan*) in case the conciliation (*chōtei*) is unsuccessful. An adjustment is conducted behind closed doors and is simpler and speedier than a litigious trial in that the court, by the authority vested in it, conducts its own fact-finding, collects necessary evidence, and announces its ruling in the form of an adjustment, one kind of decision.

In spite of its moral and ethical element, the obligation to cohabit undoubtedly involves a relationship of substantive legal right and duty, which should be tried and judgment thereof declared publicly (cf. the provision of Article 1, paragraph 1 of the Personnel Litigation Procedural Code that was later amended by the Law for the Administration of the Domestic Relations Adjustment Law). Therefore, adjustment (*shimpan*) was not designed to resolve a dispute involving substantive legal rights or duties such as the obligation between husband and wife to cohabit. Instead, an adjustment should be interpreted, first, as a disposition made possible on the basis of a substantive right or duty concerning specific issues like the time, place, and manner of cohabitation, and second, as a prescription ordering necessary offers on the basis of the disposition.

In the absence in the Civil Code of a provision for any standards concerning time, place, and manner of cohabitation, it becomes necessary for a family court to exercise its discretionary power and decide these issues in the manner that best fits a specific situation. Such a trial is nonlitigious by nature and need not be conducted and its judgment declared publicly. Article 15 of the Domestic Relations Adjustment Law clearly stipulates that an adjustment is capable of creating a legally binding effect in domestic relations, just like an adjustment ordering enforcement of a creditor's right over debtor (*saimu meigi*).

But in view of the fact that the adjustment in lieu of conciliation provided for in Article 25, paragraph 3 of the said Law, once finalized, confers the same legal effect as that of a final judgment, other forms of adjustment do not seem to be given the same legal effect as that of a final judgment. Thus construed, recourse to a public trial or to a public declaration of the judgment thereof is not closed with respect to a right or duty to cohabit, although the legally binding effect of an adjustment, once finalized, cannot be challenged. Consequently, the provision on adjustment is not in contravention of provisions of Article 32 or Article 82 of the Constitution, and the decision of the court below is not unconstitutional. The contention of unconstitutionality is groundless. The rest of the argument, which does not contest the constitutionality of the decision below, cannot be accepted as proper grounds for a special *kōkoku* appeal.

By applying Article 89 of the Code of Civil Procedure, the Court decides as stated in the Formal Judgment. This judgment is the opinion of all the justices, except for the supplementary opinions of Justices Kisaburō Yokota, Toshio Irie, and Ken'ichi Okuno, and the opinions of Justices Sakunosuke Yamada, Masatoshi Yokota, Asanosuke Kusaka, Goroku Kashiwabara, Jirō Tanaka, Jirō Matsuda, and Makoto Iwata. [All these opinions, except the following, are omitted here.]

* * *

The opinion of Justice Jirō Tanaka follows.

I concur with the judgment of the Court in dismissing the present *kōkoku* appeal, but I disagree with their reasons.

In light of both the revision of the Civil Code concerning the obligation of husband and wife to cohabit, and also the circumstances under which the domestic relations adjustment system was established, further recourse to a public trial and judgment thereby should be denied in the case of an adjustment rendered by the application of the Domestic Relations Adjustment Law to the issue of cohabitation between husband and wife, except in the case of an abrogation of the obligation to cohabit on grounds of divorce or invalid marriage. Thus interpreted, however, a judgment based on the Domestic Relations Adjustment Law should not be held in violation of Articles 32 and 82 of the Constitution. The reasons for this are as follows:

1. The provisions of Article 752 of the Civil Code clearly stipulate a general obligation of husband and wife to cohabit. As long as there exists a matrimonial relationship, it does not take a court action to prove the obligation to cohabit. A problem arises, however, when we try to determine, in each specific instance, the place, time, and manner of cohabitation in applying the legal obligation of cohabitation. Neither the Civil Code nor any other laws provide any standards concerning these issues. It may well be inappropriate to resolve these issues under a uniform standard. In light of the special nature of matrimonial life, which involves substantial ethical and moral elements and requires a great deal of privacy, the Domestic Relations Adjustment Law has left to the family courts a discretionary power to work out, as guardian of domestic relations, an

appropriate solution in each case. Thus, an adjustment under the Domestic Relations Adjustment Law is capable of creating one kind of legally binding disposition of the obligation for husband and wife to cohabit. The law should be construed to expect a family court to create a final resolution of this kind of dispute.

The majority opinion, while acknowledging the aforementioned character of the adjustment (*shimpan*), assumes the existence of a dispute involving the obligation of husband and wife to cohabit, as well as a dispute over substantive legal rights or duties. Then it argues that, constitutionally speaking, an ordinary type of recourse to litigation should be kept open for such a dispute. Is it possible, as the majority opinion contends, to distinguish clearly between a dispute involving the obligation of husband and wife to cohabit, which is based upon the assumption of a continued matrimonial relationship, and such specifics of the obligation as the place, time and manner of the cohabitation? The supplementary opinion of Justices Kisaburō Yokota, Toshio Irie, and Ken'ichi Okuno appears to state that recourse to litigation must be made available when an "obligation to cohabit is disputed in the absence of a matrimonial relationship," or when a "demand to cohabit is disputed by one of the spouses as an abuse of a right." These two are cited as examples of an "obligation to cohabit." I shall never deny the availability of ordinary litigation to the first of the two examples cited above, inasmuch as the issue under dispute is either the existence of the matrimonial relationship itself, on grounds of divorce or invalid marriage, or the absence of an obligation to cohabit, on the basis of the absence of a matrimonial relationship. Naturally, a dispute involving the absence of a matrimonial relationship should become subject to ordinary litigation, and the absence of a matrimonial relationship, once proven, should negate an obligation to cohabit. However, the second example cited above is a demand made by one party to the other to cohabit on the premise of an existing obligation, and as such is completely different from the first example. A demand such as in the second example is concerned with a concrete question of implementing such an obligation, and is always to be decided by an adjustment regardless of the propriety of the grounds for the demand. For instance, a court can rule that a spouse who is suffering from mental illness is abusing his or her right by demanding cohabitation, and that the other spouse has an abstract, but not actual, obligation to cohabit. While acknowledging the abstract obligation of the spouse, the court in this instance would exercise its discretionary judgment to implement the obligation in such a manner that, for instance, the spouse temporarily need not cohabit during the illness and recuperation of the other spouse. It would follow then, that upon recovery of the spouse from mental illness, the obligation for the other spouse to cohabit would revive. The Civil Code does not intend that the absence of an obligation to cohabit should in the final analysis be confirmed by litigation, when the continuing existence of a matrimonial relationship is still the underlying premise of the litigation. It would be hard to find rational grounds for allowing such a litigious trial.

2. A function (*Recht-sprechung*) of an ordinary civil trial is to declare what is properly the law by applying a general and abstract rule of law, which does not exclude customary laws, to a concrete dispute involving rights or duties of parties. The Constitution guarantees that such a trial be conducted and its judgment declared publicly. However, as mentioned above, there is no legal standard generally applicable to a dispute involving an obligation to cohabit. Rather, a family court in its capacity as a guardian in the realm of family matters, is expected to dissolve such disputes in an equitable manner by exercising its wide discretionary power. Therefore, a family court in making an adjustment is indeed creating one kind of legally binding decision. Inasmuch as an adjustment of such a typically nonlitigious dispute as the present one by nature differs from a trial, the function of which is to declare law, the mere absence in this type of legal disposition, i.e., an adjustment, of the principle of public trial and the confrontation of two parties, as in a civil or criminal trial, does not immediately make an adjustment unconstitutional. An adjustment conducted by a family court should not be equated with the guarantee in the Constitution that trials shall be conducted and judgment declared publicly.

Not all nonlitigious cases differ from the trial as defined above. Not all disputes involving concrete rights or duties that are nonlitigious by law are suitable to an ordinary litigious trial. Whether that which is made legally nonlitigious should be tried by litigation must be decided by examining the nature and issues involved. It is necessary to determine whether an ordinary litigious method should be made available with respect to subject matter listed in the provision of Article 9, paragraph 1 (B) of the Domestic Relations Adjustment Law. In the final analysis, this is the kind of problem that should be solved by judicial precedents.

As stated before, ordinary litigation is not denied in resolving disputes involving the obligation of husband and wife to cohabit, unless the determination regarding such an obligation will be based on divorce, invalid marriage, or the absence of a matrimonial relationship. However, as long as a continuing matrimonial relationship exists, there is no room for a dispute to arise involving a concrete right or duty that should be resolved by public, litigious trial. By its nature, a dispute over the place, time, and manner of fulfilling the obligation to cohabit, the only conceivable dispute—a temporary denial of the obligation to cohabit under specific circumstances involves only one form of such an obligation—is a domestic problem involving marriage ethics and requires the secrecy of privacy. It would be inappropriate to expose such a dispute in a public trial in which the parties confront each other. Therefore, ample reasons exist to distinguish between a typical nonlitigious dispute and an ordinary civil litigious trial, and to accord the former special treatment under a special domestic relations adjustment system. Such special treatment does not violate the intent of the Constitution.

Justices Kisaburō Yokota (presiding), Toshio Irie, Ken'ichi Okuno, Shūichi Ishizaka, Sakunosuke Yamada, Kakiwa Gokijyō, Masatoshi Yokota, Asanosuke Kusaka, Kingo Osabe, Yoshihiko Kido, Kazuto Ishida, Goroku Kashiwabara, Jirō Tanaka, Jirō Matsuda, and Makoto Iwata.

Chapter 10

Intellectual Rights and Freedoms (Seishinteki Jiyūken)

The "intellectual rights and freedoms" (seishinteki jiyūken), *or more briefly, the "intellectual freedoms"* (seishinteki jiyū), *refer to matters such as the following, guaranteed in Chapter 3 of the Constitution of Japan (see Appendix 3 for the text): freedom of thought and conscience (Article 19); freedom of religion (Article 20); freedom of expression and the right to secrecy of communications (Article 21); and academic freedom (Article 23). Based on judicial holdings, most if not all of these rights apparently may be limited to some extent if it is genuinely necessary for "the public welfare"* (kōkyō no fukushi; *Articles 12 and 13 of the Constitution of Japan); but this does not mean that freedom is casually, commonly, or severely restricted by Japan's agencies of government. The record is quite to the contrary in most issue areas.*

Case 24. Kōchi v. *Japan (1969).* The Kōchi Defamation Case*

23 *Keishū* 7 at p. 259; Supreme Court, Grand Bench, 25 June 1969; Wakayama Dist. Ct. (First Instance), Osaka High Ct. (Second Instance), [criminal defamation and press freedom].

EDITORIAL NOTE: In February 1963 the *Yūkan Wakayama Jiji* (Wakayama Evening Times) newspaper published a series of articles entitled "The Sins of the Vampire Tokuichirō Sakaguchi" (*Kyūketsuki Sakaguchi Tokuichirō no Zaigō*). Sakaguchi was a writer for the allegedly sensationalist *Wakayama Tokudane Shimbun* (Wakayama Exclusive News). In the series title, Sakaguchi's given name *Toku*ichirō was subjected to a play on Japanese ideographs: the character read as "*toku*" meaning virtue was replaced by a homonym meaning gain or profit. The article of 18 February attacked Sakaguchi for allegedly attempting to corrupt public officials. Sakaguchi, himself previously convicted of both defamation and blackmail, sought criminal prosecution for defamation against the crusading journalist, Katsuyoshi Kōchi.

In 1966 the district court convicted Kōchi of defamation under Article 230, paragraph 1 of the Criminal Code, and the Osaka High Court subsequently sustained this judgment and fined the accused 3,000 yen (ca. $8.30). On appeal, the Grand Bench unanimously reversed the conviction and remanded the case to

*The Japanese characters for 'Kōchi' can also be read 'Kawachi,' and the name is so cited by some students of this case.

district court in a decision recognizing a large measure of press freedom under such circumstances.

REFERENCES

Constitution of Japan, [ARTICLE 21 was at issue in this case. See Appendix 3 for this provision].

Criminal Code (*Law 45 of 1907*, as amended), ARTICLE 230, 1. A person who defames another by publicly alleging facts shall, regardless of whether such facts are true or false, be punished with imprisonment at or without forced labor for not more than three years or a fine of not more than 1,000 yen.

2. A person who defames a dead person shall not be punished unless such defamation is based on a falsehood.

ARTICLE 230-2, 1. When the act provided for in paragraph 1 of the preceding Article is found to relate to matters of public interest and to have been done solely for the benefit of the public and, upon inquiry into the truth or falsity of the alleged facts, the truth is proved, punishment shall not be imposed.

2. In the application of the provisions of the preceding paragraph matters concerning the criminal act of a person for which prosecution has not yet been instituted shall be deemed to be matters of public interest.

3. When the act provided for in paragraph 1 of the preceding Article is done with regard to matters concerning a public servant or a candidate for elective public office and, upon inquiry into the truth or falsity of the alleged facts, the truth is proved, punishment shall not be imposed.

FORMAL JUDGMENT

The first instance judgment and the decision below are quashed, and the case is remanded to the Wakayama District Court.

REASONS. The appeal submitted by counsel contends there has been a violation of Article 21 of the Constitution, but all aspects of the appeal are in substance no more than contentions of erroneous construction and application of law, which are not grounds for *jōkoku* appeal.

However, this Court has examined the case *ex officio* in view of the submissions. The decision below affirmed the gist of the finding of facts by the court of first instance, which was as follows: "In the *Yūkan Wakayama Jiji* of 18 February 1963, the accused published an article entitled 'The Sins of the Vampire Tokuichirō Sakaguchi,' to the effect that '*Tokuichirō*,' alias '*Toku*ichirō,'* publisher of the *Wakayama Tokudane Shimbun*, or one of his reporters on his instructions, said within hearing of others to a certain section chief in the Public Works Department at City Hall, 'That's a terrible thing to do. We could've kept it quiet if you'd

*A play on Japanese ideographs; the character in his name read as "*toku*" meaning virtue was replaced by a homonym meaning gain or profit, for purposes of insult.

shown us a little consideration, but. . . ;' and to a certain highly placed official in City Hall, 'As the saying goes, I'll rub your back if you'll rub mine. How about it? You're probably corrupt already anyway. Let's go somewhere for a drink and talk it over.' The accused published and distributed an article of such purport and thus defamed the good name of Sakaguchi." The court of first instance convicted the accused under Article 230, paragraph 1 of the Criminal Code.

On appeal, the defense argued, "since the facts were believed to be established as true on the basis of probable evidence, criminal intent to defame on the part of the accused was lacking, and guilt was not established." The decision below then held, "The accused did not establish the truth of the alleged facts; if the accused mistakenly believed the allegations to be true, this does not nullify intent and release the accused from criminal liability for defamation, as the Supreme Court has indicated (13 *Keishū* 641; 1st Petty Bench, 7 May 1959)." Thus, the decision below upheld the conviction, even though the appellant had had grounds for his mistaken belief regarding the facts.

However, Article 230-2 of the Criminal Code should be construed as harmonizing the protection of the individual's good name as a right of the person with Article 21's guarantee concerning legitimate speech. In the interests of achieving balance and harmony regarding both these elements, even if statements are not proved to be true, as specified in Article 230-2, paragraph 1, criminal intent and a crime of defamation should not be deemed present in this case, where the party mistakenly believed his statements were true and where there was sufficient reason for this mistaken belief in light of the concrete evidence presented. We hold that the above-mentioned doctrine of the First Petty Bench should be changed. Consequently, it must be said that the decision below erred in applying the laws.

Moreover, with regard to the *kōso* appeal, facts corresponding to the above finding of facts, the testimony of defense witness Sadayasu Yoshimura—to the effect that he had provided the accused with information in the article which was included in the *kōso* facts and which he had heard from officials in Wakayama City Hall—was challenged by the prosecutor as hearsay evidence. The court of first instance sustained the objection and ruled that all this evidence be stricken. As a result, the defendant had no proof related to the truth of the contents of the article in the *kōso* facts, and since the court could not find that the accused had sufficient reason for believing the alleged facts to be true, the appellant was convicted. The decision below clearly concurred in this conclusion.

However, in the court of first instance, defense counsel contended, "The actions and purposes in this case were in the public interest and acquittal is appropriate under Article 230-2." Yoshimura was a witness concerning the above *kōso* facts and was employed in the court of first instance without restriction to prove the above contention. Thus, in view of the recorded proceedings in this case, it is reasonable to interpret Yoshimura's testimony as containing matter that provided grounds for the defendant to mistakenly believe in the truth of the article's contents. In striking this evidence as hearsay regarding the question of whether the facts as presented in the article were true, the court of first instance acted correctly; but on the point of whether or not the accused mistakenly believed the contents of the instant article to be true, the above testimony cannot be called hearsay evidence, and the court of first instance erroneously construed the law with respect to the meaning of hearsay evidence, and illegally expunged evidence that should not be struck from the record. In following this lower court view, the decision below erred in interpretation of the law, was deficient in the examination of evidence, and is therefore invalid.

Since the court's judgment should have been made pursuant to serious examination of whether or not the accused had grounds for his mistaken belief that the article's contents were true, and whether or not he was free of responsibility under Article 230-2, paragraph 1, illegal aspects of the decision below materially affected the judgment, and failure to reverse it would result in a notable miscarriage of justice.

Therefore, under Article 411, paragraph 1 of the Code of Criminal Procedure, the first instance judgment and the decision below are quashed; and under Article 413 of the same Code, this case is remanded to the Wakayama District Court for thorough deliberation.

This is the unanimous judgment of the justices.

Justices Kazuto Ishida (presiding), Toshio Irie, Kingo Osabe, Yoshihiko Kido, Jirō Tanaka, Jirō Matsuda, Makoto Iwata, Kazuo Shimomura, Kōtarō Irokawa, Ken'ichirō Ōsumi, Masao Matsumoto, Yoshimi Iimura, Tomokazu Murakami, and Kosato Sekine.

Case 25. Hasegawa v. *Japan (1969)*. The Right-to-Likeness Case

23 *Keishū* 12 at p. 1625; Supreme Court, Grand Bench, 24 December 1969; Kyoto Dist. Ct. (First Instance), Osaka High Ct. (Second Instance), [the constitutional right to one's own likeness].

EDITORIAL NOTE: During an illegal student demonstration in Kyoto in 1962, the accused struck a police photographer and subsequently attempted to justify the action on grounds that the officer's picture taking violated his constitutional right to his likeness, an aspect of his right to privacy under Article 13 of the Constitution. The lower courts convicted the accused and he appealed the case to the Supreme Court.

REFERENCES

Constitution of Japan [ARTICLES 13, 21, 31, and 35 were at issue in this case. See Appendix 3 for these provisions].

Police Law (*Law 162 of 1954*, as amended), ARTICLE 2, 1. Responsibilities and duties of the police are to protect the life, body, and property of individuals, and to take charge of preventing, suppressing, and investigating crimes, as well as apprehension of suspects, traffic control, and other affairs concerning the maintenance of public safety and order.

Code of Criminal Procedure (*Law 131 of 1948*), ARTICLE 218, 2. In a case where a suspect is under physical restraint, his fingerprints or footprints may be taken, his height or weight measured, or his photograph taken without the warrant mentioned in the preceding paragraph, provided that he must not be stripped naked.

FORMAL JUDGMENT

The *jōkoku* appeal is dismissed. The costs of the proceedings in this case shall be borne by the accused.

REASONS. Concerning the contention, in number 2 of the *jōkoku* appeal of the accused and in point 1 of Counsel T. Aoyanagi's statement of reasons for *jōkoku* appeal, that Kyoto City Ordinance No. 10 of 1954, the Ordinance concerning Assemblies, Processions, and Demonstrations (hereinafter, "the ordinance in question") is contrary to Article 21 of the Constitution:

As their statement maintains, the ordinance in question stipulates that one must receive a permit from the public safety commission when one intends to hold an assembly or procession in a street or other outdoor public place, or when one intends to hold a demonstration no matter where, and has as its intent the prior regulation of these collective activities (hereinafter, simply "collective activities"). However, upon examination of the ordinance in question, we find the said ordinance provides that a permit from the public safety commission is required for collective activities (Article 2), but also that the public safety commission "must permit" the carrying out of collective activities as a matter of duty "except in cases where it is clearly recognized that it will cause direct danger to the property or freedom, life or limb of the public" (Article 6); cases of refusal of a permit are strictly limited. That an ordinance concerning public safety with such content is not in violation of the provisions of Article 21 of the Constitution is clear from the Grand Bench judgment of this Court (14 *Keishū* 1243; Sup. Ct., G.B., 20 July 1960)* regarding Tokyo Metropolitan Ordinance No. 44 of 1950, the Ordinance concerning Assemblies, Processions, and Demonstrations, whose contents are almost identical to these. Since a need to change this doctrine is not recognized, the argument is without grounds.

Concerning the contention in point 1 of counsel's *jōkoku* appeal that the ordinance in question violates Article 31 of the Constitution:

*The Tokyo Ordinance Decision. See the translation of this decision in J. M. MAKI, *op. cit.*, p. 84.

The appeal argues as follows: The ordinance in question provides that necessary conditions can be attached when granting a permit (Article 6), stipulates that the chief of police can issue a warning to the sponsors, leaders, and participants and can control their activities in cases where there is violation of or intent to violate these conditions (Article 8), and, moreover, provides for the possibility of punishment for sponsors, leaders, and others in cases of violation of conditions (Article 9). In thus leaving entirely to the police the interpretation of the contents of said conditions and the determination of violations of the conditions, the ordinance is contrary to Article 31 of the Constitution which provides for lawful procedures. Furthermore, in allowing the determination of conditions to be a matter of the convenience of the regulatory authorities, the ordinance violates that same provision, which forbids "white cloth penal law."*

However, the proviso in Article 6, paragraph 1 of the ordinance in question sets limits to the conditions that the public safety commission can attach, and based on this the conditions are determined upon in the concrete. These conditions are transmitted to the sponsor or the person responsible for liaison (Article 6, paragraph 2; Article 5 of the regulations for executing the ordinance in question), and acts in violation of these concretized conditions become the objects of warning, controls, and penalties. This is not, as the appeal contends, to allow the regulatory authorities to determine the conditions as they please; and one cannot say that the conditions necessary to constitute a crime are not prescribed or that they are unclear. For these reasons, the brief's contention of unconstitutionality is deficient in its premisses and is not legal grounds for *jōkoku* appeal.

Concerning point 3, number 4 of the appeal of the accused, the statement contends as follows: The judgment of the court below holding legal in this case acts of photographing by police, which were against the will of the party photographed and without a judge's warrant, is contrary to Article 13 of the Constitution, which guarantees one's right to his own likeness (*shōzōken*), in other words, the right not to have one's picture taken without one's consent; and it also violates Article 35 of the Constitution, which establishes the principle of requiring warrants (*reijō shugi*).

Now, Article 13 of the Constitution provides that all of the people shall be respected as individuals. Their right to life, liberty, and the pursuit of happiness shall, to the extent that it does not interfere with the public welfare, be the supreme consideration in legislation and in other governmental affairs. It can be said that this provides that the people's freedom with respect to their private lives should be protected against

***Shiraji keihō* (in German law, *Blankettrafgesets*), which provides penalties without clearly stating the nature of the illegal acts.

the exercise of state powers such as the police power. As one of the freedoms of the individual with respect to private life, it should be said that every man has the freedom not to have his face or physical appearance (hereinafter, "face") photographed involuntarily and without permission. Putting aside the question of whether or not this should be called the right to one's own likeness, it must be said at least that it violates the intent of Article 13 of the Constitution, and it is not permissible for the police to take photographs of an individual's face without proper reason. However, this does not mean that the above freedom of the individual receives unlimited protection from the exercise of state power. It is clear from provisions of the same Article that it is subject to suitable restriction when necessary for the public welfare. Furthermore, the investigation of crime is one of the state functions conferred upon the police for the sake of the public welfare. Since the police have the obligation to fulfill this function (see Article 2, paragraph 1 of the Police Law), we must say that on occasions when the police take photographs in line with necessary criminal investigation, there can be cases in which this is permissible even if the target of that photography includes the individual face not only of a criminal but also of a third party.

Consequently, when considering the permissible limits of that activity, apart from such cases as photographing suspects who are physically restrained under provisions of Article 218, paragraph 2 of the Code of Criminal Procedure, we should construe police photography of an individual's face as permissible without the agreement of the party photographed, and even without a warrant from a judge, in cases such as the following: namely, in instances where it is found that a crime is taking place or has just taken place; when there is urgency and the necessity of preserving evidence; and when that photography takes place in a suitable manner without exceeding the generally permitted limits. Police photography taking place in such cases should be interpreted as not in violation of Article 13 and Article 35 of the Constitution if, in addition to the criminal's face, the individual countenance of a third party is included in its object in a circumstance where he cannot be excluded because he is near the criminal or in the proximity of physical evidence which is being photographed.

Let us view this in the context of the present case. According to the facts ascertained by the first instance court, and sustained by the court below, the demonstration and procession in this case took place on 21 June 1962 under the sponsorship of the Kyoto-fu Federation of Student Self-Government Associations. The Ritsumeikan University Student Group, to which the accused belongs, was the group leading the way, with the accused situated outside the lines in the very front as it proceeded along. At a point about thirty meters below Miike in Kiya-cho, Chūkyō-ku, Kyoto City, a group of seven or eight people about four or five lines back from the front marched along almost in the center of the street. This situation was in violation of the permit condition attached by the Kyoto-fu Public Safety Commission that "the lines of the parade group shall be in four columns," and the condition attached by the chief of police of Kyoto-fu, pursuant to Article 77 of the Road Traffic Law, that "they shall proceed on the east side of the roadway." Consequently, Officer K. Akitsuki, who was on duty with the Yamashina Police Office of Kyoto-fu and engaged in the tasks of watching out for and gathering evidence of illegal circumstances violating permit conditions, saw this situation and concluded there were facts present contrary to permit conditions. To confirm the circumstances of the illegal procession and the offenders, he photographed the state of the procession at the front part of the group, to which the above-mentioned accused belonged, from the east sidewalk along Kiya-cho Road. That method also was not such as to impose any special burdensome duties upon the marchers.

According to the above facts, the said picture-taking of Officer Akitsuki was carried out when it was ascertained that a crime was taking place. Moreover, the urgency and the necessity of preserving evidence are recognized from the nature of collective activities in which many people are participating and the situation changing from minute to minute. And since that method is also recognized as appropriate and not in excess of generally accepted limits, we must state that, although it took place without the consent of the accused marchers and even contrary to their will, the picture-taking was a lawful act carrying out official duties. Thus, appellant's argument is groundless, since we do not find violation of Articles 13 and 35 of the Constitution, as contended in the appeal, in the first instance judgment that held this an official act authorized under Article 95, paragraph 1 of the Criminal Code and in the finding of the court below which approved of this position.

In the remaining parts of the *jōkoku* appeal of the accused there are contentions of unconstitutionality, but in substance all simply stress violation of the laws and errors in fact-finding and do not constitute grounds for *jōkoku* appeal under Article 405 of the Code of Criminal Procedure. (The same is held with respect to the remaining points in counsel's statement of reasons for appeal.)

Accordingly, pursuant to Article 408 and Article 181, paragraph 1, main text of the same Code, this Court by unanimous opinion concludes as in the Formal Judgment.

Justices Kazuto Ishida (presiding), Toshio Irie, Asanosuke Kusaka, Kingo Osabe, Yoshihiko Kido, Jirō Tanaka, Jirō Matsuda, Makoto Iwata, Kazuo Shimomura, Kōtarō Irokawa, Ken'ichirō Ōsumi, Masao Matsumoto, Yoshimi Iimura, Tomokazu Murakami, and Kosato Sekine.

Case 26. Ishii et al v. *Japan (1969)*. The de Sade Case

23 *Keishū* 10 at p. 1239; Supreme Court, Grand Bench, 15 October 1969; Tokyo Dist. Ct. (First Instance), Tokyo High Ct. (Second Instance), [the regulation of obscene literature and the freedom of expression].

EDITORIAL NOTE: In 1959 and 1960 an abridged translation of about one-third of Marquis de Sade's *In Praise of Vice* (*Akutoku no Sakae*) was published in two volumes, the second of which, *The Travels of Juliette (Jurietto no Henreki)*, became the object of litigation. The translator, a French literature specialist named Tatsuo Shibusawa, and the publisher, Kyōji Ishii, were indicted for the sale (about 2,500 copies) and possession for sale (about 290 copies) of an obscene writing. A 1962 Tokyo District Court judgment noted three conditions for the establishment of a crime of obscenity under Article 175 of the Criminal Code.* (1) wanton appeal to sexual passion; (2) offense to the average man's sense of modesty; and (3) opposition to proper concepts of sexual morality. The accused were acquitted on grounds that the brutality and unreality of the work in question were such as to preclude fulfillment of the first condition, though the other two elements of obscenity were deemed present. In 1963 the Tokyo High Court reversed the court of first instance, held that all three conditions were met by the de Sade translation, and fined both Ishii and Shibusawa.† The accused appealed to the Supreme Court, arguing violation of freedom of expression and academic freedom. The 8-to-5 Grand Bench vote to quash the appeal was attended by a series of substantial opinions.

REFERENCES

Constitution of Japan [ARTICLES 21 and 23 were at issue in this case. See Appendix 3 for these provisions].

Criminal Code (*Law 45 of 1907*, as amended),‡ ARTICLE 175. A person who distributes or sells an obscene writing, picture, or other object or who publicly displays the same, shall be punished with imprisonment at forced labor for not more than two years or a fine of not more than 5,000 yen or a minor fine. The same applies to a person who possesses the same for the purpose of sale.

Code of Criminal Procedure (*Law 131 of 1948*, as amended),§ ARTICLE 400. When the judgment below is to be quashed on any ground other than the grounds mentioned in the two preceding Articles, the case shall be either sent back to the court below or transferred to another court in the same class as the court below by means of a judgment. However, if the court of *kōso* appeal recognizes that it may immediately render a judgment on the basis of the record of court proceedings and the evidence examined by the court below and the court of *kōso* appeal, it may render the judgment for the case.

*HANREI JIHŌ, No. 318, p. 8 (Tokyo Dist. Ct., 16 October 1962).
†16 KŌSAI KEISHŪ 573 (Tokyo High Ct., 21 November 1963).
‡As translated in Ministry of Justice, Japan, CRIMINAL STATUTES, n.d., I:39.
§Based on the translation in *id.*, p. 153.

FORMAL JUDGMENT

Each *jōkoku* appeal in this case is dismissed.

REASONS. A. Regarding point 1 of the *jōkoku* appeal of Attorneys M. Ōno, M. Nakamura, H. Yaginuma, and A. Arai:

The appeal contends that the judgment below erred in interpreting and applying Article 175 of the Criminal Code and violated Articles 21 and 23 of the Constitution in this case in holding *Akutoku no Sakae* (*Zoku*) [hereinafter, *In Praise of Vice* (Continuation)] to be obscene literature first by differentiating between the dimensions of obscenity and artistry or intellectuality in a literary work, and then by making a work the object of criminal action for obscenity under Article 175 of the Criminal Code even if it is of high artistic and intellectual value.

However, we must hold that the above contention, dealt with below under numbers 1 to 5 is without merit.

1. Concerning the relationship under Article 175 of the Criminal Code between obscenity and artistic and intellectual content in literature, the judgment below clearly indicated that it would follow the views of the Grand Bench of this Court in the judgment of 13 March 1957 (11 *Keishū* 997; Sup. Ct., G.B., 13 March 1957; the so-called "Chatterley Decision").* Then the judgment below held it not impossible to consider obscenity and artistry or ideas as distinct dimensions of a work and to judge obscene in its moral and legal aspects a work that is artistic and intellectual. That court also held it appropriate to judge such a work obscene in spite of its artistry and ideas and to hold its sale and distribution liable under Article 175 of the Criminal Code. In addition to the above reasoning on this point, the above-cited judgment of the Grand Bench held: "In the name of art, one does not have any privilege to present obscene matter to the public. In the pursuit of his mission, the artist no less than the general public must not violate his duty to respect the sense of modesty [of shame] and ethical laws." The present Court agrees that all the above views should be upheld. In accordance with these views, there is no obstacle to holding obscene a literary work with artistic and intellectual value. There may be cases where the artistry and intellectual content of a work may diminish and moderate the sexual stimulus caused by its portrayal of sex to a degree less than that which is the object of punishment in the Criminal Code, so as to negate the work's obscenity; but as long as obscenity is not thus negated, even a work with artistic and intellectual values cannot escape treatment as obscene writing. This Court cannot entertain arguments which, by emphasizing the artistry and intellectuality of a work, hold that works with artistic and intellectual value cannot be liable to punishment as obscene writings, or which contend that in determining the presence or absence of a crime of

*A translation of The *Lady Chatterley's Lover* Decision can be found in J. M. MAKI, *op. cit.*, p. 3.

obscenity, legal interests damaged by obscenity in a written work should be balanced against its public benefits as an artistic intellectual writing, on analogy with a legal principle used in relation to crimes of defamation.*

2. Article 175 of the Criminal Code attempts to regulate writings and other things with respect to obscenity and is not concerned with their artistic and intellectual values as such. However, if one took the position that writings of artistic and intellectual merit, even if obscene, are beyond the reach of the above legal provision, then it might be necessary to make a determination regarding the artistic and intellectual value of a work; but as explained above under 1., this Court does not take such a position. "Under the present Criminal Code, it is enough for the courts to make a judgment on the point of whether or not a literary work is obscene under the law. In this case, the authority and function of the court lies in judging the presence or absence of obscenity in a literary work according to the prevailing ideas of the community, not in determining the artistic or intellectual value of that work. The court is not the appropriate place to render such judgments." In so holding, the judgment below was not on all points without defect in its phraseology, but what is essential is that the court, in keeping with the intent of the above legal provision, cannot be faulted for holding that its responsibility is to judge the presence or absence of obscenity in a written work and not to pass judgment on the presence or absence of its artistic and intellectual merits in themselves.

3. Since, according to the above line of thought, even artistic and intellectual writings may become liable to punishment as obscene writings, and thus the development of art and thought is indirectly restrained, it goes without saying that great care must be exercised in judging the presence or absence of obscenity. However, since the Criminal Code penalizes only the acts of distribution, sale, public display, and possession for the purpose of sale, as provided in Article 175, a finding of obscenity in a particular writing does not itself imply that it is immediately obliterated from society and reduced to meaninglessness.

4. Since each part of a passage in a writing has its meaning as part of a whole work, the presence or absence of obscenity in a portion of its passages must be judged in connection with the writing as a whole. Consequently, it is not proper to select out specific passages and to pass judgment on the presence or absence of obscenity in those parts alone, cut off from the whole; but there is no reason to consider it improper to judge the presence or absence of obscenity in a specific passage when that judgment is made in connection with the whole work. Thus, we cannot say that there is a theoretical contradiction because the judgment below held that the presence or absence of obscenity should be

*The case alluded to is Kōchi v. Japan (1969), *supra*, Case 24.

judged in connection with the whole written work, while also affirming obscenity in parts of specific passages.

5. Freedom of the press and of other expression and academic freedom are extremely important as foundations of democracy, but as held by the above-mentioned judgment of the Grand Bench of this Court on 13 March 1957, they are not absolute and without limits, their abuse is forbidden, and they are placed under limitations for the public welfare. When writings of artistic and intellectual merit are obscene, then to make them the object of penalties in order to uphold order and healthy customs in sexual life is of benefit to the life of the whole nation. Thus, we cannot say this is contrary to Articles 21 and 23 of the Constitution.

The judgment below considered the fourteen passages that it designated in the instant *In Praise of Vice* (Continuation) in relation to the entire contents of the above translation and found that the above passages are excessively frank in the portrayal of sexual scenes and lacking in normal feeling in places. Besides the fact that the content of that expression is unrealistic and fanciful, those sexual scenes are joined with scenes of brutality and ugliness, or are portrayed immediately before or after such scenes. For such reasons, when compared with the so-called "spring books,"* the work in question differs in intent on the point of stimulating and arousing passion; but we find that it suffices wantonly to stimulate and arouse sexual passion in the ordinary person. Holding that the above translation, including these passages, corresponds to obscene writing under Article 175 of the Criminal Code was appropriate. Consequently, we cannot hold there was violation of the Constitution in the judgment below, as contended.

B. With respect to point 2, the appeal argues as follows: The judgment below held that "the point of dispute in this case only has to do with a judgment of the obscenity in this translation. Since we find that judgment can readily be made with the evidence taken by the court below (the court of first instance) and the records of the proceedings, we render judgment under the proviso of Article 400 of the same law (the Code of Criminal Procedure)." Although the court of first instance did not establish the existence of the facts constituting the offense, the judgment below overturned the presumptive decision of the first instance judgment without any examination of the facts, reversed an acquittal and handed down a conviction. This is contrary to the judgment of this Court's Grand Bench (10 *Keishū* 1147, 18 July 1956) and other precedents of similar intent, and in violation of Articles 31 and 37 of the Constitution.

Upon examination of the above argument, we find that except for the judgment of the Third Petty Bench on 11 February 1958 (12 *Keishū* 187), the intent of all of the cited cases is as contended; each case in-

***Shumpon*; i.e., pornographic writings; hereafter translated as "pornography."

volved a dispute about the existence of the facts themselves that were to be the object of a judgment of law, and not even those facts had been acknowledged. However, the first instance judgment in the present case set forth the charge against the accused in the opening segment of its reasoning and then held, "according to the evidence taken by this court, virtually all of the above facts can be accepted as charged, except on the point of whether or not the volume entitled *In Praise of Vice* (Continuation): *The Travels of Juliette* (hereinafter referred to simply as "the translation in question") corresponds to obscene writing under Article 175 of the Criminal Code. While making clear *seriatim* its views on such points as the meaning, conditions, and standards for rendering judgment on obscenity to the degree necessary in order to pass judgment concerning the obscenity of the translation in question, this court will explain the reasons why none of the actions of the accused in this case are criminal." Upon examination of the record, we can fully accept all of the above charges against the accused in accordance with the evidence lawfully gathered by the court of first instance, with the exception of the judgment concerning obscenity. We must hold that the above-cited precedents that speak of "cases in which an acquittal is handed down in the absence of confirmation in the first instance judgment of the existence of the facts constituting the crime of the accused," do not apply in this case, especially because the accused accept the charge in the first instance trial, except on the point of obscenity (see the conspectus of evidence presented where the court below reversed). Consequently, with the exception of the decision of the Third Petty Bench of 11 February 1958, in all the precedents cited by the appellants there is a dispute regarding the existence of the facts that are to be the object of a judgment of law; and we must say they are not pertinent to this case in which the facts are acknowledged.

In contrast, the judgment of the above-mentioned decision below is at variance with the precedent of the above holding of the Third Petty Bench on 11 February 1958 governing a situation in which there is no dispute regarding the ascertained facts that are to be the object of a judgment of law. The precedent holds as follows: In a case where the court of first instance has handed down an acquittal without confirming the existence of facts constituting the crime of the accused, it is not permissible, under the proviso in Article 400 of the Code of Criminal Procedure for the *kōso* appellate court, without making any investigation of facts of its own, to reverse the first instance judgment and issue a conviction by directly affirming the existence of the facts constituting the crime of the accused in the case, based solely on the evidence taken in the court of first instance. However, when there is a dispute concerning the existence of the facts, which are yet to be ascertained as the object of a judgment of law, then of course it is in accord with the principles of oral proceedings and direct deliberation to provide an opportunity for the parties to argue about the existence of those facts, to examine those facts and then to pass judgment; but in cases where the facts as the object of a judgment of law are acknowledged, and only the court's judgment of law remains to be made, we cannot see the significance of letting the parties contend about the facts and of letting a court further investigate the facts. Thus, in such a case, a proper interpretation allows a *kōso* appellate court to originate a conviction under the proviso of Article 400 of the Code of Criminal Procedure without a reexamination of the facts. Consequently, pursuant to Article 410, paragraph 2 of the same Code, we change the above precedent and uphold the judgment below.

Therefore, since the above contention of opposition to precedent is groundless, and since no violations are found in the judgment below from the standpoint of appeal procedures, the contention of unconstitutionality which assumes that opposition is unfounded as deficient in its assumptions.

Moreover, the remaining related points of the appeal as set forth below under 1 and 2 are also without grounds, as explained under each item.

1. Appellants contend that the court below was at variance with the above-cited Grand Bench decision of July 18, 1956 in passing judgment on the obscenity of *In Praise of Vice* (Continuation) without investigating the facts regarding the impressions left on ordinary people in society by reading the above work, or regarding the presence, absence, or degree of its influence on them.

However, under present law, judges are charged with determining whether or not a work is possessed of obscenity by judging the work itself according to prevailing social ideas; and this determination is a judgment of law. Applying the explanation above to this case, we find an instance in which the judgment of first instance established the facts of the crime, and that the court below passed judgment directly, based on the evidence gathered by the court of first instance, thereby handing down a conviction without further fact-finding. Naturally, since the judges are charged with determining whether or not a work is obscene in accordance with prevailing social ideas, as noted above, it is desirable that the judges know the impressions of the general readership in order to know the nature of the prevailing ideas of society; but this has no significance beyond that of a reference. Consequently, the contention of variance with precedent is without foundation.

2. Appellants maintain as follows:

a. While acknowledging more clearly than the court of first instance the concept of the relativity of obscenity in determining the obscenity of a work, the judgment below in finding obscenity did not investigate directly in open court the related social facts of such matters as the methods of publishing and selling writings, and the scope, the degree and the classes of people and so on involved in the readership; and

b. While adopting the so-called "wholism" position (*zentaisetsu*) with respect to the relationships between parts of the work considered obscene and the work as a whole, the judgment below did not conduct in open court a direct investigation of the facts regarding the serious attitude with which the author handled problems, the presence or absence or the extent of the work's artistry and intellectuality, and other matters which are the facts forming the premisses for judgment concerning the obscenity of the work. In both respects, the judgment concerning obscenity is not based on lawful evidence and does not follow proper procedures, and thus violates Articles 31 and 37 of the Constitution.

However, the court below does not adopt a position based on a relativistic notion of obscenity in judging obscenity in this case. As explained above, this case should be seen as an instance in which the judgment of first instance established the existence of the facts constituting the crime. Accordingly, if the court below considers itself to be capable of passing judgment directly, based on the evidence gathered by the court of first instance, then it may also hand down a conviction without further fact-finding. Therefore, the above contentions of unconstitutionality are deficient in their premisses.

C. Regarding point 3, appellants argue as follows: While holding that the obscenity of each passage in a work should be judged in its connection with the work as a whole, the judgment below in the case at hand concerning *In Praise of Vice* (Continuation) presents no judgment regarding the relationships between the fourteen places designated in the judgment below, the attitudes of the author and the translator, or the artistry and intellectuality of the work, and holds obscene the instant *In Praise of Vice* (Continuation). This is an erroneous interpretation and application of Article 175 of the Criminal Code. The latter matter has already been judged in connection with point 1 of the appeal; the former point is simply a contention of violation of the laws, and is not proper grounds for *jōkoku* appeal under Article 405 of the Code of Criminal Procedure.

Accordingly, pursuant to Article 408 of the same Code, we dismiss each *jōkoku* appeal in this case, and decide as in the Formal Judgment.

This judgment is unanimous except for the supplementary opinion of Justice Kazuo Shimomura, the opinion of Justice Makoto Iwata, and the dissenting opinions of Justices Masatoshi Yokota, Ken'ichi Okuno, Jirō Tanaka, Kōtarō Irokawa, and Ken'ichirō Ōsumi.

* * *

The supplementary opinion of Justice Kazuo Shimomura follows.

I would like to set forth my own opinion regarding the doubts expressed by Justice Tanaka in his dissenting opinion concerning the relationship between the majority opinion in the present case and the basic position taken by the Grand Bench decision of 13 March 1957 (the judgment in the so-called Chatterley Case).

Justice Tanaka contends:

> On the issue of how the concept of obscenity in Article 175 of the Criminal Code should be understood in relation to the Constitution, which guarantees freedom of speech and expression . . . the majority opinion supports the holding of the court below, which followed the Grand Bench decision of 13 March 1957 (the judgment in the so-called Chatterley Case), to the effect that it is not impossible to consider obscenity and artistry or ideas as distinct dimensions of a work, and to judge obscene in its moral and legal aspects even a work that is artistic and intellectual; and that it is appropriate to judge that writing obscene in spite of its artistry and intellectuality, and to hold its possession and sale liable under Article 175 of the Criminal Code. . . . However, the majority opinion in the present judgment adds to this: "There may be cases where the artistry and intellectual content of a work may diminish and moderate the sexual stimulus caused by its portrayal of sex to a degree less than that which is the object of punishment in the Criminal Code, so as to negate the work's obscenity." Do these expressions perhaps intend an acknowledgement of the relativity of the concept of obscenity? Other expressions in the majority opinion might also suggest recognition of the relativity of the notion of obscenity. If this is the case, are we to surmise that the majority opinion is taking one step forward from the basic position taken by the Chatterley Decision in recognizing the relativity of the obscenity concept, while in its conclusion upholding the decision below which followed the Chatterley Decision? In the exposition of the majority opinion, the two ways of thinking are mixed up, and one might conclude that they are not entirely consistent with each other.

As Justice Tanaka asserts, the decision below follows the views of the Grand Bench decision in the above-cited Chatterley Case on the relationship between artistry or ideas and the obscenity of writings under Article 175 of the Criminal Code, and the majority opinion sustains the judgment below.

However, I do not consider the majority opinion guilty of such a confusion of thought as moving a step forward from the basic position taken in the Chatterley Decision, while in its conclusion upholding the decision below that followed the Grand Bench judgment in the Chatterley Case. Moreover, I do not think one can abruptly decide whether or not we can say that the majority opinion acknowledged the relativity of the obscenity concept. I state my reasons below. I would simply like to add here that in the majority opinion and in the explanation below, the term "obscenity" is used to encompass cases that involve obscenity in general, and cases involving a degree of obscenity which is liable to penalties under Article 175 of the Criminal Code. I think that distinction is clear on its face. Furthermore, when we speak of artistic value or intellectual value in the majority opinion and in the explanation below, this refers to works of well-established valuation—for example, classics of indispensable value in the study of intellectual history or the history of literature, East and West, or works that, if not of that stature, have earned the highest repute as literary art in a particular nation or a certain society. This usage is different from saying simply that artistry or intellectual content are present.

1. Regarding the allegation that the majority opinion takes one step forward from the basic position of the Grand Bench judgment in the Chatterley Case:

In the reasoning of the second instance judgment in the Chatterley Case (5 *Kōsai Keishū* 2429; Tokyo High Ct., 10 December 1952) on the relationship between literature and obscene writings, it is stated:

> Indeed, we can conceive of the possibility of cases in which the artistry of literature may diminish or sublimate the sexual stimulus caused by the portrayal of sex in some passages, or in which the persuasive power of its ideas or philosophy negate obscenity by diminishing or sublimating sexual stimulus. Though some portrayal of sex is involved, such cases do not fall under "obscene writings." However, instances are also possible in which the artistry of literature and the persuasive power of its ideas and philosophy are not sufficient to moderate and sublimate the sexual stimulus caused by portrayals of sex in a portion of its contents; and such literature is not extricated from the area of "obscene writings" (ibid., at 2448).

Regarding the translation of *Lady Chatterley's Lover*, for which indictment was brought, the Tokyo High Court held:

> As is clear from the preface of D. H. Lawrence, the author, and from the afterword of the translator, the accused Itō, as well as from the contents of the translation at issue as a whole, it is written in Lawrence's spirit of earnest inquiry with the intention of presenting his philosophy or ideas concerning sex, liberating sex from guilt, and promoting a better understanding of sex. Besides providing intellectual stimulus concerning these matters, the passages portraying sex also have a literary beauty that distinguishes them from pornography. The quantity of sexual material, in contrast to pornography, constitutes no more than one tenth of the whole, and there is none of the extreme obscenity of pornography; but the work has exceeded the established limits permissible in literature, as explained above, in spite of its artistic values and the intent of the author, because the portrayals of sex in the translation in question are excessively lewd and detailed, and the attendant sexual stimulation is inordinate and is neither diminished nor sublimated (ibid., at 2451).

Accordingly, the book was judged obscene writing.

In the *jōkoku* brief of the Chatterley Case, counsel naturally contended that the conclusion of the second instance judgment, holding the translation of *Lady Chatterley's Lover* to be obscene writing, was unconstitutional and illegal; but regarding the section quoted above which gave consideration to artistry and ideas in deciding upon the obscenity of the translation of *Lady Chatterley's Lover*, the *jōkoku* appeal does not deal with that part as unreasonable and illegal—perhaps because it was a judgment favorable to the accused. Consequently, there is no determination in the Grand Bench judgment in the Chatterley Case which concretely affirms that section of the High Court's reasoning. As "it was proper for the judgment below to determine that the translation itself in this case is obscene writing under Article 175 of the Criminal Code," the Supreme Court upheld the second instance judgment which determined that the translation of *Lady Chatterley's Lover* under indictment was obscene writing. Furthermore, while recognizing that *Lady Chatterley's Lover* is on the whole an artistic and intellectual work and for that reason held in very high repute in the world of English literature, the court held with respect to the relationship between the obscenity and the artistry of the work that "even a high degree of artistry does not necessarily cancel out the obscenity of a work," and "since an artistic work differs from scientific writing, which reports in a cool objective manner, in making a strong appeal to feelings and the senses, we must say that the fact that a work is artistic, far from diminishing obscenity, rather increases the degree of attendant stimulation and excitement." (The above Grand Bench judgment speaks only of the artistry of a work, but we may assume that the explanation applies as well to intellectuality. The same may be said of what follows.) Therefore, can we say that it is not in error to interpret the Grand Bench decision in the Chatterley Case as approving the intent of the above-quoted section in the second instance judgment, which explicates the other side of the same reasoning contained in the above passage in the Supreme Court decision? Justice Tanaka quotes one part of the holding of the majority opinion in the present case. . . . Since that passage has the same thrust as the passage quoted above from the second instance judgment in the Chatterley Case, we cannot say with Justice Tanaka that the above-cited passage, quoted by Justice Tanaka from the majority opinion's holding, moves one step forward from the basic position taken by the judgment of the Grand Bench in the Chatterley Case.

2. Concerning the point that the majority opinion is guilty of confused thinking, . . . I do not consider Justice Tanaka's criticism of the majority opinion as guilty of mixed-up thinking justified, since it was premissed upon the "step forward" notion; but by way of precaution, I want to add a few comments regarding the majority opinion's holding in number 1. concerning point 1 in counsel's *jōkoku* appeal.

The above-cited Grand Bench decision in the Chatterley Case, which the judgment below clearly professed to follow on the relationship between artistry or intellectual content and obscenity with respect to writings under Article 175 of the Criminal Code, judged as follows:*

> Taken as a whole, this is an artistic and intellectual book, and for that reason is held in rather high repute in the world of English letters, as stated above. The artistic nature of the present book is apparent not only in the work as a whole, but also in those sections dealing with the depiction of sex, some twelve passages as pointed out by the public prosecutor. However, artistry and obscenity are concepts that belong to different dimensions, and they can exist side by side. If it is said that obscene things cannot be called

*The translation of this passage is based on that of J. M. Maki, *op. cit.*, pp. 11–12.

> true art and that true art cannot be obscene, then we are faced with a question of concepts. . . . Even though from the standpoint of art it is an outstanding composition, it is not impossible for it to be appraised as possessing obscenity from the legal and moral standpoints, which are of a different order. We cannot approve the principle of the supremacy of art, which emphasizes only the artistic nature of a work and rejects criticism from the standpoint of law and morality.

Because the term "dimension" is very hard to interpret, the above-quoted holding is also very difficult to interpret; but in this case, it is proper to interpret dimension as the position which serves as a basis for passing evaluative judgments when observing certain things. The above-quoted holding can be construed, in summary, as clearly intending to allow even a work that is outstanding from the artistic standpoint to be liable to penalties as obscene writing if that work is perceived and judged obscene in the dimension of its obscenity. The majority opinion is based on that argument when it holds, in accordance with the views of the Grand Bench decision in the Chatterley Case, that "there is no obstacle to holding obscene a literary work with artistic and intellectual value."

The fact that artistry or intellectuality and obscenity are considered, as above, concepts belonging to separate dimensions does not mean that there is no relationship between them. When obscenity exists in an artistic and thoughtful writing, in some cases the obscenity is diminished and moderated by its artistry and ideas, and in other cases it may thereby be increased and heightened. For example, in the portrayal of matters related to obscenity, many times the obscenity may be diminished or moderated through the techniques of symbolism or rough sketching, while in many cases the obscenity may be increased and heightened by the methods of minute depiction and realism. The holding of the majority opinion quoted above clarified part of the rationale for this. . . .

Thus, the artistry and intellectuality and the obscenity of a writing are intimately related, but the majority opinion does not take a position that emphasizes the artistry or thoughtfulness of a work or its artistic and intellectual value as the basis for determining whether or not a writing is obscene. . . .

Based on the above explanations. . . , I do not consider the majority opinion guilty of confused thinking, as suggested by Justice Tanaka.

3. Regarding the point that the majority opinion acknowledges the relativity of the notion of obscenity. . . .

Justice Tanaka seems to presume that the Grand Bench judgment in the Chatterley Case does not recognize the relativity of the concept of obscenity, but that Grand Bench decision neither acknowledges nor denies the relativity of the obscenity concept. Moreover, if we look at, among other things, counsel's *jōkoku* appeal in this case, there seem to be various emphases regarding what items in the contents of the work in question should be considered relatively when deciding about obscenity.

Furthermore, these statements generally seem to be directed at acts of distributing and selling obscene writings, but it is not made clear whether or not they are to apply in the same manner to an act of possession with intent to sell, which is the charge in the present case. In the reasoning of the majority opinion in this decision, there is this passage regarding point 2 of counsel's *jōkoku* appeal: "The court below does not adopt a position based on a relativistic notion of obscenity in judging obscenity in this case." By this, I think the court below did nothing more than make clear its intention in this case not to adopt a position in judging obscenity dependent upon a relativistic notion of obscenity such as that stressed by counsel.

To my way of thinking as I look at each doctrine, I wonder if the acknowledgment of the relativity of the concept of obscenity, or in other words, the consideration of obscenity in a relative manner, cannot be appropriately construed, by inference from the meaning of the word, as the consideration of the obscenity of the work in question in connection with assessments or facts external to the work itself. From this standpoint, I wonder if it is impossible to say that the judgment, at least the part cited above by Justice Tanaka, saw obscenity in a relative manner. However, there is no disagreement among the parties in this case that the translation in question possesses, along with its obscenity, artistry and ideas; and the majority opinion does not deny the artistic and intellectual nature of the translation in question. We should say that these three elements are fused in the translation at issue, and that the three elements are created and coexist in their mutual influence on each other. If they influence each other in such a manner, then all the less do we judge that the obscenity is cancelled out to such an extent that it is less than that which is the object of punishment in the Criminal Code. In other words, if we consider as integrated with each other each essential element within the work itself that is liable to punishment, it may be because one cannot avoid thinking of those elements as integrated. If one makes of this a recognition of the relativity of the obscenity concept, that may be ascribed to a variance in usage of the words *relativity of the notion of obscenity*. Accordingly, I wish to refrain from a conclusion on the question of whether or not the intent of the above-cited part of the judgment quoted by Justice Tanaka is to acknowledge the relativity of the concept of obscenity.

* * *

The opinion of Justice Makoto Iwata follows.

I am in agreement with the conclusion of the majority opinion. . . .

As the majority opinion held, certain works can be artistically, intellectually, or academically valuable and at the same time can be obscene writings under Article 175 of the Criminal Code. However, the view is wrong which, without any inquiry into the manner of such acts, would make the distribution, sale, and public display of such works, if even slightly obscene, a crime under Article 175 of the Criminal Code, because it raises fears of an indiscriminate prohibition on the publication of writings that are valuable artistically, intellectually, or academically, and of infringement upon freedom of expression. But also mistaken is the view that if those writings have high artistic, intellectual, and cultural value—apart from cases in which obscenity is completely cancelled out for that reason—a crime is not ordinarily constituted under Article 175 of the Criminal Code even if they are at the same time obscene.

I think the question of whether or not the distribution, sale, and other acts publicly presenting obscene writings that are at the same time of artistic, intellectual, academic, or social value constitute crimes under Article 175 of the Criminal Code should be construed as follows: Upon comparative consideration of the legal interests that the public display of these writings infringes upon due to obscenity, alongside the artistic, intellectual, and academic benefits that accrue to society from their publication, when the benefit to society (public interest) from publication of those writings is greater than the legal interests infringed upon due to obscenity, then the publication of that writing for the sake of that benefit to society (public interest), as a justifiable act under Article 35 of the Criminal Code,* does not constitute obscenity.

Accordingly, even if such writings are proven to be of high artistic, intellectual and academic value, if the benefits (public interests) to society from their publication in terms of art, thought and learning are not proven to be of greater moment than the legal interests infringed upon due to the obscenity of those writings (the harm to society; in other words, the disadvantages), the publication of said writings must be said to constitute obscenity. The question of whether or not the publication of such writings is of benefit to society, and the comparative consideration of public benefits arising from the publication of such writings with the legal interests violated, should be governed by the prevailing ideas of society and based upon the degree of the writings' value and obscenity, the methods of its publication, and all other circumstances.

Looking at the present case in this light, the work in question . . . is a translation of a representative work of de Sade, and, taken as a whole, a work of intellectual and cultural value. . . . But it is also obscene writing under Article 175. . . .

Now, this work was published and sold as an ordinary literary book with the aim of general distribution, and the readership was not specially restricted. The actual readership of this book extends over every class in society and reaches into a broad age range. So much has been confirmed by the first instance judgment and the decision below. Anyone can easily

*ARTICLE 35. An act done in accordance with laws or ordinances or in pursuit of lawful business is not punishable. As translated in Ministry of Justice, Japan, CRIMINAL STATUTES, I:11.

acquire this book. Moreover, with respect to the fourteen passages in the book pointed out in the judgment below, even if we examine them in connection with the work as a whole, they graphically describe sex scenes involving sexual intercourse and sexual play in lewd, concrete detail. This wantonly excites and stimulates the sexual passions of the ordinary person, is harmful to a proper sense of modesty regarding sex, and is contrary to healthy concepts of sexual morality. In consideration of the fact that the harmful influence of this work on the general reader cannot be viewed lightly, the benefits accruing to society from the publication and sale of this book are not, in my opinion, sufficient to compensate completely for the above harmful effects. For that reason, the accused, who sold this book by the above-mentioned methods of publication, cannot escape criminal responsibility under Article 175 of the Criminal Code. . . .

* * *

The dissenting opinion of Justice Masatoshi Yokota, with which Justice Ken'ichirō Ōsumi concurs, follows. . . :

Concerning points 1 and 3 of the *jōkoku* appeal. . . .

1. We should construe the punishment under Article 175 of the Criminal Code of a person who distributes or sells an obscene writing, or who possesses the same for the purpose of sale, as prohibiting by penalty the distribution, sale, and possession with intent to sell (hereafter, distribution and other acts) out of a considerable apprehension lest writings occasioning excessive sexual stimulation curry to sexual desires rooted in human instinct, adversely influence the public moral sense concerning sex and disturb the normal social order regarding sex. However, if one takes into consideration the fact that we should rely ultimately upon the good sense of society, religion, ethics, and the like, for the maintenance of a normal social order regarding sex, because the relations between man and sexual desire involve profound and subtle matters, then we should also say with respect to writings attended by sexual stimulation (hereafter, sexual writings) that it is desirable to strictly limit the acts liable for punishment. Moreover, the freedom of speech, press, and all other forms of expression is guaranteed under Article 21 of the Constitution, and distribution and other acts regarding sexual writings are no exception to that guarantee. Furthermore, in light of the fact that this freedom of expression occupies an extremely important place among the constitutionally guaranteed freedoms, we must take ample care to avoid limiting freedom of expression more than necessary with respect to sexual writings. I think the above matters should be considered in determining the scope of application of Article 175 of the Criminal Code and in discussing the punishability of violations.

2. Considered in the abstract and apart from other factors involved in the problem, we might well define "obscene writings" in Article 175 of

the Criminal Code as the judgment below did in accordance with the Grand Bench decision of 13 March 1957 (the so-called Chatterley Decision); namely, "writings of such a nature as wantonly to stimulate and arouse the lust of the reader." Also correct is the holding of the judgment below that the standard for determining the presence or absence of that obscenity with respect to publications for general consumption like the translation in the present case should be the normal person in society at large.* The issues are (A) whether or not the translation in this case is "obscene writing" as defined above, and (B) whether or not the acts of the accused in this case can be found punishable. On these points my views are as follows.

(A) . . . .For the reasons set forth below, I have grave doubts about designating the translation in question as obscene writing.

The publication in question is the second half of an abbreviated translation of *The Tale of Juliette*, or *In Praise of Vice*, a work of eighteenth-century France by the writer Marquis de Sade. The court of first instance clearly pointed out and summarized the passages in its contents which could constitute problems.

1. The fourteen passages pointed out by the prosecution are portrayals of sex involving the heroine Juliette and a pope, a nobleman, a police chief, a notorious thief, and various other characters in debauchery, sodomy, bestiality, lewdness, and homosexuality, with the methods and styles of strange behavior set forth one after another.

2. Depictions of cruel and revolting instances of killing, flogging, torture, immolation by fire, and slaughter are found again and again in the midst of and immediately before and after sexual activities.

3. Furthermore, in and between each of the above scenes, the author of the original, Marquis de Sade, speaks through the mouths of Juliette and other characters of his own unique thought and philosophy concerning the laws of nature, or politics and religion. That philosophy made a frontal attack on both a Christian civilization fallen into decay and the enlightenment thought arising from naïve progressivism and optimism about human nature which had become the intellectual main current of eighteenth-century Europe; it exposes with thoroughness the darker dimensions hidden in human nature, casts fundamental doubt upon the established social order, religion, and morals, explodes the popular sense of values, and in this manner seeks out the essence of human nature. (For this reason, this work is also referred to as an intellectual novel.)

In judging whether or not the translation in question constitutes obscene writing with content such as the above, we follow the view presented above that a work should be seen as a whole. If one picks out only the parts of the translation in question summarized above in 1.

**Seijō na ippanshakaijin*

(which constitute about one-tenth of the translation), then the work is undeniably tainted with obscenity. But even those passages are generally vacuous, unrealistic, and abnormal, and their mode of expression is crude, dated, and solemnly vapid, and thus they are weak in obscene emotion. Not only that, but because the cruel and revolting scenes summarized above under 2. are portrayed as simultaneous with or before and after the parts referred to in 1., these sections give rise to a strong sense of loathing in the general reader rather than to obscene feelings. For that reason, we can regard as markedly diminished the obscene feelings to be expected in the general reader based on the portrayals in 1. When the ordinary person is made the standard, and the unusual, the brutal, and the cruel in sexual behavior are kept to a moderate degree, then the sexual appetite is stimulated and aroused; but in the translation at issue those elements can be regarded as clearly exceeding that limit. Not only that, but the passages summed up above under 3.—namely, the parts in which the author of the original, the Marquis de Sade, utters his own distinctive ideas and philosophy through the mouths of the characters—occupy a considerable portion of the translation in question and sharply differentiate the intent of the translation in this case from the category of pornography. When the translation in question is viewed as a whole, we cannot overlook part 3. above, which serves to diminish in large measure its obscenity. (Rather, as noted below, the fact that parts 1. and 2. referred to above are inseparably linked with part 3. can be considered as enhancing the artistry and intellectuality of the translation in question.)

In short, since the translation in question, based on the existence of the passages referred to above in 2. and 3. are not judged wantonly to stimulate and arouse lust in those who read it, it is difficult to hold that the translation in this case is obscene writing under Article 175 of the Criminal Code. If that is so, the court below erred in applying and interpreting Article 175 of the Criminal Code by finding the translation in question an obscene writing and by convicting the accused; there is reason in the argument of the appeal, and the decision below cannot escape reversal under Article 411, item 1 of the Code of Criminal Procedure.

(B) . . . .Even if one should take a view, like the majority opinion, that the translation in question is obscene writing, in this case I do not consider it appropriate to penalize the acts of the accused, for reasons that follow.

1. When part of a given work is tainted with obscenity, if the ideas, learning, artistry, and so on found in that work are not lost by excising its obscene sections, one can conclude that the deletion of the obscene parts does not give rise to a problem of improper restriction of freedom of expression. However, when the ideas and so on of that work are lost with the deletion of the obscene parts, then it must be said that the excision of

the obscene parts thereby constitutes a restriction on freedom of expression with respect to the work itself as a whole. In other words, a serious problem arises in the latter case about how to adjust the demand that distribution and other acts regarding obscene writings not be permitted, with the demands of freedom of expression with respect to writings with intellectual value and the like. Speaking in the abstract, I think distribution and other acts regarding writings with intellectual value and the like should be prohibited when it is appropriate to give priority to the former demands over the latter demands, and conversely, when it is proper to give higher priority to the latter rather than the former demands, it is appropriate to permit distribution and other acts regarding writings with intellectual value and the like, and to deny their punishability, even at the sacrifice of controls on obscene writing. In the concrete case, I think one should determine which demands should be given priority after due consideration of various circumstances, and especially of the following points:

a) Since the concept of obscenity is abstract and relative, one may find that just as there is a distinction between sexual writings that are and are not obscene, so also with obscene writings there is a distinction between those in which obscenity is strong and those in which it is weak. In the abstract, obscenity that is "strong" means something of a nature notably to stimulate and arouse the lust of the reader; with respect to publications for general consumption like the translation in question, the degree of strength should be determined according to the standard of the normal person in society at large. Concerning works containing passages strong in obscenity, I consider it unavoidable that the demands of controlling obscene writings be given priority, and that distribution and other acts be prohibited with respect to the entire work. One can regard the book involved in the so-called Chatterley Trial as belonging to this category.

b) Concerning works containing passages weak in obscenity, when the relative importance of that obscenity in the work is greater than the importance of the work's intellectual value and the like, I do not think we can avoid giving priority to the demands of controlling obscene writings and prohibiting distribution and other acts with respect to the entire work. On the other hand, when it is found that the importance of the work's intellectual value and the like is greater than the importance of the obscene passages, I think that the demands of freedom of expression should be given priority, the distribution and other acts regarding that work permitted, and liability for those acts denied. We must make a determination on whether or not the degree of importance is high, not merely on a quantitative basis, but on a qualitative basis with regard to the entire work. Above all, the guarantee of freedom of expression means that we as individuals can freely express what we believe to be of value, and other people are thus given the freedom to know that belief.

We must bear in mind that it does not always matter whether or not the content of that expression is truly of value, and whether or not it is truly superior. Consequently, even in judging the degree of importance of a work's intellectual value and the like, the court does not always need to determine the true value and excellence of that work. In light of the intent of the constitutional guarantees of freedom of expression, it is sufficient to judge whether or not, together with passages that are weak in obscenity, the intellectual values and the like in the entire work are of such a degree that their significance is recognized by its publication; moreover, it is necessary to make this much of a judgment. Thus, to say that the courts do not need to determine the true value and excellence of a work, or that a work's intellectual value and the like are acknowledged, does not imply that its distribution and other acts must be permitted. For example, intellectual value and the like may be possible even in pornography; but since we cannot ordinarily consider the importance of such values in the work to be greater than the importance of its obscene parts, its distribution and related acts should not be permitted. It is the same with regard to those who deliberately add in passages with ideas and the like in order to escape the controls on obscene writing. One can rather easily know whether or not a work is of that type from the writer's attitude toward the work, from the sales methods of the publisher, and from other circumstances.

In short, I believe the courts must make, and can make well such judgments to the degree described above. In this sense, the decision below follows the so-called Chatterley Decision in holding that the courts have responsibility for judging the obscenity of writings, but not the intellectual value and the like of writings; but to the extent that it is in conflict with the explanation above, I cannot but say that it is not correct and that it undervalues the demands of freedom of expression under Article 21 of the Constitution.

2. Applying this analysis to the present case, *The Tale of Juliette*, or *In Praise of Vice*, the original of the translation in question, is generally referred to as an intellectual novel, and the writings of de Sade, this work and others, not only continue to be rated highly as filling a blank spot in French literary history, but as the first instance judgment recognized, on the basis of testimony by so-called expert witnesses in the trial of first instance, their revolutionary ideas and their utopian ideas continue to be accorded great importance in the field of the history of social thought, in the area of medical science and psychology, and in intellectual and artistic movements that emerged in the present century, such as surrealism and existentialism. The original of the translation in question manifests de Sade's ideas most completely and is indispensable for the study of de Sade. . . . .Elements 1., 2., and 3. under (A), explained above are inseparably linked, and enhance the intellectual and artistic value of the work, so it must be said that deletion of the parts referred to in (A), 1.

would naturally diminish the intellectual and artistic values of the work in question noted above. Furthermore, . . . in light of the explanation under (A) above, the obscenity of the translation in the present case can only be called weak, and we must say that the obscene passages in the translation at issue are less important than the passages with intellectual and artistic value. If that is so, then it is appropriate from the standpoint of respect for freedom of expression to give opportunity for coming in contact with the translation in question to the experts, of course, and also to members of society at large. Consequently, I cannot consider it proper to sustain punishment of the accused for acts of selling or possessing with the intent to sell the translation in question. . . . The court below erred in interpreting Article 21 of the Constitution and, as a result, mistakenly applied Article 175 of the Criminal Code. . . .

3. Accordingly, I consider it appropriate to reverse the decision below and to acquit the accused based on Article 413, proviso of the Code of Criminal Procedure.

* * *

The dissenting opinion of Justice Ken'ichi Okuno follows. . . :

Concerning points 1 and 3 of the *jōkoku* appeal. . . .

The penal provision concerning obscene matters in Article 175 of the Criminal Code can be regarded as established with the object of controlling the genre of erotic films, so-called "springtime pictures," and pornography in general. However, undeniably there are items that are artistic, intellectual, and literary writings, pictures, and the like, and at the same time obscene. At various places in the content of this work, *In Praise of Vice*, are descriptions that stimulate and arouse lust, and the point of view must be acknowledged which is concerned about corrupting the moral sense of readers with respect to sex. Undeniably, this book has an aspect that corresponds to obscene writing, if viewed from that standpoint. Moreover, along with as well as before and after the portrayal of sex in this book, are depictions of base and brutal scenes; but these do not cause the obscenity to vanish or be erased; on the contrary, the result is to foster the stimulation and arousal of lust.

However, even the prosecution does not dispute the facts that this work *In Praise of Vice* is recognized as a representative intellectual novel in de Sade literature, and that viewed as a whole, the book is a work of intellectual and literary value. The first instance judgment also recognizes the intellectual and artistic significance of this book. The work is not one in which the obscene element and the artistic, intellectual, and literary elements are always two alternative things that are mutually exclusive. It is an artistic, intellectual, and literary work, and for that reason it is possible that it is at the same time of social value and obscene. In such cases, to fix one's attention only on the aspect of obscenity in that work, to forbid its publication and sale, and to punish contrary acts, is to deprive people in general of their right to receive the artistic, intellectual, and literary values of that work, and to violate the freedom of expression of the author. This is why many examples can be found in the legislative precedent and judicial precedent of foreign countries of not punishing as crimes of obscenity works with social value to art, thought, science, and so on.

Article 230-2 of our Criminal Code provides that speech which defames the good name of another will not be punished as a crime of defamation, when facts concerning the public interest are involved and when it was done solely for the benefit of the public, the truth of the facts being proved. Such a legal principle can be considered a generally appropriate basis for transcending legal provisions and negating illegality* with respect to the relationship between a crime involving expression and the social value and public nature of that expression. In other words, if it is proven that a certain work which is tainted with obscenity is at the same time of artistic, intellectual, and literary value and in conformity with public interests, then I do not think it should be penalized as a crime of obscenity.

But this should not be interpreted to mean that a work with the slightest bit of artistic, intellectual, and literary value can thus escape penalties for crimes of obscenity. Upon comparative consideration of the legal interests infringed upon by the obscenity of that work and the public nature which it has as an artistic, intellectual, and literary work, when there are reasonable grounds for giving priority to the demands of the former, even at the expense of the latter, only then do I think there should be punishment for crimes of obscenity.

However, the decision below holds that ". . . In the courts the assessment of artistry and ideas cannot be given priority over legal assessments concerning obscenity," thus closing its eyes completely to the artistic, intellectual, and literary values of this book, and looking solely for its obscenity without any consideration or judgment of its public nature. We should say that there is an illegality here by reason of insufficient inquiry into the question of whether there was violation of law by mistaken interpretation of Article 175 of the Criminal Code, in not effecting any inquiry or judgment regarding the possibility of escaping punishment for crimes of obscenity by reason of the public nature of that work's artistic, intellectual, and literary values. Without judgment on other issues, the decision below should be quashed and remanded under Article 411, item 1 and Article 413 of the Code of Criminal Procedure.

* * *

The dissenting opinion of Justice Jirō Tanaka follows.

Among various doubts about the majority opinion concerning points 1

*The term used is *chōhōkiteki ihō sokyaku. See* Kōchi v. Japan (1969), *supra*, Case 24.

and 3 of the *jōkoku* appeal, I find it difficult to agree readily to its fundamental way of thinking about academic freedom and the freedom of speech, press, and other forms of expression guaranteed by the Constitution, and consequently to its way of grasping the concept of obscenity established by Article 175 of the Criminal Code. My reasons are related below.

1. The majority opinion acknowledges that "freedom of the press and of other expression and academic freedom are extremely important as foundations of democracy." However, the majority opinion holds that they "are not absolute and without limits, their abuse is forbidden, and they are placed under limitations for the public welfare." Based on this position, it holds to the effect that restrictions and prohibitions and punishment of their violation cannot be termed contrary to Articles 21 and 23 of the Constitution on the grounds that "when writings of artistic and intellectual merit are obscene, then to make them the object of penalties in order to uphold order and healthy customs in sexual life is in keeping with benefit to the life of the whole nation."

At first glance, the above argument strikes a person as quite reasonable, but it appears to me that at the foundation of this way of thinking there flows the traditional approach taken by the Supreme Court, namely, that the freedom of speech, press, and other forms of expression and academic freedom can be restricted as a matter of course when it is necessary from the standpoint of the "public welfare." On this point first, I cannot shake off my doubts.

This does not mean that from the outset I consider freedom of speech, press, and other forms of expression and academic freedom to be absolute and unlimited things; nor, consequently, does it imply that I consider Article 175 of the Criminal Code unconstitutional and void. However, on the matter of assessing the meaning of the Constitution's provisions (Articles 21 and 23) guaranteeing these freedoms. . . , and consequently, on the point of the manner of thinking about the parameters of limitations on these freedoms, my views differ from those of the majority opinion. The freedom of speech, press, and all other forms of expression guaranteed by Article 21 of the Constitution, and the academic freedom guaranteed by Article 23 of the Constitution differ from many other fundamental human rights assured by the Constitution in that they surely form the basis for democracy and bring it to realization. They are extremely important and should be guaranteed in fact and not merely in formal wording. In the sense that it is not permissible freely to restrict them for considerations of legislative policy based on the pretext of demands of "the public welfare," they deserve to be called absolute freedoms; and I consider them different in nature from freedom of choice in occupation and the freedom to change one's place of residence and other freedoms the limitation of which by laws is expected based on demands of the public welfare. To put it another way, the guarantees of freedom of expression and academic freedom carry the meaning of guaranteeing the freedom to learn and the freedom to read, look, listen, and know. If restrictions can be imposed on academic freedom, and if the freedom of speech and expression can be limited with ease on the pretext of demands of "the public welfare," based on majority opinion in the Diet and the views of the government, and if in turn the freedom to learn and the freedom to read, look, listen, and know are repressed, then we cannot escape the fear that the fundamental principles of democracy are shaken in their foundations and that the development of society's culture and the pursuit of truth are improperly repressed.

Although I speak as above, I also would never contend that these freedoms are absolute and without limitation. I cannot deny the existence of intrinsic limitations that of necessity go along with these freedoms as well. On the question of what constitutes the intrinsic limitations on these freedoms in this sense, I shall comment later; but only intrinsic limitations in this sense should be seen as acceptable parameters for restrictions on these freedoms. Legal provisions with the intent of effecting external restrictions, and measures that carry them out from the standpoint of administrative policy and legislative policy on the pretext that they are based on the demand of "the public welfare" are beyond these parameters and impermissible as infringements upon these freedoms guaranteed by the Constitution.

What are the intrinsic limitations referred to above, and what restrictions can be accepted as intrinsic limitations? Such problems as these are exceedingly difficult, and it is hard to answer them, laying down general, abstract standards. But they are nothing but what can be drawn from the intent of the Constitution which guarantees these freedoms. In essence, on the premise that those who lay claim to this freedom respect among themselves the freedom of others and mutually agree on the coexistence of freedoms, it may be best to construe these freedoms as guaranteed only as freedom attended by discipline, which does not cross over into abuse, and which, using the prevailing ideas of the community as a standard, is not contrary to the sense of justice and morality of society in general in such a manner as to actually endanger that sense. Accordingly, the attendant discipline, as the intrinsic limitation on that freedom, must of necessity be respected in order to guarantee these freedoms to each person, and to violate this discipline is nothing but an abuse of freedom. However, limitations in this sense are not something external that should be established from a policy standpoint, but are approved of as limitations on freedom insofar as they are limitations *inherent in* freedom. Whether or not something should be approved of in the concrete as an intrinsic limitation on these freedoms must ultimately be decided by the courts in keeping with concrete circumstances.

Whether it be freedom of speech and expression or academic freedom, we must acknowledge that it is something which should submit to intrinsic limitations in the sense explained above. We should interpret as directed against acts that are contrary to intrinsic limitations in the above sense the punishment of acts of defaming the good name of another or acts of distributing or selling obscene writings. Moreover, as long as we can so construe those penalties, I think their constitutionality should be affirmed.

Only insofar as we can interpret the penal provisions regarding crimes of obscenity established by Article 175 of the Criminal Code as concretizing the limitations inherent in the said freedom of speech and expression and academic freedom can they escape censure as unconstitutional and void. If those provisions be taken also to carry the meaning of measures to actualize extrinsic goals of policy, on the grounds that "to make them the object of penalties in order to uphold order and healthy customs in sexual life is in keeping with benefit to the life of the whole nation," I must say there is danger of deviating from the intrinsic limitations of freedom, thus raising doubts about the constitutionality of the above provisions.

However, the provisions of laws should be interpreted in a reasonable manner, as, insofar as possible, capable of harmonizing in substance with the spirit of the Constitution. From this standpoint, the provisions of Article 175 of the Criminal Code regarding crimes of obscenity must be interpreted as capable of harmony with the various provisions of the constitution, as nothing more than one concrete expression of the instrinsic limitations of the freedom of expression and academic freedom guaranteed by the Constitution. If that is so, then the concept of obscenity in Article 175 of the Criminal Code should be construed in a rigorous and restricted manner from the start, and solicitude must be shown in the concrete application of those provisions not to contradict the spirit of the Constitution, which guarantees the freedom of speech and expression and academic freedom.

2. Next, I move to the problem of how the concept of obscenity in Article 175 of the Criminal Code should be understood in relation to the Constitution, which guarantees the freedom of expression and academic freedom.

On this point, the majority opinion upholds the judgment of the court below, which followed the Grand Bench decision of 13 March 1957 (the so-called Chatterley Case Decision), to the effect that it is not impossible to consider obscenity and artistry or ideas as distinct dimensions of a work, and to judge obscene in its moral and legal aspects a work that is artistic and intellectual, and that it is appropriate to judge that writing obscene in spite of its artistry and ideas and to hold its sale and distribution a crime under Article 175 of the Criminal Code.

The Chatterley Decision and the decision below in the present case . . . hold that the concept of obscenity is of a dimension distinct from the artistry and ideas of a book, amenable to separate judgment in its legal aspect. As noted above, fundamentally, the majority opinion also supports this viewpoint; but the majority opinion in the present judgment adds to this: "There may be cases where the artistry and intellectual content of a work may diminish and moderate the sexual stimulus caused by its portrayal of sex to a degree less than that which is the object of punishment in the Criminal Code, so as to negate the work's obscenity." Do these expressions perhaps intend to acknowledge the relativity of the concept of obscenity? Other expressions in the majority opinion might also suggest recognition of the relativity of the notion of obscenity. If this is the case, are we to surmise that the majority opinion is taking one step forward from the basic position taken by the Chatterley Decision in recognizing the relativity of the obscenity concept, while in its conclusion upholding the decision below which followed the Chatterley Decision? In the exposition of the majority opinion, the two ways of thinking are mixed up, and one might conclude that they are not entirely consistent with each other.

Be that as it may, how is the concept of obscenity understood, or how should it be understood?

The Supreme Court thus far has defined obscenity as "that which wantonly stimulates and arouses lust, offends the ordinary person's normal sense of modesty with respect to sex, and is contrary to sound concepts of sexual ethics." Applying this to concrete cases, the Court has judged works with the above three elements to be obscene writings. I intend no particular opposition to the presentation of the above three elements as a defintion of the concept of obscenity in itself. However, I must harbor grave doubts about whether that way of thinking is really appropriate which treats such a concept as something absolute and which indiscriminately holds liable to punishment as obscene writings all books which correspond to this definition.

It is a common perception, depending on one's way of looking at things, that when writings or such have sex or sexual activities as their subject matter, a good many have an element of obscenity, even if they are of a scientific, intellectual, or artistic nature. To extract this element of obscenity, to immediately conclude that the book or such in question is obscene writing and so on, and to ask whether or not it should be liable to penalties, surely this must be made an issue.

Since the question of how to deal with this problem in connection with guarantees of freedom of speech and expression and academic freedom has been agonized over for many years, both here and abroad, we must exercise ample caution in handing down judgments on this problem by tracing this agonized progress through the use of domestic and foreign academic views and judicial precedents. From this vantage point, I think we should acknowledge the relativity of the concept of obscenity from various standpoints, such as those related next. In theory, we can distinguish among these various standpoints to some extent; but of course in real life they are mutually related and we must judge the whole in an integrated manner. On this point, I must make it clear that I differ from the majority opinion.

a) First of all, in judging whether or not something corresponds to obscene writing and so on, we must take as a problem the strength or weakness of its obscenity considered precisely as a book or the like; and looking at it from the side of those who receive it and who evaluate it, we must make the issue the question of what kind of human beings should be the standard.

Taken in the abstract, the concept of obscenity, as outlined in the Chatterley Decision, is unobjectionable: "That which wantonly stimulates and arouses lust, offends the ordinary person's normal sense of modesty with respect to sex, and is contrary to sound concepts of sexual ethics." However, looked at in the concrete, many books and so on that have as their subject matter sex or sexual activities have in greater or lesser degree the essential elements of the above concept of obscenity; but we cannot deny that even where there is obscenity, in the degree of that obscenity there is variety of strength and weakness. If the essential elements of obscenity in even a slight degree are included, we may not be able to say that the writing in question corresponds to those obscene writings and so on which are liable to penalties. Or again, if we speak of the human beings who receive it and who evaluate it, usually and in general perhaps the ordinary person should judge—that is, taking the common person in society at large as the standard; but in this case as well, the very nature of man differs with place and changes with time, and with the diversity and change in environments that surround human beings, there are things difficult to judge with uniformity. It is not the case that things which should be held obscene writing and so on in one time or place, never give rise to different judgments on the question of obscenity, based on differences of environment in another time or place. Especially when the book in question, judging from its modes of expression and so on, is directed at specific people such as scientists and literateurs, perhaps the judgment as to whether or not we should see it as obscene writing must change with differences in those to whom it is directed. This said, we might do well to say that when we look at the definition of obscenity given above, in substance and in terms of its content, it is not something that shows us an absolute, unchanging, hard and fast measure or standard, but which shows us something we should see as variable and relative.

Furthermore, in judging the presence or absence of obscenity in specific writings and the like, we must of course make the writing in question as a whole the object of judgment. I shall refrain from further comment on this matter here, since the majority opinion also affirms this position.

b) Secondly, what should be attended to as especially important problems in this case are whether the artistry, ideas, or scientific nature that specific books and the like have—obviously, there are various differences of nuance in degree or situation and so on in these matters as well—and their obscenity should be construed as problems of different dimensions; and whether the obscenity of the book in question should be judged relatively in connection with its artistry, ideas, or scientific nature. On this point, the Supreme Court in its earlier Chatterley Decision denied the relativity of the concept of obscenity referred to here by putting on different dimensions the obscenity of writings and so on and their artistry, ideas, and scientific nature. However, the majority opinion in the present case uses expressions that at first sight seem to acknowledge the relativity of the concept of obscenity, as in the previously quoted passage: "There may be cases where the artistry and intellectual content of a work may diminish and moderate the sexual stimulus caused by its portrayal of sex to a degree less than that which is the object of punishment in the Criminal Code, so as to negate the work's obscenity." But continuing on, it holds:

> But as long as obscenity is not thus negated, even a work with artistic and intellectual values cannot escape treatment as obscene writing. This Court cannot entertain arguments which, emphasizing the artistry and intellectuality of a work, hold that works with artistic and intellectual value cannot be liable to punishment as obscene writings, or which contend that in determining the presence or absence of a crime of obscenity, legal interests damaged by obscenity in a written work should be balanced against its public benefits as an artistic or intellectual writing. . . .

In the end, the majority adheres to the Chatterley Decision, and upholds the judgment of the court below in saying that the presence or absence of artistic or intellectual values and the presence or absence of obscenity are problems of different dimensions.

While expounding its views in such a way as to seem at first sight not to deny the relativity of the concept of obscenity, the above majority opinion actually follows the intent of the Chatterley Decision and can also be construed as not taking one step forward from this decision. On the contrary, with an unfortunate lack of consistency compared to the Chatterley Decision, doubts about the theory and conclusions of this majority opinion are unavoidable.

By their nature, as Justice Irokawa points out, artistic works and intellectual works (and the same is true of scientific works) that have as their subject matter sex or sexual activities insert a scalpel deep into the human psyche, pursuing understanding of sexual desire, which is one of the fundamental drives of man. And since they try to depict the humanity hidden at that point, not uncommonly they cannot avoid taking as their subject matter phenomena that are at variance with the feelings and lives of common people in society at large. Insofar as that is the case, we cannot deny the existence as well of some taint of the elements of obscenity. On the other hand, on that account they bring into relief the true appetites and psychology of man; and at times, by applying a sharp scalpel of criticism to social evils, they stimulate awareness of the essential in human relations and in humanity, and provide as well an occasion for development of the culture of the community. We cannot ignore or belittle the value of such artistic works, intellectual works, and the like. If publication of these works should be prohibited solely for the reason that they are said to have the elements of obscenity, not a few artistic works and intellectual works and the like of high value would be obliterated, freedom of expression and academic freedom would be improperly repressed, and unavoidably a way to the reception of cultural values would be closed.

If we consider such points in an integrated manner, we might well say that there are many cases involving artistic works and intellectual works and the like as noted above, in which the work when assessed as a whole should not be construed as corresponding to obscene writing and so on under Article 175 of the Criminal Code even though it has elements of obscenity. In this sense, with respect to the concept of obscenity under Article 175 of the Criminal Code, assessment and judgment should be made, even when judging according to the standard of the ordinary person in society at large, in light of the degree of cultural development in that society, and various changes in the environment, as related to the artistry or intellectuality of that work. In this sense also, I think that the relativity of the concept of obscenity must be acknowledged.

c) Third, whether or not a work should be liable to penalties as obscene writing must be judged in a relative manner, in relation to the attitudes and position of the author as objectively manifested in the book or the like in question, and in relation to the methods of advertising and promotion used in its sale and distribution and so on. If the case is such that a work shows an exclusive focus on obscene elements and centers upon the stimulation of man's erotic feelings, we may often have to say that it is obscene writing under Article 175 of the Criminal Code, even if the artistry, intellectuality, or scientific nature of the writing as such is acknowledged, and even if it is of considerable value with respect to these points. When those who engage in the sale and distribution of writings and so on expressly draw out and focus on elements of obscenity in promotion, advertising and display, so that the writing in question will be taken only as an object of base interests, then for that reason they may be unable to escape punishment for the sale, distribution, and so on of obscene writing under Article 175 of the Criminal Code, even if this involves the sale, distribution, and so on of a work of considerable merit which is in substance scientific, intellectual, or artistic. Consequently, the question of whether or not something is obscene writing under Article

175 of the Criminal Code must be judged in a relative manner in connection with the various points above.

To summarize all this, I think we must judge cautiously, acknowledging the relativity in various senses of . . . the concept of obscenity. . . .

3. Looking next at the present case in the concrete, the original of the translation at issue, *In Praise of Vice*, is a representative work of the Marquis de Sade (1740–1814). . . . The translation in question is an abridged translation of that work, condensed to about one-third of the original, and is divided into two parts. What is under indictment in this case is the second part, *In Praise of Vice* (Continuation): *The Travels of Juliette*.

. . . .The problems are whether or not, looking at this work as a whole, it can be called obscene, and whether or not it corresponds to obscene writing under Article 175 of the Criminal Code by reason of that obscenity in spite of its artistry and intellectuality.

If only certain parts of this work are brought into relief, then it is undeniably tainted with obscenity; but even so, as Justice Yokota points out, its contents are generally vacuous, unrealistic, and abnormal, they are portrayed as continuous with cruel and revolting scenes before and after, and they give rise to a strong sense of loathing in the general reader rather than to obscene feelings; for that reason, the obscene feelings to be expected in the general reader are markedly diminished. Moreover, the fact that the parts in which de Sade utters his own distinctive ideas and philosophy through the mouths of the characters are quite substantial also serves to diminish its obscenity in large measure. Speaking from such a perspective, I must harbor grave doubts about concluding that this translation is sufficiently endowed with the elements of obscenity to fall under Article 175 of the Criminal Code.

However, setting aside this point for the moment, and supposing this work does have some obscene elements, if we follow my way of thinking, explained above, that we should judge whether or not that work corresponds to obscene writing under Article 175 of the Criminal Code in relation to its social value and its artistry and intellectuality, then we must hold that it does not. That is to say, this work is generally acknowledged to be an artistic and intellectual work of considerable social value. . . . The accused T. Shibusawa, who is the translator, is known as a Marquis de Sade scholar, and we can presume that he made the abridged translation in question with the perspectives of a scholar. There is no evidence therein that we should see him as attempting an abridged translation that focuses on the arousal of lascivious feelings. Moreover, it was not found that the accused K. Ishii, who engaged in sales and so on, generally and widely advertised and promoted this translation with a special emphasis on the point of its obscenity.

If we put together the various points above in making our judgment, granted this work contains obscene elements, when the work is viewed as a whole, it is highly rated for its artistic and intellectual significance, and the translation in the present case is an abridged translation of an original writing which, although embroiled in a great many troubles over a long period of well over a hundred years, has surmounted every kind of criticism. Now suddenly, it should not be removed from the scene by emphasizing its obscenity. As noted before, in light of the intent of the Constitution to respect freedom of expression and academic freedom, in view of the degree of development of the nation's culture and the changes in the environment of life which surround human beings, and in consideration of the readership that can be expected based on various conditions of this book's publication, I think that the translation in this case is not something to be hastily taken away by penalties under Article 175 of the Criminal Code, and that the freedom to possess, distribute, and sell it should be guaranteed.

. . . .I think the appeal was well grounded and that the decision below cannot avoid reversal.

From the standpoint explained above, I am unable to agree either with the conclusion of the majority opinion, which upholds the decision below, or with its reasoning.

* * *

The dissenting opinion of Justice Kōtarō Irokawa follows.

Concerning points 1 and 3 of the *jōkoku* appeal. . . .

1. Since the translation at issue is a novel, in considering the question of what kind of reading matter belonging to that genre corresponds to obscene writing under Article 175 of the Criminal Code, I would broadly divide it into two kinds. One is frankly pornographic writing, and the other is literary works and works for pleasure which are obscene, but which do not belong to the category of pornography. (What obscenity is is really the ultimate problem; but for the moment I here follow the Grand Bench decision of the Supreme Court in the Chatterley Case, on which the decision below relied. My personal views on the meaning of obscene writing are explained later.) Pornography is written from the standpoint of making sex an instrument of play and pleasure; it is indecent writing for the sake of indecency intended solely to arouse sexual interests, and that it is pornography can be easily known from the forms of expression and the contents from cover to cover. If pornography is widely offered to the public, there is a danger that it will contribute to the decay and degradation of a sound order in society regarding sex, and it has no redeeming social value; so it is unmistakably obscene writing and we must say that it is proper that its distribution and sale be prohibited with penalties. On the other hand, the second type referred to above takes sex as its subject matter and includes descriptions of sexual activities; nevertheless, we should say it differs in kind in that it is not a work which stands on the basis of arousing sensual and lascivious

preoccupations and interests. Moreover, on the matter of their relative social value, pornography differs decisively from that type. Since amusement is an essential requirement in a mass society (It doesn't take many words to say how dreary a society without amusements is!), we can recognize the existence of at least some social value even in works for vulgar entertainment. All the less can anyone deny the existence of social value in a literary work, even allowing for the differences in quantity and quality depending upon the work. I consider it impermissible to hastily judge a novel to be obscene writing under Article 175 of the Criminal Code just because it has some obscenity about it, without a very careful comparative consideration of the disvalue with which it is tainted on that account and the social value with which the work in itself is endowed.

Now the translation in this case . . . is a genuine intellectual novel. In addition, the translation in the present case is obviously not point-blank pornography, but neither is it reading matter for the purpose of pleasure; so it is enough in this case to discuss the relationship between obscenity and literary works, but, at the same time, there is no way to avoid that issue.

2. The majority opinion holds that even a book of artistic and intellectual value cannot escape treatment as obscene writing if it has something of obscenity. A literary work which has sex as its subject matter inserts a scalpel deep into the recesses of the human psyche, pursuing insight into sexual desire, which is one of the fundamental drives of man. And since it tries to depict the humanity hidden there, it often unavoidably takes as its subject matter phenomena that are at variance with the lives of ordinary citizens, such as adultery, homosexual love, rape, and consanguineous relations. If the pen portrays those activities in a suggestive manner, then we cannot deny the existence of obscenity in the work, and speaking in general, as the majority opinion explained, an artistic work can be at the same time obscene writing. However, it can be regarded as one characteristic of the techniques of modern literature to repudiate compromise with the world, to ignore or deny God, morality or law, and to depict various aspects of immorality and immoral conduct which are not permitted in the real world, searching for the truth about man, trying to draw out from depths of anguish filled with bitterness what it is that will shake the emotions of the reader. If that is so, and if such works are suppressed solely on grounds that sex is dealt with in a suggestive manner, this will become a road leading to the obliteration of many literary works worthy of the name of literature. Where that work is earnest and truthful in its subject matter, where the portrayals of sex in its narrative are fit and appropriate, inextricably related to the subject matter, and where its value as art is high, it may not be unreasonable to see also the phenomenon of a sublimation of obscenity if the work is viewed as a whole. To the extent that is so, we may be able to say that

such a work is not obscene writing under Article 175 of the Criminal Code, in spite of the existence of obscenity in form. Even if a sublimation of obscenity is not acknowledged with respect to such a work, to restrict with penal provisions its distribution and sale, and thus in fact any reading or appreciation of it, just because obscenity is present, would constitute a grave problem in the area of the nation's culture; and as explained below, the propriety of that restriction must be challenged as long as we respect freedom of expression.

How about something that is recognized as a somewhat literary work, although deficient in the conditions noted above? In this case, although there is no room for perceiving a sublimation of obscenity, the portrayals of sex in such a work are different from the modalities of pornography, they are not themselves the purpose, they are more or less subordinate to the subject matter of the work, and they are inevitably or naturally connected for the purpose of presenting the author's literary opinions.

Accordingly, to hastily deny these factors by reason of obscenity and leave it at that raises not a few doubts related to freedom of expression.

3. Probably no one will take exception if we say that freedom of expression under Article 21 of the Constitution includes not only the freedom of speech and the press, but also the freedom to know. Speaking only of phraseology, this provision differs from Article 19 of the Universal Declaration of Human Rights and Article 5 of the Basic Law of the German Federal Republic in not touching anywhere on the freedom to know; but of course we should not for that reason conclude that the freedom to know is not guaranteed by the Constitution. However, that is because freedom of expression presupposes communication with other people, and freedom of expression is meaningless without the freedom to read, listen, and see. We must consider that the freedom to seek and obtain ideas and information and the freedom to publish and distribute are bound up with and supplement each other. That is so not only from the standpoint of the individual's freedom of expression, but also from the people's right to the pursuit of happiness (Article 13 of the Constitution). In short, the freedom to appreciate a literary work and receive its values must be fully respected along with the freedom to publish, distribute, and so on. Absent special circumstances, cultural development can be anticipated precisely when both ordinary types of books and works whose great artistic or intellectual value is clear and virtually undisputed are freely published and distributed and freely read. Even if the distribution and so forth of such a work have some undesirable affect on the order in society regarding sex, as long as there is rather substantial social value in publishing that work and letting it be appreciated, seizing upon that distribution and so on as suspect under Article 175 of the Criminal Code amounts, in result, to a violation of freedom of expression. In addition, to bring charges for such acts under Article

175 of the Criminal Code is not permitted by the Constitution, and consequently, we might say that the above-noted work as well is not obscene writing under this same provision.

4. The majority opinion says:

> Freedom of the press and of other expression and academic freedom are extremely important as foundations of democracy, but they are not absolute and without limits, their abuse is forbidden, and they are placed under limitations for the public welfare. . . . When writings of artistic and intellectual merit are obscene, then to make them the object of penalties in order to uphold order and healthy customs in sexual life is of benefit to the life of the whole nation.

Certainly, freedom of expression differs from the freedoms of thought and conscience in that it necessarily involves external speech and action. When it is abused, there is injury to public social interests, or there is conflict with the rights or freedoms of other people. As explained above by the majority opinion, it should not be in essence unlimited. However, it hardly bears special mention that since free speech and a free press are foundations of democracy and basic conditions for the development of culture extending across all spheres, we must be extremely cautious about restricting them. Even when restriction for the public welfare is unavoidable, the way to fulfill the spirit of the Constitution is to give serious thought to what the public welfare is in that case, making an effort to deepen and concretize that concept. We must strictly avoid an attitude which casually uses the abstract notion of the public welfare and cuts down on freedom of expression with great dispatch. It is very regrettable that the majority opinion makes no reference at all to this point.

5. There is something I want to touch on here. The majority opinion claims that if a given book is found obscene, that does not immediately remove that book from society, because only its distribution and sale are penalized. But is that really so? By their nature literary works stimulate the imagination of readers and appeal to their feelings through the medium of words that are intelligible to people in general. Is it not impossible to have a novel with no expectation of a readership? Works that exist only in manuscript, works which are subject to seizure or confiscation in a hit-or-miss fashion if they come out, with the very few remaining copies becoming deeply cherished in the homes of the fortunate, works which are read only in secrecy; such as these have almost lost their meaning as literary works. Works which have fallen into such circumstances have been virtually erased from social existence. A confiscation based on a definite judgment may be tolerable, because it is usually preceded by a series of careful procedures, but should situations occur frequently in which a work is promptly expelled at the investigative stage from society (moreover, it is even possible that by a later definite judicial

decision that work will be held not to be obscene writing), it must be considered a grave problem. As a rule, a warrant from a court is necessary for a seizure in the course of an investigation, and to that extent, it means there is experience of a check based on "judicial authority"; but those procedures are a work carried on behind closed doors, and no opportunity is given to present contrary evidence. Besides that, since a warrant is issued if there appears to be tentative confirmation of the charges, this is clearly not comparable in circumspection to the procedures of judicial adjudication. Furthermore, if it is a case that can be regarded as a flagrant offense, there is no examination at all by the courts. Depending on the case, the seizure in question by investigating officers may go beyond the jurisdiction of judicial police, and they may even be performing their functions with preventive measures in the manner of administrative police. Not only that, but the processes of creation, publication, distribution, and so on can be restrained in advance at each stage with a pseudo-self-regulation out of fear of a hint of arrest or out of psychological compulsion by police warning. Valuable works that might become cultural treasures can even be consigned from darkness to darkness. Each restraint like the above willy-nilly gives rise to a chain reaction, and if its influence is broad in time and in place, we are in danger of inviting a serious situation attended by a substantial obstruction of the development through publications of culture, extending from the present into the future.

6. As stated above, the distribution and so on even of work with obscene passages should not be questioned under Article 175 of the Criminal Code, so long as the social value of that work predominates over the antisocial qualities of the obscenity. However, even if it is called a masterpiece, a book produced by editing such a work and altering it to extract the spicy passages and by manipulating in order to accentuate especially those parts, buries the subject matter that is the core of the work, and exists for nothing but the portrayals of sexual activities themselves. Needless to say, penalizing its distribution and so on as obscene writing does not constitute an infringement on freedom of expression. This is because it can be looked at in isolation from the original work, as virtually a separate book verging on pornography. On the other hand, even when a work is published as is without alteration, there still remain problems such as the following. Namely, when it is found that in the approach to publication, distribution, and sales for profit, the format of the printing and binding, and the methods of promotion, advertising, sales, and so on are clearly intended to appeal to base and prurient interests and preoccupations, and to arouse sexual passion in the reader, then we should conclude that there is no problem from the standpoint of the Constitution in penalizing the work's distribution and so on as obscene writing, even if the work has social value. However, the presence or absence of obscenity and the social value of the work should

be judged in light of the effect on the general reader who has read through the book in a serious-minded way, following the theme and ideas contained in the work as a whole. The very methods like those noted above, which are referred to as pandering, intend precisely the negation of such an attitude in reading; and as a result, because the obscenity of the work stands out clearly, I cannot help thinking that the social value of the work degenerates into vulgarity.

Now the decision below makes no determination concerning the social value of the translation in question. Moreover, it hardly touches on various important surrounding circumstances such as the above concerning its publication and sale. Since my own views differ with their premises this is unavoidable, but in my personal opinion, there is clear illegality in the failure of the court below to conduct a thorough inquiry, and it would consequently be proper to overrule the decision below and remand the case to the court below. However, when one reads this translation through and looks upon it as a whole, as stated below, there is no reason why one cannot see this translation from the outset as a book that does not excessively stimulate and arouse sexual desires in the general reader. If that is so, it means that in this case, without any need for added deliberations, there is nothing that should be punished as crimes of selling obscene writing and possessing the same.

7. The original work behind the translation in this case is something created by the Marquis de Sade, who uses the form of the novel in order to present his inquiry into human nature and his distinctive ideas; but if we look at the translation that is now the problem, I at least cannot avoid doubting whether its art is really of a high order. (How the question of great artistic value is judged often depends on the subjective view of the person appreciating a work. I do not consider the courts the proper place to make determinations on this matter, except in special cases, nor does it belong to their duties.) Moreover, I cannot suppress the feeling that there are portrayals of sexual activities in this book which are unnecessarily explicit. The fourteen passages in the present translation which are pointed out in the decision below, as noted in the first instance judgment, portray scenes of licentious sex involving lewd homosexual and heterosexual conduct; they intersperse descriptions of the style and manner of sexual activities with the conversation of the actors and the feelings they experience; and they are quite explicit and concrete. However, in the translation the caution was taken of using the secret language of the Edo period [ca. 1600–1868], which is now completely dead language, concerning the organs of sex and depraved sexual activities. Not only can we discover no intention at all of titillating or intoxicating the reader by currying to man's sexual interests, but if one reads through the work in a disinterested way, he can discern in the style of the writing the translator's sincerity in trying to convey faithfully to the reader the ideas and themes of the author of the original. It is particularly notable that in

this volume there is nothing about the normal sexual activities of men and women. What is described there are numerous unreal acts that are outside the experience of Japanese readers, and even what is lewd is almost entirely lacking in feeling. In the designated passages and before and after them, facts and words are repeatedly stated which deny religion and morality, and blaspheme against God, but all belong to the realm of the fantastic. They are grotesque in the extreme, and almost sufficiently filthy to make one vomit. The ordinary person cannot but find it basically something of a pain to read through the whole book. Although there are sexually stimulating elements in places, it may not be too much to say that their effects are completely deadened and erased if one looks at the work as a whole. We should not make a judgment on the presence or absence of obscenity in a work in a manner that capriciously picks out one part and magnifies its importance in weighing the problem. In the final analysis, the translation in the present case does not titillate sexual sensation and does not stimulate and arouse sexual desire. Even if we follow the views presented in the Supreme Court decision in the Chatterley Case regarding the definition of obscenity, I must contend that it is an error to hold this work to be obscene writing under Article 175 of the Criminal Code.

Justices Masatoshi Yokota (presiding), Toshio Irie, Asanosuke Kusaka, Yoshihiko Kido, Kazuto Ishida, Jirō Tanaka, Jirō Matsuda, Makoto Iwata, Kazuo Shimomura, Kōtarō Irokawa, Ken'ichirō Ōsumi, Masao Matsumoto, and Ken'ichi Okuno.

Case 27. Ōno v. *Japan (1961).* The Moxa Advertising Case

15 *Keishū* 2 at p. 347; Supreme Court, Grand Bench, 15 February 1961; Ōtsu Summary Ct. (First Instance), Osaka High Ct. (Second Instance), [constitutionality of limitations on freedom in business advertising].

EDITORIAL NOTE: A practitioner of traditional Japanese medical arts (i.e., acupuncture, moxa cautery, massage, and *jūdō* therapy) distributed thousands of fliers concerning his business. For this he was fined in summary court for violating the law regulating such occupations, and his conviction was upheld by the Osaka High Court.

He appealed to the Supreme Court, contending that appropriate advertising such as his of the benefits of moxa cautery is a matter of right under the Constitution, and that the prohibitions on such advertising in the law in question are in violation of the freedoms of thought, conscience, and expression.

REFERENCES

Constitution of Japan [ARTICLES 11, 12, 13, 19, and 21 were at issue in this case. See Appendix 3 for these provisions].

Law Regulating Practitioners of Massage, Acupuncture, Moxa Cautery, and Jūdō *Therapy* (*Law 217 of 1947*, as amended), ARTICLE 7, 1. No person shall advertise by any method any matter other than those stipulated below concerning massage, acupuncture, moxa cautery, or *jūdō* therapy, or concerning places for such treatments:

(1) Name and address of the practitioner;

(2) The type of occupation, in accordance with stipulations of Article 1;

(3) The name of the practitioner's place of business, its address, and its telephone number;

(4) The days and hours of business;

(5) Other matters prescribed by the Minister of Welfare.

2. Advertisements regarding items 1 through 3 above shall not include the method of therapy, the skill, or the personal history of the practitioner.

FORMAL JUDGMENT

The *jōkoku* appeal in this case is dismissed. The costs of the proceedings shall be borne by the accused.

REASONS. With respect to the contentions of the accused:

Article 7 of the Law Regulating Practitioners of Massage, Acupuncture, Moxa Cautery, and *Jūdō* Therapy prohibits in an advertisement, by any method, of massage, acupuncture, and moxa cautery or of places for such treatments, the inclusion of information other than that stipulated in each item of Article 7, paragraph 1. Under the same paragraph the method of therapy, the skill, and the personal history of the practitioner are also excluded from matters that may be advertised. According to the facts lawfully ascertained by the court of first instance, the accused, who practices moxa cautery, widely distributed approximately 7,030 copies of a flier stating the efficacy of moxa cautery for such ailments as neuralgia, rheumatism, dizziness, and disorders of the stomach and intestines. Since it is clear that those stated do not correspond to the abovementioned stipulated matters, we must hold that the above acts of the accused were in violation of Article 7, whether or not the above statement of alleged efficacy is found to be an advertisement of the skills of the accused, and whether or not moxa cautery is actually effective against the above ailments.

The accused contends that the advertisement at issue does nothing more than generally inform the public of the efficacy of moxa cautery; since this is in no way contrary to the public welfare, if this Article is taken as prohibiting such advertisements, then this Article is invalid as in contravention of Articles 11, 13, 19, and 21 of the Constitution. However, there are reasons why this law establishes such restrictions as the above regarding the practice and place of massage, acupuncture, and moxa cautery, and why the advertisement of their alleged efficacy is not permitted. When such is permitted without restraint, there is a danger that the general public will be misled by the tendency toward exaggeration and misrepresentation of those too eagerly soliciting patients. There is concern about inviting, as a result, loss of opportunity to receive the proper medical treatment at the proper time. Prohibiting the advertisement of other than the prescribed matters in order to prevent such ill effects beforehand must be approved as a measure unavoidable for the maintenance of the public welfare from the standpoint of the nation's health and hygiene. Thus, Article 7 does not violate Article 21 of the Constitution, and the argument to the contrary is groundless.

Furthermore, restrictions on advertising such as the above do not *ipso facto* impair freedom of thought and freedom of conscience. Since the above restrictions on advertising were established for the public welfare, as explained above, neither are the above provisions contrary to Articles 11, 13, and 19 of the Constitution. On this matter as well, the contentions of the accused are not justified.

Consequently, in accordance with Articles 181, 396, and 414 of the Code of Criminal Procedure, this Court holds as in the Formal Judgment.

This decision represents the unanimous opinion of the justices, except for the supplementary opinions of Justices Katsumi Tarumi and Daisuke Kawamura, and the dissenting opinions of Justices Yūsuke Saitō, Hachirō Fujita, Ken'ichi Okuno, and Matasuke Kawamura.

* * *

The supplementary opinion of Justice Katsumi Tarumi follows.

An expression of the mind (the will) does not necessarily correspond to the term "expression" under the provisions of Article 21 of the Constitution. This is exemplified by the conclusion of a contract regarding property, or by advertising to solicit a contract. It appears that in the United States an expression of will is construed under the Constitution to refer to freedom of expression and other intellectual activities that enjoy strong protections, and not to economic freedom, which is not afforded the same kind of protection.

A therapy such as the moxa cautery in the present case is paid for, and advertisement thereof is an economic activity and a means to making a profit. In the final analysis, therefore, it is subject to strong constitutional restrictions designed to control property rights. Such occupations as the medical and legal professions may be practiced without monetary compensation, at times on a regular basis. But it would endanger the public welfare for a person without special qualifications of knowledge and experience to make his business such a profession, which affects the lives and health of a large number of people. (A lawyer performs important functions involving human rights and freedom.) In such occupations, one should not solicit clients through advertisement, but instead, should compete in a fair and free manner on the basis of one's actual merit, as suggested in the old saying: "A fair face wins praise though its owner stays silent." A provision like Article 7 of the law in question which properly restricts the content and method of advertising this type of profession is well within constitutional limitations of economic freedom, or at least of freedom of occupation. None of the provisions of Article 7 of this law restricts the freedom of expression in Article 21 of the Constitution.

Nonetheless, does not Article 7 of the said law restrict advertisement too severely?

Is it not permissible to advertise concerning those ailments that are alleviated by moxa cautery and the like? Would not an advertisement describing ailments usually dealt with by a *jūdō* therapist be a convenience for patients who might, given the choice, go to a nearby *jūdō* therapist rather than to a doctor? These questions may be raised, but, the apparent intent of the provision of Article 7 of the law in question, which prohibits inclusion in advertisement of the names of ailments alleviated by therapy, is to prevent one engaged in moxa cautery, however well-intentioned, not only from competing with other practitioners of moxa cautery or with doctors by unfair advertisements exaggerating the efficacy of the therapy, but also from administering to a patient who is critically ill, without thorough diagnosis, treatments that are inappropriate or even dangerous. Moreover, the law appears to encourage early diagnosis and treatment by a doctor. Thus, the law does not seem to constitute unreasonable penal law in violation of the provisions of Article 31 of the Constitution.

In short, the provisions of Article 7 of the law in question neither violate nor involve the provisions of Article 21 of the Constitution. Rather, the propriety of the provisions is probably a question of legislative policy falling under the jurisdiction of the Diet.

* * *

The gist of the supplementary opinion of Justice Daisuke Kawamura follows.

If freedom of advertisement were included in Article 21 of the Constitution which protects freedom of expression, the propriety of the revision (effected by Law 116 of 1951), which resulted in a general ban under Article 1, paragraph 1 on advertisement of undesignated information, might be questioned. However, the provisions of paragraph 2 of the same Article follow the intent of provisions of Article 7 in the older law by prohibiting advertisements revealing the skills and background of the practitioner of moxa cautery and his method of therapy, which would probably be used to solicit patients. The provisions of paragraph 2 have their own significance independently of the propriety of paragraph 1. It will be sufficient to examine whether or not the restrictions prescribed in paragraph 2 constitute a reasonable restriction of freedom of expression, inasmuch as the action of the accused falls under the subject matter of the provisions of paragraph 2. The legislative intent behind the ban on advertisement of the method of therapy, the skill, and the personal history of the practitioner derives from concern lest such advertisements fall into exaggeration or misrepresentation, and thereby create the danger of public confusion. Thus, the provisions of paragraph 2 limiting advertisements are a reasonable restriction upon the freedom of advertisement growing out of the need to protect the public welfare, and do not violate Article 21 of the Constitution. The other arguments, which contend that Article 7 of the law in question is contrary to Articles 11, 13, and 19 of the Constitution, are groundless.

* * *

The gist of the dissenting opinion of Justice Yūsuke Saitō follows.

According to the facts ascertained by the court below, the advertisement in the present case merely listed neuralgia, rheumatism, dizziness, and disorders of the stomach and intestines as ailments dealt with by moxa cautery, and no exaggeration or misinterpretation was found in the advertisement. On the contrary, it is a proven fact that moxa cautery is indeed effective against such ailments. Therefore, the acts of the accused in the present case should not be held liable.

* * *

The gist of the dissenting opinion of Justice Hachirō Fujita follows.

The facts in the present case, both as presented in the indictment and as ascertained by the court of first instance, indicate that the accused "distributed fliers" that describe neuralgia, rheumatism, dizziness, and disorders of the stomach and intestines as ailments dealt with by moxa cautery. The provisions of Article 7 of the law should not be construed to prohibit the description in the present advertisement of general ailments dealt with by moxa cautery. Consequently, the facts as publicly prosecuted in the present case do not constitute a violation of the provisions of the clause in question. As far as the disposition of the present case is concerned, there is no need to argue the constitutionality of the provisions of Article 7 of the law in question, but a need to reverse the decision of the first instance and to acquit the accused.

* * *

The dissenting opinion of Justice Ken'ichi Okuno, concurred in by Justice Matasuke Kawamura follows.

There is some disagreement as to whether or not freedom of advertisement should be treated as freedom of expression protected under Article 21 of the Constitution. This provision should be construed to include advertisement inasmuch as it protects not only the expression of thought and conscience but also all other forms of expression. It cannot be argued that an advertisement that has the character of a commercial activity should lie outside the protections of the provisions of the Article in question. Granted that freedom of expression is not without its limits, and that abuses thereof are not permissible. Like other fundamental human rights guaranteed in the Constitution, freedom of expression may be restricted in favor of the public welfare. Naturally an advertisement should be prohibited or restricted when it contains false or exaggerated statements or when its form and method are contrary to the public welfare. The provisions of Article 7 of the Law Regulating Practitioners of Massage, Acupuncture, Moxa Cautery and *Jūdō* Therapy prohibit the practitioner from advertising by any method the ailments responsive to moxa cautery, and establish penalties for violations thereof. This prohibits not only exaggerated or false advertisement, but also true and reasonable advertisement of the ailments responsive to the therapy. (These provisions cannot be construed as not prohibiting reasonable advertisement of ailments responsive to the therapy.) In the first place, the law in question permits, through licensing, qualified persons to make it their profession to administer moxa cautery and similar quasi-medical therapies. In other words, the law recognizes their therapeutic effects on certain ailments and establishes licensing of moxa cautery and similar therapeutic techniques. It follows that the public is entitled, from the standpoint of health, hygiene, and the public welfare, to be informed honestly and appropriately of those ailments against which such therapy is efficacious. No justification can exist for the complete ban on true and appropriate advertisement. Such a prohibition undoubtedly constitutes unreasonable restriction of freedom of expression.

It goes beyond reasonable limits to prohibit true and reasonable advertisement simply on the grounds that, as argued by the majority, without some restraints on advertising there is the danger that the public will be confused by exaggerated or false statements designed to solicit patients. Of course prior restraints on all advertising would enable the police to prevent any false or exaggerated advertisements; but at the same time it would prevent a person from reasonable advertising, and thereby unreasonably restrict by facile police measures the freedom for proper expression. Such prior restraints are no more justified than a prohibition on demonstration marches that do not pose a clear and present danger to public safety, but involve the possible danger of occasionally disturbing the public peace. No rational grounds can be found to justify a complete ban on even reasonable advertisement of moxa cautery, especially in light of the provisions of Article 34 of the Pharmaceutical Law. This Article prohibits no advertisements except exaggerated or false advertisements of medical supplies usually considered to affect the human body more seriously than moxa cautery and the like. Furthermore, if, as the majority opinion argues, a patient "loses an opportunity to receive the proper medical treatment at the proper time" because of moxa cautery treatments he or she has undergone, then such therapy as moxa cautery should be banned from the beginning. As it is, on the one hand, the law in question is based on the argument that such therapy might cause loss of proper medical treatment at the proper time, and prohibits even reasonable advertisement; but on the other hand, it acknowledges the therapeutic effect of moxa cautery and similar treatments, and licenses it as a quasi-medical profession. In this, the law seems to contradict itself.

Moreover, there may be some doubt about whether those who have accepted the premises of the law prohibiting any kind of advertisement of ailments responsive to such therapies, and who have received licenses, can challenge the constitutionality of such restrictions. But since restricting the freedom of expression guaranteed by the Constitution cannot be made a condition for issuing a license, such a doubt cannot be real.

In short, the provisions of Article 7 of the law in question, which prohibit even true and proper advertisement of ailments related to the therapy, constitute an unreasonable restraint on freedom of expression, and should be held invalid and in contravention of the Constitution. Furthermore, the decision of the court of first instance, which convicted the defendant in accordance with the provisions of the Article in question, should be quashed as an unconstitutional judgment.

Justices Kotarō Tanaka (presiding), Katsushige Kotani, Tamotsu Shima, Yūsuke Saitō, Hachirō Fujita, Matasuke Kawamura, Katsu Ikeda, Katsumi Tarumi, Daisuke Kawamura, Masuo Shimoiizaka, Ken'ichi Okuno, Kiyoshi Takahashi, Tsuneshichi Takagi, and Shūichi Ishizaka.

Case 28. Nishida v. *Japan (1963).* The Faith Healing Case

17 *Keishū* 4 at p. 303; Supreme Court, Grand Bench, 15 May 1963; Osaka Dist. Ct. (First Instance), Osaka High Ct. (Second Instance), [constitutional limits of religious practices].

EDITORIAL NOTE: In a case arising in 1957, a mentally disturbed woman, Yoshiko, died while under the care of the accused Yae Nishida, a priestess in a bona fide Buddhist sect. Nishida took steps prescribed by her religion to cure Yoshiko and to drive an evil spirit (conceived of locally as a badger spirit) out of Yoshiko, upon the request of her family and with their participation in the proceedings. Although Yoshiko was physically weak at the time, her family had lost trust in the family physician and had turned to Nishida for assistance. Sutras were chanted, incense burned, and her body rubbed with prayer beads; she was held down when in a disturbed state about her perceived possession by a badger spirit. She did not receive hospital care and died.

Nishida alone was brought to trial and convicted of inflicting injury resulting in death. She appealed her conviction, contending there was neither criminal intent nor bodily harmful religious excesses perpetrated on the deceased. Moreover, Nishida maintained that the court of first instance manifested religious bias in reducing sincere religious beliefs and practices to superstition and ignorance. The Osaka High Court upheld her conviction, and she appealed to the Supreme Court.

REFERENCES

Constitution of Japan [ARTICLE 20 was at issue in this case. See Appendix 3 for this provision].

Criminal Code, ARTICLE 205, 1. A person, who inflicts an injury upon the person of another and thereby causes the latter's death, shall be punished with penal servitude for a limited period of not less than two years.

2. When the crime is committed against a lineal ascendant of the offender or of the spouse thereof, the offender shall be punished with penal servitude for life or not less than three years.

FORMAL JUDGMENT

The *jōkoku* appeal in this case is quashed.

REASONS. Concerning points 1, 3, and 5 of the *jōkoku* appeal presented by counsel, Y. Kobayashi:

The argument for appeal amounts simply to contentions of violation of procedural law and erroneous fact-finding, which are not grounds for *jōkoku* appeal under Article 405 of the Code of Criminal Procedure. (Moreover, the appeal contends that the court below was predisposed to bias in the taking of evidence and was seriously mistaken in its finding of fact. However, a close examination of the record did not reveal a trace of evidence that we should acknowledge bias on the part of the court below in the taking of evidence and finding of facts, as alleged by the appeal. In the final analysis, the appeal is a criticism of the acceptance and exclusion of evidence, the finding of facts, and the judgment, all of which were within the discretion of the court below. Furthermore, regarding the inspection of evidence forming the contents of a protocol of inspection prepared by the judicial police and dated 25 October 1958, point 5 of the appeal contends that such a protocol of inspection cannot stand as evidence, because it was a blasphemy against religion in trying to recreate religious acts without involving religion. Although the outward forms of religious functions, and not religious acts per se, are reconstructed in the course of necessary investigation, that one fact does not make it a blasphemy against religion, and it cannot be said that a protocol of evidence that records the circumstances of those actions does not have the force of evidence. Not only that, but regarding the use of the above protocol in evidence, it is clear from the record—Proceedings, No. 355, *chō*—that the accused agreed to it, and the appeal is mistaken in claiming there was objection to its use as documentary evidence.)

Concerning points 2, 4, and 6 of the appeal:

The portions of the argument for appeal that deal with contentions of unconstitutionality will be considered here. It goes without saying that freedom of religion is extremely important as one of the fundamental human rights. Article 20, paragraph 1, guarantees freedom of religion to all; and paragraph 2 of the same Article provides that no person shall be compelled to take part in any religious acts, celebration, rite, or practice. However, Article 12 of the Constitution prescribes that the people must not abuse the fundamental human rights, and shall always be responsible for utilizing them for the public welfare. And the intent of Article 13 of the Constitution is that, to the extent they do not interfere with the public welfare, fundamental human rights shall be the supreme consideration in legislation and in other governmental affairs. These constitutional provisions should never be referred to, as they are in the appeal, as merely didactic provisions; accordingly, the guarantee of freedom of religion is not absolute and unlimited.

According to the findings of the first instance judgment in this case, confirmed by the decision below, the acts of the accused in this instance consisted of the religious acts of offering prayers and incense in petition for the recovery of the victim, Yoshiko, from a mental disorder; but the manner, methods, and motives in practicing this faith cure, attended by a degree of violence that ended in the victim's loss of life, and so on, cannot possibly be recognized as acts of medical treatment for persons with mental disorders generally accepted in medical practice. Even if we grant that the acts of the accused in this case were, as argued, a kind of religious act, they correspond to unlawful exercise of physical force endangering the life and limb of another person, as was held by the above-mentioned judgments. Accordingly, the above acts of the accused undeniably ended in the death of the victim and were seriously inimical to society; they deviated from the boundaries of the freedom of religion guaranteed in Article 20, paragraph 1 of the Constitution, and the punishment of these acts under Article 205 of the Criminal Code in no way violates the above provisions of the Constitution. The judgments in the lower courts to the same effect are correct, and appellant's contention of unconstitutionality cannot be accepted.

The remaining points in the appeal simply bring up contentions of violation of statute and erroneous fact-finding, which do not constitute proper grounds for *jōkoku* appeal under Article 405 of the Code of Criminal Procedure. (Moreover, the determination of the decision below that the acts of the accused in this case are hard to accept as proper occupational conduct, as stipulated under Article 35 of the Criminal Code, is accepted as correct by the present Court in its affirmation of the factual relationships.) Examination of the record indicates we cannot apply Article 411 of the Code of Criminal Procedure. Accordingly, pursuant to Article 408 of the same Code, by the unanimous decision of the Justices, the Judgment is as in the Formal Judgment.

Justices Kisaburō Yokota (presiding), Matasuke Kawamura, Toshio Irie, Katsu Ikeda, Katsumi Tarumi, Daisuke Kawamura, Masuo Shimoiizaka, Ken'ichi Okuno, Shūichi Ishizaka, Sakunosuke Yamada, Kakiwa Gokijyō, Masatoshi Yokota, Kitarō Saitō, and Asanosuke Kusaka.

Case 29. Tokyo Public Prosecutor v. *Senda (1963).* The Popolo Players Case

17 *Keishū* 4 at p. 370; Supreme Court, Grand Bench, 22 May 1963; Tokyo Dist. Ct. (First Instance), Tokyo High Ct. (Second Instance), [university autonomy, academic freedom, and police investigation on campus].

EDITORIAL NOTE: The most important Supreme Court decision in post–1945 Japan regarding university autonomy and academic freedom came in 1963. On 20 February 1952, a student theatrical group at the University of Tokyo put on a political play for the university community. The group had received permission to use a campus lecture hall for the occasion on the basis of a promise in writing not to engage in political activities. The promise was not kept.

During the play students discovered four plainclothesmen in the audience and accosted two of them. In the policemen's notebooks the students found evidence of campus police inquiries concerning certain faculty members. The police had tickets to the play, but they were assaulted and forced to write a letter of apology in the presence of a university official for their campus intrusion. The accused, one of the students involved, was arrested for crimes of violence, but he was acquitted by both the Tokyo District Court and the Tokyo High Court on grounds of defending university autonomy. The prosecutor appealed to the Supreme Court, which handed down its decision eleven years after the incident.

REFERENCES

Constitution of Japan [ARTICLES 21 and 23 were at issue in this case. See Appendix 3 for these provisions].

School Education Law (*Law 26 of 1947*), ARTICLE 52. The university, as a center of learning, shall aim at teaching and studying higher learning and technical arts as well as giving broad general culture and developing the intellectual, moral, and practical abilities.

Fundamental Law of Education (*Law 25 of 1947*), ARTICLE 8, 1. The political knowledge necessary for intelligent citizenship shall be valued in education.

2. The schools prescribed by law shall refrain from political education or other political activities for or against any specific political party.

Criminal Code (*Law 45 of 1907*, as amended), ARTICLE 233. A person who injures the credit of another or obstructs his business by circulating false reports or by the use of fraudulent means shall be punished with imprisonment at forced labor for not more than three years or a fine of not more than 1,000 yen.

ARTICLE 234. A person who obstructs the business of another by the use of force shall be dealt with in the same way as provided in the preceding Article.

Law concerning the Execution of Duties of Police Officials (*Law 136 of 1948*), ARTICLE 4, 1. In case of a dangerous situation, such as a natural calamity, incident, or destruction of a structure, traffic accident . . . [or a situation] that threatens to cause an injury to the lives and persons of the people or serious damage to their property, a police official may give necessary warning to a person who happens to be on the scene . . . or order the person under threatening danger . . . and any other person concerned with it to take measures generally considered necessary for preventing the danger as well as take such measures himself as mentioned above.

2. Any action taken under the provisions of the preceding paragraph shall be reported through channels to the respective public safety commission concerned. In such cases the commission shall advise other government agencies of such action where it deems it appropriate in order to obtain proper coordination for further handling of the situation.

ARTICLE 5. A police official may, in cases where he considers any crime or offense is about to be committed, give a necessary warning to every person concerned with it in order to prevent it, and to stop an act of a person in cases where the act threatens to cause injury to the lives and persons of the people or serious damage to their property, and the case is so urgent that it admits of no delay.

ARTICLE 6, 1. In cases where any dangerous situation provided for in the preceding two Articles has come to pass, and the lives, persons, or property of the people are in jeopardy, if a police official considers it inevitably necessary for preventing the danger, holding the spread of damage in check, or giving relief to the sufferers, he may enter any person's lands, buildings, vessel, or vehicle to the limit considered reasonably required for taking such measures.

2. A keeper or any person corresponding to the said keeper of a place of performance, hotel, restaurant, railway station, or any other place to which many people have access, cannot, without sufficient reason, deny a police official entrance into his or her premises during the time when it is opened, if he or she is ordered to allow the entry by the official for the purpose of preventing a crime or danger to the lives, persons, or property of the people.

3. Upon entry as provided for in the preceding two paragraphs, a police official shall not arbitrarily interfere with the lawful operation of the business of the person concerned.

4. Upon entry as provided for in paragraphs 1 or 2, a police official, if requested, shall tell the keeper or the person corresponding to the said keeper of the reason for entry, as well as showing the person mentioned above a certificate of his identification.

FORMAL JUDGMENT

1. Both the decision below and the first instance judgment are quashed.

2. This case is remanded to the Tokyo District Court.

REASONS. With regard to the purport of the appeal presented by T. Hanai, chief prosecutor, Tokyo High Public Prosecutor's Office:

Upon examination of the contention that the judgment below erred in construing and applying the provision for academic freedom in Article 23 of the Constitution, this Court holds as follows:

The academic freedom of that Article includes freedom for academic research and the freedom to announce the results of that study. The guarantee of academic freedom under that Article intends that such freedoms should be broadly guaranteed to all the people, but especially to the university in light of its essential nature as a center of arts and sciences where truth is intensively pursued. The freedoms of education and teaching are closely related to academic freedom, but are not necessarily included therein. However, with respect to the university, it is proper to consider the freedom of professors and other research staff to teach the results of their specialized studies in the university to be guaranteed under the intent of that constitutional provision, and the parallel provisions of Article 52 of the School Education Law, which states in part: "The university, as a center of learning, shall aim at teaching and studying higher learning and technical arts. . . ." That is to say, professors and other research personnel are guaranteed the freedom to teach the results of their studies in lectures and seminars at the university. Although no such freedom can escape limitations in accordance with the public welfare, based on the abovementioned essential nature of the university, freedom is interpreted somewhat more broadly in the university than is generally the case.

University autonomy has traditionally been recognized in order to guarantee freedom of learning in the university. This autonomy is particularly recognized with respect to personnel matters affecting professors and other researchers in the university; the university's president, professors, and other research staff are selected on the basis of the autonomous judgment of the university. Moreover, a certain degree of autonomy is recognized in supervising the facilities and students of the university, and to some extent, independent authority to maintain order on campus is also recognized.

Thus, since the university's academic freedom and autonomy are based on the essential nature of the university as a center of arts and sciences where truth is intensively pursued and high learning and technical arts are studied and taught, they refer directly to the freedoms of professors and other research personnel to conduct research in the arts and sciences, and to report on and teach about the results, and to the autonomy that guarantees these activities. As a result of such freedom and autonomy, facilities are autonomously supervised by the university authorities, and students also enjoy academic freedom and the use of the university facilities. Basically, the students enjoy the same academic freedom as the people in general under Article 23 of the Constitution. However, as a result of the special academic freedom and autonomy given to university professors and other research personnel based on the essential nature of the university, the students of a university can enjoy a greater degree of academic freedom than the general public and can use the facilities autonomously administered by the university authorities.

A gathering of students in the university enjoys freedom and autonomy within the above parameters, and the fact that it involves an intramural group recognized by the university or that it is an intramural gathering held with university permission confers no special freedom and autonomy. In cases where a student gathering is not truly for academic study or for expression of the results of such, but rather engages in activities corresponding to political and social action in society at large, it cannot be said to enjoy the special academic freedom and autonomy possessed by the university. Furthermore, when that gathering is not exclusively for students, and especially when it is open to the general public, it should be regarded as a public gathering or at least should be treated as such.

According to the finding of facts in the court below, the gathering in the present case for a performance by the Tokyo University Popolo Players took place as part of a so-called anticolonialism struggle day, and the plot of the play was based on the so-called Matsukawa Case.* Before the play began a collection was taken in support of the accused in that case, and a report was given on the so-called Shibuya Incident.† These constitute activities corresponding to political and social actions of society at large; thus, it must be said that the gathering in question was not truly for the purposes of academic study and presentation. Moreover, according to the finding of facts of the same court, in the hall for the performance were visitors who were neither students nor members of the teaching or administrative staff of Tokyo University and who had bought admission tickets. The policemen in this case also bought

*On 17 August 1946, at about 3:00 A.M. a train overturned near Matsukawa Station on the Tōhoku Line of the Japan National Railways, resulting in the death of three railroad workers. Persons connected with leftist unions in the area were arrested on suspicion of sabotage resulting in deaths. After a long series of trials drawing widespread public interest and sharp political debate, the defendants were acquitted by the Supreme Court, but a number of questions remain only inconclusively answered. The definitive study of the Matsukawa Case is CHALMERS JOHNSON's *Conspiracy at Matsukawa* (Berkeley and Los Angeles: University of California Press, 1972), a mix of mystery novel, criminal law, and politics.

†Regarding the Shibuya Incident, see Justice Ishizaka's supplementary opinion below.

tickets and entered freely. From this we may judge that the general public was allowed freely to purchase tickets and enter. The gathering in question should not be referred to as a gathering only for specific students; it should rather be regarded as a public gathering, or should at least be treated as such. In light of the above factors, the gathering in question was not truly for the purpose of academic study and presentation, it involved social and political activities of society at large, and it was a public gathering or should be treated as such. We must state that such do not enjoy the academic freedom and autonomy of the university. Consequently, the entry of policemen into the intstant gathering was not an infringement upon the academic freedom and autonomy of the university.

Accordingly, the first instance judgment, which held the entry of policemen unlawful in light of the principle of university autonomy, and the decision below which upheld this first instance judgment, erred in interpreting the provision concerning academic freedom in Article 23 of the Constitution, and in construing and applying the law with respect to the limits of university autonomy. On these points, the prosecutor's argument is well founded. We do not render judgment on the other issues, but we must quash the decision below and the first instance judgment.

In accordance with Article 410, paragraph 1, Article 405, item 1, and Article 413 of the Code of Criminal Procedure, this Court renders its decision as in the Formal Judgment.

This judgment is the unanimous opinion of the justices, except for the supplementary opinions of Justices Toshio Irie, Katsumi Tarumi, Ken'ichi Okuno, Shūichi Ishizaka, Sakunosuke Yamada, and Kitarō Saitō, and the opinion of Justice Masatoshi Yokota.

* * *

The supplementary opinion of Justices Toshio Irie, Ken'ichi Okuno, Sakunosuke Yamada, and Kitarō Saitō follows.

"Academic freedom" under Article 23 of the Constitution is construed to encompass the student's freedom to learn as well as the freedoms of professors and other researchers to engage in academic research, and to report and teach about that research. In other words, at the same time that professors and other research personnel are guaranteed freedom of research, expression, and teaching without intervention by the state, students are guaranteed the freedom to receive instruction and to learn. Since the university, as a center of arts and sciences, is a place for education and a place for scholarship, we interpret this guarantee of academic freedom as a guarantee of the university's autonomy to the extent necessary to assure that freedom. If police activities were allowed such that police officers might regularly enter places of research and education of the university to observe the methods of research, presentation, and teaching of professors and other researchers and to inspect student gatherings held for academic purposes, or to collect information about such matters for police reports, then it is clear that academic freedom and university autonomy could not possibly be maintained. Accordingly, we must say it is an unlawful act in violation of the academic freedom and university autonomy guarantees of Article 23 of the Constitution for a policeman to enter the places of instruction and research of the university, particularly when it is not an exercise of the right of entry provided for in Article 6 of the Law concerning the Execution of Duties of Police Officials (at the time this case arose, the Law concerning the Execution of Duties of Police Officials, etc.), but merely for the purpose of gathering police information.

However, according to the finding of facts in the decision below, the gathering in question of the Popolo Players took place as part of a so-called "anticolonialism struggle day," and the plot of the play was based on the Matsukawa Case then pending in court; a collection was taken up for the defendants in the above case before the play began, and a report was given on the so-called Shibuya Incident. It cannot be judged a gathering truly for the purposes of academic study and presentation. Consequently, the police entry in the present cast cannot be called an unlawful act of the abovementioned type, violating academic freedom or university autonomy.

Nevertheless, it cannot be denied that at least the gathering in question was an indoor gathering at a university. Since the reason for guaranteeing freedom of assembly under Article 21 of the Constitution is to assure to the individuals in a gathering a free and mutual presentation and exchange of ideas and opinions, the freedom of expression of each individual could not be maintained and freedom of assembly would be violated if a gathering took place under the eyes of a policeman who entered the assembly for the purpose of gathering police information. Since there is no evidence that the gathering in question was not a peaceful one, and since the policemen entered to carry out police activities consisting only of gathering police information, without reference to the right of entry under Article 6 of the Law concerning the Execution of the Duties of Police Officials, it would be hard to firmly deny that any infringement on the constitutionally guaranteed freedom of assembly took place, even though the entry did not violate academic freedom or university autonomy. (The judgment below concluded that even though they had bought admission tickets, the policemen entered to carry on police intelligence activities, and not as individual private persons or as individual members of an audience. Moreover, even though the assembly in question should be treated as one open to the public, we cannot say there was no infringement upon freedom of assembly.)

However, even granting that the police entry in this case was unlawful, the manager of the premises of the gathering, or someone acting in this capacity, should have taken measures based on his supervisory authority to obstruct their unlawful acts by denying entry to the police or demanding the departure of those who had entered. In the event the police did not accede to the demand, forceful measures to obstruct or eject them would be violent acts; in that eventuality, the problem would arise of whether or not there existed grounds that nullified the illegality of those violent acts.

According to the findings of the decision below, the accused unreasonably detained the policemen and, as noted above, resorted to violence, although the police were withdrawing voluntarily. If so, the violence in this case cannot be termed conduct necessary in order to prevent the entry or to cause the removal of the police officers. When the policemen had abandoned their police activities and were on their way out, and when there was no present or imminent infringement or any connection with the removal of such, the accused assaulted the police officers. Accordingly, we cannot possibly recognize that conduct as an urgent and unavoidable necessity for the purpose of negating the unlawful acts.

Under our Criminal Code, in order to negate the illegality of an injurious act, the injurious act must be recognized as unavoidable and an urgent necessity for defense in the presence of infringement upon or danger to a legal interest, in such cases as legitimate self-defense, escape in an emergency, and so on. In the injurious act of the accused in the present case, no such urgency can be discerned. Not only that, but it is quite evident that no urgency sufficient to remove the illegality of injurious acts in this case can be acknowledged based on the past existence of illegal police activities or the prevention of illegal police activities in the future. The problem with both the first instance judgment and the decision below is that they put too much emphasis on the comparative consideration of legal interests and gave too little consideration to the above element of urgency. In short, those mistakes in interpretation of the Criminal Code materially affect these judgments; since a serious injustice would otherwise occur, we cannot but quash both the first instance judgment and the decision below.

* * *

The supplementary opinion of Justice Katsumi Tarumi follows.

1. *Academic activity* (gakumon). In its primary sense, "academic activity" in Article 23 of the Constitution refers to the specialized and systematic pursuit and elucidation of profound truths (including the fact of truth) and encompasses philosophy and all of the natural and social sciences. However, such fields as ethics, literature, and aesthetics include the search for creation of philosophical views of the world and human life, as well as beauty. Since freedom for the pursuit and creation of the higher arts should be guaranteed in the same way as academic activity in

its primary meaning, "academic activity" in Article 23 of the Constitution is understood to include the arts. (That is why Article 52 provides: "The university, as a center of learning, shall aim at . . . studying higher learning and technical arts. . . .") Contemporary arts and sciences are the product of thousands of years of human culture and civilization along with the additions of present-day scholars and artists. These constitute a foundation that makes possible for all the people a life with a healthy and a high degree of civilization and culture, and at the same time form the basis for the civilization and culture of the next generation. It is a great blessing for the nation that we have a large number of persons earnestly devoting themselves to the arts and sciences.

2. *Under the Constitution, who is to possess academic freedom?* I think the answer is, those individual scholars and artists who do specialized work in the arts and sciences with purpose and ability. Public and private universities are the perennial and organized center where many such scholars and artists study and elucidate the arts and sciences from a position of freedom and independence. The freedom for arts and sciences of the universities themselves, as distinct from the individual scholars and artists who constitute them, is guaranteed by the Constitution. But it is very difficult for one who is not a specialist to judge what is and what is not scholarship and art when he observes various schools of art and new theories and trends in art and scholarship; so in making such judgments we can only respect the common sense and good judgment of authoritative scholars and artists. However, since "academic," "arts and sciences," and "those freedoms" are legal concepts in laws and in the Constitution, when these become points at issue in litigation, must not the court, while retaining its respect for the opinions of scholars and artists, make legal judgments based in the final analysis on its own views? As long as the Diet and the executive adhere to the Constitution in making legal judgments, should they not judge within limits they themselves think constitutional, while maintaining their respect for the opinions of scholars? Is the majority opinion of this judgment not taking this position in considering academic freedom, and in distinguishing between those matters that do and do not belong to this freedom?

The second part of the majority opinion can be stated in summary as follows:

> Since academic freedom and university autonomy are based on the essential nature of the university, they refer directly to the freedoms of professors and other research personnel to conduct research in the arts and sciences and to report and teach about the results, and to the autonomy which guarantees these freedoms. As a result of such freedom and autonomy, the facilities are autonomously supervised by the university authorities, students can enjoy a greater degree of academic freedom than the general public and can use the facilities autonomously administered by the university authorities. A gathering of students in the university also enjoys freedom and autonomy within the above parameters.

However, when a given professor in the university is in the theatre or art department, students studying in that department receive instruction from that professor, or put on or appreciate a play under his guidance; all these acts are within the scope of the freedom laid down in the Constitution. However, I do not think that such acts, when engaged in by students of such Faculties as Law, Science, or Medicine who are not specializing in theatre, amount to specialized study of deep scholarship or the high arts. In providing that "the political knowledge necessary for intelligent citizenship shall be valued in education," Article 8 of the Fundamental Law of Education refers not only to university education, but also to senior high schools and so on; this is nothing more than one aspect of general education, like the above-mentioned performance of plays. Students at a university are free to make a scientific study of matters outside their majors and to develop themselves in the arts. Granted that special consideration should be given such activities because they are university students, but such activities also take place freely in junior and senior high schools and among the general populace. I do not think these activities can be referred to as falling under "the academic freedom of the university" merely because they are engaged in by university students at the university. To put on a play entirely apart from any intention or guidance of a professor or other specialist in the field is not study by a professor or researcher, nor does it necessarily correspond to specialized study of an art or science in a student's own chosen major. Furthermore, in this case, if the students received permission to use a lecture hall but did not indicate that they would be putting on a play based on the Matsukawa Case as part of an anticolonialism struggle day, if they performed such a play, and on that occasion raised funds and reported on the Shibuya Incident, then those activities were for purposes beyond those contained in the permit, and constituted unauthorized use or an abuse of the right to use the lecture hall. As held by the majority opinion, the gathering for the above-mentioned performance amounted to political and social activity in society at large and did not pertain to study in the arts and sciences. (The early years in our present-day universities are really not university but preparatory courses, and I have my doubts about whether those students are yet receiving instruction in profound and specialized learning and research.)

3. *When does a violation of the academic freedom of the university take place?* Such an infringement takes place when legislation, the courts or administrative powers are used to hamper or restrict a university, a scholar, or an artist in studying a certain subject or in presenting the results of such study, and when an individual pressures or obstructs a scholar in his research, conceals research materials, or induces him to engage in certain research and to reveal his materials. Such conduct would take place if, for example, some students arbitrarily piled desks and chairs at

the entrance to a classroom and picketed there so that the professor and the other students could not enter the classroom at classtime, or if the university authorities shut their eyes to such conduct. (It is granted, however, that since the university does not have extraterritorial rights, it cannot have its own police unit that could eliminate by force such disturbance of instruction.)

The Criminal Code does not make special provision for a crime of violating the freedom of a university. Why is this? Perhaps it is because, apart from the abovementioned examples, violations of university freedom by a private individual are generally considered in criminal law as taking place in the form of crimes against professors or other research personnel such as violence, joint violence, intimidation, compulsion, trespass, bodily injury, obstruction of business, fraud, defamation, concealment of property, and destruction of property, and can be punished as such crimes in those cases. However, entering a university campus with the intention of stealing a valuable report on academic research is not in itself yet a violation of university freedom. Or at most, it would be a violation of university freedom in an abstract sense. To take another case, would the theft of a microscope used for research at a university always constitute a crime of obstructing a researcher's business or a violation of academic freedom?

4. *Measures for protecting university freedom and the present case.* Even if it were granted that, as stated in the written indictment, the performance of a play by the Popolo Players in lecture room no. 25 of the Faculties of Law, Literature, and Economics of the University of Tokyo constituted study of the arts and sciences at the said university, and that the policemen violated the university's freedom of research in the arts and sciences by purchasing admission tickets and entering while concealing their status as policemen (this does not meet the requirements for establishing a crime of obstruction of business under Articles 233 and 234 of the Criminal Code), such violent acts as the following were not appropriate countermeasures to a violation of university freedom: When the policemen were sitting quietly in their seats or walking towards the exit on their way out, students grabbed one by the hands and punched him in the stomach, searched his pockets, pulled buttons off his overcoat, and jerked off his police notebook, which was tied to a buttonhole by a string. These acts constitute the crime under the Criminal Code set forth in the indictment. Paradoxically, this very violence is what obstructed the performance and enjoyment of the play in this case! The circumstances recognized by the decision below as grounds for nullifying the establishment of the crimes are not sufficient to negate the establishment of any of the above crimes under the Criminal Code; as a legal judgment as well, the decision below is unfounded in holding that there are grounds transcending legal provisions for negating the establishment of crime in this case. In these circumstances, the students should have stopped at

quietly making inquiries of the policemen, so as not to disturb the progress of the play, and asking them to leave with an explanation of the reasons, or promptly reporting to the university authorities and asking them to take appropriate measures. If the students nevertheless acted as stated in the indictment, it must be said that these actions were themselves unworthy of a seat of highest learning, and that the students themselves committed crimes of violence.

* * *

The supplementary opinion of Justice Shūichi Ishizaka follows.

1. The facts in the indictment in this case are as follows:

> The accused, a fourth-year student in the Faculty of Economics of the University of Tokyo, together with Shumpei Fukui and several others: (1) did violence to Yoshiteru Shiba, an officer of the Motofuji Police Station who was attending a play performed by the Tokyo University Popolo Players in lecture hall no. 25 of the Faculties of Law, Litearture, and Economics of the University of Tokyo at 1-Motofuji-chō, Bunkyō-ku, Tokyo, around 7:30 P.M., 20 February 1952, by grabbing his right hand, punching him in the stomach, searching his pockets, pulling buttons off his overcoat, and so on; and (2) did violence to Takashi Kayano, an officer of the same police station who was in like manner attending the play at the same place around this time, by grabbing his hands, searching his pockets, jerking off a police notebook that was tied to his buttonhole by a string, and so on.

In the indictment, Article 1, paragraph 1 of the Law concerning the Punishment of Acts of Violence, etc., is cited as the applicable provision.

Consequently, the court of first instance should have thoroughly inquired whether the acts of violence in the above indictment against the two policemen were perpetrated by the accused himself, whether Shumpei Fukui and several others engaged in acts of violence similar to those in the indictment, and whether there existed among the accused, Shumpei Fukui, and the others intent to act jointly in crimes against the two policemen; and if matters of joint criminal responsibility were found, the court of first instance should have made clear the concrete factual relationships involved. However, the court of first instance did not examine those questions thoroughly, held that there was no evidence which should be certified that the accused intended to act jointly with others in the commission of crime, and regarding acts of the accused admissible as evidence, limited itself to recognizing only the following: When Officer Yoshiteru Shiba was about to flee from the lecture hall, the accused caught the said policeman by the arm and along with other students apprehended him and took him to the front of the stage where he was surrounded by students. Since the policeman refused to present his police notebook, the accused grabbed and pulled him by his lapels and insistently demanded that he show him the notebook. The court below followed in the footsteps of the court of first instance by casually accepting the above facts found by the court of first instance and dismissed the contention in the prosecutor's *kōso* appeal that there had been error in the finding of facts.

However, judging from the record and the evidence, there are strong grounds for suspecting gross errors in the finding of facts in the first instance judgment and in the decision below that upheld it.

2. According to the record and the evidence, permission was granted to use a lecture hall at Tokyo University, when the applicants submitted a written request to borrow it, and on condition that it would not be used for political purposes. On 11 February 1952 a representative of the Popolo Players presented to the authorities a written request to use lecture hall no. 25 of the Faculties of Law, Literature, and Economics on 20 February from 5:00 P.M. to 9:00 P.M., and a written assurance that this meeting was not for political purposes. The program for the meeting indicated in the request included the plays "On Some Day or Other" (based on the so-called Matsukawa Case) and "A Poem to the Morning Sunlight," greetings, and commentary on the plays. The application stated that the audience would consist of students and employees of the university. Actually, there is good and sufficient reason to suspect that the accused borrowed this lecture hall on 20 February for the following concealed purposes: fund-raising; conducting a signature campaign against rearmament in conjunction with the youth sections of labor unions; putting on the play ("On Some Day or Other"), which was also performed by other organizations, as part of an anticolonialism struggle day; and other activities. Moreover, according to the finding of facts by the court below, the same evening before the play began, a collection for a relief fund on behalf of the accused in the Matsukawa Case was taken up, and a report was made on the so-called Shibuya Incident. The so-called Shibuya Incident took place in the plaza in front of Shibuya Station at almost the same time that the present case arose, and refers to a clash between police units and students resulting in some arrests. Students from the Faculty of General Education of Tokyo University and others had been conducting a signature-writing campaign against conscription and rearmament. The police had ordered them to disperse because the assembly was being carried out without the required prior notice, but the students had not complied with this order. Although the above-mentioned written request to borrow the lecture hall indicated the audience would be students and employees of Tokyo University, in actuality anyone who wished could buy a ticket and enter, and a considerable number of those who did were from outside the university. These facts can be admitted in evidence, and the gathering in question can be judged to have been open to the public. Accordingly, it must be said that there is virtual certainty in the judgment affirming that the real purpose in reserving the above lecture hall was not to use it for a study meeting falling within the parameters of constitutionally guaranteed "academic freedom" and the "university autonomy" based on this freedom, but to

hold a public meeting corresponding, in fact, to social and political action in society at large. Since this is so, there is no reason to consider the gathering in the present case of the Popolo Players within the parameters of the above "academic freedom" and "university autonomy", as maintained by the first instance judgment and affirmed by the decision below. As long as the circumstances were as explained above, it must be said that there were reasonable grounds for the police to enter the gathering in question under Article 1 of the Police Law and Article 6, paragraph 2 of the Law concerning the Execution of Duties of Police Officials, etc. (in force at the time this case arose). Not only that, but there is no basis in fact for maintaining that the above two policemen intended to interfere with the conduct of this meeting. In the light of such factual relationships, a policeman entered the gathering in question as one member of the public who had bought a ticket, and the accused had no legal interest suggesting either some defense against his entry or his removal.

In public gatherings for which an admission fee is charged, as in the present case, as long as the statements and performance stop at those activities and do not actually harm another legal interest, the persons engaging in these activities should of course be left in freedom, whatever their true intentions may be. At the same time, whatever the true intentions of someone in the audience may be, as long as he does not actually harm another legal interest by disturbing the quiet of the place, bothering other members of the audience, or interfering with the conduct of the meeting, he is to be left in freedom simply to listen to the speech or watch the performance. This rationale remains the same, whether the member of the audience is from the general public or a policeman, and there is no basis in fact for concluding that the two policemen actually intended or acted to harm another legal interest in the manner described above.

It is regrettable that the first instance judgment and the decision below that affirmed it conceived and presented, to no purpose and based on serious deficiencies in fact-finding, the theory that appropriate actions transcend legal provisions.

3. To remove the illegality of an act done in protection of a legal interest, it is not enough simply to balance the legal interest protected against the one infringed upon by the protective act; it is also necessary that the infringement of the legal interest be a present and urgent matter and the act of protection unavoidable. We can apply this to the present case as follows. Even if we grant that the police unlawfully entered the campus before the crime in the present case took place, the act of entry already belonged to the past, the infringement of a legal interest was over with, and thus there is no room for justifying acts to eliminate the infringement. Furthermore, according to the court below, Officer Shiba left his seat in the center of the room and walked quickly toward the southwest door in the rear when he felt that students in the lecture hall

had become aware that he was a policeman. Since the accused then grabbed the policeman's right hand and subsequently did violence to the said policeman, we can conclude that the accused stopped and did violence to the policeman as he was about to leave the place voluntarily. Even if we should admit that the accused had some legal interest to protect, in the absence of other special circumstances, the infringement on that legal interest was not actually an urgent matter at the time, nor can it be said that the above violent conduct arose unavoidably in defense of a legal interest. And even if we should grant with the court below that at the time of the gathering in the present case there was anxiety in anticipation of future unlawful police trespassing on campus, such trespass could not be considered actually imminent. Consequently, there is no basis under the Criminal Code for construing the conduct in this case as appropriate acts of self-defense.

In light of the views explained above, we must hold the decision below in error in interpreting the above acts of the accused in such a way that their illegality was nullified.

* * *

The opinion of Justice Masatoshi Yokota follows.

1. There is no dispute about the facts that university autonomy is recognized in order to guarantee academic freedom in the university, and that the authority of this autonomy also extends to the supervision of the facilities and students of the university. This autonomy with respect to the supervision of the facilities and students of the university has as its ultimate object the guarantee of academic freedom at the university; but that authority is never limited to purely academic research or the presentation of the results of such, that is to say, solely to matters directly connected to scholarship. With respect to the campus activities of students, students engage in various kinds of campus activities (so-called autonomous activities) besides their purely academic activities, but it must be said that even with regard to those activities the university bears some degree of authority and responsibility for guidance and supervision. The reason for the university to have such power and responsibility and to guide student activities in sound directions is so that they may result in contributions to learning. Within the area of student activities coming under the power and responsibility of the university, university autonomy should be understood to mean respect for the self-rule of the university, and the exclusion insofar as possible of interference with this self-rule from outside.

2. Another aspect is that the university does not enjoy extraterritorial rights, and of course the campus activities of students may become the object of appropriate activities on the part of police, who are charged with the maintenance of order and public safety, the arrest of suspects, and the prevention, suppression, and investigation of crime, and who

have the duty to protect the life, person, and property of the individual. Also, we must recognize that among these police activities are included so-called police intelligence activities, engaged in at the policeman's option. However, in light of the true meaning of academic freedom in the university and university autonomy, there should be strict requirements that the exercise of police powers on campus, especially police intelligence activities, is attended by greater circumspection than in other places, and that it does not exceed the bounds of necessity.

3. Adjustment of university autonomy with the exercise of police powers is a rather difficult problem, and ultimately must depend on the good sense and moderation of those involved. On this point, it is worth taking note of the circular of the vice-minister of Education mentioned in the decision below. This circular notice was issued and addressed to the presidents of universities and colleges in the Tokyo area on 25 July 1950 by the vice-minister of Education, after consultations with the Metropolitan Police Department, as a commentary at the time it went into effect on the Ordinance of Metropolitan Tokyo concerning Assemblies, Processions, and Demonstrations. If we look at the section of the circular concerning campus gatherings of university students, we find: A gathering held on campus for specific persons upon receipt of permission according to the established procedures of the university by students or their organizations is not recognized as an assembly in a public place, and consequently it clearly does not require a permit from the Public Safety Commission. At the same time, with respect to the control of such gatherings, the intent is established that the president have authority to take measures, and that the police cooperate with him upon his request. This circular can be construed as clarifying the locus of authority to give permission for an assembly, and also as touching upon the problem of adjusting university autonomy with the exercise of police power regarding campus gatherings. According to the above circular notice, the one requirement for a regular campus gathering taking place under the supervision and responsibility of the university is that it should be held for specific persons; that is to say, its nonpublic nature is thereby established in the sense that the general public is not allowed entrance. The circular does not touch specifically on purposes or programs of meetings, but it goes without saying that political activities at the university (Article 8, paragraph 2 of the Fundamental Law of Education) are per se injurious to the political neutrality that is a doctrine underlying university education; and social action contrary to the students' duty to devote themselves to learning cannot be permitted. Therefore, it is appropriate to assume that the university will impose restrictions on gatherings of such purpose and content when giving permissions (a function of university autonomy regarding the supervision of students); so it is recognized that in order to be a legitimate campus gathering, an assembly must at least fulfill the condition that it not be for such activities, in purpose or

content. Although it would be hard to regard what was set forth in the circular as itself having the binding force of law, the circular must never be regarded lightly, since it presents in outline concrete standards for adjusting university autonomy with the exercise of police power. In short, as long as a student gathering on campus at least fulfills in reality the above two conditions, the entry of police as official acts should be construed to be impermissible, except in cases where regular legal procedures have been followed, and where it does not exceed the bounds of necessity. On the other hand, when a gathering does not in reality fulfill the above conditions, the police can enter under the same conditions that apply to indoor gatherings in general. The police cannot be denied entry simply for the formalistic reasons that such a meeting took place on campus with the permission of the university. However, in the latter kind of case, if the gathering only falls short of being nonpublic in nature, we must not overlook the possibility of cases in which the sponsors of a gathering, in light of the special characteristics of policemen, have good reason to refuse entry to police for police intelligence activities, because it might interfere improperly with the movement of a campus meeting (especially an academic meeting).

4. Applying these considerations to the present case, it is clear from the record in this case that the campus gathering in question sponsored by the Tokyo University Popolo Players, an officially recognized organization in the university, in line with the above-mentioned circular notice, was held in lecture hall no. 25 of the Faculties of Law, Literature, and Economics with university permission (formally, a permission to use facilities), and that permission was granted on condition that it would be a gathering without political purpose for about three hundred students and employees of the University of Tokyo. The court below recognized, to some extent, the nature of the above Popolo Players, the content of the gathering in question, and the actual circumstances of the police entry; but in light of the records of this case, it is undeniable and regrettable that the court below did not make the thorough inquiries or the judgments necessary to make clear the true nature of the gathering in question concerning such matters as the actual nature of the Popolo Players group, the purpose of the meeting in this case, the way it was actually conducted, and how the university authorities understood the purpose and program of the gathering when permission was given. In light of what has been related above, as long as the interrelationships of these facts are not clear, it is impossible to judge whether or not the entry of the police into the gathering in question exceeded the limits of what is permissible. Therefore, the decision below is tainted with illegality by reason of insufficient examination materially affecting the judgment, at least with respect to the above mentioned points; failure to quash that judgment would be seriously incompatible with justice.

Justices Kisaburō Yokota (presiding), Matasuke Kawamura, Toshio Irie, Katsu Ikeda, Katsumi Tarumi, Daisuke Kawamura, Masuo Shimoiizaka, Ken'ichi Okuno, Shūichi Ishizaka, Sakunosuke Yamada, Kakiwa Gokijyō, Masatoshi Yokota, and Kitarō Saitō.

Case 30. Japan v. *Kanemoto et al (1964).* The Kanemoto Pamphlet Case

Hanrei Jihō, No. 396, p. 19 (1965); Supreme Court, Second Petty Bench, 21 December 1964; Gifu Dist. Ct. (First Instance), Nagoya High Ct. (Second Instance), [intent to incite insurrection by written materials].

EDITORIAL NOTE: The accused distributed politically inflammatory printed material supportive of crimes of insurrection and were convicted in the Gifu District Court of violating the Subversive Activities Prevention Law. The Nagoya High Court overturned their conviction, arguing that the court of first instance should have interpreted the political expression at issue as constituting not a concrete danger, but an abstract danger of crimes the writings encouraged. The clear intent of the law in question is to require that there be foreknowledge of a clear and present danger to public safety, and not merely "the objective of performing a crime of insurrection." The "clear and present danger" rule, the high court said, is not the sole, absolute, or universal principle to be followed, but should be recognized as one criterion for regulating freedom of expression in such cases. The prosecutor appealed the acquittal to the Supreme Court.

REFERENCES

Constitution of Japan [ARTICLES 12 and 21 were at issue in this case. See Appendix 3 for these provisions].

Subversive Activities Prevention Law (Law 240 of 1952),* ARTICLE 2. Because it has an important relation to the fundamental human rights of the people, this law must be applied only within the narrowest possible limits necessary for the preservation of public safety and it must not be interpreted to extend beyond this in the slightest degree.

ARTICLE 38, 2. Any person, as indicated below, will be sentenced to not more than five years imprisonment with or without hard labor: . . .

(2) Any person with the object of performing a crime under Articles 77, 81, or 82 of the Criminal Code† who publicly posts, distributes, or prints any document or drawing that has proclaimed the propriety or the necessity of the performance of such crime.

FORMAL RULING

The *jōkoku* appeal in this case is dismissed.

REASONS. The purport of the prosecutor's *jōkoku* appeal is to claim violation of the Constitution, violation of laws and ordinances, as well as a misconstruction of the facts.

1. Concerning the contention of unconstitutionality: The argument is

*From the translation of this law by John M. Maki in dittograph, n.d.

†These provisions deal with crimes of insurrection, subversion, and conspiracy.

made that the writings proscribed in Article 38, paragraph 2, item 2 of the Subversive Activities Prevention Law (hereafter referred to as the Subversion Law) are speech whose very contents are contrary to the public welfare, and that acts of distributing such writings without proper reason clearly constitute notable abuse of freedom of expression beyond the bounds of Article 21 guarantees. Moreover, the appeal contends that since the intent to incite a crime of insurrection is also illegal under the same provision, the limited consideration given by the court below to interpreting such intent from the standpoint of free speech guarantees involves an erroneous interpretation of Articles 21 and 12 of the Constitution.

However, what the court below explained regarding the intent to incite a crime of insurrection under Article 38, paragraph 2, item 2 of the Subversion Law is that it is not sufficient for the establishment of that crime merely to distribute, with knowledge of their contents, writings that emphasize the propriety and necessity of carrying out crimes of insurrection, but that it is necessary for such acts to be carried out with the intent to incite to the crime of insurrection. The intent of the court below is that caution should be exercised in judging the presence or absence of that motive, since it is not permissible to interpret lightly the question of motive, particularly in light of the legal intent of Article 2 of the same law which establishes a prohibition on its broad interpretation and confines application of this law to the minimum measures necessary for the preservation of public safety. The court below merely gave its opinion regarding interpretation and application of Article 38, paragraph 2, item 2 of the Subversion Law and cannot be construed, as contended, to have ruled that the interpretation and application of the above motive would be further restricted by the constitutional guarantees of free speech. Consequently, the contention of unconstitutionality is deficient in its premises.

2. Concerning the alleged violation of laws and ordinances: The contentions of error in the application and interpretation of Article 38, paragraph 2, item 2 of the Subversion Law, and of violation of the rules in the judicial taking of evidence [*saishō hōsoku*] amounts to a claim that statutes were violated, which is not grounds for *jōkoku* appeal under Article 405 of the Code of Criminal Procedure. When judging whether or not the accused in this case intended to incite to a crime of insurrection, the court below was not unreasonable from the standpoint of finding of evidence in its assessment of the objective circumstances at the time, the relationships between the accused and the recipients of the pamphlets, and so on. Moreover, based on this, we cannot construe the court below as actually employing the doctrine of concrete danger of crime,* nor can we find points of illegality elsewhere in the judgment below, as contended in the appeal.

**Kikenhan* (*Gefahrtragung* in German law)

3. Regarding the alleged erroneous fact-finding. The contention of erroneous fact-finding rests upon criticism of the court below in its judgment regarding the acceptance and exclusion of evidence, and is not proper grounds for *jōkoku* appeal under Article 405 of the Code of Criminal Procedure. We can confirm as correct the judgment of the court below in not finding that the accused in this case intended to incite a crime of insurrection under Article 38, paragraph 2, item 2 of the Subversion Law.

Furthermore, upon examination of the record, we do not find grounds for application of Article 411 of the Code of Criminal Procedure to this case.

Accordingly, pursuant to Article 414 and Article 386, paragraph 1, item 3 of the same Code, this Court by unanimous opinion rules as in the Formal Ruling.

Justices Ken'ichi Okuno (presiding), Sakunosuke Yamada, Asanosuke Kusaka, Yoshihiko Kido, and Kazuto Ishida.

Case 31. Yamagishi et al v. *Japan (1970).* The Yamagishi Poster Case

24 *Keishū* 6 at p. 280, and *Hanrei Jihō*, No. 594, p. 30 (1970); Supreme Court, Grand Bench, 17 June 1970; Ichinomiya Summary Ct. (First Instance), Nagoya High Ct. (Second Instance), [constitutionality of restrictions on political expression under the Misdemeanor Law].

EDITORIAL NOTE: The accused put up dozens of political posters concerning an international conference to support a ban on nuclear weapons on roadside telephone poles. They had not obtained permission to use the poles in this manner, and they were charged and convicted in Ichinomiya Summary Court of violating the Misdemeanor Law. The Nagoya High Court sustained this judgment. The accused appealed to the Supreme Court, arguing that the provision in question of the Misdemeanor Law is an unconstitutional abridgement of freedom of expression.

REFERENCES

Constitution of Japan [ARTICLES 21 and 31 were at issue in this case. See Appendix 3 for these provisions].

Misdemeanor Law (*Law 39 of 1948*), ARTICLE 1, item 33, first part.* A person who wantonly places a bill or poster on a house or other structure of another person, or who removes a signboard, a notice of prohibition, or other sign belonging to another person, or who defaces such structure or sign; . . . (shall be punished with penal detention or minor fine).

FORMAL JUDGMENT

Each *jōkoku* appeal in this case is dismissed.

*As translated in Ministry of Justice, Japan, CRIMINAL STATUTES, II, n.d., p. 26.

REASONS. Regarding the arguments in the *jōkoku* appeal of Attorneys N. Sakurai, K. Ōya, and K. Maejima (at present, Harayama):

According to the first instance judgment, the facts confirmed as constituting a crime are as follows: The two accused conspired in pasting handbills on Inazawa Trunk Line pole No. 61 and ten other telephone poles under the supervision of the chief of the Ichinomiya Business Office of Chūden Industries, a property of the Chūbu Electric Power Company; and on twelve telephone poles under the supervision of the head of the Telephone Pole Advertising Section, Tōkai Branch, the Electrical Communications Mutual Benefit Association, which is owned by the Japan Telegraph and Telephone Public Corporation; and, in addition, on fourteen poles under the administration of the head of the Inazawa City Agricultural Cooperative, all of which poles are installed along prefectural roadway. Without suitable cause and without obtaining the permission of the supervisors or the owners of the respective poles, they put up eighty-four copies in all of a poster (54 centimeters long and 19.5 centimeters wide) on which was printed such as: "LET'S MAKE A GREAT SUCCESS OF THE TENTH WORLD CONFERENCE TO BAN NUCLEAR BOMBS! AICHI GENSUIKYO." In so doing they spread paste over the back of the posters and stuck them fast to the poles. For these acts, both of the accused were sentenced to ten days in prison under Article 60 of the Criminal Code and Article 1, item 33, first part, of the Misdemeanor Law.

The appeal argues first of all as follows: The thrust of the judgment below is that the first part of Article 1, item 33 of the Misdemeanor Law cannot be said to violate Article 21, paragraph 1 of the Constitution, because the above legal provision has as its ultimate intent the maintenance of the public welfare. But if one maintains that the above provision of the Misdemeanor Law should be construed in this way, then acts of putting up posters, as in the present case, which are an appropriate exercise of the rights of workers and a proper exercise of the people's freedom of expression, would become subject to indiscriminate prohibition. Therefore, they contend, the above legal provision is contrary to Article 21, paragraph 1 of the Constitution.

After scrutinizing the above argument, we must hold as follows Article 1, item 33, first part, of the Misdemeanor Law should be construed as regulating wanton acts of putting up posters, generally on the houses or other structures of other persons, in order to protect property rights and the right of supervision with respect to these properties. But a means for outwardly expressing one's ideas has never been permissible if that means is such as to do unfair damage to the property rights of other persons and their right of supervision. Accordingly, this degree of restraint on the freedom of expression is permitted as reasonable and necessary restriction for the sake of the public welfare, and we cannot say that the above legal provision is contrary to Article 21, paragraph 1 of the Constitution (4 *Keishū* 1799; Sup. Ct., G.B., 27 September 1950: 9 *Keishū* 819; Sup. Ct., G.B., 6 April 1955). The holding of the judgment below to the same effect is correct, and the argument of the appeal is groundless.

Next, the appeal contends that Article 1, item 33, first part, of the Misdemeanor Law violates Article 31 of the Constitution. However, the term "wantonly" in the above provision is properly interpreted as referring to cases where appropriate reason is not found from the standpoint of the prevailing ideas of society for putting up posters on the houses or other structures of other persons. Since we do not find, with appellants, that the above term is ambiguous, or that the conditions constituting the crime are not clear, we cannot accept the contention of unconstitutionality, which is deficient in its premises.

The remaining points of the appeal amount to contentions of violation of laws and are not proper grounds for *jōkoku* appeal under Article 405 of the Code of Criminal Procedure.

Accordingly, under Article 408 of the Code of Criminal Procedure, this Court by unanimous opinion holds as in the Formal Judgment.

Justices Kazuto Ishida (presiding), Toshio Irie, Asanosuke Kusaka, Kingo Osabe, Yoshihiko Kido, Jirō Tanaka, Jirō Matsuda, Makoto Iwata, Kazuo Shimomura, Kōtarō Irokawa, Ken'ichirō Ōsumi, Masao Matsumoto, Yoshimi Iimura, Tomokazu Murakami, and Kosato Sekine.

Case 32. Kaneko et al v. *Japan (1969).* The Hakata Station Film Case

23 *Keishū* 11 at p. 1490; Supreme Court, Grand Bench, 26 November 1969; Fukuoka Dist. Ct. (First Instance), Fukuoka High Ct. (Second Instance), [constitutionality of a court order to present evidentiary TV film.]

EDITORIAL NOTE: In August 1969 a district court ordered presentation to the court of all the film taken during the Hakata Station Incident, which had occurred on 16 January 1968. About three hundred activist students from the Tokyo and Osaka areas had gone to Sasebo in southern Japan to protest the visit of the American nuclear-powered aircraft carrier, the U.S.S. *Enterprise*. When they detrained at Hakata Station for a side visit to Kyushu University, their way was impeded by some 870 mobile police and railroad security personnel. Four students were arrested; one was indicted, but later acquitted in the Fukuoka District Court.* Lawyers, politicians, and others supporting the students brought countercharges against the Prefectural Police Commissioner and others for abuse of police authority. After lengthy unsuccessful negotiations between the Fukuoka District Court and the four TV companies that filmed the incident regarding use of footage as evidence, the court issued an order to present (*teishutsu meirei*) the film. Amidst heated national debate, the appeal of the companies against the order as a violation of press freedom was dismissed by the

*HANREI JIHŌ, No. 562, p. 23 (1969) (Fukuoka Dist. Ct., 11 April 1969).

high court on 20 September,* and the case went to the Grand Bench, Supreme Court.

REFERENCES

Constitution of Japan [ARTICLE 21 was at issue in this case. See Appendix 3 for this provision].

Code of Criminal Procedure (*Law 131 of 1948*, as amended),† ARTICLE 99, 1. When it is necessary, a court may seize any articles that it believes should be used as evidence or liable to confiscation, except as otherwise provided in this and other laws.

2. A court may designate articles to be seized and order the owner, possessor, or custodian thereof to produce such articles.

ARTICLE 262, 1. If, in a case with respect to which complaint or accusation is made concerning the offenses mentioned in Articles 193 to 196 of the Criminal Code or Article 45 of the Subversive Activities Prevention Law (Law 240 of 1952), the complainant or accuser is dissatisfied with the disposition made by a public prosecutor not to prosecute, he may apply to a district court having jurisdiction over the place of the public prosecutor's office to which that public prosecutor belongs for committing the case to a court for trial.

2. The application mentioned in the preceding paragraph shall be made by submitting a written application to the public prosecutor who made the disposition not to prosecute, within seven days from the day on which notice mentioned in Article 260 was received.

ARTICLE 265, 1. Trial and decision on the application mentioned in Article 262, paragraph 1 shall be conducted and delivered by a collegiate court.

2. The court may, if it deems necessary, cause a member of a collegiate court to investigate the facts, or requisition a judge of a district or summary court to do so. In this case a commissioned judge or a requisitioned judge shall have the same authority as the court or a presiding judge has.

FORMAL RULING

The special *kōkoku* appeal in this case is dismissed.

REASONS. Regarding the complainants' grounds for *kōkoku* appeal, the added reasons of their counsel T. Murata, and the first of the supplementary reasons of their attorneys, A. Senō and two others:

The appeal alleges violation of Article 21 of the Constitution as follows: The freedom of information forms a basis for the democratic society upheld by the Constitution, and occupies an important position in Article 21 of the Constitution, which guarantees freedom of expres-

**Id.*, No. 569, p. 23 (Fukuoka High Ct., 20 September 1969).

†As translated in Ministry of Justice, Japan, CRIMINAL STATUTES, II, n.d., pp. 84, 122, and 123.

sion. The freedom to gather news must also be guaranteed under Article 21 of the Constitution as indispensable for the realization of the freedom of information. The broad assurance to the mass media till now of the freedom to gather news is due to the achievements and the conviction of the mass media in gathering news solely for the purpose of informing, and in not offering the results of their news-gathering for any other purpose, and to the trust in this on the part of the people. However, if it is held in cases like the present one that a court order to present film for use as evidence in a criminal trial is lawful, and that the mass media have a duty to comply with this, then the people's trust for the information media will be lost and their cooperation will become unobtainable. As a result, the freedom to report the truth would be obstructed, and in turn, the materials on which the people base their judgments in exercising their sovereignty would become inadequate, and perhaps inevitably the people's "right to know," the other face of the freedom of expression, would be improperly affected. In conclusion, they say, the order to present evidence in this case is contrary to Article 21 of the Constitution, which guarantees freedom of expression.

In response, this Court holds as follows: As the appeal points out, in a democratic society the reports of the mass media provide the people with important materials on which to base their judgments as they participate in the nation's politics, and they serve the people's "right to know." Consequently, it goes without saying that the freedom to report facts, along with the freedom to express ideas, is grounded in the guarantees of Article 21 of the Constitution, which provides for freedom of expression. Moreover, in order that the contents of the reports of such mass media may be correct, the freedom to gather news for informational purposes, as well as the freedom to report, must be accorded due respect in light of the spirit of Article 21 of the Constitution.

In this case, the object of the court order is the film gathered in preparation for a broadcast, which includes some film already broadcast. With that broadcast, the news-gathering activities of the mass media have already reached their fruition; so the order to present that film is not directly related to the above film-gathering activities themselves. Indeed, film footage gathered by the mass media is taken by the mass media as something to be used for reporting purposes; and where film gathered for such a purpose is used for another purpose, namely, for evidence in a criminal trial as in the present case, it is not unreasonable for them to be concerned about future hindrances to the news-gathering activities of the mass media.

However, the freedom of news-gathering is by its nature not unlimited. For example, when there is involved a constitutional demand, as for the attainment of a fair trial, it cannot be denied that there is some degree of limitation.

In this case, the issue is precisely whether or not limitation of the freedom of news-gathering is permitted for the attainment of a fair criminal trial. It goes without saying that the attainment of a fair criminal trial is a fundamental demand upon the state, and that the discovery of the actual truth is imperative in criminal proceedings. In order to assure the achievement of such fair criminal trial, it should be said that some measure of limitation on the freedom of news-gathering may be unavoidable, when materials gained by the news-gathering activities of the mass media are deemed necessary evidence. However, even such cases should be determined by comparing and balancing, on the one hand the necessity and the value, as evidence, of the gathered materials for the attainment of a fair criminal trial, in light of the seriousness, circumstances, and nature of the alleged crime under deliberation, and on the other hand the degree to which the freedom in news-gathering of the mass media and the freedom of information may be hindered by presentation of the gathered items as evidence, and various other factors. Even when the evidentiary use of this material is deemed unavoidable, care must be taken that the disadvantages accruing to the mass media on that account do not exceed the bounds of necessity.

Viewing the present case from the above perspective, the object of deliberations in the appeal from a doubtful judgment* of this case is whether or not crimes of abuse of authority by public officers and violence and cruelty by special public officers† on the part of the mobile police and others took place on the occasion of a confrontation between a number of mobile police (*kidōtai*) and university students. At present, those deliberations are at an especially difficult stage for both the suspects and the victims. Nearly two years have passed since the case arose, and no new third-party testimony can be expected. Consequently, we find ourselves in a situation in which the film of the mass media at issue, taken as it was at the scene from an impartial standpoint, has very great value as evidence and is deemed well-nigh indispensable for determination of the guilt or innocence of the suspects. On the other hand, the film in this case, including material already broadcast, was prepared for the purpose of broadcasting. We interpret this to mean that the disadvantage accruing to the mass media from the evidentiary use of that film does not involve the freedom of reporting itself, but is confined to anxiety about future obstacles to free news-gathering. This is a case of appeal from a doubtful judgment; while we take the view that the position of the mass media should be accorded due respect, we hold that this degree of disadvantage must be endured in order to be sure that the criminal trial in this instance will be fairly conducted. Furthermore, the Fukuoka District Court, which issued the subpoena, has indicated it will take care not to interfere with use by the mass media of the film in this case, by

***Fushimpan seikyū*. An appeal to the courts against a prosecutorial refusal to support allegations of abuse of police authority. Article 262, Code of Criminal Procedure.

†Articles 193 and 195, Criminal Code.

such measures as temporarily returning the film if needed, once the court has taken legal possession. When we consider together the various points above and each of the other circumstances, we find the issuance of the order in this instance to present the film for use as evidence in the case of an appeal from a doubtful judgment to be genuinely unavoidable.

Considered in the manner described above, the order to present film in this case neither violates Article 21 of the Constitution nor conflicts with its intent; the judgment below was reasonable in upholding the order as appropriate, and the contention of appellants is groundless.

Regarding the second of the supplementary reasons of counsel for the complainants, A. Senō and two others:

They allege violation of Article 32 of the Constitution, but in substance assert no more than a violation of procedural law which does not constitute lawful grounds for a special *kōkoku* appeal.

Accordingly, pursuant to Articles 434 and 426, paragraph 1 of the Code of Criminal Procedure, by unanimous opinion this Court rules as in the Formal Ruling.

Justices Kazuto Ishida (presiding), Toshio Irie, Asanosuke Kusaka, Kingo Osabe, Yoshihiko Kido, Jirō Tanaka, Jirō Matsuda, Makoto Iwata, Kazuo Shimomura, Kōtarō Irokawa, Ken'ichirō Ōsumi, Masao Matsumoto, Yoshimi Iimura, Tomokazu Murakami, and Kosato Sekine.

Appendix 1

Supreme Court Justices of Japan: 1961–70

Name	*Date of Appointment*	*Date of Retirement*	*Education*	*Occupation at Time of Appointment*
Shima, Tomatsu	4 Aug. 1947	24 Aug. 1961	Tokyo University	Judge (before 1945, Department Head, The Court of Cassation)
Saitō, Yūsuke	4 Aug. 1947	20 May 1962	Tokyo University	Public Prosecutor (Chief Prosecutor, Osaka Court of Kōso-Appeals)
Fujita, Hachirō	4 Aug. 1947	4 Aug. 1962	Tokyo University	Judge (Chief Judge, Osaka Court of Kōso-Appeals)
Kawamura, Matasuke	4 Aug. 1947	31 Dec. 1963	Kyoto University	Professor, Kyūshū University
Irie, Toshio	30 Aug. 1952	9 Jan. 1971	Tokyo University	Director, Legislative Bureau, House of Peers
Ikeda, Katsu	2 Nov. 1954	22 May 1963	Tokyo University	Prosecutor (Director, Prosecutors Office, Ministry of Justice)
Tarumi, Katsumi	26 May 1955	14 Nov. 1963	Tokyo University	Judge (Chief Judge, Tokyo High Court)
Kawamura, Daisuke	22 Nov. 1956	1 June 1963	Nihon University	Attorney

Name	*Date of Appointment*	*Date of Retirement*	*Education*	*Occupation at Time of Appointment*
Shimoiizaka, Masuo	22 Nov. 1956	28 Jan. 1964	Tokyo University	Judge (Chief, Osaka High Court)
Okuno, Ken'ichi	22 Nov. 1956	17 Nov. 1968	Tokyo University	Director, Legislative Bureau, House of Councillors
Takahashi, Kiyoshi	30 Jan. 1957	29 Dec. 1961 (Death)	Tokyo University	Attorney
Takagi, Tsuneshichi	28 June 1958	14 Mar. 1963	Waseda University	Judge (Chief Judge, Nagoya High Court)
Ishizaka, Shūichi	28 June 1958	13 Sep. 1965	Tokyo University	Judge (Chief Judge, Osaka High Court)
*Yokota, Kisaburō	25 Oct. 1960	5 Aug. 1966	Tokyo University	Professor, Tokyo University
Yamada, Sakunosuke	27 Dec. 1960	21 Apr. 1966	Tokyo University	Attorney
Gokijyō, Kakiwa	26 Aug. 1961	31 Dec. 1966	Chūō University	Judge (Chief Judge, Osaka High Court)
*Yokota, Masatoshi	28 Feb. 1962	10 Jan. 1969	Tokyo University	Judge (Chief Judge, Tokyo High Court)
Saitō, Kitarō	29 May 1962	9 Aug. 1964 (Death)	Tokyo University	Director, Legislative Bureau, House of Councillors
Kusaka, Asanosuke	12 Aug. 1962	24 Oct. 1970	Kyoto University	Prosecutor (Chief Prosecutor, Osaka High Prosecutors Office)
*Ishida, Kazuto	6 June 1963	19 May 1973	Tokyo University	Judge (Chief Judge, Tokyo High Court)
Osabe, Kingo	5 Apr. 1963	31 Mar. 1971	Tokyo University	Prosecutor (Deputy Chief, Supreme Public Pr[illegible]

Kido, Yoshihiko	6 June 1963	19 Dec. 1970	Nihon University	Attorney
Kashiwabara, Goroku	13 Dec. 1963	19 Sep. 1967	Chūō University	Attorney
Tanaka, Jirō	16 Jan. 1964	31 Mar. 1973 (Resignation)	Tokyo University	Professor, Tokyo University
Matsuda, Jirō	31 Jan. 1964	29 July 1970	Tokyo University	Judge (Chief Judge, Osaka High Court)
Iwata, Makoto	31 Aug. 1964	25 Nov. 1972	Tokyo University	Judge (Judge, Tokyo High Court)
Shimomura, Kazuo	14 Sep. 1965	1 Jan. 1973	Tokyo University	Judge (Chief Judge, Tokyo High Court)
Irokawa, Kōtarō	10 May 1966	29 Jan. 1973	Tokyo University	Attorney
Ōsumi, Ken'ichirō	9 Sep. 1966	1 Oct. 1974	Kyoto University	Professor, Kyoto University
Matsumoto, Masao	17 Jan. 1967	5 Dec. 1971	Hitotsubashi University	Attorney
Iimura, Yoshimi	29 Sep. 1967	26 Apr. 1971	Tokyo University	Attorney
*Murakami, Tomokazu	19 Nov. 1968		Tokyo University	Judge (Chief Judge, Tokyo High Court)
Sekine, Kosato	17 Jan. 1969		Tokyo University	Judge (Chief Judge, Osaka High Court)
Fujibayashi, Ekizō	31 July 1970		Tokyo University	Attorney
Okahara, Masao	28 Oct. 1970		Tokyo University	Prosecutor (Chief Prosecutor, Osaka High Prosecutors Office)
Ogawa, Nobuo	22 Dec. 1970		Tokyo University	Attorney

*Chief Justices: K. Yokota served as Chief Justice from 1961 to 1966, M. Yokota from 1966 to 1969, K. Ishida from 1969 to 1972, and T. Murakami from 1972.

Appendix 2
Organization Chart of Japan's Judicial System

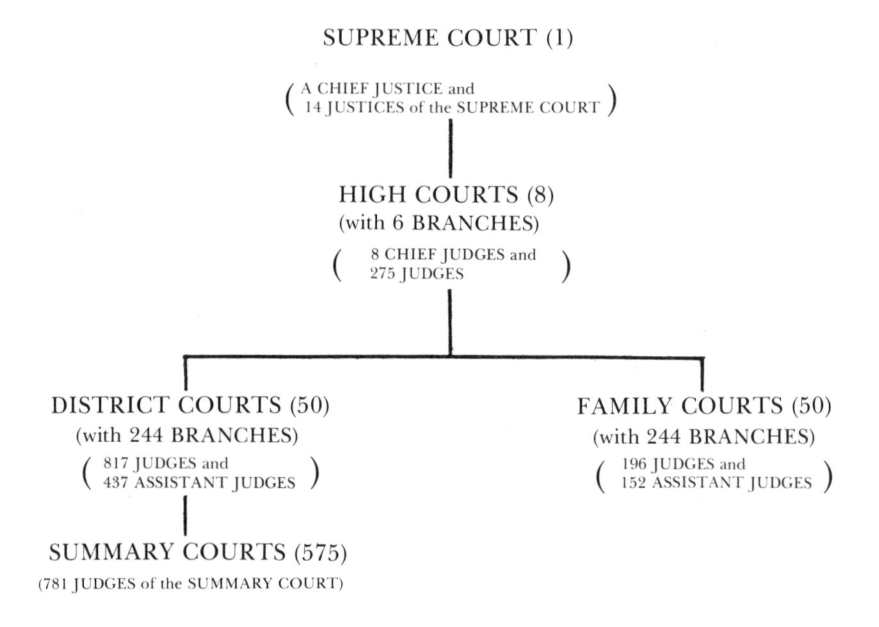

Fixed Number of Judges and Supporting Personnel (1972)

Classification	Number
Chief Justice of the Supreme Court	1
Justice of the Supreme Court	14
Chief Judge of the High Court	8
Judge	1,288
Assistant Judge	589
Judge of the Summary Court	781
Court Clerk	6,568
Family Court Probation Officer	1,502
Court Stenotypist	935
Court Secretary	6,900
Bailiff	1,883
Other	3,831
Total	24,300

Map of Court Jurisdictions in Japan

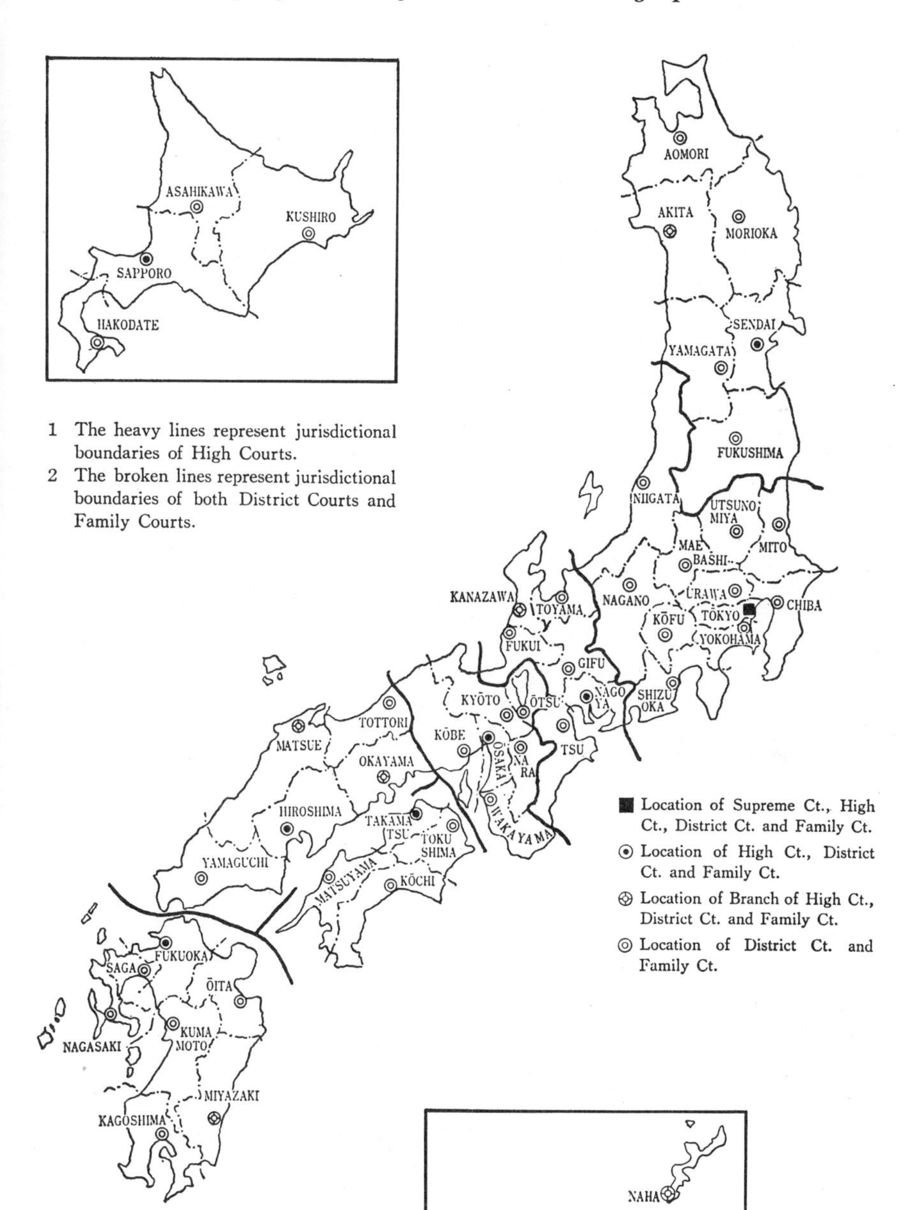

Appendix 3
The Constitution of Japan (Nihonkoku Kempō)

From The Constitution of Japan and Criminal Statutes. *Compiled by the Ministry of Justice, Tokyo, 1958.* (This is an authoritative translation; but no official translation into English has been made. Because of the source of this translation, spelling, punctuation, and so forth are exactly as they are in the version issued by the Ministry of Justice.)

We, the Japanese people, acting through our duly elected representatives in the National Diet, determined that we shall secure for ourselves and our posterity the fruits of peaceful cooperation with all nations and the blessings of liberty throughout this land, and resolved that never again shall we be visited with the horrors of war through the action of government, do proclaim that sovereign power resides with the people and do firmly establish this Constitution. Government is a sacred trust of the people, the authority for which is derived from the people, the powers of which are exercised by the representatives of the people, and the benefits of which are enjoyed by the people. This is a universal principle of mankind upon which this Constitution is founded. We reject and revoke all constitutions, laws, ordinances, and rescripts in conflict herewith.

We, the Japanese people, desire peace for all time and are deeply conscious of the high ideals controlling human relationship, and we have determined to preserve our security and existence, trusting in the justice and faith of the peace-loving peoples of the world. We desire to occupy an honored place in an international society striving for the preservation of peace, and the banishment of tyranny and slavery, oppression and intolerance for all time from the earth. We recognize that all peoples of the world have the right to live in peace, free from fear and want.

We believe that no nation is responsible to itself alone, but that laws of political morality are universal; and that obedience to such laws is incumbent upon all nations who would sustain their own sovereignty and justify their sovereign relationship with other nations.

We, the Japanese people, pledge our national honor to accomplish these high ideals and purposes with all our resources.

CHAPTER I. THE EMPEROR

ARTICLE 1. The Emperor shall be the symbol of the State and of the unity of the people, deriving his position from the will of the people with whom resides sovereign power.

ARTICLE 2. The Imperial Throne shall be dynastic and succeeded to in accordance with the Imperial House Law passed by the Diet.

ARTICLE 3. The advice and approval of the Cabinet shall be required for all acts of the Emperor in matters of state, and the Cabinet shall be responsible therefor.

ARTICLE 4. The Emperor shall perform only such acts in matters of state as are provided for in this Constitution and he shall not have powers related to government.

2. The Emperor may delegate the performance of his acts in matters of state as may be provided by law.

ARTICLE 5. When, in accordance with the Imperial House Law, a Regency is established, the Regent shall perform his acts in matters of state in the Emperor's name. In this case, paragraph one of the preceding article will be applicable.

ARTICLE 6. The Emperor shall appoint the Prime Minister as designated by the Diet.

2. The Emperor shall appoint the Chief Judge of the Supreme Court as designated by the Cabinet.

ARTICLE 7. The Emperor, with the advice and approval of the Cabinet, shall perform the following acts in matters of state on behalf of the people:

(1) Promulgation of amendments of the constitution, laws, cabinet orders and treaties;
(2) Convocation of the Diet;
(3) Dissolution of the House of Representatives;
(4) Proclamation of general election of members of the Diet;
(5) Attestation of the appointment and dismissal of Ministers of State and other officials as provided for by law, and of full powers and credentials of Ambassadors and Ministers;
(6) Attestation of general and special amnesty, commutation of punishment, reprieve, and restoration of rights;

(7) Awarding of honors;
(8) Attestation of instruments of ratification and other diplomatic documents as provided for by law;
(9) Receiving foreign ambassadors and ministers;
(10) Performance of ceremonial functions.

ARTICLE 8. No property can be given to, or received by, the Imperial House, nor can any gifts be made therefrom, without the authorization of the Diet.

CHAPTER II. RENUNCIATION OF WAR

ARTICLE 9. Aspiring sincerely to an international peace based on justice and order, the Japanese people forever renounce war as a sovereign right of the nation and the threat or use of force as a means of settling international disputes.

2. In order to accomplish the aim of the preceding paragraph, land, sea, and air forces, as well as other war potential, will never be maintained. The right of belligerency of the state will not be recognized.

CHAPTER III. RIGHTS AND DUTIES OF THE PEOPLE

ARTICLE 10. The conditions necessary for being a Japanese national shall be determined by law.

ARTICLE 11. The people shall not be prevented from enjoying any of the fundamental human rights. These fundamental human rights guaranteed to the people by this Constitution shall be conferred upon the people of this and future generations as eternal and inviolate rights.

ARTICLE 12. The freedoms and rights guaranteed to the people by this Constitution shall be maintained by the constant endeavor of the people, who shall refrain from any abuse of these freedoms and rights and shall always be responsible for utilizing them for the public welfare.

ARTICLE 13. All of the people shall be respected as individuals. Their right to life, liberty, and the pursuit of happiness shall, to the extent that it does not interfere with the public welfare, be the supreme consideration in legislation and in other governmental affairs.

ARTICLE 14. All of the people are equal under the law and there shall be no discrimination in political, economic or social relations because of race, creed, sex, social status or family origin.

2. Peers and peerage shall not be recognized.

3. No privilege shall accompany any award of honor, decoration or any distinction, nor shall any such award be valid beyond the lifetime of the individual who now holds or hereafter may receive it.

ARTICLE 15. The people have the inalienable right to choose their public officials and to dismiss them.

2. All public officials are servants of the whole community and not of any group thereof.

3. Universal adult suffrage is guaranteed with regard to the election of public officials.

4. In all elections, secrecy of the ballot shall not be violated. A voter shall not be answerable, publicly or privately, for the choice he has made.

ARTICLE 16. Every person shall have the right of peaceful petition for the redress of damage, for the removal of public officials, for the enactment, repeal or amendment of laws, ordinances or regulations and for other matters, nor shall any person be in any way discriminated against for sponsoring such a petition.

ARTICLE 17. Every person may sue for redress as provided by law from the State or a public entity, in case he has suffered damage through illegal act of any public official.

ARTICLE 18. No person shall be held in bondage of any kind. Involuntary servitude, except as punishment for crime, is prohibited.

ARTICLE 19. Freedom of thought and conscience shall not be violated.

ARTICLE 20. Freedom of religion is guaranteed to all. No religious organization shall receive any privileges from the State nor exercise any political authority.

2. No person shall be compelled to take part in any religious acts, celebration, rite or practice.

3. The State and its organs shall refrain from religious education or any other religious activity.

ARTICLE 21. Freedom of assembly and association as well as speech, press and all other forms of expression are guaranteed.

2. No censorship shall be maintained, nor shall the secrecy of any means of communication be violated.

ARTICLE 22. Every person shall have freedom to choose and change his residence and to choose his occupation to the extent that it does not interfere with the public welfare.

2. Freedom of all persons to move to a foreign country and to divest themselves of their nationality shall be inviolate.

ARTICLE 23. Academic freedom is guaranteed.

ARTICLE 24. Marriage shall be based only on the mutual consent of both sexes and it shall be maintained through mutual cooperation with the equal rights of husband and wife as a basis.

2. With regard to choice of spouse, property rights, inheritance, choice of domicile, divorce and other matters pertaining to marriage and the

family, laws shall be enacted from the standpoint of individual dignity and the essential equality of the sexes.

ARTICLE 25. All people shall have the right to maintain the minimum standards of wholesome and cultured living.

2. In all spheres of life, the State shall use its endeavors for the promotion and extension of social welfare and security, and of public health.

ARTICLE 26. All people shall have the right to receive an equal education correspondent to their ability, as provided by law.

2. All people shall be obligated to have all boys and girls under their protection receive ordinary educations as provided for by law. Such compulsory education shall be free.

ARTICLE 27. All people shall have the right and the obligation to work.

2. Standards for wages, hours, rest and other working conditions shall be fixed by law.

3. Children shall not be exploited.

ARTICLE 28. The right of workers to organize and to bargain and act collectively is guaranteed.

ARTICLE 29. The right to own or to hold property is inviolable.

2. Property rights shall be defined by law, in conformity with the public welfare.

3. Private property may be taken for public use upon just compensation therefor.

ARTICLE 30. The people shall be liable to taxations as provided by law.

ARTICLE 31. No person shall be deprived of life or liberty, nor shall any other criminal penalty be imposed, except according to procedure established by law.

ARTICLE 32. No person shall be denied the right of access to the courts.

ARTICLE 33. No person shall be apprehended except upon warrant issued by a competent judicial officer which specifies the offense with which the person is charged, unless he is apprehended, the offense being committed.

ARTICLE 34. No person shall be arrested or detained without being at once informed of the charges against him or without the immediate privilege of counsel; nor shall he be detained without adequate cause; and upon demand of any person such cause must be immediately shown in open court in his presence and the presence of his counsel.

ARTICLE 35. The right of all persons to be secure in their homes, papers and effects against entries, searches and seizures shall not be impaired except upon warrant issued for adequate cause and particularly describing the place to be searched and things to be seized, or except as provided by Article 33.

2. Each search or seizure shall be made upon separate warrant issued by a competent judicial officer.

ARTICLE 36. The infliction of torture by any public officer and cruel punishments are absolutely forbidden.

ARTICLE 37. In all criminal cases the accused shall enjoy the right to a speedy and public trial by an impartial tribunal.

2. He shall be permitted full opportunity to examine all witnesses, and he shall have the right of compulsory process for obtaining witnesses on his behalf at public expense.

3. At all times the accused shall have the assistance of competent counsel who shall, if the accused is unable to secure the same by his own efforts, be assigned to his use by the State.

ARTICLE 38. No person shall be compelled to testify against himself.

2. Confession made under compulsion, torture or threat, or after prolonged arrest or detention shall not be admitted in evidence.

3. No person shall be convicted or punished in cases where the only proof against him is his own confession.

ARTICLE 39. No person shall be held criminally liable for an act which was lawful at the time it was committed, or of which he has been acquitted, nor shall he be placed in double jeopardy.

ARTICLE 40. Any person, in case he is acquitted after he has been arrested or detained, may sue the State for redress as provided by law.

CHAPTER IV. THE DIET

ARTICLE 41. The Diet shall be the highest organ of state power, and shall be the sole law-making organ of the State.

ARTICLE 42. The Diet shall consist of two Houses, namely the House of Representatives and the House of Councillors.

ARTICLE 43. Both Houses shall consist of elected members, representative of all the people.

2. The number of the members of each House shall be fixed by law.

ARTICLE 44. The qualifications of members of both Houses and their electors shall be fixed by law. However, there shall be no discrimination because of race, creed, sex, social status, family origin, education, property or income.

ARTICLE 45. The term of office of members of the House of Representatives shall be four years. However, the term shall be terminated before the full term is up in case the House of Representatives is dissolved.

ARTICLE 46. The term of office of members of the House of Councillors shall be six years, and election for half the members shall take place every three years.

ARTICLE 47. Electoral districts, method of voting and other matters pertaining to the method of election of members of both Houses shall be fixed by law.

ARTICLE 48. No person shall be permitted to be a member of both Houses simultaneously.

ARTICLE 49. Members of both Houses shall receive appropriate annual payment from the national treasury in accordance with law.

ARTICLE 50. Except in cases provided by law, members of both Houses shall be exempt from apprehension while the Diet is in session, and any members apprehended before the opening of the session shall be freed during the term of the session upon demand of the House.

ARTICLE 51. Members of both Houses shall not be held liable outside the House for speeches, debates or votes cast inside the House.

ARTICLE 52. An ordinary session of the Diet shall be convoked once per year.

ARTICLE 53. The Cabinet may determine to convoke extraordinary sessions of the Diet. When a quarter or more of the total members of either House makes the demand, the Cabinet must determine on such convocation.

ARTICLE 54. When the House of Representatives is dissolved, there must be a general election of members of the House of Representatives within forty (40) days from the date of dissolution, and the Diet must be convoked within thirty (30) days from the date of the election.

2. When the House of Representatives is dissolved, the House of Councillors is closed at the same time. However, the Cabinet may in time of national emergency convoke the House of Councillors in emergency session.

3. Measures taken at such session as mentioned in the proviso of the preceding paragraph shall be provisional and shall become null and void unless agreed to by the House of Representatives within a period of ten (10) days after the opening of the next session of the Diet.

ARTICLE 55. Each House shall judge disputes related to qualifications of its members. However, in order to deny a seat to any member, it is necessary to pass a resolution by a majority of two-thirds or more of the members present.

ARTICLE 56. Business cannot be transacted in either House unless one-third or more of total membership is present.

2. All matters shall be decided, in each House, by a majority of those present, except as elsewhere provided in the Constitution, and in case of a tie, the presiding officer shall decide the issue.

ARTICLE 57. Deliberation in each House shall be public. However, a secret meeting may be held where a majority of two-thirds or more of those members present passes a resolution therefor.

2. Each House shall keep a record of proceedings. This record shall be published and given general circulation, excepting such parts of proceedings of secret session as may be deemed to require secrecy.

3. Upon demand of one-fifth or more of the members present, votes of the members on any matter shall be recorded in the minutes.

ARTICLE 58. Each House shall select its own president and other officials.

2. Each House shall establish its rules pertaining to meetings, proceedings and internal discipline, and may punish members for disorderly conduct. However, in order to expel a member, a majority of two-thirds or more of those members present must pass a resolution thereon.

ARTICLE 59. A bill becomes a law on passage by both Houses, except as otherwise provided by the Constitution.

2. A bill which is passed by the House of Representatives, and upon which the House of Councillors makes a decision different from that of the House of Representatives, becomes a law when passed a second time by the House of Representatives by a majority of two-thirds or more of the members present.

3. The provision of the preceding paragraph does not preclude the House of Representatives from calling for the meeting of a joint committee of both Houses, provided for by law.

4. Failure by the House of Councillors to take final action within sixty (60) days after receipt of a bill passed by the House of Representatives, time in recess excepted, may be determined by the House of Representatives to constitute a rejection of the said bill by the House of Councillors.

ARTICLE 60. The Budget must first be submitted to the House of Representatives.

2. Upon consideration of the budget, when the House of Councillors makes a decision different from that of the House of Representatives, and when no agreement can be reached even through a joint committee of both Houses, provided for by law, or in the case of failure by the House of Councillors to take final action within thirty (30) days, the period of recess excluded, after the receipt of the budget passed by the House of Representatives, the decision of the House of Representatives shall be the decision of the Diet.

ARTICLE 61. The second paragraph of the preceding article applies also to the Diet approval required for the conclusion of treaties.

ARTICLE 62. Each House may conduct investigations in relation to government, and may demand the presence and testimony of witnesses, and the production of records.

ARTICLE 63. The Prime Minister and other Ministers of State may, at any time, appear in either House for the purpose of speaking on bills, regardless of whether they are members of the House or not. They must appear when their presence is required in order to give answers or explanations.

ARTICLE 64. The Diet shall set up an impeachment court from among the members of both Houses for the purpose of trying those judges against whom removal proceedings have been instituted.

2. Matters relating to impeachment shall be provided by law.

CHAPTER V. THE CABINET

ARTICLE 65. Executive power shall be vested in the Cabinet.

ARTICLE 66. The Cabinet shall consist of the Prime Minister, who shall be its head, and other Ministers of State, as provided for by law.

2. The Prime Minister and other Ministers of State must be civilians.

3. The Cabinet, in the exercise of executive power, shall be collectively responsible to the Diet.

ARTICLE 67. The Prime Minister shall be designated from among the members of the Diet by a resolution of the Diet. This designation shall precede all other business.

2. If the House of Representatives and the House of Councillors disagree and if no agreement can be reached even through a joint committee of both Houses, provided for by law, or the House of Councillors fails to make designation within ten (10) days, exclusive of the period of recess, after the House of Representatives has made designation, the decision of the House of Representatives shall be the decision of the Diet.

ARTICLE 68. The Prime Minister shall appoint the Ministers of State. However, a majority of their number must be chosen from among the members of the Diet.

2. The Prime Minister may remove the Ministers of State as he chooses.

ARTICLE 69. If the House of Representatives passes a nonconfidence resolution, or rejects a confidence resolution, the Cabinet shall resign en masse, unless the House of Representatives is dissolved with ten (10) days.

ARTICLE 70. When there is a vacancy in the post of Prime Minister, or upon the first convocation of the Diet after a general election of members of the House of Representatives, the Cabinet shall resign en masse.

ARTICLE 71. In the cases mentioned in the two preceding Articles, the

Cabinet shall continue its functions until the time when a new Prime Minister is appointed.

ARTICLE 72. The Prime Minister, representing the Cabinet, submits bills, reports on general national affairs and foreign relations to the Diet and exercises control and supervision over various administrative branches.

ARTICLE 73. The Cabinet, in addition to other general administrative functions, shall perform the following functions:

(1) Administer the law faithfully; conduct affairs of state;
(2) Manage foreign affairs;
(3) Conclude treaties. However, it shall obtain prior or, depending on circumstances, subsequent approval of the Diet;
(4) Administer the civil service, in accordance with standards established by law;
(5) Prepare the budget, and present it to the Diet;
(6) Enact cabinet orders in order to execute the provisions of this Constitution and of the law. However, it cannot include penal provisions in such cabinet orders unless authorized by such law.
(7) Decide on general amnesty, special amnesty, commutation of punishment, reprieve, and restoration of rights.

ARTICLE 74. All laws and cabinet orders shall be signed by the competent Minister of State and countersigned by the Prime Minister.

ARTICLE 75. The Ministers of State, during their tenure of office, shall not be subject to legal action without the consent of the Prime Minister. However, the right to take that action is not impaired hereby.

CHAPTER VI. JUDICIARY

ARTICLE 76. The whole judicial power is vested in a Supreme Court and in such inferior courts as are established by law.

2. No extraordinary tribunal shall be established, nor shall any organ or agency of the Executive be given final judicial power.

3. All judges shall be independent in the exercise of their conscience and shall be bound only by this Constitution and the laws.

ARTICLE 77. The Supreme Court is vested with the rule-making power under which it determines the rules of procedure and of practice, and of matters relating to attorneys, the internal discipline of the courts and the administration of judicial affairs.

2. Public procurators shall be subject to the rule-making power of the Supreme Court.

3. The Supreme Court may delegate the power to make rules for inferior courts to such courts.

ARTICLE 78. Judges shall not be removed except by public impeachment unless judicially declared mentally or physically incompetent to perform official duties. No disciplinary action against judges shall be administered by any executive organ or agency.

ARTICLE 79. The Supreme Court shall consist of a Chief Judge and such number of judges as may be determined by law; all such judges excepting the Chief Judge shall be appointed by the Cabinet.

2. The appointment of the judges of the Supreme Court shall be reviewed by the people at the first general election of members of the House of Representatives following their appointment, and shall be reviewed again at the first general election of members of the House of Representatives after a lapse of ten (10) years, and in the same manner thereafter.

3. In cases mentioned in the foregoing paragraph, when the majority of the voters favors the dismissal of a judge, he shall be dismissed.

4. Matters pertaining to review shall be prescribed by law.

5. The judges of the Supreme Court shall be retired upon the attainment of the age as fixed by law.

6. All such judges shall receive, at regular stated intervals, adequate compensation which shall not be decreased during their terms of office.

ARTICLE 80. The judges of the inferior courts shall be appointed by the Cabinet from a list of persons nominated by the Supreme Court. All such judges shall hold office for a term of ten (10) years with privilege of reappointment, provided that they shall be retired upon the attainment of the age as fixed by law.

2. The judges of the inferior courts shall receive, at regular stated intervals, adequate compensation which shall not be decreased during their terms of office.

ARTICLE 81. The Supreme Court is the court of last resort with power to determine the constitutionality of any law, order, regulation or official act.

ARTICLE 82. Trials shall be conducted and judgment declared publicly. Where a court unanimously determines publicity to be dangerous to public order or morals, a trial may be conducted privately, but trials of political offenses, offenses involving the press or cases wherein the rights of people as guaranteed in Chapter III of this Constitution are in question shall always be conducted publicly.

CHAPTER VII. FINANCE

ARTICLE 83. The power to administer national finances shall be exercised as the Diet shall determine.

ARTICLE 84. No new taxes shall be imposed or existing ones modified except by law or under such conditions as law may prescribe.

ARTICLE 85. No money shall be expended, nor shall the State obligate itself, except as authorized by the Diet.

ARTICLE 86. The Cabinet shall prepare and submit to the Diet for its consideration and decision a budget for each fiscal year.

ARTICLE 87. In order to provide for unforeseen deficiencies in the budget, a reserve fund may be authorized by the Diet to be expended upon the responsibility of the Cabinet.

2. The Cabinet must get subsequent approval of the Diet for all payments from the reserve fund.

ARTICLE 88. All property of the Imperial Household shall belong to the State. All expenses of the Imperial Household shall be appropriated by the Diet in the budget.

ARTICLE 89. No public money or other property shall be expended or appropriated for the use, benefit or maintenance of any religious institution or association, or for any charitable, educational or benevolent enterprises not under the control of public authority.

ARTICLE 90. Final accounts of the expenditures and revenues of the State shall be audited annually by a Board of Audit and submitted by the Cabinet to the Diet, together with the statement of audit, during the fiscal year immediately following the period covered.

2. The organization and competency of the Board of Audit shall be determined by law.

ARTICLE 91. At regular intervals and at least annually the Cabinet shall report to the Diet and the people on the state of national finances.

CHAPTER VIII. LOCAL SELF-GOVERNMENT

ARTICLE 92. Regulations concerning organization and operations of local public entities shall be fixed by law in accordance with the principle of local autonomy.

ARTICLE 93. The local public entities shall establish assemblies as their deliberative organs, in accordance with law.

2. The chief executive officers of all local public entities, the members of their assemblies, and such other local officials as may be determined by law shall be elected by direct popular vote within their several communities.

ARTICLE 94. Local public entities shall have the right to manage their property, affairs and administration and to enact their own regulations within law.

ARTICLE 95. A special law, applicable only to one local public entity, cannot be enacted by the Diet without the consent of the majority of the voters of the local public entity concerned, obtained in accordance with law.

CHAPTER IX. AMENDMENTS

ARTICLE 96. Amendments to this Constitution shall be initiated by the Diet, through a concurring vote of two-thirds or more of all the members of each House and shall thereupon be submitted to the people for ratification, which shall require the affirmative vote of a majority of all votes cast thereon, at a special referendum or at such election as the Diet shall specify.

2. Amendments when so ratified shall immediately be promulgated by the Emperor in the name of the people, as an integral part of this Constitution.

CHAPTER X. SUPREME LAW

ARTICLE 97. The fundamental human rights by this Constitution guaranteed to the people of Japan are fruits of the age-old struggle of man to be free; they have survived the many exacting tests for durability and are conferred upon this and future generations in trust, to be held for all time inviolate.

ARTICLE 98. This Constitution shall be the supreme law of the nation and no law, ordinance, imperial rescript or other act of government, or part thereof, contrary to the provisions hereof, shall have legal force or validity.

2. The treaties concluded by Japan and established laws of nations shall be faithfully observed.

ARTICLE 99. The Emperor or the Regent as well as Ministers of State, members of the Diet, judges, and all other public officials have the obligation to respect and uphold this Constitution.

CHAPTER XI. SUPPLEMENTARY PROVISIONS

ARTICLE 100. This Constitution shall be enforced as from the day when the period of six months will have elapsed counting from the day of its promulgation.

2. The enactment of laws necessary for the enforcement of this Constitution, the election of members of the House of Councillors and the

procedure for the convocation of the Diet and other preparatory procedures for the enforcement of this Constitution may be executed before the day prescribed in the preceding paragraph.

ARTICLE 101. If the House of Councillors is not constituted before the effective date of this Constitution, the House of Representatives shall function as the Diet until such time as the House of Councillors shall be constituted.

ARTICLE 102. The term of office for half the members of the House of Councillors serving in the first term under this Constitution shall be three years. Members falling under this category shall be determined in accordance with law.

ARTICLE 103. The Ministers of State, members of the House of Representatives, and judges in office on the effective date of this Constitution, and all other public officials, who occupy positions corresponding to such positions as are recognized by this Constitution shall not forfeit their positions automatically on account of the enforcement of this Constitution unless otherwise specified by law. When, however, successors are elected or appointed under the provisions of this Constitution, they shall forfeit their positions as a matter of course.

Selected Bibliography

1. *Publications in English*

A bibliography of some 3,500 Western-language writings on Japanese law has been compiled by Rex Coleman and John O. Haley, *An Index to Japanese Law* (1867–1973), special issue of *Law in Japan: An Annual*, University of Tokyo Press, 1975 (available through Asian Law Program, University of Washington, Seattle, Wash. 98195). Legal journals regularly containing material on Japanese law are *Law in Japan: An Annual* (Japanese American Society for Legal Studies, since 1967), and *Lawasia* (Law Assoc. for Asia and the Western Pacific, since 1969).

Adams, L. Jerold. *Theory, Law and Policy of Contemporary Japanese Treaties*. Dobbs Ferry, N.Y.: Oceana, 1974.

Beer, Lawrence W. "Freedom of Information and the Evidentiary Use of Film in Japan." *American Political Science Review* 65, no. 4(December 1971):1119–34.

———. "Defamation, Privacy and Freedom of Expression in Japan." *Law in Japan: An Annual* 5(1972):192–208.

———. "Education, Politics and Freedom in Japan: The Ienaga Textbook Review Cases." *Law in Japan: An Annual* 8(1975):67–90.

———. "Freedom of Expression in Japan with Comparative Reference to the United States." In R. P. Claude, ed., *Comparative Human Rights*. Baltimore: The Johns Hopkins University Press, 1976.

——— and Hidenori Tomatsu. "A Guide to the Study of Japanese Law." *American Journal of Comparative Law* 23, no. 2(1975):284–324.

——— et al, "Asian Legal Studies in the United States: A Survey Report," 29 Journal of Legal Education, no. 3(1977).

Dando, Shigemitsu. *The Japanese Law of Criminal Procedure*, B. J. George, trans. South Hackensack, N.J.: Fred B. Rothman and Co., 1965.

Danelski, David J. "The People and the Court in Japan." In *Frontiers of Judicial Research*. Edited by Grossman and Tanenhaus. New York: John Wiley & Sons, 1969, pp. 45–72.

Henderson, Dan F. *Conciliation and Japanese Law: Tokugawa and Modern*. 2 vols. Seattle: University of Washington Press, 1965.

———, ed. *The Constitution of Japan: Its First Twenty Years, 1947–67*. Seattle: University of Washington Press, 1969.
Itoh, Hiroshi, ed. *Japanese Politics: An Inside View*. Ithaca, N.Y.: Cornell University Press, 1973.
———. "How Judges Think in Japan." *American Journal of Comparative Law* 18(1970):775–804.
———. "Judicial Decision-Making in the Japanese Supreme Court." *Law in Japan: An Annual* 3(1969):128–61.
———. "The Scalogram Analysis of the Judicial Behavior of the Japanese Supreme Court: 1947–58." *Journal of Political Studies* (1970):1–24.
Maki, John M. *Court and Constitution in Japan: Selected Supreme Court Decisions, 1948–60*. Seattle: University of Washington Press, 1964.
Miller, Frank O. *Minobe Tatsukichi: Interpreter of Constitutionalism in Japan*. Berkeley and Los Angeles: University of California Press, 1965.
Okudaira, Yasuhiro. "The Japanese Supreme Court: Its Organization and Function." *Lawasia* 3, no. 1(April 1972):67.
Oppler, Alfred C., *Legal Reform in Occupied Japan*. Princeton, N.J.: Princeton University Press, 1976.
Seymour, Robert L. "Japan's Self-Defense: The Naganuma Case and Its Implications." *Pacific Affairs* (Winter, 1974–75):421–36.
Shubert, Glendon A., and Danelski, David J., eds. *Comparative Judicial Behavior: Cross-Cultural Studies of Political Decision-Making in the East and West*. New York: Oxford University Press, 1969.
Tanaka, Hideo, assisted by M. D. H. Smith, *The Japanese Legal System: Introductory Cases and Materials*. Tokyo: University of Tokyo Press, 1976.
Von Mehren, Arthur T., ed. *Law in Japan: The Legal Order in a Changing Society*. Cambridge: Harvard University Press, 1963.

2. *Some Major Legal Journals in Japanese Covering Constitutional Law*

Hanrei Jihō (The Case Reporter), *Hanrei Taimuzu* (The Law Times), *Hōgaku Seminā* (The Law Seminar), *Hōritsu Jihō* (Law Review), *Hōsō Jihō* (Lawyers Association Journal), *Jurisuto* (The Jurist), *Kōhō Kenkyū* (The Public Law Review).

3. *Some Selected Publications in Japanese Covering Constitutional Law*
(Most publishers are in Tokyo. See also the items mentioned in Beer and Tomatsu, cited above under I.)

Ashibe, Nobuyoshi, ed. *Jurisuto, No. 44, Kempō Hanrei Hyakusen* (Jurist, no. 44, 100 selected constitutional cases) 3d. ed. Yūhikaku, 1974.
———, and Masaaki Ikeda. *Enshū Hōritsugaku Taikei 2, Enshū Kempō* (Seminars on legal studies 2; Seminars on the constitutional law). Edited by Seirin Shoin Shinsha, 1973.
Chiba, Yujirō, *Shiru Kenri* (The Right to Know). Tokyo University Press, 1972.
Hasegawa, Masayasu. *Kempōgaku no Kiso* (Fundamentals of the study of the Constitution). Nihon Hyōronsha, 1974.
Itō, Masami. *Puraibashii no Kenri* (The right of privacy). Iwanami Shoten, 1963.
———, and Shimizu, Hideo, eds. *Masu Komi Hōrei Yōran* (Survey of laws and regulations concerning the mass media). Gendai Jānarizumu Shuppankai, 1966.

Kiyomiya, Shirō. *Hōritsugaku Zenshū 3: Kempō I (Shimpan)* [A compendium of legal studies 3: The Constitution I (new edition)]. Yūhikaku, 1971.

Kobayashi, Naoki. *Nihonkoku Kempō no Mondai Jōkyō* (Problem areas of the Japanese Constitution). Iwanami, 1964.

———. *Kempō Kōgi (Kaiteiban)* (Lectures on the Constitution) (revised edition). Tokyo University Press, 1972.

Miyazawa, Toshiyoshi. *Hōritsugaku Zenshū 4: Kempō II (Shimpan)* [A compendium of legal studies 4: The Constitution II (new edition)]. Yūhikaku, 1971.

Okudaira, Yasuhiro. *Hyōgen no Jiyū towa Nanika* (What is the freedom of expression?). Chūō Kōronsha, 1970.

Satō, Isao. *Kempō Kenkyū Nyūmon* (Introduction to constitutional studies). 3 vols. Nihon Hyōronsha, 1964–66.

———, ed. *Kempō Kihon Hanreishū (zoku)* (A basic collection of constitutional cases), sequel. Ichiryūsha, 1976.

Shimizu, Hideo. *Shisō-Ryōshin oyobi Genron no Jiyū* (The freedoms of thought, conscience and speech). Ichiryūsha, 1961.

———. *Hō to Masu-Komyunikēshon* (Law and mass communication). Shakai Shisōsha, 1970.

——— ed. *Hō to Hyōgen no Jiyū* (Law and freedom of expression). Gakuyō Shobō, 1972.

Suekawa, Hiroshi. *Hō to Jiyū* (Law and freedom). Iwanami Shoten, 1969.

Suzuki, Yasuzō. *Kempō Riron Kenkyū Sōsho; Nihon no Kempōgaku* (Collection of studies of constitutional principles: Japanese studies on the Constitution). Hyōronsha, 1968.

Tokioka, Hiromu, ed. *Jinken no Kempō Hanrei* (Constitutional cases concerning human rights). Seibundō, 1973.

Ukai, Nobushige. *Kempō ni okeru shōchō to daihyō* (symbols and representation in the Constitution). Iwanami Shoten, 1977.

Wada, Hideo. *Kempō Taikei* (The constitutional system). Keisō Shobō 1967.

———. *Gendai Nihon no Kempō Jōkyō*, (The contemporary Japanese constitution). Hōgaku Shoin, 1974.

4. Selected Japanese Commentaries on the Translated Supreme Court Decisions

Case 1. Japan v. *S. Matsumoto (1961)*

Akira Mitsui in 14 *Hōsō Jihō* 2(February 1962):123–26.

Kimimoto Hashimoto in 34 *Hōritsu Jihō* 2 (February 1962):60–63.

——— in *Toki no Hōrei* No. 417(March 1962):40–48.

Case 2. T. Matsumoto v. *Japan (1962)*

Tadashi Wakida in 14 *Hōsō Jihō* 7(July 1962): 178–81.

——— in *Toki no Hōrei* No. 431(July 1962):42–48.

Shūzō Hayashi in 38 *Jichi Kenkyū* 8(August 1962):3–12.

Taizō Yokoi in *Kenshū*, no. 170 (Aug. 1970):61–65.

Yoshio Kaneko in 36 *Hōgaku Kenkyū* 4(April 1963):97–102.

Teruya Abe in 73 *Hōgaku Ronsō* 2(May 1963):135–39.

Kazushi Kojima in *Jurisuto* No. 276–2(June 1963):259–60.

Itsuo Sonobe in *Jurisuto, zōkan* issue (November 1966):185–89.

——— in *Jurisuto, zōkan* issue (May 1971):225.
Hideo Wada in 4 *Jurisuto* 5, *bessatsu* issue (December 1968):236–37.
Chūichi Fukase in 6 *Jurisuto* 3, *bessatsu* issue (October 1970):73–74.

Case 3. Shimizu v. *Governor, Osaka Metropolis (1962)*

Yoshio Ōnishi in 47 *Minshōhō Zasshi* 4(January 1963):135–44.
Jirō Tanaka in *Jurisuto* No. 276–2(June 1963):194–96.
Kazushi Kojima in 6 *Jurisuto* 3, *bessatsu* issue (October 1970):213–14.

Case 4. Japan v. *Kobayashi et al (1963)*

Yoshitaka Watabe in 15 *Hōsō Jihō* 5(May 1963):97–107.
Ryokichi Arikura in 35 *Hōritsu Jihō* 5(May 1963):50–51.
Ryūichi Arai in 16 *Hōritsu no Hiroba* 5(May 1963):30–33.
Yoriaki Narita in *Jurisuto* No. 273(May 1963):18–25.
Fumio Endō in *Jurisuto* No. 276–2(June 1963):228–30.
Yoshiaki Yoshida in *Meiji Daigaku Hōseishi Kenkyūjo Kiyō* No. 7(September 1963):127–37.
Hisao Oka in 4 *Kōnan Hōgaku* 2(October 1963):93–120.
Hide Ara in *Jurisuto, zōkan* issue (November 1966:168–73.
——— in *Jurisuto, zōkan* issue (May 1971):208.

Case 5. Takano v. *Director, Osaka Office, National Tax Bureau (1961)*

Masaya Numa in *Hōgaku Seminā* No. 68(November 1961):66–70.
Masaji Tanaka in 13 *Hōsō Jihō* 11(November 1961):116–20.
——— in *Toki no Hōrei* No. 405(November 1961):49–51.
Hirohisa Kitano in *Jurisuto* No. 276–2(June 1963):221–23.
Kiyoshi Igarashi in 3 *Jurisuto* 1, *bessatsu* issue (February 1967):48–49.

Case 6. Koshiyama v. *Chairman, Tokyo Metropolitan Election Supervision Commission (1964)*

Nobushige Ukai in *Hanrei Hyōron* No. 66(March 1964):1–3.
——— in *Toki no Hōrei* No. 490(March 1964):50–55.
Takasuke Kobayashi in 17 *Hōritsu no Hiroba* 4(April 1964):4–8.
Nobuyoshi Ashibe in *Jurisuto* No. 296(April 1964):48–58.
——— in *Jurisuto, zōkan* issue (November 1966):20–24.
Kazuhiro Hayashida in 51 *Minshōhō Zasshi* 5(February 1965):114–21.
Seiichi Taguchi in 38 *Hōgaku Kenkyū* (Keio University) 3(March 1965):79–84.

Case 7. Nakamura et al v. *Japan (1962)*

Tadashi Wakida in 15 *Hōsō Jihō* 1(January 1963):131–38.
Masataka Taniguchi in *Jurisuto* No. 266(January 1963):48–51.
——— in *Hanrei Hyōron* No. 54(February 1963):1–4.
Atsushi Nagashima in *Kenshū* No. 175(January 1963):73–81.
Hideo Fujiki in 16 *Hōritsu no Hiroba* 2(February 1963):4–8.
Masami Itō in 35 *Hōritsu Jihō* 2(February 1963):36–41.
——— in *Jurisuto* No. 268(February 1963):10–29.

Tadashi Uematsu in 50 *Hitotsubashi Ronsō* 2(August 1963):55–59.
Shintarō Kawai in 70 *Hōgaku Shimpō* 12(December 1963):55–67.
Tatsuo Kagawa in *Jurisuto, zōkan* issue (November 1966):92–96.
——— in *Jurisuto, zōkan* issue (May 1971):108.
Hiroshi Tamiya in 6 *Jurisuto* 2, *bessatsu* issue (July 1970):122–23.

Case 8. Japan v. *Iida et al (1963)*

Kazuo Fujii in 15 *Hōsō Jihō* 8(August 1963):160–73.
Ichirō Ogawa in *Jurisuto* No. 280(August 1963):12–16.
——— in *Toki no Hōrei* No. 471(August 1963):59–64.
Ryūichi Arai in 16 *Hōritsu no Hiroba* 9(September 1963):32–37.
Ryōkichi Arikura in *Toki no Hōrei* No. 472(September 1963):53–61.
Teruya Abe in 74 *Hōgaku Ronsō* (Kyoto University) Nos. 5/6(February 1964):137–43.
Hiroshi Maeda in 36 *Keisatsu Kenkyū* 9(September 1965):103–22.
Yoriaki Narita in *Jurisuto, zōkan* issue (November 1966):76–80.
——— in *Jurisuto, zōkan* issue (May 1971):98.
Narikazu Imamura in 4 *Jurisuto* 3, *bessatsu* issue (May 1968):198–99.
Shōzaburō Ichihara in 4 *Jurisuto* 5, *bessatsu* issue (December 1968):72–73.
Chūsei Fujita in 6 *Jurisuto* 3, *bessatsu* issue (October 1970):191–93.

Case 9. Yoshida v. *Japan (1965)*

Takuma Hyōgo in 37 *Keisatsu Kenkyū* 7(July 1966):164–68.

Case 10. Kozumi v. *Japan (1963)*

Ikuo Ichikawa in 16 *Hōsō Jihō* 2(February 1964):128–31.
——— in *Toki no Hōrei* No. 487(February 1964):50–54.
Kazuhiko Tokoro in 38 *Keisatsu Kenkyū* 9(September 1967):109–12.
Yoshio Kanazawa in 4 *Jurisuto* 5, *bessatsu* issue (December 1968):64–65.
Minoru Onoe in 7 *Jurisuto* 4, *bessatsu* issue (November 1971):192.

Case 11. Japan v. *Ki et al (1970)*

Yoshio Ogino in 43 *Hōritsu Jihō* 1(January 1971):63.
Tatsu Tomizawa in 23 *Hōsō Jihō* 2(February 1971):174.
Hideo Wada in *Jurisuto, zōkan* issue (May 1971):91.
Masahiko Kakutani in 48 *Jichi Kenkyū* 1(January 1972):162.

Case 12. Toyama et al v. *Japan (1966)*

Mitsuo Minemura in 19 *Rōdō Hōrei Tsūshin* 29(November 1966):1–25.
——— in *Rōdō Hōritsu Jumpō* Nos. 615/616(November/December 1966):3–75.
Naomi Maekawa in *Chihō Kōmuin Geppō* No. 40(December 1966):17–27.
Tadashi Hanami in *Hanrei Hyōron* No. 97(December 1966):15–18.
Yoshie Tahara in *Jurisuto* No. 359(December 1966):63–81.
Kiyoshi Gotō in *Jurisuto* No. 362(January 1967):67–71.
Heiji Nomura in 39 *Hōritsu Jihō* 1(January 1967):55–63.
Kazuhisa Nakayama in *Hōgaku Seminā* No. 130(January 1967):41–45.

Naofumi Murakami in 20 *Hōritsu no Hiroba* 1(January 1967):33–39.
Katsumi Ueda in 18 *Dōshisha Hōgaku* 3(January 1967):110–33.
Tsuneo Yoshida in *Jurisuto* No. 363(February 1967):92–96.
Tsugio Nakano in 19 *Hōsō Jihō* 3(March 1967):178–95.
Yasutsugu Tomita in 16 *Sōsa Kenkyū* 5(May 1967):46–58.
Ryōji Ishimatsu in 8 *Sangyō Keizai Kenkyū* 1(May 1967):37–68.
Nobuo Hayashi in 33 *Nihon Hōgaku* 1(May 1967):56–74.
Masami Itō in 3 *Jurisuto* 2, *bessatsu* issue (May 1967):14–15.
Yoshikatsu Naka in 6 *Jurisuto* 2, *bessatsu* issue (July 1970):28–29.
Toshimasa Sugimura in *Jurisuto, zōkan* issue (May 1971):156.
Ken'ichi Tatenuma in *Jurisuto, zōkan* issue (December 1972):16.

Case 13. Japan v. *Sakane et al (1969)*

Mitsuo Minemura in 22 *Rōdō Hōrei Tsūshin* 11(May 1969):46–47.
Shinrō Watabiki in 21 *Hōsō Jihō* 6(June 1969):214–37.
Inejirō Numata in 19 *Kikan Rōdohō* 2(June 1969):100–31.
Kunio Sōshi in *Hanrei Hyōron* No. 126(July 1969):14–20.
Ken Murakami in 7 *Jurisuto* 3, *bessatsu* issue (June 1971):84.
Tetsuo Takezawa in *Hō to Minshushugi* No. 60(September 1971):37.

Case 14. Asahi v. *Japan (1967)*

Isao Kikuchi et al in *Hanrei Jihō* No. 481(June 1967):3–8.
Kunio Yano in 6 *Jurisuto* 3, *bessatsu* issue (October 1970):244–45.
Takanori Sumino in *Jurisuto, zōkan* issue (May 1971):142.

Case 15. Katō v. *Japan (1964)*

Ryūichi Arai in 17 *Hōritsu no Hiroba* 4(April 1964):20–24.
Yoshitaka Watanabe in 17 *Hōritsu no Hiroba* 4(April 1964):25–29.
——— in 16 *Hōsō Jihō* 4(April 1964):109–13.
Takeshi Takagi in 8 *Tōyō Hōgaku* 1(July 1964):79–84.
Toyoji Kakudō in 51 *Minshohō Zasshi* 1(February 1965):135–39.

Case 16. Taniguchi v. *Japan (1967)*

Yasuo Tokikuni in 7 *Jurisuto* 3, *bessatsu* issue (June 1971):206.

Case 17. Iwasaki v. *Japan (1962)*

Yoshitaka Watanabe in 14 *Hōsō Jihō* 5(May 1962):88.
Kazuo Kojima in *Jurisuto* No. 254(July 1962):44–47.
Shinji Tanaka in 15 *Senkyo* 10(October 1962):17–18.
Katsuhisa Yano in 47 *Minshōhō Zasshi* 5(February 1963):49–56.
Kunio Kamata in 16 *Senkyo* 6(June 1963):5–8.

Case 18. Kojima v. *Japan (1966)*

Fumio Aoyagi in *Hanrei Hyōron* No. 97(December 1966):45–47.
Shin'ichi Ebihara in *Jurisuto* No. 377(August 1967):96.

——— in *Toki no Hōrei* No. 619(August 1967):120–24.
Taizō Yokoi in *Kenshū* No. 230(August 1967):39–46.
Jirō Nakano in 20 *Hōritsu no Hiroba* 9(September 1967):21–27.
Hidemi Sugiyama in 74 *Hōgaku Shimpō* Nos. 11/12(December 1967):85–103.
Ken Toyota in 41 *Hōgaku Kenkyū* (Keio University) 10(October 1968):120–25.
Hiroshi Tamiya in 4 *Jurisuto* 5(December 1968):88–89.

Case 19. Japan v. *Arima (1961)*

Tadashi Kurita in 14 *Hōritsu no Hiroba* 6(June 1961):915.
——— in 13 *Hōsō Jihō* 8(August 1961):123–31.
Akio Date in *Jurisuto* No. 231(August 1961):4–9.
Taizō Yokoi in *Kenshū* No. 159(September 1961):65–72.
Shōichi Mikami in 69 *Hōgaku Shimpō* 9(September 1962):68–75.
Akira Morii in 72 *Hōgaku Ronsō* 2(November 1962):83–92.
Takuji Takada in 1 *Jurisuto* 1, *bessatsu* issue (January 1965):48–49.
——— in 7 *Jurisuto* 2, *bessatsu* issue (May 1971), p. 64.

Case 20. Ichikawa et al v. *Japan (1961)*

Tadashi Kurita in *Jurisuto* No. 232(August 1961):50–58.
——— in 13 *Hōsō Jihō* 9(September 1961):135–42.
Ryō Masaki in *Hōgaku Seminā* No. 66(September 1961):54–56.
——— in *Toki no Hōrei* No. 401(October 1961):44–49.
Kazuhiko Tokoro in 34 *Keisatsu Kenkyū* 4(April 1963):89–95.
——— in *Jurisuto* No. 307-2(October 1964):104–5.
——— in *Jurisuto* 2, *bessatsu* issue (July 1970):120–21.
Narikazu Imamura in *Jurisuto* No. 276-2(June 1963):245–46.
Yutaka Hiratsuka in 37 *Hōgaku Kenkyū* (Keio University) 1(January 1964):3–38.

Case 21. Saitō v. *Japan (1962)*

Yoshie Tahara in 14 *Hōsō Jihō* 7(July 1962):154–64.
Taizō Yokoi in *Kenshū* No. 169(July 1962):59–63.
Takuji Takada in *Hōgaku Seminā* No. 78(September 1962):41–45.
Hideo Fujiki in *Jurisuto* No. 276-2(June 1963):111–13.
——— in 4 *Jurisuto* 2, *bessatsu* issue (April 1968):216–17.
Hiroshi Tamiya in *Jurisuto, zōkan* issue (November 1966):108–13.
——— in *Jurisuto, zōkan* issue (May 1971):130.

Case 22. Abe v. *Japan (1966)*

Takeshi Sakamoto in 18 *Hōsō Jihō* 10(October 1966):135–39.
Tōyō Atsumi in *Hanrei Hyōron* No. 98(February 1967):40–43.
Masataka Taniguchi in *Jurisuto* No. 373(June 1967):337–40.
Tatsumi Tamura in 16 *Sōsa Kenkyū* 8(August 1967):41–47.
Hideo Niwayama in 7 *Jurisuto* 2, *bessatsu* issue (May 1971):170.

Case 23. Yoshimura v. *Yoshimura (1965)*

Nobuo Miyata in 17 *Hōsō Jihō* 8(August 1965):110–15.

Noboru Koyama in *Hanrei Hyōron* No. 84(October 1965):3–7.
——— in *Toki no Hōrei* No. 550(November 1965):54–58.
——— in *Toki no Hōrei* No. 551(November 1965):54–62.
Ichirō Iikura in 3 *Kokugakuin Hōgaku* 3(January 1966):89–97.
Tomohei Taniguchi in 54 *Minshōhō Zasshi* 2(May 1966):72–83.
Sakae Wagatsuma in *Hōgakukyōkai Zasshi* (June 1966):169–77.

Case 24. Kōchi v. *Japan (1969)*

Taira Fukuda in *Jurisuto* No. 432(1969):103.
——— in *Jurisuto, bessatsu* issue No. 27(July 1970):202–3.
——— in *Jurisuto, bessatsu* issue No. 31(February 1971):42–43.
Hideo Fujiki in 86 *Hōgakukyōkai Zasshi* 10(1969):1103.
Tomio Nishiyama in *Jurisuto* No. 456(20 July 1970):127–29.

Case 25. Hasegawa v. *Japan (1969)*

Kinuko Kubota in *Jurisuto, zōkan* issue, No. 456(20 July 1970):27–29.
Kageaki Mitsudō in *Jurisuto, bessatsu* issue No. 31(February 1971):150–51.

Case 26. Ishii et al v. *Japan (1969)*

Yasuhiro Okudaira in *Jurisuto*, No. 440(15 December 1969):66.
Zenji Ishimura in *Jurisuto, zōkan* issue, No. 456(20 July 1970):18–20.
Shinjirō Maeda in *Jurisuto, bessatsu* issue No. 27(July 1970):174–75.
Lawrence Beer in *Amerika Hō*, 1970–2(1971):173–86.
Hisatomo Tanaka in *Jurisuto, bessatsu* issue No. 31(February 1971):34–37.

Case 27. Ōno v. *Japan (1961)*

Kinuko Kubota in *Jurisuto, zōkan* issue (November 1966):40–44.
Zenji Ishimura in *Jurisuto, bessatsu* issue No. 21(December 1968):38–39.
Ichirō Hokimoto in *Jurisuto, bessatsu* issue No. 31(February 1971):152–53.

Case 28. Nishida v. *Japan (1963)*

Hiroshi Chiba in 16 *Hōritsu no Hiroba* 8(August 1963):21–24.
Ichirō Yamamoto in 15 *Hōsō Jihō* 9(September 1963):152–54.
Hisashi Aizawa in *Jurisuto, bessatsu* issue No. 21(December 1968):32–33.
——— in *Jurisuto, bessatsu* issue No. 37(July 1972):10–11.

Case 29. Tokyo Public Prosecutor v. *Senda (1963)*

Naoki Kobayashi in 35 *Hōritsu Jihō* 7(July 1963).
Isao Satō in *Jurisuto, bessatsu* issue No. 21(December 1968):58–59.
Shin'ichi Takayanagi in *Jurisuto, bessatsu* issue No. 21(December 1968):65–70.
Ryōkichi Arikura in *Jurisuto, bessatsu* issue No. 41(April 1973):16–17.

Case 30. Japan v. *Kanemoto et al (1964)*

Symposium in 41 *Hōritsu Jihō* 13(November 1969):4–63.

Case 31. Yamagishi et al v. *Japan (1970)*

Teruya Abe in *Jurisuto, bessatsu* issue No. 31(February 1971):156–57.
Kazuyuki Takahashi in *Jurisuto, bessatsu* issue No. 44(June 1974):52–53.

Case 32. Kaneko et al v. *Japan (1969)*

Zenji Ishimura in 41 *Hōritsu Jihō* 13(November 1969):78–89.
Yoshito Obuki in *Jurisuto, zōkan* issue, No. 456(20 July 1970):15–17.
Shigetsugu Suzuki in *Jurisuto, bessatsu* issue No. 31(February 1971):14–15.
Japan Federation of Bar Associations, 22 *Jiyū to Seigi* 10(October 1971):1–65.

Index

Academic freedom, 175, 186, 203–5, 226–41 *passim*
Accused: rights of, 20, 23–36, 154–61, 164–68
Acupuncture: regulation of, 217–23
Adjustment (*shimpan*) of disputes, 169–74
Administrative Litigation Law of 1962: 82–84, 137, 139; text of Art. 9, 82
Advertising: regulation of, 217–23
Aliens: right of reentry, 82–84
Appeals: *jōkoku*, xvi, 224–25; *kōkoku*, xvi; *kōso*, xvi, 183; from a doubtful judgment (*fushinpan seikyū*), 249–50
Arrest: under conditions of urgency, 157–61
Assembly: freedom of, 19, 103, 130, 231
Automobile accidents: reporting of, 164–66

Baker v. *Carr*, 55–56
Bias: allegation of judicial, 224
Bribery, 78–79; for votes, 149–53; and prosecutorial interrogation, 167–68
Bureaucracy in Japan, 4, 7

Cabinet, 4, 7
Capital punishment, 19, 161–63
Chatterley Decision (Supreme Court of Japan), 184, 190–94, 197, 205–9
Civil Code: marriage rights under, 50–52, 169–74
Civil law tradition in Japan, 8
Civil Procedure, Code of: text of Arts. 89 and 95 (trial costs); text of Art. 208 (inheritance), 133
Classification: of cases, xii
Clear and present danger: as judicial standard, 107, 150, 242–44 (concrete danger)
Codes, in Japanese law, 8–9
Collective bargaining rights, 90, 124–29
Commission on the Constitution, 6
Conciliation (*chōtei*), 170
Concrete danger doctrine, 243
Confession: evidentiary use of, 167–68
Conscience: freedom of, 175, 217–23
Conspiracy: punishment of, 105; definition of, 107
Constitution of 1889 (Meiji Constitution): imperial sovereignty, 4; courts, 9; effect of pursuant laws under Constitution of 1947, 162–63
Constitution of 1947 (Constitution of Japan): 3, 5–21; pacifist provisions of, 5, 13–14; judiciary of, 7–11; judicial powers of, 8, 58, 70, 246–50; "judicial crisis" of, 16–21
Councillors, House of, 16, 53–57
Court of Cassation (Meiji Constitution), 9
Court system, 7–11, 254–55
Creditor: rights of, 170
Criminal Code: 78, 90, 176–78, 183–217, 224, 226–27; text of Art. 35, 90; text of Arts. 197-2 and 197-4 (bribery), 78; text of Arts. 230(1) and 230-2 (defamation), 176; text of Art. 175 (obscenity), 183; text of Art. 205 (injury resulting in death), 224; text of Arts. 233 and 234 (obstruction of another's business), 226–27
Criminal intent, 177
Criminal Procedure, Code of, 154–61 (double jeopardy; method of administering death penalty), 181–82 (photography during criminal investigation; *see also* Case 32); text of Art. 198 (criminal investigation), Art. 239 (lodging an accusation), Art. 311 (questioning the accused),

Art. 337 (grounds for acquittal), Art. 396, Art. 404, and Art. 414, 23–24; text of Art. 405(1) (grounds for *jōkoku* appeal), 59; text of Art. 317(1) (ascertaining facts), Art. 319(2) (inadequacy of confession as evidence), 154–55; text of Art. 210 (arrest under conditions of urgency), Art. 220 (conditions of arrest), Art. 309 (lodging an objection to taking of evidence), and Art. 326 (written or oral evidence), 158; text of Art. 319(1) (confession under duress), 167; text of Art. 218(2) (taking evidence without warrant), 179; text of Art. 400 (judicial actions on *kōso* appeal), 183; Article 405 (*jōkoku* appeal) discussed, 224–25; text of Art. 99 (court seizure of articles), Art. 262, and Art. 265 (appeal from a doubtful judgment), 247
Criminal record: effect on sentencing in separate case, 154–57
Criminal trial: fairness of, 246–50
Cruel punishment, 161–63
Customary law, 173
Customs Law, 58–72; text of Art. 118 (confiscation of criminal cargo), 59

Defamation, 20, 175–78, 184, 202
Demonstrations ("collective activities"): regulation of, 19–20, 179–82
De Sade, Marquis, 183–217 *passim*
Diet: House of Peers (Meiji Constitution), 4; House of Representatives, 4, 7; House of Councillors, 7, 16, 53–57
"Dispute activities": restraints on public employees, 20, 85–130; defined, 122, 126; Law Regulating the Methods of Dispute Activities in the Electrical, Coal and Mining Industries, Arts. 2 and 3, 122
Dissenting opinions (Supreme Court), 19
Domestic Relations Adjustment Law, 169–74; text of Arts. 7, 9(1), and 15, 169
Double jeopardy, 154–57
Due process (Art. 31, Constitution), 22–23, 26–36, 39, 58, 60–72, 78–79, 110–11, 115, 154–74, 179–80, 246

Economic rights, 58–81, 218–23
Edo Period (Tokugawa), 3–4, 216
Education: right to, 147–48; textbooks, 14, 20, 147–48; School Education Law (tuition), 148; Fundamental Law of Education, Art. 4(2) (tuition), 148, text of Art. 8 (political education), 226; School Education Law, text of Art. 52 (university purposes), 226; Ministry of Education and university autonomy, 240–41
Elections: of a ward mayor, 45–49; apportionment of Diet seats, 19, 53–57; crime of campaign manager, 151–53
Emperor of Japan, 4–7, 14
Equality: of women's rights, 50–52; of value of a vote, 53–57
Evidence: confiscation of, 18–19, 58–61; third-party possessions, 18–19, 58–71; expert opinion, 160–61; hearsay, 177–78; judicial taking of, 243–44; court order to present (*teishutsu meirei*), 246–50; television film, 246–50
Expression, freedom of: (election canvassing), 149–50; (press freedom), 175–78; (obscene publications), 183–217; inherent limits of, 204, 243; in advertising, 217–23. *See* Press freedom

Faith-healing, 223–25
Family courts, 10, 170–74, 254–55
Forms of law (*kokuhō no keishiki*), 22
Frankfurter, U.S. Justice Felix, 56
Freedom. *See* Academic freedom; Advertising; Assembly Conscience; Expression; Economic rights; Information; "Intellectual rights and freedoms"; News-gathering; Press freedom; Privacy; Religion; Speech; Thought; Travel
Fujita, Justice Hachiro: opinions of, 26, 221

German Federal Republic, Art. 5 (freedom to know) of the Basic Law of, 213
Gluckman, Max, 13n44
Grand Bench of Supreme Court, xv, 10
Guardians: duties of, 147–48

Hanging: as method of execution, 161–63
Hanreishū, xv
Health and Welfare Minister, 130–47 *passim*
Hearsay evidence, 177–78
Hiraga Incident, 17
Homicide: by negligence, 164–66; inflicting injury resulting in death, 223–26

Ienaga Saburo: textbook review cases, 14, 20
Ikeda, Prime Minister Hayato, 12
Immigration Control Ordinance: text of Art. 26 (alien reentry), 82
Incitement to crime, 116–30 *passim*; definition of, 106–7
Indirect incitement, 109, 112–13
Information: freedom of, 213, 246–50
Injury: crime of inflicting, 232–41 *passim*
Instigation of crime, 116–30 *passim*; definition of, 107
Insurrection: crime of, 242–44
"Intellectual rights and freedoms" (*seishinteki jiyūken*), 175
Interpretation: judicial methods of, 8
Investigation (criminal): by a public procurator, 22–36; by police during demon-

stration, 178–82; by police on university campus, 229–41
Irie, Justice Toshio: on investigation of political organizations, 32; on confiscation of third-party property, 62; on public employee rights, 113; on academic freedom, university autonomy, and political activities, 230
Irokawa, Justice Kotarō: on alien reentry rights, 84; on public employee rights, 121; on the obscenity question and freedom, 211
Ishida, Justice Kazuto: on public employee rights, 98, 119
Ishizaka, Justice Shūichi: on academic freedom, university autonomy, and campus political activities, 236
Ito, Masami, xiii
Iwata, Justice Makoto: on public employee rights, 117; on obscenity and freedom of expression, 194

Jōkoku appeal, xvi
Judicial review in Japan, 8–9, 58–70 *passim*
Judiciary: 7–11, 254–55; types of appeal to, xvi; "judicial crisis," 16–18; and Hiraga incident, 17; trends in decision-making by, 18–20; and National Judicial Employees Union, 103, 106–30 *passim*

Kawamura, Justice Daisuke: on confiscation of property of an accused, 63; on advertising and freedom of expression, 220
Kawamura, Justice Matasuke: on advertising and freedom of expression, 221
Kobayashi, Naoki, xiii
Kōkoku appeal, xvi
Kōso appeal, xvi
Kusaka, Justice Asanosuke: on public employee rights, 98, 119

Labor law: the "Three Labor Laws", 122; post–1945 history of, 122–27
Labor Relations Adjustment Law (LRAL), 122–30 *passim*
Labor Relations Commission, 122–24
Labor Union Law: text of Art. 1 (purposes of the law), Art. 7 (prohibited employer actions), and Art. 8 (limits on employer indemnity claims), 87–88
Lawrence, D. H., 191
Laws (*hōritsu*), 7
Lawyers: advertisement by, 219–20
Legal training, 10
Liberal-Democratic Party (LDP), 7, 11, 15, 17
Licensing: of taxis, 80–81; of medical arts practitioners, 223
Livelihood Protection Law, 130–47 *passim*; text of Arts. 2, 3, 8, 9, 24, 59, 64, 65 (welfare rights and procedures), 131–32
Local autonomy, 14, 42–49
Local Autonomy Law: text of Art. 2 (administrative jurisdiction of local public entities) and Art. 14 (local sublegislative powers), 37, 74; text of Art. 243-2 (official corruption), 42; text of Art. 281-2 (election of a ward mayor), 45
Local Public Employees Law (LPEL), 95, 119–20, 122; text of Art. 31(1) (duty performance oath), 37 (restraints on activities of local public employees), and Art. 61(1) (penal provisions), 86–87

MacArthur, Gen. Douglas, 124–26
Malapportionment, 16 (1975 election law changes), 19, 53–57
Marbury v. *Madison*, 9
Maritime Employees Law, 122
Marriage: taxation of family income, 50–52; adjustment of domestic disputes, 169–74
Massage: Law Regulating Practitioners of Massage, Acupuncture, Moxa Cautery, and *Jūdō* Therapy, 217–23; text of Art. 7 (restraints on advertising), 217–18
Mass media, 175–78, 183–216, 246–50
Matsukawa Case, 229, 231, 234, 237
Matsumoto, Justice Masao: on illegality of public employee dispute activities, 119
Meiji Constitution (1889), 3–5, 7–9; present effectiveness of 1873 Cabinet Order issued under, 161–64
Mental illness: effect on legal obligations, 172, 225
Mikazuki, Akira, 8
Military: of Japan, 4–6, 17–18; of U.S., 105
Misdemeanor Law, 244–46; text of Art. 1(33) (poster hanging), 244
Mistaken belief: as evidence, 177
Moxa cautery, regulation on, 217–23

Naganuma Missile Site Case, 17–18
Narcotics: Drug and Narcotics Law, 34–35; seizure of, 157–61
National Personnel Authority, 86, 125
National Public Employees Law: text of Art. 98 (rights of public employees) and Art. 110(1) (penalties for illegal dispute activities), 86; text of Art. 98(5) and Art. 110(1), 105
News-gathering: freedom of, 248–50
North Korea, 82–83

Obscenity: regulation of, 183–217
Occupation: right to, 80–84
Occupation Period, 3, 5, 8, 88; regulation of political organizations in, 22–36; ordinances of, 22–36, 124–26

Okinawa: reversion to Japan, 13
Okuno, Justice Ken'ichi: on procurator's investigation, 30; on notice of confiscation of evidence, 63; on public employee rights, 98, 119; on freedom of advertising, 221; on obscenity regulation, 201; on academic freedom, freedom of assembly, and university autonomy, 230
Ordinances, 7; during Occupation, 22–36; punishment under, 37–39, 76; as sublegislation of local public entities, 38, 73–77
Organization Control Ordinance, 22–23, 26–36; text of, 24–26
Ōsumi, Justice Ken'ichirō: on obscenity regulation, 196

Peers, House of (Meiji Constitution), 4
Petty Bench of Supreme Court, xvi, 10
Pharmaceutical Law, Art. 34 (freedom of advertising), 222
Police: Police Law, 41, 44, 181–82; photography, 178–82; text of Art. 40 (maintenance of local police forces) of Police Law of 1947 and of Art. 36 (prefectural police forces) of Police Law of 1954, 42–43; text of Art. 2(1) (police duties), of 1954 Law, 179
Political parties, 5–7, 15–16
Political Organization Control Ordinance (Occupation), 22–26
Political writings: restraint on distribution of, 242–46
Pornography, 186, 191, 201, 211–12, 215
Postal employees: rights of, 20, 85–103; mail theft by, 154–57
Postal Law, text of Art. 1 (purposes of law) and Art. 79 (penal provision for employee misconduct), 89
Posters: illegal hanging of, 244–46
Potsdam Cabinet Orders, 29, 124
Potsdam Declaration, 24
Precedent: binding power of, 9; changing of, 9, 177, 187–88; application of under Criminal Code, 168; allegations of change, 190, 203–11
Press freedom, 175–78, 186–217, 246–50
"Prevailing social ideas": as legal standard, 188–217 *passim*
Privacy: right to, 20, 180–82; of certain trials, 170–74
"Procedure established by law" (Constitution, Art. 31). *See* Due process
Procurator: investigative powers of Supreme Public Procurator, 27–29, 32, 35
Property rights: limits of, 60, 73, 76–77
Prostitution, regulation by ordinance and law, 36–40
Public employees: rights of, 20, 85–130
Public Enterprise Labor Relations Law (PELRL, 1948), 129–30; text of Art. 3 (object of law), Art. 17 (prohibition of dispute activities, which *see*), and Art. 18 (penalties for dispute activities), 87; text of Art. 17, 122
Public Office Election Law (1950), 16, 53–57, 149–53; text of Art. 138(1) (prohibition on canvassing), Art. 239 (penal provision), Art. 211 (grounds for invalidating election), and Art. 251–52 (effect of campaign manager's crime), 150–52
Public safety commission, 179
Public welfare doctrine (*kōkyō no fukushi*), as qualifying rights and freedoms, 19–20, 149–53, 175, 180–82, 186–217 *passim*, 219–22, 225, 243

Religion: freedom of, 175, 223–25
Reporting (media): freedom of, 247–50
Representatives, House of, 4, 7
Revision of the Constitution, 3, 5–6
Rights: under Meiji Constitution, 7–8; Universal Declaration of Human Rights, Art. 19, 213; rights of workers, 245; "right to know," 248–50; "right to likeness" (*shōzōken*), 178–82. *See also* Public employees and freedom
Road Traffic Control Law (1956), 164–66; text of Art. 24(1) (duties at traffic accident site) and Art. 28(1) (penal provision), 164; Enforcement Ordinance (1960), text of Art. 67 (duties at traffic accident site), 164–65; Art. 77, 182

Saitō, Justice Kitarō: on judicial review and apportionment, 55–57; on academic freedom, freedom of assembly, and university autonomy, 230
Saitō, Justice Yūsuke: on Occupation ordinance and administrative investigation, 35; on effectiveness of moxa cautery, 221
Satō, Prime Minister Eisaku, 13
Schools. *See* Education
Search and seizure: consent to, 157–61; without warrant, 159–60; warrants for, 215
Secrecy of communications: right to, 175
Security Treaty (United States–Japan, 1960): Crisis of 1960, 13; opposition to, 13, 103, 108, 127–29; constitutionality of, 103, 110–111; text of, 104–5
Seizure: warrants for, 215
Self-defense: as legitimizing injurious acts, 232, 235–236
Self-Defense Forces, 5. Self-Defense Forces Law, Art. 64, 122. *See also* Military
Self-incrimination, 164–66
Self-regulation: of obscenity, 215
Shibuya Incident, 229, 231, 234, 237

Shimoiizaka, Justice Masuo: on administrative investigation, 35; on judicial review of confiscation judgment, 68
Shimomura, Justice Kazuo: on public employee rights, 119; on obscenity regulation, 189
Socialism, in Japan, 5
Sovereignty, locus in Japan: Emperor, 4; people, 6
Speech: freedom of, 150
Standards of living: right to minimum, 130–31, 134–36, 139–47
Strike: the right to, 92–103 *passim*; 105–30 *passim*
Student politics, 178–82, 226–41, 249–50
Subversive Activities Prevention Law, 22, 29, 242–44; text of Art. 2 (restriction of application of law) and Art. 38(2) (penalties for illegal distribution of printed material), 242
Sunagawa Case, 55, 111n
Supreme Command, Allied Powers, 124–25
Supreme Court: of Japan, 10–11; of U.S., 55, 65–66, 70–71

Takahashi, Justice Kiyoshi: on procurator's investigation, 26
Takagi, Justice Tsuneshichi: on procurator's investigation, 32
Tanaka, Justice Jirō: on welfare rights and administrative litigation, 137; on nonlitigious trials and marital disputes, 171; comment on his obscenity opinion by Justice K. Shimomura, 189–94; on obscenity regulation, 202
Tarumi, Justice Katsumi: on constitutionality of political organization ordinance, 35; on constitutionality of confiscation judgment, 64; on restraint on advertising, 219; on academic freedom and university freedom, 232
Taxation: of income, 50–51
Taxi cabs: licensing of, 80–81
Television companies: and freedom of information, 246–50
Textbooks: government review of, 14, 20; fees for, 147–48
Thought: freedom of, 175, 217–23
Tokyo Central Post Office Decision, Case 12, 106, 115, 116
Travel: freedom to, 81–84
Trial methods: nonlitigious, 169–74

Unconstitutionality, 8
Unindicted crime, 155–57
Unions: National Tax Agency Union, 109; National Judicial Employees Union, 103, 106–30 *passim*; National Government and Public Enterprise Employees Union, 124
University autonomy, 226, 228–41
Urgency: conditions of in criminal matters, 157–61, 181–82; as defense for injuring another, 232

Vote: right to, 149, 151–53; illegality of canvassing, 149–51

"Wanton," in law, 244–46
Welfare payments, Case 14, 130; inheritance of right to, 134, 137–39
Women's rights: under tax law, 50–52

Yamada, Justice Sakunosuke: on academic freedom, freedom of assembly, and university autonomy, 230
Yokota, Justice Kisaburō: on constitutionality of political organization ordinance, 35
Yokota, Justice Masatoshi: obscenity regulation, 196; university autonomy and academic freedom, 239
Young Lawyers Association (*Seihōkyō*), 16–17